HEGEL, MARX, AND THE ENGLISH STATE

This work, now brought back into print, is an insightful intellectual portrait of Hegel and Marx that challenges standard interpretations of their
political theory and places their political thought directly into social and
historical context. David MacGregor reveals the revolutionary content
of Hegel's social theory and the Hegelian themes that underlie Marx's
analysis of the English state in *Capital*, and shows how the transformation of the Victorian state in the nineteenth century influenced the
mature Marx to reclaim Hegelian arguments he had earlier abandoned.
These ideas included a theory of politics and social class that coloured
Marx's view of capitalist and working-class opposition to government
reform initiatives.

MacGregor criticizes interpretations of state action that present government solely as a tool of capitalist and patriarchal interests. Noting the
essential significance of child labour in the growing industrialization
during Hegel's and Marx's time, the author contends that 'alienation,' as
the two thinkers understood the term, assumes a labour force in which
many workers are socially powerless children and women. Given these
conditions, the centrality of the English Factory Acts to workers' lives
becomes obvious, a centrality acknowledged by Marx but forgotten by
his followers. The author concludes his discussion with an assessment
of current debates about state and civil society, relating these arguments
to Hegel's conception of the rational state.

DAVID MACGREGOR is a professor in the Department of Sociology at
King's College, University of Western Ontario. His previous book, *The
Communist Ideal in Hegel and Marx*, received the John Porter Memorial
Prize of the Canadian Sociology and Anthropology Association.

Hegel, Marx, and the English State

David MacGregor

UNIVERSITY OF TORONTO PRESS
Toronto Buffalo London

© University of Toronto Press Incorporated 1996
Toronto Buffalo London

Printed in Canada

ISBN 0-8020-7842-7

Printed on acid-free paper

First published in 1992 in the United States of America by Westview
Press, Inc. This edition is published by arrangement with the author.

Canadian Cataloguing in Publication Data

MacGregor, David, 1943–
    Hegel, Marx, and the English state

    Includes bibliographical references and index.
    ISBN 0-8020-7842-7

    1. Hegel, Georg Wilhelm Friedrich, 1770–1831 –
    Contributions in political science.   2. Marx, Karl,
    1818–1883 – Contributions in political science.
    3. Great Britain – Politics and government –
    19th century.   I. Title.

    JC233.H46M34 1996   320′.01   C95-933050-X

For Patricia and Ethan

Contents

1

Introduction

Classics are earlier works of human exploration which are given a privileged status vis-à-vis contemporary explorations in the same field. The concept of privileged status means that contemporary practitioners of the discipline in question believe that they can learn as much about their field through understanding this earlier work as they can from the work of their own contemporaries. . . . It is because of this privileged position that exegesis and reinterpretation of the classics—within or without a historical context—become conspicuous currents in various disciplines, for what is perceived to be the "true meaning" of a classical work has broad repercussions.
—Jeffrey C. Alexander, *"The Centrality of the Classics" (1987: 12)*

They sentenced me to twenty years of boredom
for trying to change the system from within. I'm
coming now I'm coming to reward them. First we
take Manhattan, then we take Berlin.
—Leonard Cohen, *"First We Take Manhattan" (1988)*

1. Hirschman's Riddle

Almost twenty years ago A. O. Hirschman (1973; 1981) pointed to the remarkable similarity between the theory of imperialism developed by J. A. Hobson and Rosa Luxemburg in the early twentieth century, and the brief but lucid account of imperialism in Hegel's *Philosophy of Right*. "There are a number of puzzles here," Hirschman wrote. "First of all, how did Hegel come to express these 'premature' thoughts?" Why, he wondered, had Marx missed the striking implications of Hegel's text? Moreover, why had Marx's followers themselves ignored Hegel in this regard? Adding to the original mystery, the quandary opened up by the eminent economist has been ignored ever since by Marxists (and by many Hegelians).

The theory of imperialism is largely outside the scope of this study, which concentrates on the English domestic scene between

1831 and 1867. But the book does explore an enigma closely related to the one unearthed by Hirschman. I argue that Hegel developed a profound and radical critique of nineteenth century English capitalism, and offered a theory of politics that addresses many of the deepest problems of advanced industrial society. I contend further that Marx was aware of this critique, and employed Hegel's political insights in his epic account of the British state in *Capital*. As in the example of Hegel and imperialism, however, a signal aspect of Marx's (Hegelian) confrontation with the English state is its almost total absence from the bulky literature on both Marx and Hegel.

The version of the Hegel-Marx relationship constructed in these pages may confuse readers familiar with the conventional view. Am I trying to build a right-wing Marx or a left-wing Hegel?[1] Perhaps the best answer is to describe how I came to this investigation in the first place. Afterwards, I will briefly outline the background and argument of the book, and acknowledge the many debts incurred in the seven years spent writing it.

2. Influences

As a twenty year-old university student in 1963 I went to bed almost every night with Volume One of *Capital*, a glass of milk, and some cheese and crackers. Until long afterward, I never thought of Marx without remembering my delicious nighttime snack. Nevertheless, I was not studying Marx simply as a gourmand. It made perfect sense for me to scrutinize him as preparation for entering the Public Service of Canada. Like many young people at the time, I thought problems of poverty and economic depression could be solved by an activist government staffed with socially-aware, highly educated and zealous civil servants. Marx (spiked with a bit of Keynes) should be a perfect guide for such an effort, I thought, especially with the way he wrote about the heroic factory inspectors in *Capital*. Marx's civil servants were role models who would, I hoped, illuminate my career in government.

After studying under Z. A. Jordan, John Porter, and others at Carleton University who knew a lot about Marx and Weber,[2] and bureaucracy,[3] I became a public servant, and—as a sociologist evaluating innovative social programs for the poor in the early 1970s—got to know and admire many dedicated women and men in the Ottawa bureaucracy. This was the state machine that produced the universally respected Canada Medicare program, among others, and which initiated radical community-run job creation projects. By the mid-seventies, however, the steam had gone out of the reforming impulse; disappointment in the limitations of government stimulated my departure. I went to the London School of Economics, where Professor Donald MacRae introduced me to Hegel.

Later, while teaching at King's College (University of Western Ontario), I couldn't shake a nagging question. Where were the factory inspectors in the commentaries about Marx? Why did no one mention the clear affinity between Marx's activist civil servants in *Capital*, and Hegel's celebration of bureaucrats in the *Philosophy of Right*? There were some hints about this in Stanley Hyman's (1962) excellent but now forgotten *The Tangled Bank*, and a few other places, such as Hobsbawm's *Industry and Empire* (1972). That was all. It occurred to me that if such a book were to exist I would have to write it.

While an important ingredient in this study, the story of Marx and the factory inspectors (Chapter Nine) forms only part of a larger canvass. I interpret the role of public servants in *Capital* in the context of Marx's social and political theory, and its relation to Hegelian thought. Wherever possible, I have tried to illustrate Marx's and Hegel's project with historical examples. I have done this to help elucidate difficult ideas, and also to keep in the forefront Marx and Hegel as beings in time, persons with their own history.

3. Problems of British History

I am not an historian or a specialist in historical sociology, and professionals in the field may smile or wince at errors that occur in this book, despite my efforts and the guidance of concerned colleagues. The problem is compounded because I have had to intrude into many of the "burgeoning and proliferating sub-specialisms" that now characterize the study of England's past, including "social history, urban history, family history, women's history, the history of childhood, [and] the new economic history" (Cannadine 1990: 5). Still, there is an historical point of view that will become obvious from citations in the text. I have been influenced by the school of British history that, according to Professor Cannadine (1987: 173, 190), produced "a welfare state version of the past." Chief among the "welfare-state Whigs" to whom this study is indebted are David Roberts (1960), Oliver MacDonagh (1977), Maurice Walton Thomas (1948), D. Fraser (1984) and the women who chronicled the Factory Acts, B. L. Hutchins and A. Harrison (1966). Like countless other toilers in this branch of British history, I have also profited from the writings of Norman Gash, Asa Briggs, Ivy Pinchbeck, Wanda Neff, Cecil Driver, Martha Hewitt, J. T. Ward, Eric Hobsbawm, E. P. Thompson, Neil Smelser, F. M. L. Thompson, Michael Brock, John Cannon, and (especially) Harold Perkin.

Tom Nairn (1988) has charted the morass of names of the small group of islands off the coast of Europe with which this study is concerned. As Nairn shows, there is much that is political in the decision whether to name them (or some of them) Britain, Great Britain, Britannia, the United Kingdom, England, or the British Isles. Neither Hegel nor Marx had this problem. For them, England was England, and included (most of the time) Scotland, Ireland and Wales.[4] I have adopted their terminology, with a few exceptions, because it reflects their understanding of the times. The convention unavoidably falsifies things, of course. Most of the "English" thinkers who influenced Hegel, including Smith, Steuart, Ferguson, and Hume were Scots. Leonard Horner, chief factory inspector, a founder of the University of London and leading member of the Geological Society, brother of the famous economist and parliamentarian Francis Horner, and long-time intimate of Charles Darwin, was from Edinburgh.

Similarly, I have adopted the nineteenth century demarcation between infants and children. One hundred years ago the term infant could mean a child up to age six or seven. The distinction was critical in the era of the factory when employment of children under the age of seven was common, even though their physical and mental capacities were much inferior to older cousins and siblings. In Victorian Britain, most factory operatives were female, but the masculine pronoun is widely used in theoretical and historical works. I have abandoned this convention, and mostly use the female pronoun when referring to the English worker.

4. The Approach to Hegel and Marx

Perhaps because Hegel is the greatest of all modern thinkers, and therefore the most troubling, the quality of commentary on him differs from that which obtains with such classic writers as Rousseau, Kant, Hobbes, Montesquieu, and even Marx. Interpreters might differ with these latter authors, but a hushed solemnity prevails nevertheless. With Hegel, useful commentary often comes mixed with gratuitous faultfinding.[5] Pelczynski (1964: 136) suggests this is because Hegel's romantic metaphysics repels contemporary readers. It may also indicate a robust freedom of opinion in Hegel studies lacking elsewhere, at least if freedom is understood as divergence from, and hostility to, a thinker. In any event, you will find few criticisms of Hegel in this book. I intend to show the strength of Hegel's politics, not its weakness; to praise Hegel rather than deconstruct him. Similarly, with Marx my differences are few, and these mostly relate to his misunderstanding of Hegel.[6]

Some readers may dismiss this study as yet another entry into what Harold Perkin (1981: 228) calls, "the sociological hagiography of 'great thinkers.'" Indeed nothing could be easier than to detect errors of fact and interpretation in the writings of a long-dead philosopher who like everyone else, was "a child of his time" (Hegel 1976: 11). Further, it would be absurd to make out that Hegel (or Marx) did not make mistakes. What I want to suggest is that their contributions illuminate, as well as reflect, their own period, and they point to a new understanding of our own epoch.

Hegel (1975: 36) defined metaphysics as *"the science of things set and held in thoughts*—thoughts accredited able to express the essential reality of things." I take this to mean that Hegel (as well as Marx) wrote for the future as well as for his own time, that he intended his writing to have an impact on generations after him (Smith 1989: 14). This is the spirit I have found in studies on Hegel that have guided my own view, including the text and commentaries of the great English translators of Hegel, William Wallace, J. B. Baillie, T. M. Knox, and A. V. Miller; and the exemplary scholarship of H. S. Harris, Duncan Forbes and Z. A. Pelcynski.[7] I have learned also from the grand tradition of "Western Marxism" (Anderson 1976)—the Russian, Italian, French, German and East European scholars who kept alive the radical vision of Hegel and Marx. The magnificent Hegel journal *The Owl of Minerva*, edited by Lawrence Stepelevich, has been an indispensable resource in writing this book.

R. N. Berki (1983) has exposed the controlling problem of Marx's thought: how can one be scientific and yet work with a vision of the future? How can empirical analysis be made to conform with political desire? To deal with this dilemma Marx borrowed the Hegelian dialectical method, which brings shifting levels of analysis into a single whole. Hegel's own success with the procedure is indicated by the conflicting interpretations that have been made of his thought. You can find the conservative, or the liberal, or even the communist Hegel. Especially regarding a theory of the state, Marx decided to contend with the tension between realistic analysis and political vision by not directly saying anything at all.

Now that communism as a system of government has collapsed almost everywhere in the world, Marx's dilemma is with us even more urgently than before. When the Soviet Union or Hungary or Poland existed as functioning communist republics it was at least possible for the theorist to point to something real, even if this was just to debunk communism, or show what communism should not be, or what it inevitably must be. With the disappearance of communism as a reality, the ideal must again take its place. This is why, I think, scholars will eventually join Marx in turning back to Hegel for guidance. Hegel showed how to account for the existing world while constructing an ideal. The alternative to his dialectic is to rest comfortably with an eternally unchanging capitalist world, the end of history.

5. Structure of the Argument

Interpretations of the relation between Hegel and Marx once hinged on what was held to be a seismic difference between their respective historical periods. Hegel was assumed to have written in, and about, an almost feudal Germany, while occasionally peeking out from the continent to dimly espy a still embryonic industrial England. By contrast, Marx lived in the era of high capitalism, surrounded by the clamor of a mighty commercial machine. The standard periodization of Hegel and Marx exaggerated the differences between their historical experience, and understated Hegel's deep fascination with England. It also missed a momentous societal change. The industrial revolution in England was fifty years old by the time Hegel wrote the *Philosophy of Right*; the phenomena of industrial capitalism that subsequently captured Marx's attention were already in place. What was missing in Hegel's time, however, and what did appear in Marx's, was the new interventionist state.

Chapter Two interprets Hegel's 1831 article on the English Reform Bill in light of recent scholarship on Victorian England. I show that Hegel's essay relied upon, and illustrated, some pivotal concepts in his political theory, including property, social class, democracy, elite rule, and the nature of the state. His essay also demonstrated a better understanding of the character of English politics than Marx was able to achieve. While the latter proposed that capital ruled the English state, Hegel saw that aristocrats were firmly in charge, and likely to remain so for some time. Hegel remarked often on the absence of a real state in England, the lack of an effective countervailing force to the sway of the market. He predicted that electoral reform, however inadequate, might unleash a new type of state power.

This novel form of political power took shape as the English Factory Acts, the first effective legislative interference in the workings of a mature capitalist economy. I argue in Chapter Three that Hegel's influence helped the German revolutionary exiled in London to see the vast significance of the English political experiment, a significance that Marx's contemporaries failed to grasp.

Chapter Four begins a detailed exploration of the key concepts in Hegel's political theory that assisted Marx in his trailblazing account of the first interventionist state. Hegel's notion of the sovereignty of the individual, and the vital importance of personality, are crucial for understanding Marx's emphasis on the value of time for human development, and the world-historical import of the English Factory Acts. Yet Marx mishandled a major component of the Hegelian legacy. He replaced Hegel's concept of private property, which includes the right of the worker to the product of labor, with the notion of surplus value and the negation of private ownership under communism. This meant that Marx's ideal society lacked not only a state, but also most of the institutions in civil society required to ensure personal freedom and prevent arbitrary rule by a dominant elite.

Marx's chronicle of factory legislation was underpinned by an egalitarian vision of family life that resembled Hegel's concept of the family in the *Philosophy of Right*. Chapter Five presents Hegel's theory of the family, a theory indebted to the scholarship of Theodor Gottlieb von Hippel, top Prussian bureaucrat and family law expert, who published a landmark text on the emancipation of women two centuries ago, in 1792, the same year as Mary Wollstonecraft's world-shattering *A Vindication of the Rights of Woman* (1967).

Both Marx and Engels were profoundly affected by the feminism that emerged from the German romantic period, but Hippel and Hegel are ignored in Engels's *Origin of the Family, Private Property and the State* (1985). However, Hegel's ideas on love, the fundamental duty of parents to support and educate offspring, and the role of the state in asserting the rights of children and women against those of dominant men have clear counterparts in Marx's treatment of the struggles around factory regulation. For Hegel, individuals come to the capitalist market economy with personalities nourished within the family; and they make contracts with one another as property owners, including property in their own labor. Chapters Six and Seven explore Hegel's theory of property, contract and social class, showing areas of contrast and agreement between the *Philosophy of Right* and *Capital*. These chapters demonstrate that Hegel provided a more powerful understanding of modern society than Marx; but they also reveal some previously unrecognized Hegelian elements in *Capital*.

One of these Hegelian borrowings, as displayed in Chapter Eight, is Marx's three-stage development of the labor contract. In the first stage, the contract between capitalist and worker is a bargain between equals; in the second, free exchange is transformed into its opposite. On one hand, the worker gives up all her time to the capitalist in return for a bare subsistence; on the other, the proletarian sells his wife and child into wage slavery. Government intervention marks the third stage of contract. The state regulates the working day, providing workers with free time for self-development; it prevents fathers from selling little children, and limits exploitation of older children and adult women.

Chapter Nine presents Marx's saga of the struggle to impose the Factory Acts on Victorian capitalism. The chapter highlights the overwhelming importance of the state in *Capital*, along with the dramatic role played by factory inspectors, especially Leonard Horner. We see that Hegel's concepts of the interventionist state and the universal class are central to Marx's account, as are Hegelian notions of personality, education, and the family.

In the concluding chapter, Hegel's theses on political power are evaluated in the context of late twentieth century politics. I argue that Hegel's emancipatory project was based on worker-owned, democratic corporations; he replaced majority voting and mass-based political parties with corporate representation in parliament. The corporation-based business class, on one side, and government bureaucracy on the other, are major contenders for political power in the modern state. Yet unlike Weber, who concentrated on the ominous side of politics, both Hegel and Marx were optimistic about the future of government. For Hegel, as for Marx, the state is the manifestation of the principle of love and caring. This was the principle carried forward by Marx's factory inspectors; and it is also the ethic that underlies the growth of the modern welfare state.

6. Acknowledgments

Contrary to received economic wisdom, burgeoning debt is not always bad thing, especially when it comes to getting help on writing a book. Peter Findlay hired me in 1970 as a sociologist to evaluate what was then called the Canada Manpower Training Program; this was my entry into the Public Service of Canada. Sue Findlay, who in the mid-seventies became the first Director of the Women's Program at the Secretary of State, taught me a lot about the struggle for women to enter the corridors of state power. Discussions about Marxism, and the role of the state with Martin Loney and John Conway over the last two decades, and with Eric Liggett, Logan Murray, Susan Chamberlain, Bill Kaye, Chris Poulter, Helen Masson, Stan Staple, Stan Marshall and Leo Panitch helped me to think about many of the issues addressed in this volume.

When I began serious research on this book in 1984 my friends Gerry Nixon and Jane Baigent showed me it was important; so did my colleagues Kathy Kopinak, Ken Westhues, Karen Anderson, Joe Lella, Bernie Hammond, Sandra Aylward, David Flynn, Alan Pomfret, Cathy Mendler and Al Koop. Elizabeth Russell, Linda Jarvis, Norma Pizzey, Susan Evans and others at King's College library located cartloads of books and articles for me. I owe a great deal to David Skilton, Dillard Hunley, David Ellerman, and Timothy Sellner who inspired me with their own work on, respectively, English industrial fiction, the biographies of Marx and Engels, the labor theory of property, and Theodor Gottlieb von Hippel.

Randall Collins proffered many kind suggestions; he taught me the value of twentieth century sociological theory when I was certain that Hegel and Marx had already said it all. Dillard Hunley amiably corrected me on matters of style and substance; Sam Clark tried to steer me away from historical error; I trust their efforts were not in vain. H. S. Harris and Duncan Forbes gave me encouragement early in this project. Jay Drydyk offered advice on earlier versions of Chapters Two and Four, as did my friend Daniel Francis. Harold Perkin submitted some sage advice on the proper scholarly approach to great thinkers.

As this book went to press I learned of the death of Professor R. N. Berki. Professor Berki read an early version of this book and offered many valuable suggestions. His passing is a great loss.

In a lengthy and memorable telephone conversation Dorothy E. Smith suggested some substantial changes to an earlier version of the chapter on Hegel and the family. Jane Roland Martin's *Reclaiming a Conversation* (1985), gave me a wonderful scholarly ideal to emulate, and I am grateful also for her counsel on Chapter Five. Sue Findlay extended helpful criticism of the ms., and so did Bonnie Easterbrook, Maureen Waechter, and Barb Pratt.

R. I. K. Davidson prompted me to write this book; John Wilson and Scott McNall helped me to think about the best way to present the argument. I wish to thank the anonymous reader at Westview Press who recommended significant amendments to the text. The reader's comments have made this a better book than it would have been otherwise. Ellen Williams and Dean Birkenkamp, my editors at Westview Press, were gentle, thoughtful, and enthusiastic; they made the long journey to publication a pleasant experience. Research for this study was financed by the Research Grants Committee of King's College, and by the Social Science and Humanities Research Council of Canada.

My students at King's College encouraged me to bring Hegel and Marx down to earth, and showed me how to teach a feminist Hegel. Laurie Rushbrook, Allan Griffiths and Jim Hood provided invaluable assistance for my research on the English Factory Inspectorate.

As a commuter to London, Ontario I am very lucky to have my dear friends Lesley DePauw and Jessica DePauw to stay with; I still miss the friendship of Mark DePauw, who died suddenly in 1986.

When the Berlin Wall crumbled my mother, Jean Nethercote, called to ask what I had to say about *that*? She always thinks my opinions are worth listening to, even if generally wrong. This has given me confidence to assert things others are disinclined to believe. My sister Betty MacGregor has done more for me than she knows. Felled by a heart attack in February 1965—a week before Malcolm X was assassinated in the Audubon Ballroom—my father, Ted McGregor, had faith in the promise of modern liberalism which later caused me to doubt the benefits of total revolution.

While writing a book partly about the history of legislation against child labor, it was very instructive to become a happy father. Marx said you should learn from your children, and my four year-old son, Ethan MacGregor Bishop, is teaching me a lot. Patricia Bishop, my spouse of sixteen years, is schooling me in the politics of equality in the family; she says I'm not a quick study. This book is dedicated with love to them both.

Notes

1. Commenting on an earlier version of my argument, David Duquette (1990: 123) remarks that "it is certainly astonishing that the same Hegel, who has often been interpreted as a defender of authoritarianism, reactionism, and even totalitarianism, should here be viewed as a sort of leftist with a revolutionary program for social change . . . [MacGregor] turns Hegel's *Philosophy of Right* into a 'Hegelian critique of the Philosophy of Right.'"

2. Gertrud Neuwirth, John Harp, Dennis Forcese, and Donald Whyte.

3. John Hofley, Charles Gordon, Bruce McFarlane, Stephen Richer, John DeVries, Victor Valentine, and Frank Vallee.

4. Hegel addressed this problem directly in the *Philosophy of Right* (1976: 182). "Any people whatever is self-subsistent *vis à vis* other peoples, and constitutes a state of its own, like the British people for instance. But the peoples of England, Scotland, or Ireland, or the peoples of Venice, Genoa, Ceylon, &c., are not sovereign peoples at all now that they have ceased to have rulers or supreme governments of their own." Although Hegel sometimes used the term Britain in the inclusive sense, he more often used England.

5. A review of Francis Fukuyama's *The End of History and the Last Man* (1992) offers a recent and convenient example. Acknowledging that Fukuyama's book is really about Kojève, rather than Hegel, the reviewer nevertheless mocks *The End of History*'s "exotic Germanic garb" and concludes, that going "'back to Hegel' . . . is reactionary in the true sense of the word" (McNeill 1992: 15).

6. Leo Strauss's (1973: 7, 143) "sociology of philosophy" displays a useful distinction between "interpretation and explanation." "By interpretation we mean the attempt to ascertain what the speaker said and how he actually understood what he said, regardless of whether he expressed that understanding explicitly or not. By explanation we mean the attempt to ascertain those implications of his statements of which he was unaware." In this book, I am attempting to interpret rather than explain the views of Hegel and Marx.

7. I have given page numbers only in references to Hegel's works to avoid confusion in the science-style citation format used in this book.

2

"Not Reform but Revolution"

Take the case of <u>England</u> which, because private persons have a predominant share in public affairs, has been regarded as having the freest of all constitutions. Experience shows that that country—as compared with the other civilized states of Europe—is the most backward in civil and criminal legislation, in the law and liberty of property, in arrangements for art and science, and that objective freedom or rational right is rather <u>sacrificed</u> to formal right and particular private interest.

        —G. W. F. Hegel, *Philosophy of Mind* (1971: 273)

It now appears almost inconceivable that only five years ago there was an innovative, radical Labor local authority in London, which broke new ground in developing and implementing policies. [Before it was abolished by the Thatcher government] the Greater London Council pioneered equal opportunities in British public institutions, initiated preventive health work among pensioners, developed forms of ethnical trade with Third World countries. . . . Now it stands empty, bleak and abandoned still waiting for its bidder, a visible symbol of what it means to transfer public property onto the market, an empty shell of social wastefulness.

  —Sheila Rowbotham, *"The Greater London Council"* (1991: 61)

1. Introduction

Hegel died of cholera on 14 November 1831. The end came amidst revolutionary upheaval in Europe and political turmoil in England. An economic depression gripped Germany. During the last months Hegel watched events with growing anxiety. The English situation dismayed him; the government's Reform Bill was grossly inadequate. Although the proposed reform was illusory, Hegel feared it would make England's free market experiment even more attractive to radicals on the continent. Liberal economic ideology dominated political thought, and many looked to Adam Smith's *Wealth of Nations* for guidance in constructing a new society.[1] Like East

European admirers of American democracy in the 1990s, Hegel's contemporaries had a rose-colored view of English freedom. Hegel believed this was dangerous. A few years after his death, Germany embarked on its own industrial revolution; profits and production soared, but so did unemployment, poverty and hunger (Kocka 1986: 293).

Earl Grey's Whig government placed the Reform Bill before Parliament on March 1, 1831. Later that month, Hegel drew on his deep knowledge of England to write a four-part series on the reform crisis for the *Prussian State Gazette*. The journal was widely read by the educated classes in Germany, and Hegel's piece—published in April—attracted much attention. For reasons that remain unclear, the king himself suspended publication of its very controversial final section (Petry 1984: 146, 296).

Hegel's sketch of England on the eve of the Great Reform Act serves as a bench mark for the argument of this book. The regulatory power of the English state grew prodigiously between the time of Hegel's death and the publication of *Capital* in 1867.[2] I contend that Hegel's political philosophy anticipated the main lines of this growth, and inspired Marx to document the transformation of government in England.

While providing a basis of comparison with Marx's England, Hegel's article on parliamentary reform also offers a unique opportunity to integrate his views on contemporary politics with the *Philosophy of Right*. Hegel the journalist relied heavily on Hegel the political philosopher, and vice versa (Pelczynski 1964: 113).

The present chapter will contribute to the larger theme of this book: what is the nature of the capitalist state? The English political system Hegel discussed was an example of what he called, "the state external." Wealth and power in civil society are overwhelming forces in an external state. By contrast, representative institutions in the Hegelian "social state" unite government with all groups in civil society. Marx witnessed the "becoming" of the English political administration, its transformation from an external regime, to a form of government that incorporated some elements of the social state. I argue that the Hegelian distinction between these two faces of the state is vital for an understanding of modern government.

An important, but frequently overlooked, aspect of Hegel's political theory is underscored by his commentary on parliamentary reform. Great Britain's military prowess, vast colonial holdings, and surging economy encouraged the English to see themselves as the new Romans.[3] While Hegel shared this view, he did not believe it placed the English in a flattering light. The comparisons he drew between Rome and England usually emphasized the worst features of English capitalism. In works subject to censorship, such as the *Philosophy of Right*, Hegel often employed the Roman example to disguise critical remarks about England. I will point to instances of this throughout the book.

2. The Prussian Background

Before discussing Hegel's article in detail, it may be useful to outline the context within which he was writing. England's politics and economic theory had long been objects of great fascination on the continent.[4] The Germans were envious of English industrial progress, and eager to apply the lessons of political economy to the backward economies of the German states. So it was not surprising that Germany's leading philosopher should attempt to decipher the strange political events unfolding in England.

While its economy was backward compared to England's, Germany was progressive in other ways. England, for example, did not adopt compulsory education for children until late in the nineteenth century; Prussia legislated compulsory schooling in 1763 (Frevert 1989: 83). As H. S. Harris (1988) points out, Berlin in Hegel's time "was . . . without dispute, the intellectual capital of the world." Prussia had constructed a university system that would serve as a world model for the next century. Reform in Prussia, following the country's defeat by Napoleon in 1806, had resulted in an efficient public service based on merit that was far more representative of the various classes in society than that of England (Mueller 1984: 122). Serfdom was eliminated, legal equality was established for all citizens, the Jews were emancipated, and the aristocratic caste system in the military was swept away. "More radical proposals by Stein, Hardenberg, Scharnhorst, and other ministers . . . pushed unsuccessfully for the abolition of the aristocracy and for democratic self-government;" most of the reformers, notes Randall Collins (1987: 62), rejected Christianity and looked forward to "a new national culture, based on education and embodying freedom." I will touch on other aspects of Germany's "revolution from above" later in this chapter.

Hegel was hardly the grizzled apologist of a repellent reactionary order, as claimed by Karl Popper and many others. He is best seen as a representative of the rising middle class, which in Germany meant not the standard bourgeoisie of Marxist legend, but rather a "new class" of intellectuals, academics, and government officials. In Hegel's day, this "'aristocracy of experts' . . . was still something of a counterelite pitting its ideology of cultivation against the claims of mere nobility" (Mueller 1984: 163-4). Hegel was the most prominent member of a whole generation of highly educated Germans who suffered career blockage at the close of the eighteenth century, and eagerly embraced the new order promised by the French Revolution and the reforms of Napoleon Bonaparte (Toews 1985: 26). This generation's fondest hopes were dashed by the dark period of reaction that was signalled by Napoleon's defeat in 1815, and would dog Hegel's final years. The disillusioned bureaucrats and academics who read Hegel's 1831 article on reform in England prefigured the members of this class who would help make the German revolution of 1848.

Within the new class, however, there was considerable division. Many German nationalists wanted a liberal economic system and a weak central authority, along with popular democracy. In the person of Hegel's enemy and rival, J. F. Fries, a leader of the nationalist movement, this liberal tendency coexisted with "chauvinism, xenophobia and antisemitism" (D'Hondt 1988: 95). A strong conservative opposition grew during the period of reform, and with the fall of Bonaparte, reactionaries came to power in Prussia and elsewhere. German idealists, like Fichte and Schelling, had already become conservative or nationalist prior to Waterloo. "In later years of the Idealist movement," writes Collins (1987: 65), "Hegel remained the only liberal thinker." As such, he attracted the lightning bolts of Restoration thinkers like Friedrich Ancillon, K. L. von Haller, and others close to the Prussian throne, and to the Austrian Prince Metternich. Some of Hegel's students were arrested, and his work, like that of other writers, was subject to stringent censorship by the Prussian state after the Carlsbad Decrees of 1818/19. This has led Jacques d'Hondt (1988) to speak of the "secret Hegel," who was forced by the reaction to live in hiding during the last fifteen years or so of his life. Certainly Hegel had reasons to avoid statements that might be interpreted as seditious by the authorities in Berlin.

Contrary to the myth that Hegel ingratiated himself with the Restoration monarchy by attacking England's political system, this was actually a sure way of currying disfavor. England was the leader of the reactionary alliance of great states sealed by the Treaty of Paris in 1815. The Prussian nobility admired the English aristocracy's domination of politics, and hoped to duplicate that success in Germany. Free markets, a renewed unity of the crown with Christian faith, and a refurbished aristocracy, with landholdings managed on a capitalist model, were all part of the restoration agenda in Prussia (Raff 1988; Sagarra 1977).

Throughout the nineteenth century, England consolidated its global power by posing as the champion of freedom and democracy. Hegel's essay challenged this claim to superiority, noting especially the retarded development in England of a concept of the state. This feature of British politics has survived to fascinate modern scholars.[5] He also indicated the dangers of parliamentary oligarchy unencumbered by a government-guaranteed system of civil and human rights. His criticisms have been interpreted as predictable outgrowths of Hegel's Prussian anglophobia, but they have a modern ring today, now that British violations of civil rights are widely acknowledged (Perkin 1989: 476).

Compared to its European counterparts, as Hegel (1964: 300) observed, the early nineteenth century English political system was "remarkably far behind." Bureaucrats in Germany influenced by the French example had swept away most of the aristocracy's ancient privileges. Many similar privileges persisted in England.[6] Admirers on the continent trumpeted the virtues of English justice and rights. In fact, these were hostage to property and wealth. Slavery was practiced in the colonies (until the Whigs abolished it in 1833); and colonial landowners were prominent among those who were allowed to buy seats in Parliament (Bentley 1984: 90; Hegel 1964: 299). No central authority existed to watch over the administration of law, which was entirely the prerogative of the local gentry.[7] The consequent "financial loss and the physical and spiritual misery suffered by the people of the parishes and towns of England," notes Herman Finer (1961: 756-7), "was enormous and terrible." The main energy of English constitution-making was aimed at limiting the power of the Crown, and preventing the emergence of an autonomous public service (Mueller 1984: 91).

Still, Hegel's review was far from the despairing jeremiad of an old man. Despite its shortcomings, he saw chances in the Reform Bill for a massive alteration of English society. Political change might dislodge the existing order, and install a government more responsive to the needs of workers and the poor. This would be the result, he argued, not of the Reform Bill itself, but rather of the expectations it aroused in the English people.

Hegel's own death may help illustrate the pressures combining to bring about a new type of state. Alarmed by the encroaching epidemic, he retreated from Berlin. "I . . . prefer to endure the storm here," Hegel (1984: 679) wrote from the family vacation home at Kreuzberg. Although his flight proved futile, it was based on a rational calculation. Berlin was crammed with the poor and homeless, conditions that everywhere invited cholera. In fact, the close connection between cholera and economic distress led many to suspect the rich were poisoning the poor. Successive waves of the disease dating from 1826 had shaken European authority structures (Evans 1990). In the decades following Hegel's death, eradication of epidemics became a chief contributor to the rise of the modern state (Swaan 1988; Finer 1952)).

3. England on the Eve of the Reform Bill

Commentators have awarded mixed reviews to Hegel's foray into English politics. For Avineri (1972: 219)—who provides an excellent account—Hegel's essay "is . . . one of the most informed and radical critiques of English social conditions." Others describe the "remarkably incisive and penetrating" piece as "strongly anti-English" (Pelcynski 1964; 23); as "somewhat ill-tempered" (Butler 1984: 669); and as degenerating "into something closely resembling polemic" (Petry 1984: 138). Rosenkranz, one of Hegel's earliest editors, suggested that the "abusive" tone of "The English Reform Bill" may have resulted from an early rush of choleric fever (quoted in Pelczynski 1964: 24).

This reaction is puzzling. Few have described Marx, for example, as anti-French because he disliked the regime of Louis Napoleon. Engels wrote some critical commentaries on the English, but nobody has called him "ill-tempered," or suggested he must have been sick. Why single out Hegel? Part of the answer lies in what Jacques d'Hondt (1988: 1) called, "the traditional . . . but false" view of Hegel as a "Prussian chauvinist." Another factor may be that until recently the negative comparison made by Hegel between social relations in England and those on the continent was simply not acceptable to scholars. Among historians the English aristocracy was seen as an oddity, differing from the continental nobility in its lesser degree of privilege, greater openness to reform, larger distance from the state, and so forth. With the work of Michael Bush, David Cannadine (1990), and others, this picture is beginning to change. For Bush (1984: 5-6), the English aristocracy, like the nobility elsewhere in Europe, "was a ruling class with a special function in running the state." Compared to the continental elite, the topmost level of the English aristocracy was "overprivileged" rather than "underprivileged."

In any case, Hegel's article was not Prussian "propaganda" (Petry: 1984: 24). It was a profound critique of the English political system and a model of class analysis. His judgements on large-scale corruption in Britain—and the consequent rise of revolutionary agitation—were largely accurate. Hegel sketched an inert English state that forms a strong contrast, as we shall see, with the interventionist government described a generation later in *Capital*.

If Hegel was angry, there is little wonder. The ugly scene he described contradicted publicity on freedom and rights retailed by England's apologists. In many countries on the continent, including Prussia, tithes had been abolished. In England, poor people were forced to give up ten percent of their income to the free-spending and corrupt Anglican Church. In Ireland, the Church collected its tithes from an embittered Catholic populace, whose own houses of worship were deliberately left in ruins (1964: 304-6). "Even the Turks," wrote Hegel,

> have generally left alone the churches of their Christian, Armenian, and Jewish subjects; even where these subjects have been forbidden to repair their churches when dilapidated, they were still allowed leave to buy permission to do so. But the English have taken all the churches away from their conquered Catholic population.

R.F. Foster (1988: 292) observes that this "spectacularly inequitable treatment" led to escalating agrarian violence in Ireland; Whig authority responded with "coercive legislation [that] reached its apogee in the 1830s."

Everywhere in Britain, Hegel (1964: 307-8) pointed out, large landowners had an iron monopoly on land. "The moment of transition from feudal tenure to property has slipped by without giving the farmer class the chance to own land." He was not exaggerating. In 1872, the first national survey of manorial holdings revealed that 7,000 individuals owned eighty percent of the land. "A quarter of England was occupied by large estates of over 10,000 acres," writes Norman Gash (1979: 17). "In Wales and Scotland the

greater part of the soil belonged to the gentry and aristocracy."
Distribution of land had changed little since 1700; "indeed, nine-
tenths of the richest owners . . . lived on an accumulation of wealth
that predated the industrial revolution" (Beckett 1986: 87).

"English legislation about property," wrote Hegel (1964: 309),
" . . . has gone too far away from the freedom enjoyed in this matter
by continental countries." While European status systems nourished
a bewildering complexity of noble titles, landownership was the
primary measure of status in England. According to Beckett (1986:
42), land "represented not merely wealth, but stability and continuity, a fixed interest in the state which conferred the right to govern."
The English law of primogeniture—that is, the inheritance of all
family property by the eldest son—ensured the aristocratic monopoly
of land. By contrast, property laws that reinforced a powerful noble
elite had been struck down on the continent. The enormous
concentration of land in the hands of aristocrats and gentry was
unique to England. Their holdings were double and triple those of
the landed elites of France, Prussia, Russia and Spain, in which there
was a strong tradition of a landholding peasantry. "It was the
preponderance of land in the British case that most stands out"
writes David Cannadine (1990: 21). "In no other country in Europe
were wealth, status, and power so highly correlated or so territorially
underpinned."

Hegel (1964: 307, 308) observed that few in England questioned
the rights of property, but most people had been "incapacitated for
the possession of property in land and reduced to the status of
tenants or day labourers." In England and Scotland the propertyless
"agricultural class" could turn to factory labor. "But what really
keeps it from the consequences of extreme indigence is the poor law
which imposes on every parish the obligation to look after its poor."
In Ireland there was neither factory work or the poor law. English
landowners and their agents had burned many Irish poor off their
lands and left them to starve. "Those who already own nothing are
deprived of their birthplace and hereditary means of livelihood—in
the name of justice."

Hegel (1964: 310, 309) referred to legislation that made hunting of
edible game such as deer, rabbits and pheasants an exclusive
privilege of the nobility, and gave hunters unrestricted access to the
land of tenant farmers. Since foxes were seen as noxious and
disgusting animals, countryfolk and the bourgeoisie could join nobles
in fox-hunting packs "with a string of hounds and twenty, thirty, or

more riders and with still more on foot." The chase often took place over the sown fields of tenant farmers, a practice banned elsewhere in Europe. Social mixing in the hunting pack disguised the reality of class warfare in the countryside. The poor tenant, or commoner in the hunt, might the day after a chase be sentenced to death for poaching by offended aristocrats. "It is just the aristocrats," Hegel wrote, "who made the laws and who then sit in court in their capacity as magistrates and jurymen." The Game Law Act, which weakened noble prerogatives, was passed the year Hegel died, but hunting privileges for the nobility survived well into the nineteenth century (Bush 1984: 23; Beckett 1986: 343-4).

Prospective civil servants on the continent had to take public examinations and prove professional ability. English public administration, Hegel (1964: 310-11) argued, required nothing except immense wealth or good family connections. "Nowhere more than in England is the prejudice so fixed and so naive that if birth and wealth give a man office they also give him brains." The Reform Bill would do nothing to provide England an expert public service instead of government by "the crass ignorance of fox-hunters and landed gentry."

A distinguished contemporary of Hegel's made similar comments. "The whole of English society," said Alex de Toqueville in 1834,

> is based on privileges of money . . . . There is not a country in the world where justice, that first need of the peoples, is more the privilege of the rich . . . . Intelligence, even virtue, seems of little account without money. Everything worthwhile is somehow tied up with money. It fills all the gaps that one finds between men, but nothing will take its place" (quoted in Marcus 1985: 62).

Engels's 1844 article on the English Constitution (which bears an unmistakable resemblance to Hegel's 1831 piece) also complained of "the repugnant and disgusting . . . respect for the aristocracy" prevalent in England (Marx and Engels 1953: 37-8).

4. English Civil Society and the Owl of Minerva

Jeremy Bentham asserted that England had no constitution (Pelczynski 1964: 55), Hegel (1964: 330) felt that the English lacked a state. The central government had a negligible influence "on the particular circles of social life, on the administration of counties, cities, &c., on ecclesiastical establishments, and even on other public concerns such as road-making." There was no state in Britain because the state and civil society were the same; in fact, civil society *was* the state.

In the *Philosophy of Right* Hegel (1976: 126, 176, 178) defined civil society as the system of business and agriculture, the courts, and public works, connected with making a living. Ideally, this arrangement stands apart from the "the state as a political entity": the representative structure of government, the Crown and the bureaucracy. The English, however, recognized no separation between the two. Civil society's external state ruled England. "In this type of constitution, political life rests on privileged persons and a great part of what must be done for the maintenance of the state is settled at their pleasure." National affairs, noted Hegel (1964: 325, 300, 309), were "in the hands of a privileged class," and Parliament was just a talking shop for aristocrats and large capitalists. "The governing power lies in the hands of those possessed of so many privileges which contradict a rational constitutional law and true legislation." Advocates argued that the Reform Bill would widen representation, distribute seats fairly, and end much electoral abuse. Hegel disagreed. Under the Whig proposals "parliamentary legislation remains in the hands of the class which has its interest, and still more its fixed habits, in the hitherto existing law of property." Nor was there hope of positive intervention by the monarch, for "the power of the Crown is too weak."

Tom Nairn (1988: 110, 321, 170-71) makes an analogous argument about the collapse of the state into British civil society. "The anglo-British oligarchy," he writes, attained unmatched political dominance after Waterloo which gave it "far greater purchase over the development of civil society than that enjoyed by struggling *anciens regimes* . . . or by the precarious new-bourgeois states that took over from them." From the early nineteenth century onward, the glamour of the monarchy has been the mystical glue that sealed identification of the English state (monarchy, peerage, houses of parliament) with civil society. "Great Britain herself is *the* stately home: the State which is also Home, a power-structure which could not be so convincingly either of these things without the Crown, and a family still in residence." Moreover, the identity of crown and civil society rests precisely on the political powerlessness of the monarch. This leaves the way clear for the ruling party in parliament to take up arbitrary monarchical powers, without undue interference from the royal figurehead.

A significant stage in the long decline of monarchy had already been reached in 1830, Hegel (1964: 326-8) warned. This was the Whig government's successful bid to separate payments for civilian government from the Crown's Civil List. The Civil List made up budget items for the monarchy. Before the Whig innovation, it included royal household expenses plus all government payments, except those for defence and servicing the national debt. The List was mostly a formality. "Nevertheless there . . . remained an appearance of monarchical influence on this small part of the British expenditure, even though this influence was subject to the Cabinet."

Apparently, Hegel's judgment on this issue was correct. The Whig government action," writes Norman Chester (1981: 79), "carried the implication that those hitherto dependent on the king's money and favour were now dependent on that of the House of Commons." The Duke of Wellington's Tory government resigned in 1830, after defeat on an opposition motion to refer the Civil List to a House of Commons committee. This prepared the way, said Hegel, for reform and absolute supremacy of Parliament.

A frightened cabinet committee drafted the Reform Bill in secret during the winter of 1830-31 (Brock, 1973: 136). In France, the 1830 July revolution had toppled the king; in Belgium insurgents occupied Brussels. "The revolutionary fever took possession of the Swiss Cantons, the free city of Hamburg, Hesse, Saxony, and Brunswick" (Halévy 1961a: 6). The "Captain Swing" risings of the autumn and winter of 1830 in southeast England had created "hysteria" in London. Concerned "that 'peasant' disturbances might touch off a far more dangerous conflagration among industrial workers in the north and west," Home Secretary Melbourne ordered arrests and speedy trials. The courts hanged nineteen men, transported 500, and jailed 600 more (Hobsbawm and Rude 1975: 282, 257, 262).

Hegel (1964: 295) noted drily that events in France were a catalyst for reform in England. "A sense of justice," he wrote, "now mastered the obstinacy of privilege." The aristocratic regime was trembling at the brink and Hegel knew it.[8] He (1976: 13) had already reached this conclusion in 1821. "When philosophy paints its grey in grey," he wrote in the *Philosophy of Right*, "then has a shape of life grown old. By philosophy's grey in grey it cannot be rejuvenated but only understood. The Owl of Minerva spreads its wings only with the falling of the dusk."

Many commentators have interpreted this famous passage as Hegel's confession that philosophy cannot bring about change. He was saying the opposite. Philosophy can offer little to a dying order, but it can display the image of a better future. "History's inescapable lesson," he contended, is that the future remains invisible until current arrangements have exhausted all of their potential. Hegel's article on the Reform Bill is an example. On one hand it described the decay of the aristocratic system; on the other, it presented a glimpse of events to come.

5. The English Class System

Many of Hegel's interpreters assume that Germany was the primary focus of the *Philosophy of Right*. I argue that the book concentrates on the English system rather than the German one.[9] A summary of the work appeared in the 1830 version of the *Encyclopedia of the Philosophical Sciences* (1971). There, Hegel used England—not Germany or France—for a discussion of constitutional structure. His remarks on the Reform Bill, therefore, offer important clues about his political theory.

According to the standard version of Hegel, he was a conservative Prussian nationalist with a marginal interest in England. Since German society preoccupied him, his writings were about a capitalist economy barely emerged from feudalism. Recent revisionist interpretations discover a liberal Hegel, but continue to see his focus as post-feudal Germany. G. A. Kelly (1978: 113), for example, counsels that "we should put out of our minds the notion that Hegel's 'civil society' has much to do with our own"; Steven Smith (1989: 140) reaches a similar conclusion. A growing body of evidence shows that Hegel was no conservative; moreover, his politics were closer to modern democratic socialism than to liberalism (Bellamy 1986, 1987; MacGregor 1984, 1989a,b; Drydyk 1991, 1991a). Further, he was not dealing with Germany's early mode of industrialism, but with England's relatively advanced capitalist economy. During Hegel's period the English political and social landscape contained "new and important truths." Among these, writes Norman Gash (1979: 1-2), were "the special problems of the industrial working classes [which] were struggling for recognition."

An important section of the *Philosophy of Right* dealt with civil society, and its system of social classes. As we have seen, the economic order is a vital component of civil society. "The English Reform Bill," however, mentioned the economy—or as Hegel called it, the system of needs—only in passing. While Hegel (1964: 302) noted that "the interest of trade [was] the basis of England's existence," he devoted merely a single phrase to English industry—the wonder of the world. Even so, by detailing the class structure, his essay indirectly highlighted the concept of civil society.

Hegel used the term, "class" (*Klasse*) in the Reform Bill article, rather than "estate" (*Stand*). According to Z. A. Pelcynski (1964: 67), he was making an important point. In German, class has "economic implications of income or wealth, or the relations of production." Estate carries mostly political connotations. Although Hegel rarely utilized class to discuss social relationships on the continent, it was a key concept in the *Philosophy of Right*. Therefore, in this book—as in his piece on parliamentary reform—Hegel was usually referring to the mature English network of social classes.

Hegel's (1964: 295, 297, 328-9, 301, 312) article marked several "different classes and divisions." A basic economic boundary line separated the small number who owned property and the mass of propertyless people. Politically, the country was split between "the democratic element" and the "aristocratic" "power." Democrats desired change on the basis of individual rights while aristocrats opposed even minor alterations to a system founded on privilege. The Reform Bill, Hegel felt, was likely to shift the balance between these bitter opponents in favor of democrats. Although the bill would actually increase landlord representation, it would also bring in a "new class . . . new men and different principles." The new current of men and ideas would flow from a large middle group, located between "those who own much" and the destitute. This group included merchants, small manufacturers, shopkeepers, professionals, teachers, and artisans. These people questioned "the foundation of existing rights, a [position] to which external need, and the need of reason thereby aroused, has driven people who find existing rights oppressive."

Because Hegel did not explicitly call attention to his class analysis, the following is my own reconstruction. He discussed six social classes directly or indirectly in "The English Reform Bill." These are defined by property ownership or state relationships. The landed aristocracy occupied the leading position. Capitalists made up the second tier of society. Industrial and agricultural workers formed two separate classes in Hegel's scheme. At the bottom of the scale were the very poor, those without any means of earning an income. Bureaucrats and professionals took up the middle position between workers and the upper classes. Hegel's arrangement differs from the classical Marxist one, but it is similar to those recently proposed, for example, by R. S. Neale (1981) and Harold Perkin (1969, 1981).

Aristocrats combined material wealth with exclusive rights in the hierarchy of church and state. According to Hegel (1964: 323), most were "incompetent and ignorant"; they dissipated their lives in fox-hunting, social gatherings, pointless parliamentary debates, and newspaper reading. Like other members of what Perkin (1981: 103, 104) calls, "the professional class," Hegel "could not separate unearned luxury from the idea of sin." Thus his characterization of the English nobility was probably unfair, but it does not stray too far from that offered by historians. Bush (1984: 75, 195), for example, points to the nobility's "cult of amateurism which rested upon a belief in unpaid and untrained aptitude," and its enthusiasm for the virtue of non-involvement in any type of productive activity. Although F. M. L. Thompson (1963: 17) paints a much more flattering portrait than Hegel, he nevertheless observes that for many in the landed elite, "participation in the pleasures and engagements of social life was occupation enough in itself. The chief interest of others lay in hunting, racing or shooting."

Hegel (1964: 323, 326, 324) suggested that aristocratic leadership came from a small band of "brilliant men wholly devoted to political activity and the interest of the state." These individuals enjoyed little independence from the dominant class. Even exceptional personalities had to join one of the ruling political parties, all of which "[stood] within the same general interest."[10] Parliament had no room for "ideas which are opposed to the interest of the class and which therefore have not yet entered its head".

The vast wealth of the Anglican Church, said Hegel (1964: 304-6), provided "a sort of private property revenue" for the ruling aristocracy. Access to lucrative Church posts was in the hands of the government, which dispensed these to "younger sons or brothers [of aristocrats] who are left without capital because landed property in England goes to the eldest son." The Reform Bill, Hegel thought, would change nothing "so far as the wealth of the Church and its patronage are concerned." Indeed it did not. Cannadine (1990: 255-6) shows that until the mid-twentieth century, Church of England appointments, from lowly vicarships to bishoprics and deaneries, "were in the gift of the crown, which effectively meant that they were in the hands of the patrician political classes." For the younger sons of peers and gentry, appointment to the church meant, at the very least, "a big house and an assured income for life."

Hegel's emphasis on aristocratic power differed radically from the classic Marxist model; for him, aristocrats rather than capitalists were the ruling social group. Following the usual pattern for Marxists to blame the master's errors on Hegel, Nairn (1977: 15) avers that Marx derived his mistaken view of the English bourgeoisie as a ruling class from Hegel. Clearly, this is doubtful. In any event, Marx and Engels (1953: 38, 110) themselves sometimes portrayed the aristocracy as the English ruling class. Perry Anderson (1987: 24) shows that Marx and Engels "oscillated" between this, and two other views. Sometimes they saw the bourgeoisie as the English ruling class; at others, they felt capitalists shared state power with the nobility. The longer they were in England, however, the more likely they were to see the aristocracy alone as the governing stratum. As noted above, modern scholarship has gone in much the same direction.

Thompson (1977: 23) warns against confusing parliamentary democracy in nineteenth century England with domination by the bourgeoisie. Indeed, Thompson—along with Anderson (1987), Nairn (1977), Bush (1984), Cannadine (1990), Mayer (1981) Perkin (1981) and many others—argue for "the continued dominance of the landed elite until the First World War." J. V. Beckett (1986: 467) agrees that "The First World War proved to be the straw which broke the camel's back, and from which aristocracy emerged permanently weakened."

Long before 1831, the English aristocracy abandoned manorial ties with those who worked the land (Anderson 1987: 28). Landowners instead adopted strict capitalist standards of profit and loss, as Hegel (1976: 270) noted in the *Philosophy of Right* and (with Ireland as an example) in the "English Reform Bill" (1964: 307-8). Wrigley (1987: 189, 218) documents that from 1680 to 1820, England experienced huge gains in agricultural productivity combined with an "unprecedented rise" in population growth. "Between 1791 and 1831, English population rose from 7.74 to 13.28 million, at a rate of 1.36 per cent per annum, and in the peak decade 1811-21 the rate rose as high as 1.52 per cent per annum." The result of this increase, which greatly exceeded population growth anywhere else in Europe, was a landless rural stratum dependent on outdoor work and the Poor Law, and a large mass of people in the overcrowded slums of industrial towns. The first of these, the agricultural class, appeared several times in Hegel's (1964: 307) commentary. He referred only once to the urban class of "day labourers," or factory operatives.

However, the working class played a prominent role in the *Philosophy of Right*, as I will show in later chapters.

The near absence of the urban proletariat from Hegel's essay may have been due to the political climate. The working class was the most dangerous adversary of the existing order. Unrest in manufacturing towns was a constant headache for rulers in England and on the continent. In Germany, urban weavers and spinners "participated in riots directed against early factories, machines, and the houses of capitalists and civil servants." During the depression of 1830-31, almost half of the population of many German cities "could not live without some support from public funds or private charity" (Kocka 1986: 305, 293). In spite of this, Hegel (1964: 321) wrote provocatively about the working class in France.

> Since the [French] have been roused to take things and their share in them more seriously [than the English] they have seized a share in things for themselves in insurrections, clubs, associations, &c., and have thus gained a right and found compensation for the triviality of the part which their individual sovereignty plays in public affairs.

So far I have discussed three of the classes in Hegel's essay. The landless agricultural class and the working class were close to the bottom of the ladder, the aristocracy stood on the uppermost rung. Capitalists rivalled the aristocracy's economic reach, though not its political dominance. Members of this group ranged from small traders to "the leading bankers in London" (Hegel 1964: 312-13). Even before the Reform Bill, Hegel observed, the wealthiest capitalists—"the moneyed, trading, shipping, and colonial interests"—had secured political representation. Bank directors, "directors of the East India Company . . . great plantation owners in the West Indies and other business men, who dominate great branches of trade" shamelessly bought their way into Parliament. They did this "so that attention would be paid to their interests, and those of their associates, which in any case are of course so important for the national interest in England." Far from controlling English politics, however, this class felt itself endangered by the Reform Bill's provisions outlawing purchase of parliamentary seats.

Hegel (1964: 308) briefly discussed two other classes. One was the group of "beggars" and "surplus poor." This fluctuating heap was distinct from workers and farm laborers because it had no legal employment or income. There were proposals to send a million poor people from Ireland to the colonies, but Hegel doubted this would solve the problem. "The empty space thus produced would quickly be filled in the same way as before if laws and circumstances remained otherwise the same." Fifteen years later the Potato Famine wiped out a half-million Irish poor, but the country remained destitute, as Hegel predicted.

Another class was remarkable for its relative nonappearance in England, the universal class, or class of civil servants. There were, of course, naval and army officers, ambassadors, tax collectors, teachers, clerics, lawyers and doctors. But an independent public service, drawn from the middle layers of society and trained in public administration, was not present. There was hardly any executive power in Britain, little real authority rested with the Crown. The English division of powers between the monarch and parliament was based on an illusion; real executive authority rested not with the king, but with the majority party in parliament. A bureaucracy like that of France or Prussia was unnecessary in a country where parliament ruled supreme, and noble amateurs filled all the required government posts. "In defeating royal absolutism and avoiding popular revolution," writes Michael Bush (1984: 198), "the English aristocracy preserved a political system in which the presence of the state was weakly felt."

6. The External State

A central motif in Hegel's commentary on the Reform Bill is the almost invisible presence of a real state in England. The English system was a classic example of "the external state, the state based on need, the state as the Understanding envisages it." Here, Hegel (1976: 156) wrote, "the state is confused with civil society, and its specific end is laid down as the security and protection of property and personal freedom." Because the external state appeared only as an instrument to achieve particularistic ends, it lost its moral character, its connection with inner, spiritual meaning. Freedom or autonomy for everyone, regardless of wealth or family, was not a concern.

Carole Pateman (1988: 10, 25) notes that there is an "inherent ambiguity" in political thought about the term, civil society. Most theories attempt to define civil society by contrasting it with something else. "One contrast," she suggests, "is between civil society and the state of nature." Civil society represents civilization, while "state of nature [is] pre-social or asocial." For Locke, civil society restored the natural rights individuals once possessed in the state of nature, before these rights were lost to the despotic monarchical state. In Locke's view the free market is the "model for natural behavior, including the assertion of rights and the conclusion of agreements." (Hinchman 1984: 10)

Hegel rejected the idea that human rights originated in the state of nature; and he did not believe that civil society restored these rights. Just as the external state is another term for civil society, Hegel's state of nature doubles as civil society. The state of nature, for Hegel, represents a Hobbesian contest between unequal individuals. The contest is adjudicated by naked force. The result is what Hobbes called, "a little body politic," consisting of a master, on one hand, and a servant on the other (Hobbes 1966: 149-50, quoted in Pateman 1988: 47).

In Hobbes's "natural state," Hegel (1990: 181, 182) wrote, "all have the will to injure one another, and equally the will to secure themselves against the pretensions of others and to acquire greater rights and advantages for themselves. So there is mistrust of all toward all." Hobbes felt that despotic rule by a monarch was the only exit from the natural state. Hegel objected. The way out of the state of nature, he claimed, is a state based on reason, that is, "on the foundation of human nature, of human characteristics and inclinations." These rational, human qualities are lacking in the external state, which must be based "on force, must be held together by force." According to Hegel (1956: 284), ancient Rome provided the first historical instance of an external state; here subjectivity had some scope, but it was ultimately the plaything of a despot. Like Rome, the English state in 1831 was "not a moral, liberal connection, but a compulsory condition of subordination."

England's was the sort of state Marx would later define as the executive committee of the bourgeoisie (although here "aristocracy" should displace "bourgeoisie"). The English had a system of law, but wealth controlled it. Government itself was of, by, and for the rich. The aristocratic regime, noted Hegel (1964: 302), utilized England's hefty military machine to pursue economic interests overseas, and to handle "the danger of internal revolts." As indicated by the Peterloo massacre of 1819, and the repressive Six Acts which followed (Bentley 1984: 44-5), violence and coercion were major means of government. Neither bureaucracy or an independent executive were available to limit the sway of aristocrats and capitalists. This indeed was the "*state external*" (Hegel 1971: 257).

The nineteenth century English political administration reflected an important aspect of Hegel's concept of the external state. An external regime is not "weak," i.e. unable to use force and intimidation effectively to achieve elite goals.[11] In fact, the external state is distinguished by its capacity to employ coercion on a vast scale. Between 1756 and 1815, for example, Britain fought four long wars; about one-fifth of the male population of England, Scotland and Wales served in the military in the struggle against Napoleon. Unlike its continental rivals, remarks Linda Colley (1986: 106), "the British state was highly compact and immensely strong . . . [I]t showed an unrivalled capacity to raise men, levy taxes, conquer territory abroad and maintain stability at home."

The English state resembled what Hegel (1976: 110) called in the *Philosophy of Right*, "an association" to bring about "particular and common interests [of] self-subsistent individuals." In England, many felt that as a mere servant of particular interests, government should not interfere with virtuous wealth-creators; certainly, it should not dig too deeply into their pockets. Given this popular view, it was not surprising that—as Hegel (1964: 302, 301, 324) pointed out—"the enormous national debt" haunted the English mind. Supporters argued that the Reform Bill would bring "economies in administration." Even Henry Hunt, the lone independent voice in Parliament, called for smaller government. In this, as in other things, he was a proper representative of the radical cause. "Radical politicians of the years after 1815 rarely if ever showed any appreciation that increased State action financed by higher taxation might prove a beneficial agency of social improvement" (McCord 1991: 26). Writing in 1817, David Ricardo anticipated the prevailing mood. His textbook on political economy denounced big government, twice repeating J. B. Say's "golden maxim . . . 'that the best of all plans of finance is to spend little, and the best of all taxes is that which is least in amount'" (Ricardo, 1966: 242).

This argument did not impress Hegel. In the *Philosophy of Right* he (1976: 127) criticized the "subjective aims and moral fancies . . . [the] discontent and moral frustration" that led to political economy's distorted grasp of the state. Economists, however, had no corner on hypocrisy. The parliamentary opposition demanded government cutbacks and relief from high taxes. "These declamations," noted Hegel (1964: 301-2) in the *Prussian State Gazette*, "have been repeated in similar words every time taxes have been reduced in the last fifteen years." Extravagant spending was scandalous, Hegel admitted, but "if we bring under consideration the chief heads of public expenditure in England, it appears that there is no great room for economy."

Interest on the national debt swallowed a major part of revenue. Payments for the military soaked up much of the remainder.

> The cost of the army and navy, pensions included, is most closely connected not only with the political situation . . . but also with the habits of the military and naval men and their demand not to fall behind other classes in good living and luxury; and thus in this field there can be no cuts without risk (1964: 302).

Even if Parliament abolished the notorious sinecures in government and the Church, this would hardly reduce the debt. Anyway who would support a measure targeting the friends and family of aristocrats? For all the wailing, "Members of Parliament are of course protected [against taxes] by their wealth." There was a way to reduce the national debt, and taxes in the bargain. The state could simply decline to honor its commitments to debt-holders. Unfortunately, Parliament would not take this action because "it would . . . trespass too deeply on the inner constitution of particular rights." The power of wealthy individuals in England ensured there would be no "serious arrangements for diminishing the prodigious national debt substantially" (1964: 302-3).

Was Hegel right to doubt excessive spending by government? According to Norman Gash (1986: 47), over 70 per cent of state payments at the time went to charges for debts incurred during the Napoleonic Wars. The armed forces consumed most of the rest. Cheap government was a major factor in agitation for parliamentary reform. However, the English enjoyed a very low rate of taxation, and had one of the least costly administrations in the world. Nor did Reform bring inexpensive government. In the decade after the Act, cost-cutting Whigs managed a saving of only £3.75 million "compared with £11 million net savings achieved by the reviled 'tory' governments of 1820-30. They were scraping the bottom of a barrel from which their predecessors had long ago removed most of what was disposable."

Breast-beating about taxes and the debt concealed the reality that England had scarcely any government at all. The goals of a real state were never on the parliamentary agenda. These included, Hegel (1964: 300, 330) explained, "such principles as the state's well-being, the happiness of their subjects, and the general welfare, as well as and above all else the sense of an absolute justice." Securing these ends meant "giving them reality in face of merely positive privileges, traditional private interest, and the stupidity of the masses." A weak state gave the British a "freer and more concrete condition of civil life," but it also exposed them to the unchecked power of the rich.

7. The Second Roman Rule in Britain

In *The Philosophy of History*, Hegel (1956: 287) made a direct comparison between England's sacrifice of public welfare to private interest, and the "passive severity" of Rome. For Hegel, Roman domination of Britain—like many other historic events—happened twice. It occurred once as the conquest of Great Britain by ancient Rome. The icy dictatorship of what Marx (following Carlyle) labelled, the "cash nexus" (quoted in Prawer, 1976: 72). marked the second coming of the Roman principle. According to Hegel, English emphasis on property and individual rights carried with it the decay of political life. This was the same dynamic, he (1956: 308) said, that ruined Rome. "As when the physical body suffers dissolution, each point gains a life of its own, but which is only a miserable life of worms; so the political organism is here [in Rome] dissolved into atoms—viz., private persons."

I argue that the connection between England and Rome illuminates Hegel's political theory. Roman subjectivity made a unique contribution to world history, and Hegel acknowledged this in the *Philosophy of Right*.[12] Rome also appeared in that book as a substitute for English capitalism; the "Roman principle" (Hegel 1956: 308) was identical with the principle of English civil society. "The Roman principle . . . exhibits itself as the cold abstraction of sovereignty and power, as the pure egotism of the will in opposition to others, involving no moral element of determination, but appearing in concrete form only in the shape of individual interests." There is no discussion of this similarity in Hegel's article on the Reform Bill. But seen in the context of his writings on Roman authority, the resemblance is unmistakable. Who knows whether Hegel sensed "The English Reform Bill" would be his political testament?

Heinrich Heine (quoted in Lukács 1975: 462) claimed that Hegel lived in fear that his students might finally grasp the subversive implications of his lectures. Heine took classes with Hegel, and was probably just half-joking. Nevertheless, Hegel was more candid in the classroom than he was in print. His lectures on the philosophy of religion commented directly on resemblances between modern civil society (that is, England) and Rome. Combined with statements in the *Philosophy of Right*, the lectures offer useful insights on Hegel's view of England's political system.

Hegel (1984: 150-51) lectured that the breakdown of the modern world demanded philosophy's effort to find and preserve truth. Here—as in ancient Rome—"all the foundations have been tacitly removed." Under capitalism, "moral views, individual opinion and conviction without objective truth, have attained authority . . . [T]he pursuit of private rights and enjoyment is the order of the day." Hegel despaired of an immediate improvement in social conditions. A union of reason and reality was possible only in the realm of philosophy. "How the present-day world is to find its way out of this state of disruption, and what form it is to take, are questions which must be left to [the world] itself to settle." Salvation, he thought, was not likely to come from the external state, or the ministration of a corrupt clergy. "The rigidity of an objective command, an external direction, the power of the State can effect nothing here; the process of decay has gone too far for that." The people, Hegel insisted, "are nearest to the condition of infinite sorrow; but since love has been perverted to a love and enjoyment from which all sorrow is absent, they seem themselves to be deserted by their teachers."

Many references to Roman law appear in the *Philosophy of Right*. These include legal enslavement of children and women by fathers and husbands. As I demonstrate in Chapter Five, Hegel had in mind not only Rome, but England as well. In his Berlin lectures of 1818/19, Hegel condemned the mortifying English trade in little children (1983a: 107).[13] Contemporary writers compared exploitation of children in the factories to the ancient slave system (MacDonagh 1977: 27). Richard Oastler was following an established formula when, in 1830, he wrote his electrifying articles on "Yorkshire Slavery" in the *Leeds Mercury* (Finer 1952: 50).

The old Roman republic contained a mass of propertyless individuals, dependent on the state for their livelihood. Marx used the Latin term, "proletariat" to refer to a working class separated from the means of production, and at the mercy of capital. Hegel, too, was reminded of the Roman proletariat when he surveyed the terrible conditions of dispossessed English children, women and men.

The final section of the *Philosophy of Right* outlined the major phases of world history. Its brief discussion of "the Roman Realm" resonated strongly with Hegel's article on the Reform Bill. The stages of world history are also aspects of the reality of Hegel's time.

Roman society, wrote Hegel (1976: 221), is divided by the extremes of "private self-consciousness . . . and abstract universality. This opposition begins in the clash between the substantial intuition of an aristocracy and the principle of free personality in democratic form." Besides describing Roman conditions in this passage, Hegel appears to be summarizing the conflict between the aristocracy and the movement for parliamentary reform. "As the opposition grows, the first of these opponents develops into superstition and the maintenance of heartless self-seeking power, while the second becomes more and more corrupt until it sinks into a rabble." Was Hegel referring to the morally bankrupt Anglican Church, and aristocratic despotism? He may well have been, since (as he pointed out in his essay on England) these went together with exploitation and degradation of the English working class, a leading force in the movement for reform.

Conditions similar to those Hegel (1976: 221) found in England led to the fall of Rome: "Finally the whole is dissolved and the result is universal misfortune and the destruction of ethical life." According to Hegel, the choice for England in 1831 was between reform or revolution. Ten years earlier, when the *Philosophy of Right* was published, the reform movement in England looked hopeless (Brock 1973: 1). Like many others at that time (Cannon 1973: 165-7), Hegel may have felt that revolution, not reform, was in store for England. "The government," writes John Cannon in *Parliamentary Reform,* "preached resignation and practiced repression." In any event, Hegel's (1976: 221-2) final verdict on Rome also applied to English civil society. "All individuals are degraded to the level of private persons . . . possessed of formal rights, and the only bond left to hold them together is abstract insatiable self-will."

8. "Badges, Roasts, Beer, and a Few Guineas"

Hegel divided the Reform Bill article into four main parts. The first two outlined issues surrounding reform of the franchise; the last installments criticised the limitations of the proposed Act. The second half of Hegel's essay has mystified and irritated many critics. M. J. Petry's influential commentary is typical. Instead of discussing "the benefits" of reform, Petry (1984: 138) writes, Hegel "proceeds to condemn it . . . as subversive and dangerous, potentially revolutionary."

Was Hegel mad, as some critics have argued? Was he taking the side of the Tory opponents of reform, as others have claimed? I do not think so. Throughout his commentary, Hegel (1964: 298) vigorously supported "thorough-going reform," and questioned aspects of the Bill that would compromise this goal. The last two sections of Hegel's piece reproached the Whig proposals because they would not go far enough (Avineri, 1972: 208). While England desperately needed profound social and economic change, the Whigs offered a deceptive political solution. Hegel's appraisal pertains to modern democracy, as well as a dramatically altered English Parliament. Moreover, it forms a bridge between the world of 1831 and the very different one analyzed by Marx in 1867.

The Reform Bill was not a measure for perfect democracy; reforming Whigs and reactionary Tories alike used democracy as a term of abuse (Gash 1953: 4). The Whig leadership believed reform would strengthen an aristocratic parliament, weaken the king, and avoid democracy (Hawkins 1989: 649). They believed universal suffrage and representation by population were dangerous utopian fantasies. "There was nothing democratic about the Whig reforms," writes Norman McCord (1991: 137), "nor is there any reason why they should have been so."

Hegel was commenting on the March, 1831 Reform Bill. The government put forward three versions of the Bill before it became law in June, 1832. There were important differences between the Bill Hegel wrote about, and the one that actually became law. This is crucial to understanding what Hegel was saying about reform (thus Pelcynski [1964: 315n-317n] misinterprets Hegel by confusing the 1832 Act with the 1831 Bill). The discussion which follows refers mainly to the Bill of March, 1831.

Most commentators agree that the first version of the Reform Bill prescribed a very modest decline in aristocratic power. Some, like D. C. Moore (1961, 1966, 1976), argue that it offered less than this. According to Moore (1966: 44-5), reformers were trying "to correct the conditions from which they believed the demands for reform had arisen—not to yield to these demands." Even in its later versions, writes Moore (1976: 232), "the Bill was not a 'concession' whose essential 'conservatism' would lie in the paucity of the things 'conceded' but an effort to impose a 'conservative' 'cure.'"

Hegel's evaluation complements that of Moore and others who believe the Reform Bill cemented aristocratic privilege. The Bill would not bring England a step closer to democracy; it would abolish features of the ancient system that favored the common people while maintaining many of the old inequities. Hegel mentioned the Duke of Wellington's famous speech against Reform. The ill-timed oration ultimately crippled Wellington's Tory government and handed victory to the Whigs (Cannon 1973: 201). Hegel (1964: 314-15) quoted the Duke's claim in that speech, "that the present House of Commons is so formed that no better could be elected." The unfortunate Duke was right, Hegel remarked with heavy irony.[14] "[I]n fact there lies in the Reform Bill itself no further guarantee that a House elected with its provisions and in transgression of the previously existing positive rights would be any more excellent."

Moore's interpretation of the Reform Bill is controversial, although it has gained increased acceptance since he first proposed it.[15] The standard approach is that the Whigs drafted the Bill to attract support from the urban middle classes. Reform would satisfy public opinion, and draw the middle group away from its dangerous anti-aristocratic alliance with the working class (Gash 1979; Brock 1973). Concessions to democracy may have been moderate, and based on ulterior motives, but they were concessions nonetheless.

Hegel's critics take the standard view as a basis for their disapproval of "The English Reform Bill." Yet Hegel's interpretation had plenty of support from his contemporaries. Reforming Whigs consistently argued that the Bill would strengthen the landed interest. Moreover, a radical wing of the working class opposition claimed that reform would buttress the aristocratic regime, and was not worthy of support (Brock 1973: 165-9).

The unreformed system may not have reached "such excellence" as attributed to it by the ill-starred Duke of Wellington. But it was not an unmitigated evil, especially considering the Whig legislation that replaced it. O'Gorman (46-52, 37) claims that the pre-reform "electorate was somewhat more representative of several of the major social movements of the time than we have perhaps believed." Under the old rules, more than half the voters were artisans or semi-skilled and unskilled workers. The system accurately expressed in many ways the prevailing political culture. "An electoral system in which the middling orders could play such an indispensable political role also enabled their ideas . . . to gain acceptance and legitimacy."

Even the most plausible benefit of reform, an increase in the number of voters, has been exaggerated. The standard version of Reform suggests that the electorate almost doubled, but as O'Gorman shows the rise in voters was "strikingly less" than this. "The Reform Act of 1832 . . . hoist[ed] the size of the electorate to a limit of 620,000 . . . an increase of between 35 and 50 per cent." The increase of about 200,000 voters was minuscule in comparison with the total population of England, Scotland and Wales of more than 16 million (Bentley 1984: 88).

As introduced by Lord John Russell, the Reform Bill outlawed many (though not all) of the "rotten boroughs." These were constituencies too small to escape the influence of government patronage, or that of a single family, or a handful of corrupt voters. The Whig package granted a few large manufacturing cities like Manchester and Birmingham—with populations of 182,000 and 144,000 respectively (Mingay 1986: 4)—two parliamentary seats, some smaller towns, one. Since the reformed Parliament would have almost 600 seats,[16] this allocation was not generous.

The Bill featured a network of voter qualifications which differed for boroughs and counties; far from simplifying the electoral system, it greatly added to the complexity of the old one (Seymour 1915: 20-21). A uniform borough franchise gave the vote to any adult male who lived in a home with a yearly rental value of £10. O'Gorman (1986: 47) explains that "The £10 householder of 1832 was, by comparison with his freeman and other predecessors, a wealthy man." Accordingly, this measure risked disenfranchising many voters, and as a result, it would take effect in stages. In the counties, so-called forty shilling freeholders would keep the vote. These were mostly tenant farmers "dependent in some way or other on their landlord's good will. Thus, the voters of an English county were not far from the ideal electorate of the propertied classes" (Brock, 1973: 29). The Whig proposal retained steep property qualifications for M.P.'s. Reform would not limit election campaign expenses, which exceeded £100,000 in some constituencies. As noted above, the Bill did make it more difficult for capitalists to purchase seats.

The landed aristocracy, Hegel (1964: 312) averred, would benefit from these measures; the urban middle class would lose. "Big cities or the trading interest" stood to gain only twenty-five seats, against eighty one to the landlord-dominated countryside. Many shared Hegel's view. Whig reformers themselves counted it "in the Bill's favour, that landlord's and the agricultural interest will lose nothing of their influence, but will more likely gain a relative increase." According to the first Bill (Moore 1976: 143; Brock, 1973: 138-9; Gash, 1953: 13). twenty-two seats would go to eleven boroughs with a population over 100,000 each. Hegel counted these—and three of the 20 additional borough seats—as urban, middle-class constituencies. The remaining seventeen new boroughs and sixty-four county seats (including nine in Wales, Scotland, and Ireland) would reinforce aristocratic power.

9. Results of the 1832 Reform Act

The 1832 Act dramatically increased urban representation from that proposed in the first Bill. Twenty-two new boroughs received two seats each; most were large, urban constituencies. Another twenty new boroughs received one seat each, but these were mostly non-industrial, small towns. Moore (1976: 180-81) concludes that even this liberalized redistribution was heavily weighted toward the aristocracy.

Hegel admitted the first version of the Bill would give twenty-five seats to the urban interests. Wasn't this better than nothing? The problem was that the old system itself had already changed, without any reform. Radical shifts in population and wealth made the ancient setup obsolete, but they also undermined aristocratic control. These changes meant that many counties now included large urban population centres. Thus, under the old system, people from sprawling towns like Manchester, Sheffield and Leeds could vote in county elections. As a result, urban voters swamped county seats that the aristocracy dominated, and threatened a take-over. By assigning borough seats to these cities Whig reformers were isolating the urban vote. The government was not succumbing to urban pressures, but trying to derail them.

Hegel (1964: 315-16) observed—a point on which Pelczynski thinks he was mistaken[17]—that the change from county to borough in the first Bill raised the property qualification for many urban voters from forty shillings to £10 (Cannon 1973: 247; Moore 1976: 149; Seymour 1915: 15); the many borough electors with a franchise based on so-called "ancient rights" rather than a property qualification also stood to lose the ballot. Strangely, said Hegel (1964: 317), this brought few protests from "the large class" of disqualified voters. The Whigs, it is true, proposed a compromise (Cannon 1973: 247) that allowed forty-shilling freeholders resident in the new boroughs to vote in surrounding counties (this became law under the 1832 Act). As Hegel pointed out, however, this weakened their rights. They had to travel to cast their ballot in an unfamiliar constituency; and the impact of their vote was likely to be negligible. A factor that Hegel did not mention is that the first version of the Bill prevented £10 borough voters from casting their ballots in the county, even if they had property outside the town (Seymour 1915: 21). As Moore emphasizes (1976: 151), this meant that many middle class voters would be disqualified from influencing the result in the counties.

The Reform Bill abolished voting qualifications that mostly favored poor people, as Hegel maintained. Ancient rights voters lost the ability to pass their vote onto their children, and many were disqualified by residence requirements (O'Gorman 1986: 39). Charles Seymour's (1915: 88) classic study claims that reform "weakened enormously. . . [t]he electoral strength of the working classes." The overall result of the 1832 Act, John Cannon (1973: 257) confirms, "was to reduce the electorate in a considerable number of towns, and particularly to cut the working-class vote." Significantly, the Bill disenfranchised women, an exclusion angrily noted by contemporary feminist reformers like Anna Wheeler (Taylor 1983: 61). Under the old law a small number of adult females had the vote because of ancient rights and freeholder qualifications. The Whigs excluded women along with minors, the insane, and civil servants.

Reform would inflate aristocratic power at the expense of capital, urban voters, male workers, and women. This contradicted "the modern principle" of one person, one vote (Hegel 1964: 313, 316). It also went against the peculiar English notion that major interests should have representation in Parliament. Further, the Bill did not require a secret ballot. As a result "numerous weeks of feasting and drinking" paid for by candidates would continue to characterize British elections. This was especially true in rural areas, where ballot-peddling was a major industry. (Open voting was the rule in England until 1872.) The £10 requirement was unlikely to prevent wealthy landowners from recruiting propertyless but willing borough voters who could be easily bribed with a badge and some alcohol. "Hundreds and thousands of propertyless tenants" who once posed as forty-shilling freeholders, could do just as well "in the disguise of £10 freeholders."

The vote itself belonged to electors with only geography (and property qualifications) in common. Ordinary voters would have little leverage against the elite that selected and fielded candidates. Moreover, the wishes of constituents had no impact on the behavior of M.P.'s Like feudal monarchs, legislators would be answerable "to no one for the fulfilment of their duties" (Hegel 1964: 319).

In any event, a single vote carried little weight. Hegel (1964: 318, 321) calculated that in France, for instance, "one vote is a two-hundred-thousandth part of the total voting power and the ninety-millionth part of one of the three branches of the legislative power." It is "no wonder at all," he reflected,

> that in England a great number of individuals . . . require to be stimulated by candidates before they will take what is to them the trifling trouble of voting, and for their trouble, which advantages the candidates, they have to be compensated by them with badges, roasts, beer, and a few guineas.

Hegel's (1964: 318-19) critical analysis of representative democracy has not lost its validity. In the United States, for instance, there is widespread indifference to the vote. Yet it is the only means for "people to participate in public affairs and in the highest interests of the state and the government." As long as the vote is a disconnected ballot cast along with thousands of others, it has limited meaning. A century and a half after Hegel, a single ballot is still worth much more to the candidate than to the voter. Moreover, a successful life in politics remains prohibitively expensive. I will discuss Hegel's recommendations for a democratic politics in the final chapter.

10. Reform or Revolution?

The Reform Bill, Hegel argued, would not touch the sources of aristocratic power. Parliament would remain supreme; courts of justice would still belong primarily to the rich; the Crown would grow even weaker; and wealthy amateurs would continue to run the tiny public service. All sorts of privileges in the Church and government would endure. Yet Hegel (1964: 301) thought reform might rejuvenate English society. Aristocratic domination was so complete that even the minor setback promised by the Bill would likely come as "a shock" for a section of the ruling group. Perhaps he was thinking of the widely reported outburst of scornful laughter that swept opposition Tory benches after Lord John Russell's opening speech on reform. Still, there was another, even more important reason for his assessment.

Hegel (1976: 135-6) suggested that the "positivity" of English law exposed it to sudden, radical change. Let us look more closely at his sometimes perplexing use of the terms, positive law and positivity. In the *Philosophy of Right*, Hegel employed the English example to define positive law, comparing the "monstrous confusion" of England's legal system with that of the "later Roman Empire." Thus, he saw irrationality and positivity to be closely related. This, if you will, is the negative side of positivity. However, law is also positive in Hegel's sense whenever it is written down and enforced by an administrative system. Codification allows every individual to be aware of the law, to consider its validity, and to act accordingly. This is the favorable side of positivity.[18]

Hegel (1976: 135) contrasted positive law with the philosophical concept of right. Unlike positive law, the philosophical concept conforms to universal principles. Every order of positive law may contain some elements, at least, of the concept, but no existing system is likely to embrace them all. Positive law also differs from tradition and custom, which "are known only in a subjective and accidental way, with the result that in themselves they are less determinate and the universality of thought is less clear in them."

Hegel (1964: 135-6) was contemptuous of English "unwritten law." After all, the law was written in the form of judicial precedents that filled "numerous quartos." Further, the concept of an "unwritten law" gave judges authority to make up any interpretation of the law they wished. English claims of superiority were fraudulent.

> No greater insult could be offered to a civilized people or to its lawyers than to deny them the ability to codify their law; for such ability [is] . . . only that of apprehending, i.e. grasping in thought, the content of existing laws and then applying them to particular cases.

Every system of law is time-bound, and subject to distortions of influence and authority. In Hegel's terms, the closer an existing law is to the concept, the less positive it is. Accordingly, Hegel (1969: 299; 1976: 17) separated "the purely positive . . . *content*" of English statutes from the rights of real freedom. This "very important" contrast was crucial for Hegel's evaluation of the Reform Bill.

"Positivity" infected English statutes because the law had drifted away from philosophical considerations of justice and truth (Hegel 1964: 329, 299). As Hegel (1976: 136) put it in the *Philosophy of Right*, there was "a discrepancy between the content of law and the principle of rightness." So, English law had lost its "obligatory force."

Hegel inferred that the Reform Bill carried the seeds of significant change. Of course, it was inadequate. However, it forced rationality into an absurd legal system; the English people, he (1964: 315, 330) thought, would now employ democratic standards to judge future proposals. "The Bill contains an internal contradiction between positive rights and an abstract theoretical principle [which] . . . carried out logically would produce revolution rather than a mere reform." By denying legitimate rights while appearing to affirm them, the Reform Bill demonstrated in an even more "crude" fashion than the old system the true disjunction between equal rights and formal privilege. Reform, Hegel predicted, would bring "into the heart of government . . . principles opposed to the system existing hitherto." The king was not strong enough to mediate between a small, but radical opposition and an entrenched aristocracy. As a result, the opposition might "look for its strength to the people, and then introduce not reform but revolution."

11. Aftermath

The test of wills came more quickly than Hegel expected, and it did not require any radicals in Parliament. Popular pressure for reform grew rapidly after introduction of the Whig proposal. The House of Commons carried the Reform Bill on 23 March 1831, with 302 voting for the government and 301 against (Hegel, 1969: 327). Defeat on an opposition amendment allowed the Whigs to press William IV for dissolution of Parliament. The ensuing election created a solidly pro-reform Lower chamber. After a summer in committee, a large majority of the House approved a modified version of the Bill in September, 1831.

The House of Lords threw out the Bill in the early morning of 8 October, about a month before Hegel's death. For eight dramatic months the aristocracy skated on the edge of disaster. As Hegel (1964: 325) foresaw, England did "indeed have to fear an extreme shattering of the bonds of its social and political life."

Reformers blamed the Bill's defeat on Anglican bishops in the Upper chamber. The bishops voted almost unanimously against the Bill; had they gone the other way, they would have produced a majority in favor. For the first time anti-clerical sentiments swept the country (Halévy 1961a: 42). A pattern of violence striking at opponents of reform quickly emerged. "Serious riots broke out at Derby and Nottingham; and Nottingham Castle which belonged to the [anti-reform] Duke of Newcastle was burned." Bloody disorders occurred in Bristol where mobs looted and destroyed the Bishop's palace, torched the city's jails and the town hall. Regular cavalry units suppressed the protest after four days of rioting; there were more than 400 casualties (Brock 1973: 253).

Artisans and workers mounted large demonstrations in London and Birmingham that frightened the rulers at Westminster. Rebellions in manufacturing centres shook the north of England. Wherever a group of operatives met, the conversation turned to *"whether it would be more advantageous to attack the lives or the property of the rich"* (Thompson 1968: 889, 898).

The government hesitated in reintroducing the Reform Bill after its October defeat by the Lords. This created suspicion in middle class political unions, like those of Thomas Attwood in Birmingham and Francis Place in London. They put pressure on Earl Grey's government, including threats to unite with working class radicals. Founded early in 1831, the National Union of the Working Classes "rejected the Whig Bill entirely" (Fraser, 1970: 43). There were a dozen active branches in London alone when the Lords turned down the Bill.

The government began to negotiate with Tory "waverers," the moderate opponents of reform in the House of Lords. Fearing the Whigs might introduce a watered-down Bill, Attwood proposed to put the Birmingham Political Union on a military footing. He claimed the idea was not to fight the government. Instead, the middle class would defend authority against reprisals from extreme elements, enraged by the failure of reform. Attwood's plan attracted other reform leaders, and rumors of private armies drilling in the streets terrified the cabinet.

The Whigs reached a secret agreement with Attwood, promising an undiminished version of the Reform Bill. Then the government called out the troops. It banned the worker's National Union along with middle class reform organizations. "By then what Attwood had wanted had been achieved. The Cabinet was revitalised in its determination to get the Bill through and, significantly, Parliament was recalled early in December and the Bill was reintroduced" (Fraser, 1970: 45).

In the bleak winter of 1831-32 the cholera epidemic that killed Hegel cut through the unskilled masses in London; an economic depression spread over the whole country. The government pushed the Bill through the Commons, which passed it, again by a decisive majority, in late March, 1832. It was now more than a year since Lord John Russell's opening speech on reform. Unfortunately, popular feeling had not yet sufficiently chastened the House of Lords. On 7 May, the peers voted down the Bill a second time, 151-116. Grey asked the King to create 50 new peers to guarantee passage of the Bill in the Upper House. William IV refused, and the Whig Prime Minister resigned.

Wellington accepted the monarch's offer to command a new government, but he had difficulty assembling a cabinet. The man who would succeed Wellington as Tory leader, Sir Robert Peel, refused a post. Peel could not agree to join a government committed, in William IV's words, to "extensive Reform;" others were reluctant to follow the Duke down a path he had once blocked (Brock 1973: 292-4). While Wellington struggled to form a credible administration, fury burst over the capital. "On the 11th [of May, 1832] monster petitions reached London from Birmingham and Manchester." Jeering protesters surrounded the royal coach on the way to St. James Palace, and King William faced the prospect of exile (Halévy 1961a: 55-6). "'I feel the crown tottering on my head,' he is supposed to have said" (Nairn 1988: 283).

Reform leaders organized a tax strike (Brock, 1973: 299). Francis Place's Political Union advocated withdrawing deposits to provoke a run on the Bank of England. Posters with Place's slogan, "To stop the Duke, go for gold," were everywhere in London. A run on the Bank actually developed, though perhaps due more to panic than to political action. "This does not imply that devices such as Place's were ineffective. The placard may have intensified the scare." In any event, middle class tactics alarmed City financial leaders. They wanted Grey and his Reform Bill to come back.

Attwood and others plotted to overthrow the Duke if he became prime minister (Thomis and Holt 1977: 90-91). In the middle of May the Commons made clear that a government led by Wellington was unacceptable. The King turned reluctantly to Grey. The Whig leader reclaimed power with a promise from William IV to create 50 peers if necessary to pass the Bill. The Lords admitted defeat. The Reform Bill became law on 4 June 1832, almost seven months after Hegel's death.

12. Hegel's Assessment of Reform

Was Hegel exaggerating when he said a revolution was possible in England? Some critics think so. Petry (1984: 158) claims that Hegel "allowed himself to be misled . . . by Utilitarian propaganda" in the *Morning Chronicle*. This newspaper was one of Hegel's main sources of English news, and a chief organ for supporters of reform. Cannon's (1973: 239) *Parliamentary Reform* throws a skeptical light on the "heroic quality" of the "days of May," but there are many historians who believe that the Reform Bill narrowly averted revolution in 1831-32. In the autumn of 1831 and in the "days of May," writes E. P. Thompson (1968: 898), "Britain was within an ace of revolution." Halévy (1961a: 43) compared the situation in Britain with the events of July, 1830 which overthrew France's Charles X. "If there had been no Reform Act," declares Michael Brock (1973: 334), the old system "would have been overthrown by more or less revolutionary means."

Hegel (1964: 315) was certain that if the Bill became law, it would save the existing order. The English were too practical, too focused on economic realities, to take the French alternative. Even though few would get the vote, "the middle and lower classes in the three kingdoms seem to be very generally satisfied with the bill." Moreover, he contended, the terms of the Bill made sure there would be no rapid change in the makeup of Parliament. This prediction also was born out. "The social composition of the 1832 Parliament hardly differed from its predecessor. Representatives of the aristocracy (particularly its eldest sons) and gentry still dominated the Commons" (Evans 1983: 216).

This result underlines the complexity of the Reform crisis. "It is not surprising," writes John Cannon (1973: 242), "that historians should have found difficulty in reaching agreement on the Reform Act when contemporaries themselves were so divided." The Bill favored the interests of landowners, but it split them along party lines. In particular, Whigs had long felt that the system of rotten boroughs was skewed toward the Tories (Davis 1964: 99-100). "Though less obviously creatures of agricultural pressure than the Tories, they owned more acres and were entrenched in county seats"

(Bentley 1984: 73). Popular protest in 1830 created the opportunity for the Whigs to bring to fruition a program of reform they had first proposed many years before. The framers of the Bill naturally were tempted to construct an electoral map that would increase their party's standing, and whether or not they actually did so, the Tories certainly suspected it. For example, Hegel (1964: 315) mentioned the opposition charge that the Bill deliberated left "untouched the boroughs belonging to the Duke of Bedford, whose brother, Lord John Russell, had introduced the Bill in the Commons." The stalemate within the aristocracy between Whigs and Tories meant that the Bill could not pass without intervention from outside Parliament. The great mass of people normally absent from the policy process suddenly found itself with the balance of power. As resistance to reform increased in Tory ranks, popular demand for the Bill, regardless of what it really contained, expanded dramatically (Bentley 1984: 78). Cannon (1973: 253) offers a compelling summation: "Though in motivation [the Reform Bill] was anti-democratic, in appearance it was democratic, and won for Grey the support of his own militants and the vast majority of radicals in the country."

The aftermath of reform bitterly disappointed the working class, and stimulated the Chartist movement. Yet something else happened as well. "To step over the threshold, from 1832 to 1833," writes Thompson (1968: 887), "is to step into a world in which the working class presence can be felt in every county in England, and in most fields of life." David Roberts (1979: 49) comments,

> While no one believed that England [after the Reform Act] was a *tabula rasa*, one free of the House of Lords, the Church of England, and law courts, there was a sense that England's oligarchies had lost their sovereign veto on further reform and that now rational men could end irrationalities and injustices.

Hegel (1964: 301) had expected a shift like this. "One instinctively suspects that more far-reaching change will issue from this subversion of the formal basis of the existing order." Having once been given a chance to weigh a central public issue on the basis of fairness and equality, the English people would no doubt demand to do this again in the future.

Reform brought a few radicals to Parliament. It also loosened the age-old structure of the House of Commons and opened opportunities for leadership (Evans 1983: 218). Contests over the spoils of office persisted. However, they were displaced in importance by "all the problems of social reform which the unreformed House had systematically shelved" (Davis 1964: 218). While the power of the landed interest was undiminished after 1832, Parliament experienced a new vulnerability to the feelings of ordinary people. "After its signal demonstration during the reform crisis," says Norman Gash (1953: 28), public opinion "exercised ultimate control over the extent and direction of [aristocratic] rule." This outcome conformed to Hegel's (1964: 329) expectations.

> When claims of a new kind, which hitherto have scarcely come to halting and involuntary expression and have not been so much demanded as vaguely feared, come to be increasingly discussed in Parliament, the opposition changes its character: the parties have an object other than that of getting the Ministry.

For Hegel (1964: 329), "general ideas about freedom, equality, the people, its sovereignty, &c." could not resolve the impasse of modern politics. Instead, the times required a real state. This meant "a more fully detailed legislation, an organization of the powers of the state and the hierarchy of administrative officials, and the subordination of the people to these authorities." Avineri (1972: 219) points out that Hegel's "essay reads like an agenda for social reform in England." This project was largely realized in the years following Hegel's death. "Late Victorian England was a very different society from that of the early nineteenth century precisely because it moved along the path described by Hegel as necessary if England were to achieve the stage of a modern, more rationally ordered society."

The most spectacular accomplishment of the reformed Parliament was the Factory Act of 1833, and the Inspectorate created to enforce the law. "In some ways," writes Michael Brock (1973: 334), "the new House was more oppressive than the old." The Factory Act tipped the balance toward the working class. Significantly, three of the foremost Whig reformers—Lord John Russell, Viscount Althorp, and Sir James Graham—became strong supporters of factory legislation. As leader of the House in 1833, Althorp successfully proposed the 8-hour day for children under fourteen. This measure went beyond the demands of the working class Factory Movement. While Home Secretary, Graham (by then having converted to Sir Robert Peel's Conservative Party) introduced the 1844 Factory Act, which contained "revolutionary proposals concerning the provision of schools" for factory children (Thomas 1970: 194) and protected women as well.

"Lord John Russell supported the Ten Hours' Bill both in Opposition (1846) and when himself Prime Minister (1847)" (Davis 1964: 297).[19]

In 1831, Hegel surveyed a wide chasm lying between the English people and their government. Two years later it began, almost imperceptibly, to narrow. The closing of the divide between the working class and the state is a decisive theme in *Capital*. Relying heavily on the *Reports of the Inspectors of Factories*, Marx chronicled the upheavals that shook Britain after 1833. I will argue in the following chapters that an Hegelian conception of government and the universal class found its way into Marx's classic. The factory inspectors began the attack on capitalist property rights that created the modern welfare state.[20]

Notes

1. In Hegel's Germany, *"Smithianismus* became a cult, while [*The Wealth of Nations*] was likened to the New Testament in its social significance." (Finer 1961: 43).

2. In his influential "Figures of Descent," Perry Anderson (1987) contends that the British state stagnated between 1830 and 1870. Anderson confuses physical size with extension and effectiveness, and overlooks the work of such writers as Polanyi (1957), Finer (1961), Roberts (1960), MacDonaugh (1977), Thane (1990) and many others, including Marx (1976), who insist on the fundamental change registered in the English administration during those years. However, Anderson is in accord with a recent trend in British history that down plays the role of the state in the nineteenth century. "The Welfare State is not a way of seeing history any more," notes David Cannadine (1990: 181), "it *is* history."

3. I owe this observation to a personal note from Mr. Duncan Forbes. According to Forbes, Edinburgh-born David Hume was the first to remark on this English penchant.

4. Admittedly, using "England" in this context is an especially egregious misnomer. The real fount of political and economic thought was Scotland, of course. As Waszek (1988) has shown in brilliant detail, the Germans were fascinated with Scottish intellectual culture, and Hegel was no exception. The writers who influenced Hegel and other German thinkers included David Hume, Adam Smith, Adam Ferguson and Sir James Steuart.

5. "Whereas the continental European concept of the state referred to a living entity and inspired that entity, the Crown [in Britain] remained a theoretically undeveloped and lifeless abstraction" (Dyson 1980: 43).

6. Professor Sam Clark (1991: 6) observes that the term "aristocracy" had different connotations in England than in France or Germany. "In France the landed aristocracy consisted of a large 'nobility' recognized by the state

and enjoying legal privileges, while in England it consisted of a very small number of 'peers', who had the right to sit in the House of Lords, plus a much larger number of landed 'gentlemen,' most of whom did not possess a title." The state played a larger role in the control of aristocratic status in Western Europe than it did in England, where state interference was minimal.

7. Thane (1990: 5, 11, 13) argues that the central apparatus of the mid-eighteenth century English state was "comparable with most European states." The government influenced the lives of its citizens "in a variety of ways . . . [but] it did so by methods markedly less visible than those of its European counterparts." However, the streamlining of government after 1815, especially under the Tory regimes of the 1820s, "stripp[ed] away the great pre-modern weight of intrusive legislation, custom and regulation especially in relation to economic activity." The "Tory approach" was reversed by the Whigs after 1832.

8. The popular urban protests "of 1816-19," writes Richard Price (1986: 49), "were highly politicised illustrations of the extent to which élite hegemony had eroded and could no longer be taken for granted."

9. "That Hegel from his youth onwards," writes Duncan Forbes (1988: xiii) "was consciously and avidly observing the theory and practice of what he knew to be the most advanced commercial and industrial country in the world makes nonsense of one recent, very large and elaborate and apparently influential English book on Hegel that sees his political and social thinking as essentially German-bound and therefore backward looking and indeed medieval."

10. Hegel's characterization of the English landed aristocracy strikingly resembles Domhoff's (1987: 160; 1967: 5-9) analysis of the U.S. power elite. "Not all members of the upper class are members of the power elite. There are many jet-setters, sportsmen and -women, and coupon clippers within the upper class who cannot be considered 'active and working,' and they have very little to do with the exercise of power. Put another way, not all members of the upper class are members of the power elite, and not all members of the power elite are members of the upper class."

11. Professor Clark (1991: 85-6) points to the lack of conceptual tools required to measure the relative power of states. "We need to develop better conceptual frameworks for comparing states. We cannot contrast England and France [for example] merely as strong versus weak. In some ways England [in the eighteenth century] was the stronger state, in other ways France. Strength and weakness need to be broken up into different dimensions, such as the extent to which power is concentrated in the head of state, the powers of representative institutions, the centralization of these institutions, the military power of the state vis-a-vis other states, the magnitude of intra-state conflict, the size of the state bureaucracy, the size of the armed forces, the size of the territory and population over which the central state rules, and so on."

12. Remarking on this passage in a letter to me, Jay Drydyk writes that "one gets a different view from the vantage point of the philosophy of history. In Rome some are free. There is on one hand the emperor. He enforces Roman legality, and does so entirely arbitrarily. But this legality gives a restricted, private freedom to legal persons, -- citizens. Citizenship really meant something in the Roman empire; Hegel wasn't just making this up. Still, the power and caprice of the Emperor stripped this legal status of the practical personal or economic security that might attach to it. Hence people were driven to express themselves, subjectively, in the other world rather than this. Enter Christianity. Hegel saw the democratisation of modern Europe as part of the tendency to make this other-worldly subjective freedom secular, realizable in political and civil society ... In this light, Rome is more than a stand-in for England. It epitomizes the institution of private right at the expense of security in pursuing one's welfare and participation in political life. The historical tendency is for subjective freedom to achieve greater security and participation. England is simply slower, i.e. closer to Rome than to the future."

13. As already noted, Prussia adopted compulsory schooling for children in 1763; by 1816 60 percent of Prussian children under 13 were in school, by 1880 all children were attending school (Frevert 1989: 83-4). Children and women were employed in Prussia as well, of course; the first Prussian law regulating employment of children was passed in 1839. However, abuses on the scale of England's did not emerge until mid-century when the German industrial revolution was in full swing. Children under the age of thirteen were finally banned from German factories in the 1890s (Raff 1988, pp. 101-2, 188).

14. G. A. Kelly (1978: 17) along with many other commentators, suggests that Hegel actually agreed with "some of the positions of the Duke of Wellington regarding the English Reform Bill." This may well be true. There is no doubt, however, that Hegel dissented from the Duke's recalcitrant opposition to reform, and his sanguine views about the "excellence" of the English electoral system. The lines immediately following Hegel's ironic remark make clear his rhetorical intent: the Duke's speech, said Hegel (1964: 315), put "the previously existing positive rights ...on the same footing as the right on the strength of which he [Wellington] could as little lose his seat in the Upper House as the Prime Minister, Earl Grey, could be deprived of his properties in Yorkshire."

15. Bentley (1984), Bush (1984) and Cannadine (1990), for example, accept Moore's account; Brock (1973), Cannon (1973), Stone (1984), Beckett (1986), Gash (1979) and Thompson (1988) disagree with it. A good summary of the debate appears in Beckett's *The Aristocracy in England* (1986: 451-6).

16. The 1832 Act left the House of Commons unchanged from its pre-reform number of 658.

17. Pelczynski's (1964: 315-16) two misleading editorial notes to Hegel's article dealing with the electoral qualification show once again that editors should interfere as little as possible with an author's posthumous text. Pelczynski claims that Hegel misread the Bill's property requirement, confusing it somehow with the 1829 electoral reform in Ireland which accompanied the Catholic Emancipation Act, and which replaced the forty-shilling freehold with a £10 qualification. True, Hegel might have specified more clearly that under the English Reform Bill the 40-shilling requirement remained in the counties (although his readers would have known this in any event, since the issue was widely debated: Hegel was *interpreting*, not *reporting* the Bill). But the £10 borough qualification was the new feature brought by the Bill, and in the first versions of the reform legislation it did mean that many thousands would be disenfranchised. That Hegel knew the 40-shilling requirement was not abolished is clear from the sentence (1964: 317) in which he speaks of borough voters having to vote in the counties; the only borough voters affected in this way were the 40-shilling free-holders.

18. Hegel (1971: 259) pointed out that positive law is likely to be wrong even when it is right. For example, today statutes exist which rightly restrict consumption, purchase and sale of drugs deemed to be hazardous to health. However, some drugs included in these statutes, such as marijuana, pose little danger to health, while others, such as cigarettes, which are very dangerous, are not restricted. This sort of injustice, counselled Hegel, "happens and has from old happened in all legislations: the only thing wanted is clearly to be aware of it, and not be misled by the talk and the pretence as if the ideal law were, or could be, to be, at *every* point, determined through reason or legal intelligence, on purely reasonable and intelligent grounds."

19. Peter Mandler (1984: 85) argues in favor of "a genuine whig tradition of social reform," but he doubts Althorp's and Graham's commitment to the factory cause, while recommending Lord John Russell and Palmerston as the key Whig promoters of the regulated working day.

20. Asa Briggs defines the welfare state as "organized power deliberately used through politics and administration to modify the play of market forces" (quoted in Cannadine 1989: 182). By limiting the nature and quantity of labour available to capitalists, and enforcing these limits within the private confines of the factory, factory legislation considerably narrowed the property rights of capital. The conception of property rights used in this book resembles that developed by Campbell and Lindberg (1990: 635). "[T]he state shapes the organization of the economy by manipulating and enforcing property rights ... Property rights actions are state activities that define and enforce property rights, i.e., the rules that determine the conditions of ownership and control of the means of production."

3

A Hegelian Marx

When a delegation from the British National Union of Mineworkers visited the Soviet Union a few years ago, their hosts explained that Soviet Mineworkers begin their day at 6 a.m., work until noon, when they get a 15-minute break for lunch, then work again until 6 p.m.—six days a week. On hearing this, the British union boss observed: "You wouldn't catch British miners working like that. We're all communists."

—Globe and Mail (1989)

One of the key features of the post-communist world, indeed, is the vindication of Hegel against Marx, that there can be no higher freedom than that achieved by the rule of law in a constitutional state.
—Richard Sakwa, "The Hegelian Triumph" (1991: 15)

1. The Mystery of *Capital*

"Leonard Horner has resigned his post," Marx wrote to Engels (Marx and Engels 1985: 5) in January, 1860. Marx was referring to the chief inspector responsible for administration of the Factory Acts. "His last brief report is replete with bitter irony. Could you find out whether the Manchester MILL-OWNERS had a hand in his resignation?" There is no record of a reply from Engels, but the request stemmed from Marx's deep fascination with the "history, the details, and the results of the English factory legislation." This peculiar love affair reached full bloom and "occupied a great deal of space" in *Capital* (Marx 1976: 92). An unprecedented example of government regulation, the Factory Act of 1833 announced "the first beginnings of the welfare state" (Roberts 1960: 326).

Halévy (1961b: 172) called Marx "the great historian of the struggle to secure a legally restricted working day." Certainly, the German communist exiled in London was a unique observer and theorist of the interventionist English state. This chapter will provide a preliminary exploration of the role of the state in *Capital*, and examine some of the questions raised by the overwhelming and favorable presence of government in Marx's *magnum opus*.

The triple pattern and twist of dialectic that Hegel found so compelling are also features of what I shall call, the mystery of *Capital*. First, there is the story of the factory inspectors and the key role they play in Marx's chronicle of English social history. Given the accepted portrayal of Marx as an enemy of bureaucracy and liberal government, just what are the inspectors *doing* in *Capital*?

Another mysterious element is the general silence among commentators about the nature and significance of Marx's lengthy discussion of state intervention. The silence cannot be "innocent," since Marx himself called attention in the opening pages of *Capital* to his treatment of the Factory Acts.

Perhaps the most baffling aspect of the mystery embedded in *Capital* is Marx's own failure to draw explicit theoretical conclusions from his account of Victorian government. I will propose a tentative solution for this enigma in section four. Of course, there can be no completely satisfactory explanation without testimony from Marx himself. What I hope to show, however, is that had Marx decided to develop a political theory to explain the Victorian experience discussed in *Capital*, it would have been a Hegelian one. A key argument of this book is that Marx's masterpiece stands as the first test case of Hegelian principles in the analysis of a modern state.

State intervention in *Capital* brings to light a previously obscure piece of the puzzle formed by Marx's relation to his teacher, Hegel. The hidden Hegelian hand is present in many passages where Marx praises factory legislation, and "exalt[s] the marvellous success of this working man's measure" (Marx and Engels 1978: 517). For Marx (1976: 915), the regulatory state serves the interests not of capital, but the working class. Workers' "physical, moral, and intellectual" development is a key concern of "state intervention in factory affairs" (Marx and Engels 1978: 519; Marx 1976: 520). Marx's pivotal argument underscores his agreement with one of Hegel's major theses. According to Hegel, government as an independent power surfaces primarily as a counterpoise to class rule in civil society (Pelczynski 1964: 107). The modern state, wrote Marx in a similar vein (Marx and Engels 1978: 519.), arose chiefly in opposition to the "criminal folly" of the capitalist class.

Marx's Hegelian approach sets him apart from the earliest British writers on interventionist politics. The English, notes Sidney Webb in his introduction to Hutchins and Harrisons's classic study of factory legislation, "began with no abstract theory of social justice or the rights of man. We seem always to have been incapable even of taking a general view of the subject we were legislating upon" (Webb 1966: ix). His English contemporaries may not have been capable of such a view, but Marx was.

Capital is the most Hegelian of texts, not only because of its dialectic method and frequent use of Hegelian language, but because it takes the state seriously. Like other German political exiles of the time, Marx regarded with "admiration and envy . . . the [English] parliamentary system of elections and representation." Thus Marx outshone the political economists because he used empirical sources that they mostly ignored. The Hegelian dialectician was also a keen collector of neglected government reports and statistics.

> That Marx knew at first hand the neglect of such reports is testified by his disciple and son-in-law Paul Lafargue, who tells how Marx picked up the reports and parliamentary blue books cheaply from a waste-dealer in Long Acre, members of the House of Commons being in the habit of disposing of the books either in that way or by using them for shooting practice (Ashton 1989: 6).

Marx's attitude toward government in *Capital* contrasts strongly with another view both he and Engels expounded throughout their careers. In this version the state appears as a strong ally of the dominant class. As we saw in Chapter Two, Marx and Engels came to see the aristocracy rather than the capitalists, as England's governing class. This raised important questions about the character of the nineteenth century state that Marx and Engels tended not to pursue. Instead they focused their attention on the nature of government under communism "in which there would be no more conflict" (van den Berg 1988: 67). Given its function as an instrument—or partner—of the ruling class, the state in a future communist society ultimately "dies out" (Marx and Engels 1978: 713), since there are no longer any ruling groups to serve.[1]

In the Hegelian scheme, the state becomes more prominent, not less, with the march of history. Hegel's *Philosophy of Right* (1976: 160-61) urges that government is an entirely different phenomenon from civil society. The state has its own dynamic and its own goals. These derive from government's nature as an organized moral force, a source of identity for its citizens, and guardian of universal interests. The state is "the actuality of concrete freedom." It opposes caprice and selfish behavior in civil society, which is "subordinate to the [the state] and dependent on it."

This is also the notion of politics that surfaces in *Capital*. Marx (1976: 626, 915, 610) acknowledged that the English state is everywhere restricted by the parliamentary strength of the ruling classes. Nevertheless government enacts laws that will outlive the contemporary order. The state is no subservient player; nor is it a helpful partner of capitalists or the aristocracy. The state's "extraordinary and extensive measures against the excesses of capitalist exploitation" make it an antagonist of arrogant wealth and reckless authority. Government, said Marx , is the "concentrated and organized force of society;" factory legislation is the "first conscious and methodical reaction of society against the spontaneously developing system" of capitalism.[2]

In Hegelian political theory the state is more than a legislative and representative organization. As a special form of the social division of labor, it includes a particular group of individuals, the bureaucracy or universal class (MacGregor 1984, 1989a,b). The bureaucratic aspect of the state is mentioned in similar terms in Marx's (1974: 356) "Critique of the Gotha Programme," where he spoke of "the government machine . . . or . . . the state in so far as it forms through the division of labor a special organism separate from society." Hegel's universal class comes largely from the educated middle layer of society (the stratum to which Marx himself belonged). Bureaucrats have a unique structure of consciousness and represent interests different from those of landlords and capitalists, and also from those of peasants and workers. For Hegel, only the universal class is capable of a viewpoint that embraces the interests of an entire nation.

The young Marx poked fun at the *Philosophy of Right's* description of public servants as "upright, dispassionate and polite" (Hegel 1976: 193). Wrote Marx (1970: 125), "it is evident that [Hegel] is thoroughly infected with the miserable arrogance of Prussian officialdom, which, distinguished in its bureaucratic narrow-mindedness, looks down on the self-confidence of the subjective opinion of the people regarding itself." Denying that bureaucrats are blessed with a universal world view, he substituted the proletariat as his own "universal class." In *Capital*, however, the Hegelian universal class comes back with a vengeance. Marx (1976: 91) emphasized in the first few pages that the "competent" and non-partisan English bureaucracy was instrumental in exposing desperate conditions among workers. A primary difference between England and the Continent, he argued, was that Europeans lacked the formidable regulatory apparatus and personnel of the Victorian state.

> We [Europeans] should be appalled at our own circumstances if, as in England, our governments and parliaments periodically appointed commissions of inquiry into economic conditions; if these commissions were armed with the same plenary powers to get at the truth; if it were possible to find for this purpose men as competent, as free from partisanship and respect of persons as are England's factory inspectors, her medical reporters of public health, her commissions of inquiry into the exploitation of women and children, into conditions of housing and nourishment, and so on.

In the unfolding mystery story of *Capital* the factory inspectors are handed a crucial part. They are the ones who ferret out the clues of the crime, i.e. gross exploitation of women, children and men in factories and mills. Inspectors record the dismemberment and death of operatives in mills, the degradation of humanity in noisy factories filled with deadly cotton dust, the retailing of infants and children in big city flesh markets. Factory Act bureaucrats pursue the wrong-doers and bring them to justice, while ridiculing capital's powerful accomplices in the ranks of political economy. Most important, the Inspectorate is a leading force behind the solution to overwork and unsafe working conditions in industry: factory legislation. "No poison," said Marx (1976: 605), "kills vermin with more certainty than the Factory Act.

2. "A Remarkable Foreshadowing of *Capital*"

Marx's focus on factory legislation, and the Hegelian approach he adopted, closely followed the method employed in Engels's masterpiece *The Condition of the Working Class in England*. The young Engels's book, writes Stanley Hyman (1962: 162), "is a remarkable foreshadowing of the sociology of *Capital*." Stephen Marcus (1985: 139) observes that it brought "a Hegelian style of analysis to . . . an English social reality notorious for its capacity to withstand theoretical incursions." In an important study demonstrating the similarity between Marx's and Engels's method, Hunley (1991: 83) comments that "Marx cited blue books, factory inspector's reports, even newspaper accounts ad infinitum and quoted from them at length in exactly the same way that Engels had done." Engels's book, much read by, and influential upon, German radicals who had no personal knowledge of modern industrial life in 1845, was the first public assessment by a philosophically trained communist German observer of nineteenth century capitalist conditions . . . [Marx's] *Capital* completed the historical picture of the rise of capitalism in England for which Engels's work might have been a preparatory sketch (Ashton 1989: 5-6).

Factory inspectors are almost invisible in *The Condition of the Working Class*, but the Hegelian universal class is represented by crusading physicians and Children's Employment Commissioners, including Drs. Peter Gaskell, James Kay and Thomas Southwood Smith. Gaskell "is a Liberal," Engels (1969: 98) admitted, "but wrote at a time when it was not a feature of Liberalism to chant the happiness of the workers. He is therefore unprejudiced and can afford to have eyes for the evils of the present state of things, and especially for the factory system."

Engels based his account on English government reports,[3] and provided what must have been the first historical survey of factory legislation. From our standpoint, however, the most striking feature of the young Engels's narrative is the role of the state. "As we shall see," Engels (1969: 178, 126) wrote, "the power of the State intervened several times to protect [children] from the money greed of the bourgeoisie." There was no need, he felt, to explain the peculiar character of political authority to "*German* readers. If I were writing for the English bourgeoisie," he commented, "the case would be different." (In a note to the English edition of 1886, Engels lamented that German capitalists were now "fully up to the English level" in their ignorance of the nature of the state.)

It is unfortunate that Engels did not discuss the character of political authority. In failing to do so he set a precedent followed by Marx and him in all their writings.[4] Nevertheless, Engels (1969: 126-27) declared that his entire condemnation of the misery of the workers rested on a (Hegelian) view of "society as a responsible whole, having rights and duties." As "the ruling power of society . . . the bourgeoisie is charged with the duty of protecting every member of society . . . to see to it, for example, that no one starves." Holders of state power, therefore, "bear[] the responsibility for the condition of those to whom it grants no share in . . . social and political control." Engels's Hegelian politics meant in effect that the English bourgeoisie's shameless exploitation of the working class made it guilty of "social murder": "that [the bourgeoisie] *knows* the consequences of its deeds; that its act is, therefore, not mere manslaughter, but murder, I shall have proved, when I cite official documents, reports of Parliament and of the Government, in substantiation of my charge."

In the New Year's letter of 1860 in which he asked Engels about the fate of Leonard Horner, Marx (1985: 5) wrote that he had just "re-read" *The Condition of the Working Class* "at the Museum." "The state of health of the workers (ADULTS) has improved since your [book]," Marx opined, ". . . whereas that of the children (mortality) has deteriorated." The "miraculous progress" made by "industry in England . . . since 1850," he continued, has been documented by "the 'Factory Inspectors' Reports (of '1855'-'1859 first six months')." The conjoining of *The Condition of the Working Class* and the *Reports of the Factory Inspectors* in this missive may have signalled the turn in Marx's thinking on the state that reached maturity a few years later in *Capital*. "Marx's work," writes Rosemary Ashton (1989: 7),

> is a remarkable fulfilment of Engels's early boastful claim in his prefatory addresses to *The Condition of the Working Class in England*: namely, that the English, having ignored the reports and blue books which they alone in Europe are privileged to have available to them, have "left it to a foreigner to inform the civilized world of the degrading situation you [i.e. the working classes of Great Britain] have to live in."

Engels was still a Young Hegelian when he wrote *The Condition of the Working Class*, and this certainly explains the book's Hegelian overtones. "This book," Engels (1969: 26) wrote almost fifty years later, "exhibits everywhere the traces of the descent of Modern Socialism from one of its ancestors, German philosophy." But his Hegelian faith in government intervention remained constant. Thus it was Engels who emphasized in the 1886 "Preface to the English Edition" of *Capital* (Marx 1976: 113) that Marx's "whole theory . . . led to the conclusion that, at least in Europe, England is the only country where the inevitable social revolution might be effected entirely by peaceful and legal means." The example of factory legislation was without doubt a major factor in both Marx's and Engels's optimistic assessment of the future of English politics.

One thing is certain: Marx's view of the English state changed dramatically at some point after 1855. For example, in his 1855 description of the English parliament in dispatches to the *Neue Oder-Zeitung* there is no trace of sympathy for government. "The Reform Bill of 1831," Marx (1973: 282, 286) ventured, "opened the door to . . . the *millocracy*, as they are called in England: the high dignitaries of the *industrial* bourgeoisie." As a result of parliamentary change, "legislative history since 1831 is the history of concessions made to the industrial bourgeoisie, from the Poor Law Amendment Act to the repeal of the Corn Laws, and from the repeal of the Corn Laws to the Succession Duty on Landed Property." "Factory legislation," according to Marx in 1855, along with "the Septennial Act [and] . . . the most recent Poor Law," are examples of "the laws directed against the people . . . initiated by the Whigs."

If the language of "concessions" to the bourgeoisie and "laws directed against the people" characterized Marx's political vocabulary in 1855, his discourse had a Hegelian coloration by 1867. Thus the state appears as a third force in *Capital*. Government intervenes sometimes on the side of capitalists, more often on behalf of the working class, but always with its own discrete agenda.

3. "Converting Social Reason into Social Force"

Actually Marx (1973: 74-5) had prepared the stage for the new reformist-Hegelian language of *Capital* in the "Inaugural Address of the International Working Men's Association."[5] His 1864 Address practically began with the findings of a medical officer commissioned by the House of Lords to investigate nutritional standards among the working classes. Marx then quoted at length from "the *Sixth Report on Public Health,* published by order of Parliament in the course of the present year." The *Report* concluded that its "painful reflections" concerned "not the deserved poverty of idleness," but "in all cases . . . the poverty of the working masses." Throughout the "Address" Marx used "official statements published by order of Parliament in 1864" to ridicule a pronouncement by Gladstone, then Chancellor of the Exchequer. "The average condition of the British labourer," Gladstone claimed, "has improved in a degree we know to be extraordinary and untrampelled in the history of any country or any age." For a corrective to Gladstone, expostulated Marx, "look to the picture hung up in the last *Public Health Report* . . . Compare the *Report of the Children's Employment Commission* of 1863 . . . Glance at Mr Tremenheere's blue book on *Grievances Complained of by Journeymen Bakers!*"

Already Marx sounds like a herald for the English bureaucracy rather than an implacable enemy of the state. Any doubts in this regard are dispelled once Marx (1973: 78-9) comes in the Address to "the English Factory Act." "The immense physical, moral, and intellectual benefits accruing to the factory operatives, half yearly chronicled in the reports of the inspectors of factories, are now acknowledged on all sides." Marx proclaimed that "this working men's measure" represented "the first time that in broad daylight the political economy of the middle class succumbed to the political economy of the working class." It would be difficult to imagine a more laudatory view of state intervention, or a more portentous vision of its meaning.

> This struggle about the legal restriction of the hours of labour raged the more fiercely since, apart from frightened avarice, it told indeed upon the great contest between the blind rule of the supply and demand laws which form the political economy of the middle class, and social production controlled by social foresight, which forms the political economy of the working class.

The implications for political theory of Marx's paean to Victorian state intervention are clear enough. But it is worth emphasizing that even the use of government statistics to back up a case for social transformation has Hegelian-revolutionary significance. This was precisely the tactic of the young Engels when he used government documents to condemn the state itself for "social murder." Moreover, the power to name, to find the categories to describe in detail something otherwise obscure or invisible to onlookers, was a unique and radical achievement of the social reformers, report writers, and census takers of Victorian government. "The exposure of the actual state of things in particular fields," asserts MacDonagh (1977: 6), "was in the long run probably the most fruitful source of reform in nineteenth-century England." Significantly, when the reforming impulse disappeared among senior bureaucrats in the Factory Inspectorate and Home Office during the late nineteenth century, they lost interest in developing innovative data on the factory labor force (Davidson 1985: 183-5: Pellew 1982: 155).[6]

Thus arises the historical paradox that this achievement of the Victorian state contributed immensely to revolutionary politics. "The Victorian compromise," writes George Lichtheim (1971: 306), "offered radicals of that age a chance of turning philosophy into science." Earnest public servants made Engels's *The Condition of the Working Class* possible to write in the form it has come down to us, and, as I will show in this book, they played an important part in *Capital* itself. Moreover, both Marx and Engels were intensely aware of the significance of this aspect of Victorian government. "Only in

England," Engels (1969: 18) wrote in 1844, "has the necessary material been so completely collected and put on record by official inquiries as is essential for any in the least exhaustive presentation of the subject." Recording a similar sentiment in *Capital*, Marx (1976: 91) observed that Europe's lack of "social statistics" reminded him of "Perseus [who] wore a magic cap so that the monsters he hunted down might not see him. We draw the magic cap down over our own eyes so as to deny that there are any monsters."

Marx (1974: 86) emphasized the potentially radical character of data collection in his 1866 "Instructions for the Delegates to the Geneva Congress." There he recommended the kind of statistical procedures pioneered by English bureaucrats, especially the factory inspectors.

> One great "international combination of efforts" which we suggest is a *statistical inquiry into the situation of the working classes of all countries to be instituted by the working classes themselves.* To act with any success, the materials to be acted upon must be known. By initiating so great a work, the workmen will prove their ability to take their own fate into their own hands.

The "Instructions to Delegates" also included a discussion of laws to regulate the working day "without which all further attempts at improvement and emancipation must prove abortive." This account underscores Marx's familiarity with the experience of the factory inspectors. Virtually all his recommendations follow existing English legislation, or proposals put forward in the *Reports of the Factory Inspectors.* "Children and juvenile workers," he (1974: 89) advocated,

> must be saved from the crushing effects of the present system. This can only be effected by converting *social reason* into *social force,* and under given circumstances, there exists no other method of doing so, than through *general laws,* enforced by the power of the state.

George Lichtheim (1971: 99, 101) suggests that Marx had a much different view of the English situation than he harbored about conditions on the Continent. Thus, commentators who look primarily to his writings on European politics, miss the lessons contained in his accounts of the English system. "*Capital,*" contends Rosemary Ashton (1989: 7) in her book on London's German immigrant community, "is the supreme document to emerge from among the German political exiles in England in the mid nineteenth century, and its peculiar qualities are traceable in part to its German author's peculiar translation to England at a particular historical moment."

Nevertheless, the statist streak in Marx's writings is unmistakable even in some of his publications on Europe. A cogent example is provided by his "Critique of the Gotha Programme," a piece widely regarded as extremely anti-government. The 1875 Gotha Programme was the founding document of the new German Socialist Workers' Party (later the German Social-Democratic Party). It contained some formulations by the followers of the deceased Ferdinand Lassalle. These incensed Marx, but also prompted him to reveal his favorable sentiment toward government. Marx (1974: 357) criticized "the Lassallean sect's servile belief in the state." Yet he made use of American and English government experience to counsel the German workers on laws regulating education and the working day. There is nothing wrong with

> specifying the means available to . . . schools, the qualifications of
> . . . staff, the subjects to be taught, etc. by a general law, as is
> done in the United States, and having state inspectors to supervise
> the observance of these regulations, [but this] is something quite
> different from appointing the state as the educator of the people!

Similarly, Marx relied on the model provided by factory inspection in Britain for a system of working day regulation in a socialist republic. He (1974: 358-9) praised the (English) combination of education for children with "strict regulation of [their] working hours," as "one of the most powerful means for the transformation of present society" (a theme returned to in *Capital*). In addition, he recommended forming an army of state inspectors. These civil servants would be "removable only by a court of law" and would be liable to be taken to court by a worker "for neglect of duty." Moreover, he underlined the need for credentials for these bureaucrats: "inspectors should only be recruited from the medical profession." He also pointed out "that, in speaking of the normal working day," the Gotha Programme overlooked "the section of the factory laws relating to health regulations, safety measures, etc."

It must have struck Marx as ironic that German socialists forgot to include in their proposed factory law what every English bureaucrat in the field would have regarded as a basic right of workers! From a Hegelian point of view, however, ignorance among the German proletariat's representatives about the work actually done by bureaucrats should have been no surprise.

4. Ferdinand Lassalle

The Lassallean connection represented by the Gotha Programme actually offers a clue to the most perplexing mystery in *Capital*. If Marx had a favorable view of the state, why didn't he say so? What prevented him from shaping a political theory that took account of the Victorian experience? I believe at least part of the answer lies in the character of Marx's relationship with Ferdinand Lassalle[7], revolutionary *bon vivant*, romantic, and undisputed founder of German social democracy.

A follower and admirer of Marx, Lassalle fashioned Marx's revolutionary writings into a program of social change. He was much influenced by Hegel's theory of the state, and his consciously Hegelian politics infuriated Marx, who believed Lassalle placed altogether too much trust in the Prussian regime. Two years before his death in a duel, Lassalle developed the famous Workers Programme of 1862, which launched the German social democratic experience. In 1863 he became president of the newly founded German General Workers' Association. The Association was based on Lassalle's "Open Letter to the Central Committee for the Convention of a General German Workers' Congress in Leipzig." Lassalle's political platform called for integration of workers' organizations with the state, government aid for workers's cooperatives, and a complete democratization of representative institutions. The thrust of Lassalle's politics are revealed in two characteristic paragraphs.[8]

> Thus the purpose of the state is to bring about the positive unfolding and progressive development of man's nature, in other words, to realize the human purpose, i.e. the culture of which the human race is capable; it is the education and development of the human race into freedom. ("Workers' Programme".)
>
> The task and purpose of the state consists exactly in its facilitating and mediating the great cultural progress of humanity. That is its job. That is why it exists; it has always served, and always had to serve, this very purpose . . . ("Open Letter".)

There are many sentences celebrating the Victorian state buried in *Capital*'s vast bulk that sound as though they were written by Lassalle. Yet Marx's hatred (Raddatz, 1978: 185; McLellan 1973: 315-25) for the "Jewish Nigger" (as he once called Lassalle) and his jealousy of Lassalle's leadership of the German workers were enough, I think, to prevent Marx from exploring the implications of his own positive assessment of English politics. After all, for many at the time (perhaps even including Marx himself), "the crucial difference between Marx and Lassalle [was] their diametrically opposed views on the role of the state in the emancipation of the working class" (Grebing 1985: 36).

Lassalle's untimely end in 1864 may have spurred Marx once again to take an active part in proletarian politics. His Inaugural Address to the new International, written a few months after Lassalle's death, contained Marx's first published acknowledgement of the progressive role of the Victorian state. Political action later brought Marx sharply against Bakunin, who never doubted the statist streak in his antagonist. Indeed, Bakunin had no hesitation in linking Marx's political theory with that of Lassalle. The Russian anarchist's insistence on connecting them might have provided an additional motivation for Marx to avoid an explicit statement of his political theory.

In a private notebook, Marx copied out the passage in Bakunin's *Statism and Anarchy* which expressed "deep opposition to the theory of Lassalle and Marx." According to Bakunin, both of the German communists were advocating state dictatorship by the working class (Quoted in Marx 1974: 333). In his notes, Marx admitted that the proletariat might have to resort to governmental action in order to construct a communist society; significantly, however, he did not object to Bakunin's linkage of his political theory with Lassalle's.

5. "Too Ignorant to Understand the True Interest of His Child"

Whatever the reasons for Marx's suppression of an important part of his political outlook, his enthusiastic portrait of Victorian government reveals an unexpected strength in his analysis. Unlike many of his followers, Marx avoided treating the male working class Ten Hours' movement as entirely admirable in its motivations and aims. As a result, he presented a picture of the struggle for a restricted working day that conforms closely with recent findings.

Neil Smelser wrote a pioneering study of social change in the British textile industry. He showed that a Marxian two-class model was inadequate as an explanation for factory reform. Very often, Smelser (1959: 392) contended, the working class itself joined capitalists in opposing Parliamentary legislation. "After the Factory Act of 1833 was passed, it was *both* workers and capitalists who cooperated to evade the Act, lengthen hours, overwork children, and thereby increase the level of worker exploitation." In place of class struggle, Smelser suggested that threats to the traditional family structure were the most important factor behind the movement for factory reform.[9]

E. P. Thompson's *The Making of the English Working Class* provided what became the standard Marxist response to Smelser. Thompson (1968: 373) admitted that adult male factory operatives made an ambiguous contribution at best to factory legislation. However, he denied they "were indifferent to humane considerations," and argued that in employing child labor "the factory community expected certain standards of humanity to be observed."

Thompson's apologetics merely evaded Smelser's objection. They also ignored Marx's position in *Capital* that operatives and parents were among the worst exploiters of child labor. "The worker is no free agent," noted Marx (1974: 89). "In too many cases, he is even too ignorant to understand the true interest of his child, or the normal conditions of human development." In common with the factory inspectors themselves, Marx puts more blame on factory occupiers than on male workers for the sweating of children and women. There were good political reasons, as well as moral ones, for turning the spotlight on factory masters. Missing in both Smelser—who "did not refer to the 'state' at all as a theoretical category" (Alford and Friedland 1985: 145)— and Thompson, but not in Marx, is the cumulative role of the state in the struggle for factory reform.

Because Marxists have ignored, or dismissed the positive role of the state in Marx's work, they have stumbled into an error he warned against in 1872. In an article called "Political Indifferentism," Marx (1974: 327-8) scornfully outlined various criticisms of reformist working class politics. These criticisms suggest that any form of political compromise, especially the movement for government regulation of the working day, is "contrary to eternal principles."

> All peaceful movements, such as those in which English and American workers have the bad habit of engaging, are therefore to be despised. Workers must not struggle to establish a legal limit to the working day, because this is to compromise with the masters, who can then only exploit them for ten or twelve hours, instead of fourteen or sixteen. They must not even exert themselves in order legally to prohibit the employment in factories of children under the age of ten, because by such means they do not bring to an end the exploitation of children over ten: they thus

commit a new compromise, which stains the purity of eternal principles.

The words Marx sarcastically puts in the mouths of partisans of "political indifferentism" are similar to those many commentators bring forward as Marx's own position on the state.

> In the practical life of every day, workers must be the most obedient servants of the state; but in their hearts they must protest energetically against its very existence, and give proof of their profound theoretical contempt for it by acquiring and reading literary treatises on its abolition; they must further scrupulously refrain from putting up any resistance to the capitalist regime apart from declamations on the society of the future, when this hated regime will have ceased to exist!

6. Heroes and Villains in *Capital*

Like any classic mystery story, *Capital* has good characters and evil ones. Marx's opus, Stanley Hyman (1962: 138-9) affirms, "is crammed with heroes and villains." The English proletariat is "the true dramatic hero of *Capital*." Only a few of the heroes in *Capital*, however, are actual, living individuals. Among the most notable of these are "the factory inspectors . . . particularly their chief, Leonard Horner . . ." Marx (1976: 334) lavished rare praise on this Scottish bureaucrat, whose

> services to the English working class will never be forgotten. He carried on a life-long contest, not only with the embittered manufacturers, but also with the Cabinet, to whom the number of votes cast in their favour by the masters in the House of Commons was a matter of far greater importance than the number of hours worked by the "hands" in the mills.

The chief inspector, and many other public servants honored in *Capital*, may not have been forgotten by the proletariat. However, there is slight recognition of them in Marxist literature. Thompson's account of the English workers does not mention Horner or the Inspectorate. E. J. Hobsbawm's *Industry and Empire* contains a reference to "the admirable factory inspectors" (1972: 124), and there the matter ends. A recent neo-Marxist history of English government points out that Marx's treatment of the Factory Acts illustrated that he "did not . . . unproblematically treat states as obedient tools or creatures of a monolithic ruling class." However, the authors also relate their strong disagreement with Marx's commendatory analysis of Victorian interventionist politics (Corrigan and Sayers 1985: 184-5.)

Comprehensive studies on Marx's theory of the state, such as those of Miliband (1977), Hunt (1984), and Draper (1977: 514) offer nothing on the Acts, or the famous English government Blue Books. According to Draper, "Marx labored under the complication of feeling passionate hostility to everything the state bureaucracy represented. It was not merely an institution to be studied but an enemy to be fought." Writing on what he calls, Marx's and Engels's "blind spot," Tom Nairn (1977: 9) inadvertently submits a remarkable testament to Marxism's own blocked vision in this regard.

> From mid-century onwards the main theorists of the following century's revolutions lived in the most developed capitalist society, and the central part of their main achievement, *Capital*, was based to a great extent on study of its economy. Yet they wrote very little on its state and hegemonic structures . . . Marx's own general political ideas were formed before his exile in England . . . There were to be no further experiences compelling them to a more searching inquiry into the prior universe of the British state: their long exile coincided largely with an era of quiescence and growing stability in Britain, and this seems to have rendered them largely incurious about their immediate political milieu.

What accounts for Marxism's shyness about the factory inspectors, and the other bureaucrats mentioned in *Capital*? We find what we look for, said Hegel, and Marxists have not been looking for heroic government workers in *Capital*. Even if they could find them, Marxists have no theoretical framework within which to fit members of what Harold Perkin (1981: 103) has called, "the professional class". Neither workers or capitalists, and hardly the same as the compromised petty bourgeoisie of classical Marxism, the inspectors elude Marxist pigeon holes.

Marxists have done considerably better at delineating the dark figures in *Capital*, especially its foremost villains, the English bourgeoisie. This group is not, Marx (1976: 92, 97, 533) admitted at the beginning of *Capital*, "by any means depict[ed] in rosy colours." Nevertheless, Marx's portrait of capitalists is positively cheerful compared to the gray faces of his political economists, the women and men Marx lambasted as the bourgeoisie's "hired prize-fighters." These accessories to the crime, he observed, "preach the slavery of the masses in order that a few crude and half-educated parvenus might become 'eminent spinners,' 'extensive sausage-makers' and 'influential shoe-black dealers.'"

Marx's assessment of capitalists and political economists agreed with that offered by factory inspectors. Here, as on many other points, the communist and the Whitehall bureaucrats were of similar mind. After a few years experience with the Inspectorate, Horner and his colleagues formed a measure of contempt for the factory occupiers (as mill-owners called themselves) and their ideological cheerleaders among political economists. Writing to his daughter in 1837, Horner described a typical cotton master, Mr. Horsfield, of Hyde. This elderly capitalist

> is said to be worth at least £300,000 and can hardly write his own name . . . He took me to his house, as he was going to dine, it being *twelve* o'clock. He had a piece of cold beef and potatoes, no wine; he keeps one woman servant, and his daughter, whom I saw, was not much in appearance above the maid. He told me that at eighteen years of age he had not five shillings in the world, beyond his weekly wages; that out of his wages of fifteen shillings, he saved £28, bought a spinning jenny, and made £30 the first year. In 1831, he made a £24,000 profit; he employs about 1200 people. His is not a solitary case; there are many not very unlike him in this part of the country (Quoted in Thomas 1970: 4).

If *Capital*'s civil servant protagonists have been given short shrift by Marxist writers, the opposite is true of Fabian and socialist historians, who have produced important works on Victorian state intervention. As Smelser (1959: 394-5) suggests, these writers "are not far from Marx" in their sympathy for the workers, "and their explanation of many historical events" as instances of class struggle. But "in other ways" he continues,

> . . . these historians differ radically from Marx. Their outlook is neither so explicit nor so elaborate, and one finds no long streams of logic to connect notions such as "surplus value," "exploitation," etc., even though these and similar words are used by socialist historians. Furthermore, because these scholars are perhaps more nearly "straight" historians than Marx, it is more difficult to locate their guiding assumptions.

Still, the Hegelian view of state intervention that emerges from *Capital* is closer to that of socialist and some bourgeois historians than it is to the perspective of Marx's followers. Marx would have concurred with Maurice Thomas's (1948: 5-6) conclusion in his *Early Factory Legislation*. The factory masters "were ruthless, hard, and selfish;" these men of power and immense wealth "knew no scruples, they acknowledged no claims of humanity, they cared little, if at all, for the welfare of the men, women and children who came crowding to their mills." Capital's own cruelty inspired the rise of the state.

> It was this indifference to the needs of the operative classes that made state intervention necessary, and the story of factory legisla- tion . . . is the story of the gradual imposition of regulations and controls upon those who conceived that regulation and control would involve them in ruin.

Although Marx's view of state intervention accords with the standpoint of Fabian and socialist historians, it is based on "long streams of logic" foreign to these thinkers. The next chapter will begin the search for the Hegelian motivations that lie behind Marx's championing of the Factory Acts. We shall see also that there are crucial differences between Marx and Hegel in their outlook on the state. Nevertheless, these dissimilarities are not the ones usually mentioned by commentators. Hegel turns out to be more radical than Marx, not less.

Notes

1. This is the view commonly accepted as definitive by Marx commen- tators. See, for example, Ralph Miliband's entry on the state in *A Dictionary of Marxist Thought* (Harris et. al 1983: 464-8.)

2. An argument similar to that put forward in this chapter appears in Booth (1989), "Gone Fishing: Making Sense of Marx's Concept of Commu- nism,": "Marx lauds [the Ten Hours Act] as a 'social barrier' to capital, that is, as an instance of the subordination of the economy to the purpose of the community rather than to the requirements of the valorization process ... [T]he principal issue for Marx is the relationship between the 'blind power' of the autonomous economic process of capital and the community it governs, rather than the relationship between the bourgeoisie and the proletariat, both of which are governed in different ways by laws not of their own making." (p. 219-220.)

3. "The main sources of [Engels's] descriptions were his own firsthand experience of Manchester ... the English factory commissioners' reports for 1843, and Carlyle's 'Chartism' (1839) and *Past and Present*" (Ashton 1989: 5).

4. As Axel van den Berg (1988: 42) concludes, "the writings of Marx and Engels do not contain a coherent theory of politics and the state."

5. George Lichtheim (1971: 99,105) also noted a change in Marx's attitude toward politics that occurred by the 1860s, although he emphasized Marx's new-found belief in the representative aspect of the state, rather than a fundamental transformation in Marx's political theory. "The Marx of 1864 was the theorist of a *labour* movement and therefore committed to democratic socialism, however much this circumstance was clouded in his mind by the continuing struggle to overthrow the old regime." For Lichtheim this view of politics remained stable in Marx's mind, except during the period of the Paris Commune, when "under its influence Marx temporarily abandoned his realistic outlook of 1864 and reverted to the utopianism of the *Communist Manifesto.*"

6. Writes Davidson (1985: 245), "the 'social context' therefore determines the content as well as the pace of theoretical advances in statistical methodology. Such advances are goal-orientated and the choice of quantitative techniques is conditioned to a significant extent by the culture and ideology of dominant groups within society, and in particular by the economic and social philosophy . . . of the statisticians and social scientists involved."

7. A revealing account of Marx's relationship with Lassalle is provided in Fritz J. Raddatz , *Karl Marx, A Political Biography* (1978: 167-190).

8. This discussion, and the quotations from Lassalle, are drawn from Helga Grebing (1985: 35-37), *History of the German Labour Movement.* An interesting account of Lassalle's politics is provided in Anton Menger's *The Right to the Whole Produce of Labour: The Origin and Development of the Theory of Labour's Claim to the Whole Product of Industry* (1962: 117-125).

9. Smelser's thesis about the connection between changes in the family, factory work, and legislation on the working day has been decisively challenged at many points by Anderson (1976), and Calhoun (1982), among others. Nevertheless, Smelser's classic study offered a novel perspective on the factory cause. Burawoy (1985: 116) implies that Smelser's thesis has been revived by feminist writers who "delineate the family as a site of male domination . . . with a distributive function."

4

"Personality"

Mutual recognition by property owners is achieved through contract: "contract presupposes that the parties entering it recognize each other as persons and property owners"—the words are Hegel's, the greatest critic of contract theory, who lays bare the presuppositions of contract.
—Carole Pateman, *The Sexual Contract* (1988: 56)

It will not be forgotten that, where the labour of children is concerned, even the formality of a voluntary sale vanishes.
—Karl Marx, *Capital* (1976: 724)

1. Introduction

Parliamentary reform, and the 1833 Factory Act that followed, mark a profound divide between Hegel's and Marx's world. They also furnish a vital link between the two thinkers. The spectacle of political change at Westminster fascinated both men; and both were convinced of the importance of factory regulation. They realized that state intervention would alter the terms of the employment contract: "the *absolute foundation* of capitalist production" (Marx 1976: 1005). This chapter outlines the Hegelian critique of the assumptions underlying the employment contract. Marx accepted Hegel's critique—which centers on the idea of individual personality—only in part, with fateful results for his social theory.

The link between the contract for wages and the extraordinary analysis of poverty in Hegel's 1818/19 Berlin lectures on the Philosophy of Right is the subject of the first section. I argue that his account of the roots of mass impoverishment in civil society clarifies the role of the Hegelian "social state." The next two sections show that a fundamental goal of Hegel's state is regulation of the labor contract, including abolition of child labor and restrictions on working hours.

The remainder of the chapter explicates the meaning of "personality" in Hegel. The notion of personality reveals a dissimilarity between the latter's concept of the employment contract and that of Marx. We shall see that the difference hinges on a key distinction made by both thinkers between "means" and "ends." The development of human personality, not profit, is the true foundation and goal of the economic system. This philosophical and juridical ideal, originally developed by Hegel and by Thomas Hodgskin, was dropped by Marx. He replaced it with a materialist analysis of "surplus value," an analysis which has recently come under intense criticism. The concluding section sketches the Hegelian connection between property and abstract personality, and prepares the way for the next chapter, which deals with Hegel's theory of the family.

2. "Insanity of Personality"

Hegel saw the employment contract as the defining instance of bourgeois "insanity of personality" (1976: 50). The so-called free contract was, in reality, an insane agreement to make one person a slave for wages, and the other rich.[1] This was the source of the contradictions of wealth and poverty that threatened civil society's "external state" ("the state of nature"), and called forth the powers of the rational or "social state." These Hegelian terms for the state are important, and worth exploring. In Chapter Two, I argue that Hegel's terminology in the *Philosophy of Right* is illuminated by his 1831 analysis of electoral reform. The categories underlying the Reform Bill article are drawn from Hegel's political theory; similarly, Hegel's discussion of the actual English state reflects upon, and highlights, these categories. An example is Hegel's notion of the external state: it is at once a category of political analysis, and a label for a particular kind of government exemplified by England in 1831.

An external state, like the aristocratic-capitalist administration that ruled England, lacks means of representation and administration that would bring the interests of people with little or no property into government. Without these mechanisms state power is monopolized by the ruling circles of civil society. The social state, on the other hand, offers channels of influence for all classes and groups, so everyone can enjoy the benefits and wealth of civil society. In the *Philosophy of Mind*, Hegel (1971: 248) used the terms "law of nature" and "state of nature" as a code for capitalist property law, and the external state that enforced it.

> The law of nature is . . . the predominance of the strong and the reign of force, and a state of nature, a state of violence and wrong, of which nothing truer can be said than that one ought to depart from it. The social state, on the other hand, is the condition in which right alone has actuality: what is to be restricted and sacrificed is just the wilfulness and violence of the state of nature.

The best available commentary on this paragraph comes from Hegel himself in his 1819/20 Berlin lectures on political philosophy, where he described the situation of impoverished English workers.[2] These early lectures were given "by a Hegel who was not encumbered by fear or repression" (Avineri 1985: 201). He was considerably more frank about conditions in Britain than he would be after the Carlsbad Decrees imposed censorship throughout the German states. As Hegel's Berlin lectures are not well known, there is justification for a few excerpts.

First, Hegel (1983b: 194-5; Avineri 1985: 205-6) described the conditions giving rise to extremes of wealth and poverty in the external state, using England as his focus. (Notice the part played by lucrative government contracts in the generation of private riches.)

> The emergence of poverty is generally a consequence of civil society and grows necessarily out of it. Thus there accumulate wealth without measure or limits on one hand, and want and misery on the other. The spread of wealth and poverty go hand in hand .... Wealth accumulates in the hands of owners of factories (*Inhaber der Fabriken*). If one works for the state, the accumulation becomes even more significant through the business of suppliers and contractors. With the accumulation of wealth, the possibility for further extension of the enterprise through the accumulated capital (*gesammelten Kapitalien*) becomes even greater. The owner of large capital can be satisfied with smaller profits than those whose capital is more limited. This is one of the main reasons for the greater wealth of the English.
>
> With the amassing of wealth, the other extreme also emerges — poverty, need and misery. In England, the work of hundreds of thousands of people is being carried out by machines. Inasmuch as the industry of any country extends its products into foreign lands, the welfare of single branches of industry is becoming exposed to many accidentalities. In all these ways need and poverty accumulate. At the same time, the individuals become more and more interdependent through the division of labour.

Hegel (1983b: 195; Avineri 1985: 206-7) then outlined the consequences of this extreme division of rich and poor. One outcome is the destruction of culture in the working class, which is discussed below. Another concerns the lack of political freedom experienced by workers, and their consequent right to overthrow an oppressive government. A fascinating aspect of Hegel's approach is that while he grants that poverty is due to objective economic conditions ("mere being"), on one hand, it also arises, on the other hand, from the naked greed of the rich ("arbitrariness . . . human accidentalness"). This two-sided assessment of the nature of poverty and wealth in civil society underscores Hegel's skepticism about the prize hobbyhorse of political economists: the "neutrality of free markets."

> There is another gap which appears among the poor—the gap which distances them from civil society. Most of all, the poor person feels himself excluded and despised, and thus an inner revulsion and revolt . . . arises within him. He has a consciousness of himself as infinite and free, and out of this arises the demand that external existence should correspond to this consciousness. Within civil society it is not only natural need . . . which the poor person has to combat; that nature, which confronts the poor person is not mere being—it is my will. The poor person feels himself beholden to arbitrariness, to human accidentalness, and it is this which, in the last resort, is revolting . . . that he is thrown into this duality . . . by arbitrariness.
>
> It appears that self-consciousness is pushed to this extreme where it does not possess any rights, where freedom has no existence. From this point of view, where the existence of freedom becomes purely accidental, inner revulsion and revolt (*Empörüng*) become necessary. Because the freedom of the individual has no existence, there disappears the recognition of universal freedom. It is out of this situation that arises the kind of shamelessness which we discern among the rabble.[3]

Hegel's sentiment is clear: without freedom, revolt becomes necessary. Unless workers can develop "towards the self-consciousness of their right," i.e. organize and struggle against class domination, they risk remaining "stuck in their limitless poverty," and becoming a "rabble . . . [for which] the variations of self-respect disappear." As already pointed out, the plight of the poor is only partly due to impersonal mechanisms of the bourgeois economy. A more direct cause is the sheer evil of the ruling classes.

In this development of poverty, the power of the particular against the reality of the free person comes into existence. This implies that the infinite verdict against the criminal be taken into account. Criminal acts can be punished, but this punishment is accidental. In the unity of the substantive in its full scope lies the unity of objective right in general (Hegel 1983b: 196; Avineri 1985: 206-7).

Hegel was saying that the rich are guilty of the kind of crime Engels would later call, "social murder." To be sure that his students didn't miss this implication, Hegel went further. In the process he made it clear that the famous master-slave dialectic of the *Phenomenology* has direct bearing on the relationship between workers and capitalists.

Just as poverty appears, on the one hand, as the basis of the descent into the rabble, this non-acknowledgment of right, so a similar descent into ruffian-like behavior appears on the side of the rich. The rich person regards everything as something which can be bought by him, because he knows himself as the particularity of self-consciousness. Wealth can thus lead to the same disrespect and shamelessness to which the poor rabble has recourse. The consciousness of the master toward the slave is the same as that of the slave. The master knows himself as power, just as the slave knows himself as the actualization of freedom, of the idea. Inasmuch as the master knows himself to be master over the freedom of another, the substantive of this consciousness disappears. Bad conscience is here not only something internal, but an actuality (*Wirklichkeit*) which is being acknowledged.

If the poor are forced by "the corruption (*Verderben*) of civil society" into misery and shamelessness, or prompted to revolt to secure their freedom, shouldn't the authorities also have a right to respond with force? In a single sentence Hegel (1983b: 197; Avineri 1985: 207) revealed once for all what side he was on: "As for the rabble itself, one might think that it should be restrained by disciplinary measures: but in this way the essential rights of the citizens (*die wesentliche Rechte der Bürger*) would be affected." Hegel's account of the English working class is radical and compelling. Were it just a description of the conditions of the poor, it would be a remarkable narrative for its time, but it is more than that. Hegel's analysis rests on an understanding of the causes of poverty and degradation among workers that is superior to the one offered by Marx. The focus of Hegel's theory is the employment contract.

3. "A Duty to Protect the Children"

The contract for wages conceals antagonisms which threaten the stability of civil society. The wage bargain contains an *internal* contradiction that will occupy our attention in Chapter Seven. Yet it also may be *externally* voided, in two ways. *These external violations account for the ferment around factory legislation throughout the nineteenth century.* First, those who enter a contract must be mature, self-conscious individuals; in Hegel's terms, they must have a "personality." "Personality is that which struggles to lift itself above this restriction [of being merely subjective] and to give itself reality, or in other words to claim that external world as its own" (Hegel 1976: 37-8). Children—who have only an implicit, an undeveloped, personality—are automatically excluded from contract. This external violation of the wage bargain was also the first one recognized by the English Parliament.[4] However, legislators had much more difficulty accepting the second external negation of contract.

Hegel (1976: 54) argued that a worker must have some elementary control over conditions of employment. Children cannot make a contract for wages; adults must be capable of setting the terms for entering one. The most essential condition is the length of time a person may be normally required to work. Without definite time limits, the sale of labor becomes slavery. Along with abolition of child labor, regulation of working hours must be a key goal of Hegel's social state. Both forms of capitalist exploitation targeted by the state absolutely stifle the development of free personality.[5]

Factory legislation succeeded after lawmakers became convinced that the wage bargain could not apply to children. Parliament decided that children were in no sense "free agents," capable of making autonomous and rational decisions about their personal welfare. In the words of the Factory Commission of 1833, children in the mills

> are not free agents, but are let out to hire, the wages they earn being received and appropriated by their parents and guardians. We are therefore of the opinion that a case is made out for the interference of the legislature in behalf of the children employed in factories (quoted in Thomas 1948: 51).

Workday legislation was no bolt from the blue. As we shall see in Chapter Nine, controversy over child labor had occupied Parliament in one form or another at least since the beginning of the nineteenth century. By 1831 Parliament had passed seven Factory

Acts , including Sir Robert Peel's ground breaking legislation of 1802 and 1819. Because these statutes lacked machinery for adequate enforcement, they were ineffective. Hegel reflected directly on the movement for factory reform in England. In his lectures on law and the state given at Heidelburg in 1817-18, Hegel spoke openly on the issue. Significantly, his remarks came as Sir Robert Peel's bill to limit child labor and educate factory children—an effort inspired by Robert Owen and accompanied by agitation in the cotton districts—was before Parliament. "Parents," Hegel (1983a: 107, my translation) observed,

> should have neither the goal or advantage to drag their children out to work; here the state has a duty to protect the children. Thus in England children from six years old must sweep narrow chimneys, and in English manufacturing towns all little children must work, and only on Sundays does anyone care about their education. Here the state has the absolute duty to insist that the children be educated.

There is no mention of child labor in writings published during Hegel's lifetime. We must consider why. Advocating restrictions on working hours for children was already part of a radical working class program. Doubtless, Prussian censors would also have been sensitive to the intimate connection between factory agitation and limits on exploitation of children. This may have compelled Hegel to leave aside direct comment on the issue. He omitted the Heidelburg lines on child labor in the *Philosophy of Right*. However, he (1976: 148) did suggest that "in its character as a universal family, civil society has the right and duty of superintending and influencing" the education of children.

Hegel was well aware of the connection between shorter hours for children and education, a linkage already made by followers of Robert Owen and other reformers. Children could hardly be educated while confined for twelve hours and more behind factory walls. Speaking to a Philadelphia audience in 1829, the Scottish socialist Frances Wright observed,

> In your manufacturing districts you have worked children twelve hours a day .... What leisure or what spirit may [the] children find for visiting a school, although the same should be open to them from sunrise to sunset? Or what leisure have usually the children of your most thriving mechanics, after their strength is sufficiently developed to spin, sew, weave, or wield a tool?

Provision of universal education isn't enough, Wright concluded. "To build school houses now-a-days is something like building churches. When you have them, you need some measure to ensure their being occupied" (quoted in Roediger and Foner 1989: 22).[6] Hegel would have agreed.

4. "Alienation of Personality"

An early hint of the Hegelian inspiration[7] of Marx's treatment of the Factory Acts appears in a key chapter of *Capital*, "The Sale and Purchase of Labour-Power," which refers directly to Hegel's discussion of the wage contract. Marx (1976: 271, 272) saw that a free labor market, as opposed to a system of slavery, rests upon the worker's ability to limit the time she works for the capitalist. A worker's capacity to labor is her only property; it can remain such just so long as she restricts its employment. "In this way [the worker] manages both to alienate . . . his labour-power and to avoid renouncing his ownership over it." To support this argument Marx footnotes the following passage from the *Philosophy of Right*.

> Single products of my particular physical and mental skill and of my power to act I can alienate to someone else and I can give him the use of my abilities for a restricted period, because, on the strength of this restriction, my abilities acquire an external relation to the totality and universality of my being. By alienating the whole of my time, as crystallized in my work, and everything I produced, I would be making into another's property the substance of my being, my universal activity and actuality, my personality (Hegel 1976: 54).

Marx did not follow Hegel explicitly on this point: nevertheless, both saw the worker's private property in herself as a primary element in developing a personality, the ability to join the universe of culture and society. This Hegelian idea lies behind Marx's (1976: 270) definition of labor-power as "the aggregate of those mental and physical capabilities existing in the physical form, the living personality, of a human being ..." The substance of an individual's personality, according to Hegel (1976: 80, 54, 63), is her private property in herself. If she loses the ability to control employment of her labor—her "power to act," or "productive capacity"—she loses her personality, her faculty of creating herself. Marx (1976: 271) made the same point. "In order that its possessor may sell [labour-power] as a commodity, he must have it at his disposal, he must be the free

proprietor of his own labour-capacity, hence of his person."
Marx (1976: 1033) expanded on this in the addition to *Capital* entitled
"Results of the Immediate Process of Production." Within the wage
relationship, Marx wrote, the worker *"learns to control himself, in
contrast to the slave,* who needs a master." Opportunity for self-
development makes the "worker's work more intensive, more
continuous, more flexible and skilled than that of a slave;" it also
prepares her "for quite a different historical role." Revolutionary
consciousness itself is a product of the sale of labor-power.

Peter Archibald (1989: 63) emphasizes the paradox that to
become class-conscious a worker first has to develop a conception of
selfhood. "Unless individuals . . . distinguish themselves from their
social relations, activities, instruments of production, and products
to begin with, they are not likely to see themselves as having
produced them or to become dissatisfied enough . . . to want to
change them." The important point, however, is that if the sale of
labor-power is unrestricted, then there is no opportunity for self-
reflection, let alone revolutionary consciousness. An exhausted
worker has little time for self-cultivation or politics.

Workers in mid-nineteenth century England suffered what Hegel
(1976: 53, 241) called, "alienation of personality and its substantive
being." Labor is intrinsic to growth of personality, but work without
pleasure is slavery. A person confined in a factory fourteen or
fifteen hours a day, six or seven days a week, has lost control of
himself. For the English worker of Hegel's time there was no space
for pleasure, for the play of personality. Like the Athenian slave,
the worker "had alienated to his master the whole range of his
activity."[8]

"To industrial civilizations," write David R. Roediger and Philip
S. Foner (1989: 1), "few propositions seem more obvious than the
idea that twelve or more hours of daily labor are too many and that
workers can be expected to organize against so taxing a schedule."
Certainly many of Hegel's contemporaries shared this belief, but is
there evidence that Hegel himself felt that industrial capitalism steals
the worker's time, and leaves her bereft of culture? The passage
quoted by Marx indicates there should be limits to work time in civil
society; it does not say that such limits are absent. The *Philosophy of
Right* includes a discussion of the cultural degradation of the poor,
but the working day is not specifically mentioned. In the Berlin
lectures, however, there is direct reference to workload issues.
Hegel (1983b: 194-5; Avineri 1985: 206) noted that capital gave

workers no rest, compelling them to go to work even on Sundays. The exhausted English working class lacked both the means and the time for leisure, education, and health care. Even the doubtful consolations of religion ("religious institutions cannot be the immediate answer. Religious activity cannot confront immediate nature and needs") are beyond the reach of the proletariat.

> Poverty is then a state of civil society meaning an all-encompassing misery and deprivation. It is not only external need which burdens the poor; it is combined also with moral degradation. The poor mostly lack the consolation of religion; frequently they cannot go to church because they lack clothes or because they have to work Sunday as well. Furthermore, the poor participate in a divine service which is meant mainly for an educated public. Christ, on the other hand, says [Matthew 11: 5] that "the poor [should] have the gospel preached to them." The university training of most pastors is mainly of the sort which makes most teachers of religion more learned than able to speak to the heart and reveal the inner life *(das Innere zu offenbaren)*.
>
> Moreover, it is very frequently most difficult for the poor to enjoy the benefit of the law. The same applies to matters relating to their health. Even if the poor person is taken care of when ill, he still lacks the wherewithal for the regular maintenance and care of his health. If one would like to suggest to the poor to enjoy the pleasures of art, they would equally lack the means for such an enjoyment and would look upon such an injunction to enjoy art as a sorry joke.

Can there be any doubt that Hegel (1976: 54) was describing a class of individuals who have made "into another's property the substance of [their] being, [their] universal activity and actuality, [their] personality"?

Marx noted that many countries regulated the maximum length of a labor contract. This conformed with his and Hegel's theory. A worker was hired by the day, or month, or year, but never for an indefinite period. However, such legislation could suffice only in the abstract. More than the maximum total duration of employment has to be settled to make free labor possible. The state must also fix a reasonable daily and weekly maximum for work time. This idea has ancient lineage. During the feudal era, for example, "the ideal day [was] divided into three parts: work, pleasure and rest . . . [T]his three-fold and three-functional vision of time" was the basis of the "famous 'Three Eights' which became a rallying cry" for French workers at the close of the nineteenth century (Perrot 1984: 146).

In line with the Hegelian idea of personality, the working class in England and the United States saw shorter hours as a way to enrich their lives. A regulated working day would enhance workers' opportunities not only for leisure, but also for performing family duties, education, and participating in political life. Moreover, restrictions on the duration of work also increased workers' control over the labor process (an issue discussed further in Chapters Eight and Nine). Thus in the United States,

> employers perceived as early as the 1830s that exercising power over when to work could go hand in hand with exercising power over how to work . . . [S]tandardized hours helped remove from lower management one source of arbitrary control over workers: the manipulation of long days, layoffs, and unfavorable shifts (Roediger and Foner: ix).

Thirty years after the first effective Factory Act, Marx (1976: 1033) wrote "that newspapers . . . form part of the essential purchases of the urban English worker." The revolution in time required before English workers could have the pleasure of reading a newspaper is the primary subject of *Capital*.

5. "Means" Versus "Ends"

Concrete details like the length of the working day and child labor come later in the dialectical argument of *Capital*. At the point of sale of labor-power, considered abstractly, the capitalist and worker are equals, participators indeed in a free contract. "The only force bringing them together, and putting them into relation with each other, is the selfishness, the gain and the private interest of each. Each pays heed to himself only, and no one worries about the others (Marx 1976: 280, 283). Here is the world of the "free-trader *vulgaris*," the stamping ground of political economy. Child, woman or man, it doesn't matter; a contract is a contract. This is a most peculiar contract, however, for its outcome involves a subsistence wage for the worker and an enhanced holding for the capitalist. Labor-power, wrote Marx, turns out to be "a source not only of value but of more value than it has itself." The strange quality of the labor contract stems from the creative character of human labor and its diverse relationships with nature. Through the movement of labor, the individual "acts upon external nature and changes it, and in this way he simultaneously changes his own nature, and subjects the play of its forces to his own sovereign power."

Hegel's *Science of Logic* is a profound philosophical statement on the creative power of labor. As we shall see, Marx's failure in *Capital* thoroughly to rehearse Hegel's metaphysics of work accounts in part for the difficulties now faced by his theory of surplus value.[9] The philosophical concept of human creativity hinges on the distinction between "means" and "ends". The distinction goes back at least to Kant, but receives the fullest airing in Hegel (MacGregor 1984: 90-97, 244). Unlike human personality, machinery, capital, money and the like are only "things." They are not ends in themselves, but simply a means to something else. A book, for example, has no meaning aside from that invested in it by a reader; without a reader, the book is nothing. The same is true for any other "thing"—its vocation, as it were, is provided by its human user.[10] Human beings have a will, and are creatures of purpose and responsibility. Machines lack these qualities. The distinction is especially important in courts of law; a machine cannot be found guilty of breaking a law because a machine, unlike a woman or man, has no will, no purpose within itself.[11] Human action, for Hegel, is primarily "ideality," the transformation of ideas into concrete reality through mental and physical effort. The best example of ideality is *work*:

> work is a social relationship—a collective enterprise—whereby nature is subordinated and made a *means* to the diverse ends of men and women. Precisely because labour transforms natural objects into instruments and expressions of human will, work is also a chief aspect of the transcendental, creative quality of consciousness (MacGregor 1984: 13).[12]

The "means-ends" distinction underlies the term "means of production," as employed by both Hegel (1976: 129) and Marx (1976: 287). This economic-philosophical expression contrasts human labor, as an end in itself, with "things" that are a "means" to something else. However, both theorists recognized that tools and other instruments consumed in the process of production are more important than commodities directly used up by individual consumers. As Hegel (1989: 747) argued in the *Science of Logic*, the means of production are the points through which the rationality of the producer are conveyed to the end product.[13]

> But the *means* is the external middle term of the syllogism which is the realization of the end; in the means, therefore, the rationality in it manifests itself as such by maintaining itself in *this external other*, and precisely *through* this externality. To this extent the

means is *superior* to the *finite* ends of *external* purposiveness: the *plough* is more honourable than are immediately the enjoyments procured by it and which are ends. The *tool* lasts, while the immediate enjoyments pass away and are forgotten. In his tools man possesses power over external nature, even though in respect of his ends he is, on the contrary, subject to it.

Bourgeois economics claims that machinery, capital stock, and the like, are productive of value and profit. This is a denial of human creativity, and stems from an alienated thought process that confuses people with things. Marx (1976: 163) called this "the fetishism of the commodity." An early critic of political economy—Thomas Hodgskin (quoted in King 1983: 355), who is discussed further in Chapter Six—provided in 1827 one of the best analyses.

The language commonly in use is so palpably wrong, leading to many mistakes, that I cannot pass it by altogether in silence. We speak, for example, in a vague manner, of a windmill grinding corn, and of steam engines doing the work of several millions of people. This gives a very incorrect view of the phenomena. It is not the instruments which grind corn, and spin cotton, but the labour of those who make, and the labour of those who use them . . . The fact is that the enlightened skill of the different classes of workmen . . . comes to be substituted in the natural process of society, for less skilful labour . . . By the common mode of speaking, the productive power of this skill is attributed to its visible products, the instruments, the mere owners of which, who neither make nor use them, imagine themselves to be very productive persons.

"It is remarkable," writes David Ellerman (1990: 18), "that the human science of 'Economics' has not been able to find or recognize any fundamental difference between the actions of human beings . . . and the services of things." Two strategies are used to obliterate the notion of human will and responsibility. The first—which Ellerman calls, "the poetic view,"—is to treat things as people and vice versa. This is the strategy criticized by Hodgskin. The other is "the engineering view," which makes ingenious use of the passive voice: "Given so much land, labor, and capital, the product is produced." The economic position carries a grain of truth. Machinery and the like are certainly things, but the capacity to labor is both "a thing and not a thing," as Hegel (1976: 40-41) put it. Like other commodities, labor-power can be bought and sold. Thus it is easy to forget its character as a non-thing, i.e. as creative human personality. Under capitalism, noted Hegel in a deliberately ironic passage, everything comes within the scope of a contract.

> Mental aptitudes, erudition, artistic skill, even things ecclesiastical (like sermons, masses, prayers . . .), inventions, and so forth, become subjects of a contract, brought on a parity, through being bought and sold, with things recognized as things."

Like all commodities labor-power contains two forms of value, value in exchange and value in use. A razor, for example, has a certain use-value—it is helpful in the maintenance of a smooth appearance, wherever this is desired by a consumer. It also has an exchange-value—it may be exchanged on the market for a certain sum of money that represents its worth in terms of other commodities. Every "thing or performance," Hegel (1971: 245) wrote, referring to the "abstract universal thing, or commodity," contains a distinction between its immediate specific *quality* and its substantial being or *value*, meaning by value the quantitative terms into which that qualitative feature has been translated."

For Marx, the exchange-value of a razor, or any other commodity, is determined by the amount of socially useful labor necessary to produce it. Squandering labor-power with obsolete machinery and inadequate materials will not increase the razor's value, for exchange-value is based on the most efficient means of employing labor-power.

An individual's capacity to work differs from other commodities in one crucial respect: its exchange-value, which expresses the cost of maintaining the worker, amounts to less than its use-value—the worth of the commodities the worker can produce. Given appropriate market and production conditions, a person can produce commodities worth more than the combined total of the capital allocated to machinery, raw materials, and the worker's wages. "Therefore," wrote Marx (1976: 300-1), "the value of labour-power, and the value which that labour-power valorizes . . . in the labour process are two entirely different magnitudes."

Marx (1976: 378, 382) called the length of labor-time required for the worker to offset wages and costs of production, necessary labor-time. When the worker is employed for a period in excess of necessary labor-time, she creates "surplus-value." Accordingly, every capitalist has a built-in desire to keep the worker employed each day far beyond the point at which the value of commodities produced equals the costs of production and wages. This is only part of the story. Since the labor supply is infinitely elastic, that is, since there is almost always an ample supply of labor for capital, there is also a tendency to restrict wages. In mid-nineteenth century capitalism there was usually an over-supply of workers, whether they were women, children, or men. Capitalists faced a most desirable situation. The so-called free contract meant the worker was "compelled by social conditions to sell the whole of his active life, his very capacity for labor, in return for the price of his customary means of subsistence, to sell his birthright for a mess of pottage." A similar idea is expressed by Hegel. In civil society, he (1976: 128) wrote,

> dependence and want increase *ad infinitum,* and the material to meet these is permanently barred to the needy man because it consists of external objects with the special character of being property, the emodiment of the free will of others, and hence from his point of view its recalcitrance is absolute.

6. The Labor Theory of Value

At this point Marx's and Hegel's concept of the employment contract part company. So far we have seen it as an unequal exchange in which the worker is forced to labor for as long as the capitalist wishes, and for wages that are scarcely enough to keep her alive. But as Carole Pateman (1988: 58) argues, this is not a critique of the labor contract. Instead, it is a critique of the terms of the contract. Conceivably if the worker received full value for her work, this would validate the deal between capitalist and worker, although obviously the employer might quickly lose interest in the bargain. For Ellerman (1985: 303), the Marxist value theory is "quite irrelevant to the debate over capitalist production. Capitalism is not a particular type of price system or a particular set of value relations." The key issue is that under capitalism, the employer has the right to take the whole product of production. The best of value theories would only determine the value of the assets and liabilities in the whole product, but would not determine who ought to appropriate that bundle of property rights and obligations in the first place."

Marx (1976: 300) referred briefly to the possibility of a fair wage bargain representing "value for value." Nevertheless, he insisted that such a contract is impossible. Capitalists are solely interested in exchange based on exploitation, a relationship enforced by the societal power of the bourgeoisie. Recently, his theory of exploitation has fallen on hard times. The concept of surplus value deployed by Marx in *Capital* to prove the sole creative capacity of labor is flawed (Ellerman 1983; Wolff 1984; Winfield 1988; Macy 1988). Using similar empirical assumptions *any* essential unit in the productive process could be shown to be eminently creative. As a result, Neo-Marxist theory has abandoned the labor theory of value, or important elements of it. Some theorists argue that exploitation boils down to a positive interest rate; if the rate of interest is positive, workers are being exploited. But this removes the theory from any account of workplace power relations (Ellerman 1990). Another version of the theory, a "game-theoretic" model developed primarily by John Roehmer, "locate[s] the exploitative mechanism within the distribution of productive assets and not the purchase and sale of labor" (Macy 1988: 149). Accordingly, Roemer ends up with little to say about "the experiential dimension of class."

Marx believed the theory of surplus value was a scientific account of the worker's alienation, and the need for revolt; he never wanted to jettison the Hegelian themes that occupied his youth. "Historical materialism was only one of the bases," concludes Jerrold Seigel (1978: 372) in his probing biography of Marx,

> on which his economic theory rested; the other [was] the return to Hegel . . . By refusing to acknowledge this second guiding thread in his life—the philosophical and abstract as opposed to the materialistic and empirical one—Marx also covered up the labyrinth within which he had taken hold of it.

The exploitation theory has led Marxism away from the Hegelian vision, apparently against the intentions of Marx himself. What happened?

The answer lies, I think, in Marx's failure to grasp Hegel's own diagnosis of poverty and dislocation in civil society. As Drucilla Cornell (1989: 1597) suggests, Marx did not consider the connection, emphasized by Hegel, between the wage contract and the socio-philosophical theory of property. This absence still afflicts Marx's modern followers. "Despite the pivotal significance of a juridically articulated and enforced concept of property," Marxists offer nothing "but the vaguest indication of what they mean by property as a legal term" (Woodiwiss 1987: 515).

For Marx, the answer to capitalist exploitation lies in overthrow of the bourgeoisie and establishment of communism. Private property vanishes amidst a singular revolutionary upheaval. Revolution, it is true, results from workers forming themselves into a social class with a definite political organization, a process that takes place within capitalism. Nevertheless, the outcome is total abolition of the bourgeois system. In Marx's (1976: 929) pithy phrase, "the expropriators are expropriated." *Capital*, however, offers another prospect, one grounded in Hegel's political thought. Here the transformation of capitalism is an incremental development, based on change in the character of the state and in class relationships within civil society. Gradual transformation is hinted at in the first few pages of *Capital*, where Marx (1976: 92) wrote that "apart from any higher motives . . . the most basic interests of the ruling classes dictate to them that they clear out of the way all the legally removable obstacles to the development of the working class." The Factory Acts are a classic example of the slow but radical change Marx was talking about.

Marx was enigmatic about the linkage between state intervention and the development of the proletariat. Later chapters of this book will show that the connection appears in *Capital* but is not spelled out. The difficulty results from a lacuna in Marx's analysis of the labor contract. His discussion ends too early, or rather, begins too late. Marx shows that the free contract is faulty, but he does not investigate the roots of contract in private property. While he relates defects in the labor contract to government intervention, he does not directly fuse the wage contract to a theory of the state. For Hegel, distortions in the employment contract are legal-philosophical ones. They are not simply a matter of unequal exchange, although this is very significant. The partial working out of these deformations through a basic change in the wage contract is exactly what English factory legislation was all about.

7. "The Infinite Self-Relation"

A dialectical treatment of the wage contract in *Capital*, showing gradual change marked by state intervention, is perhaps the book's most Hegelian feature. Yet it is almost Hegelian in spite of itself since Marx's narrative is incomplete. A preliminary survey of the *Philosophy of Right*'s theory of property and contract should make plain the Hegelian sources of *Capital*. It will also, I think, cast a revealing light on Marx's notion of the state.

Hegel disagreed with Locke (Stillman 1989: 1040-41) that there is anything natural about private property. The right of property, it is true, expresses the substantive basis of human personality. For Hegel, however, property is a social right that people had to win through long struggle. Initially, the battle for property rights was unconscious and evolutionary; its definition and refinement in law were pivotal moments in the struggle (Maker 1987: 5). Thus, an important victory in this battle was limitation of the working day by the Victorian state; without such limits the individual had no time to develop as a personality. For Marx, as we have seen, the purpose of this legislation was to allow for self-development of the individual worker, which was impossible with an unregulated workday. Stillman points out that Hegel's understanding of personality as "dynamic and developmental" distances him from many modern political theorists who are not concerned with what "constitutes a mature individual who is able sensibly to choose for himself or herself." This contemporary lack of sensibility may account for the neglect of the role of factory legislation in *Capital*.

Macpherson (1983: 10) argues that the concept of property, narrowly considered as a right to exclude others from use or benefit of a thing, also includes the right not to be excluded. The property right means that an individual cannot be denied an unpolluted environment, means for self-support, or certainty that objects in everyday use are as safe as possible. Hegel also was aware of this contradiction, and its implications for politics. Property is clearly a right to exclude, to prevent others from enjoyment of a thing; it is also a right not to be excluded (Cornell 1989: 1590). The value of a thing, Hegel (1977: 448-9) wrote in the *Phenomenology of Spirit*, "lies in being *mine*, which all other acknowledge and keep themselves away from. But just in being acknowledged lies rather my equality, my identity with everyone—the opposite of exclusion."

As Hegel (1976: 30) initially developed it in the *Philosophy of Right*, property is abstract. That is, the concept applies only to the individual, and takes no account of social institutions. Nevertheless, it is integral to human freedom. Hegel's usage reflected one of the earliest meanings of property, where it referred not only to things, but also to a right in one's life and liberties. Slaves and serfs lacked such rights. A slave had no claim to her body or person; a serf was defined entirely in terms of his link to the land. Deprived of the rights of a person, devoid of personality, the slave and serf could develop no self-consciousness. "The slave does not know his essence, his infinity, his freedom; he does not know himself as human in essence; and he lacks this knowledge of himself because he does not think himself."

Property is the chief means through which human beings become aware of themselves and achieve recognition from others. Stephen R. Munzer (1990: 70)—whose book is an example of the new interest in Hegel among legal scholars—offers an interesting discussion of Hegel's theory of property. But Munzer objects to "Hegel's view [that] it is only, or even mainly, as owners that persons exist for one another." This is a common misinterpretation. Hegel said that outside of more concrete social relationships, like those of family or friendship, people encounter one another, and are important to each other, mainly as property owners.

We react to strangers primarily through the ritualized signs they offer as property owners; and we expect them to react the same way to us. This is one of the lessons of Erving Goffman's sociology. "Instead of worshiping the whole society or group, as symbolized by its gods and other public sacred objects . . . everyday rituals express regard for each person's self as a sacred object" (Collins 1988: 252). At a party, for example, strangers ask one another, "What do you do?" That is, they want to know one another's status with respect to occupation and life style. These are property questions, in Hegel's terms. Another lesson from Goffman is that modern capitalism vastly increases the individual's ability to build upon, and display the self as property. The vital resources of time, privacy and social space necessary to construct an image of the self were absent in earlier societies. "A wealthy capitalist society provides more material assets, including more of a repertoire of clothes, better housing, more private rooms, autos and other transport," observes Randall Collins (1988: 253).

> All these can be used as staging devices, so that individuals can show themselves to audiences when and how they choose. There is more material control of frontstages on which to present the individual self and more privacy into which the performers can retire when they do not wish to be viewed.

Property is more than an instrument for satisfying personal needs; people were able to fend for themselves long before the concept unfolded. Property stands for the relationship between person and thing, but this relationship can be fulfilled only in the presence of other persons. You may find your personality confirmed by possession of a certain object, but true consummation comes only with acknowledgement by others (Elster 1989: 136-7). That is why we like to try out our new clothes in public; it's no fun alone. "Property," writes Dudley Knowles (1982: 57),

> is a social relation akin to language in interesting ways; a medium of social transparency, it permits both self-expression and public intelligibility, both self-identification and mutual recognition. Like language, a consciousness which determines itself cannot be a private object of introspection.

The relation between a person and her property is abstract and external. However wonderful a piece of property might be, it is still only a thing. The connection between thing and person lacks the significance and warmth of a human relationship. The property relationship gains its real meaning through the eyes of other individuals, who validate this connection. "I, the infinite self-relation," wrote Hegel (1971: 244), "am as person the repulsion of me from myself, and have the existence of my personality in the *being of other persons*, in my relation to them and in my recognition by them, which is thus mutual." Modern anthropology has adopted a similar standpoint. Thus Polanyi (1957: 46) notes that "an individual does not act so as to safeguard his individual interest in the possession of material goods; he acts so as to safeguard his social standing, his social claims, his social assets." Property, says Lévi-Strauss (1987: 46), represents "not only physical objects, but also dignities, responsibilities, privileges—whose sociological role is nevertheless the same as material goods." The social function of property is to give expression to and obtain recognition for individual personality.

Strictly speaking, property refers to an individual's connection with an external thing, "something not free, not personal, without rights" (Hegel 1976: 40, 236). A thing, as we have seen, lacks an end in itself. It appears only as a means to an end. "This is made manifest when I endow the thing with some purpose not directly its own." How does this affect the relationship between an individual and an animal, say, a family pet? "When the living thing becomes my property, I give to it a soul other than the one it had before, I give to it my soul." For Hegel, then, the responsibility we owe as property owners to living things is akin to that which we hold for our own self.

Peculiar difficulties are involved in the connection between person and thing. Even a person's "capacity to act," his or her labor-power, can be treated in civil society as a thing. Moreover, confusion between what is a thing and what is not extends well beyond the employment contract. Under capitalism it runs even to barter in family members. Chapter Five will present the Hegelian concept of the family. It prepares the stage for the full emergence in Hegel's theory of the autonomous individual as a member of civil society, unencumbered by family connections and ready to appear as a property holder.

Notes

1. Hegel borrowed this idea from Rousseau. "Rousseau," writes Carole Pateman (1988: 75-6), "thinks that anyone who entered a contract to be another's slave would not be in his right mind. . . Rousseau argued that the story told by his fellow contract theorists was about a fraudulent contract that merely endorsed the coercive power of the rich over the poor." The connection between Hegel's property theory and that of Rousseau is explored further in Chapter Seven.

2. The 1819/20 Berlin lectures were among the recently discovered lectures on politics given by Hegel in Heidelberg and Berlin. The text quoted was translated by Shlomo Avineri (1985), who also provides an excellent introduction to the controversy surrounding these important lectures. Tony Smith (1990: 220) asserts that the lectures indicate that "Hegel . . . held radical positions that anticipate Marx to an astonishing degree." However, Smith attributes these positions to Hegel's "youth"! Perhaps at age forty-nine, after having finished the *Science of Logic*, and while preparing the *Philosophy of Right*, Hegel might still be described as being in his youth, but few would join Smith in doing so.

3. T.M. Knox observes in his "Translator's Notes," to the *Philosophy of Right* (Hegel 1976: 361) that "rabble" may also be translated as "proletariat."

4. The government was to decide in 1844 that women—like children—were not "free agents," capable of negotiating a fair contract with employers. This decision has been a key focus of debate among feminists; the controversy surrounding employment legislation for women will be discussed in later chapters.

5. Commenting from a legal perspective on the relation between Hegel's theory of property and the employment contract, Drucilla Cornell (1989: 1600) writes, "It is easy to conclude from Hegel's remarks on the damaging effect of poverty and unemployment on the self-conception of the person that the distress of factory work should be minimized through the public authority."

6. "The most notorious feminist radical in America," Frances Wright was the first woman to speak on a public platform in the United States (Taylor 1983: 66; Foner 1992: 13).

7. Richard Winfield (1988: 99, 76, 103-4, 87, 127) agrees that Marx and Hegel differed on the wage contract, but he sees much larger differences between the two thinkers than I do. On his view, Marx wrongly relied on the notion of exploitation and falsely assumed that the relationship between capital and labor was the key antagonism in civil society, while Hegel regarded the wage contract and profit-making as structures of freedom. Winfield overlooks the dialectic of property ownership in Hegel, and the key part played by the notion of personality in the *Philosophy of Right*. As a result, he fails to recognize Marx's dependence on Hegel, and presents a distorted picture of both thinkers. According to Winfield, Hegel's bourgeois society lacked the bourgeoisie, while Marx's mistake was to present English capitalism as an historical entity, instead of doing what Winfield does, and offering an ahistorical "just economy." For Winfield, "it makes no difference whether a factory be privately run, worker self-managed, or state-owned, or whether it employ wage earners, dividend receiving partners, indentured workers, forced labor or slaves." Profit depends only on "the break-even price of the product." Winfield avers that compared to his theory, Hegel's "efforts are fragmentary and often misguided," but Winfield makes a better case for the opposite conclusion.

8. In the additions to the *Philosophy of Right* drawn from students' notes on Hegel's lectures, Hegel (1976: 241) actually says that the "modern day labourer" is *unlike* the Athenian slave, because the latter "had alienated to his master the whole range of his activity." I believe that Hegel's point here is the opposite of what appears on the surface. Ideally the worker who contracts to exchange a limited period of labor for wages is different from the slave, whose whole being is the property of the slaveholder. But the modern worker who cannot restrict her hours of labor is precisely *like* the slave, except that the latter (as Hegel notes ironically) "perhaps had an easier occupation and more intellectual work." As we have seen, Hegel makes a direct comparison of the factory worker to a slave in his Berlin lectures.

9. "The conscious directedness and purposefulness of human action is now called the '*intentionality*' of human action ... Marx failed to connect intentionality to his labor theory of value and exploitation. This is in part because Marx tried to develop a labor theory of value as opposed to a labor theory of property" (Ellerman 1990: 22).

10. "Because a thing is essentially external, its notion is not contradicted if it is given a purpose from outside. In other words, what is essentially external *can* be used *merely* as a means; its end can be given to it by something that is other than it" (Benson 1989: 1164).

11. "While Marx did not use the word 'responsibility,' he nevertheless clearly describes the labor process as involving people as the uniquely responsible agents acting through things as mere conductors of responsibility. The responsibility for the results is imputed back through the instruments to the human agents using the instruments. Regardless of the 'productivity' of the burglary tools (in the sense of causal efficacy), the responsibility for the burglary is imputed back through the tools solely to the burglar" (Ellerman 1990: 22-3).

12. E. L. Doctorow's (1989: 10) *Billy Bathgate* contains a nice illustration of what Hegel meant by ideality. The youthful hero, on the way to watch a gangster launched into the sea with feet encased in cement, notes the sturdy, rational arrangement of the ship. "I had never been on anything bigger than a rowboat so all of this, at least, was good news, that something like a boat could be so much of a construction, all according to the rules of the sea, and that there was a means of making your tenuous way across this world that clearly reflected a long history of thought." (New York: Random House, 1989), p. 10.

13. The argument that the dialectics of labor are an integral part of the *Science of Logic* is fairly recent. For a discussion see my *The Communist Ideal in Hegel and Marx* (1984), and David Lamb's "Teleology: Kant and Hegel" (1987).

5

"The Father's Arbitrary Will Within the Family"

[Man's] two ruling animal propensities [are] sexual desire and love of domination
—William Thompson [and Anna Wheeler], *Appeal . . . (1970: 189-90)*

Kreon: Everything is second to a father's will.
—Sophocles, *Antigone (1973: 46)*

1. Introduction

In the last chapter we learned that Hegel's concept of individual personality is closely connected to the notion of property. Yet Hegel would have disagreed with modern libertarian theorists, such as Robert Nozick, who discuss property solely as a relationship between individuals (Munzer 1990: 153). Property has a social context. Practically everyone belongs to a family, the first social relation; an individual's personality begins and grows within a network of family ties. This chapter examines Hegel's theory of the family.[1] I will look at the theory partly as a conversation between Hegel and other theorists, and as a reflection on family relations in Victorian England.

Hegel's period, like ours, was marked by an historic upheaval around ideas about women and men, the family, and marriage. At the close of the Napoleonic wars, the surge of romantic radicalism, which began in the 1790s, dwindled in Germany and fell under seige in England; but it left a profound impression on Hegel. If early feminism influenced his theory, so did the empirical evidence of social change in England. In many ways, the structure of the modern family was forged by the wrenching transformations Hegel discussed. I try to show that his theory is pertinent to an understanding of the family at the close of the twentieth century.

Jane Roland Martin (1985: 7-8) suggests that the philosophy of women's education is the result of a "conversation over time and space" about "marriage, home, family" between rival philosophers. "My image of a conversation," she writes,

> derives from the fact that in *Emile* Rousseau was addressing what Plato had to say about women's education in the *Republic* and, in turn, Wollstonecraft, in *A Vindication of the Rights of Women*, was directly responding to Rousseau's *Emile*. Thus, history yields a natural conversational triad.

Hegel's concept resulted from a similar conversation. The radical sexual egalitarianism of Plato contributed to his theory, as did the misogynist constructions of Rousseau and Kant, and the feminism of Mary Wollstonecraft and Theodor Gottlieb von Hippel. Of all these theorists, however, Hippel—a writer Hegel appreciated "from his university days" (Knox 1975: 584)—may have had the greatest impact. While Hegel does not explicitly call attention to this, many aspects of his concept of the family have their counterparts in Hippel's (1979) "amazingly neglected" classic, *On Improving the Status of Women* (Dawson 1980: 31-2). These include, as adumbrated in sections two and three of this chapter, Hippel's delineation of the characteristics of women and men, his "ingenious reinterpretation" of the Edenic myth, and his analysis of German and Roman family law. Section four deals with the place of *Antigone* in Hegel's theory. I suggest that Hegel's interpretation of Sophocles's tragedy throws an unexpected light on his own conception of the character of women and men, and their domestic roles. Sections five and six focus on Hegel's concept of love, and the contradictions involved in this most intense and intimate relationship. The remainder of the chapter deals with the domestic power struggle between women and men. For most nineteenth century writers, consensus among family members, rather than antagonism, was the normal assumption. Until the 1980s, modern historical research shared this conception. Even among feminist historians, write Louise Tilly and Joan Scott (1987: 9), the supposition was "that a kind of collective ethos—a notion of shared interest—informed the behavior of individual family members." But Hegel's theory profoundly questioned complacent beliefs about family unity and mutual interest.

Sections seven and eight demonstrate that, for Hegel, the interests of the two sexes collide over issues of property and personality. The rights of the male head of family are in sharp conflict with those of his spouse and children. According to Hegel, this power struggle is so corrosive that the state must intervene to assert the rights of family members against those of dominant men. Sections nine and ten highlight issues identified by Hegel's theory that continue to define personal and family experience in the modern era. In the final section I contend that Hegel provided the opening that would eventually free women and children from domestic tyranny.

2. The Puzzle of Theodor Gottlieb von Hippel

Hegel's celebration in his lectures on fine art of T. G. von Hippel's comic romance *Careers in an Ascending Line* has "shocked" and "astounded" modern German literary opinion (Knox 1975: 584). Hippel, Hegel affirmed, was "a master in depicting and representing ... [the] monotony in buttoned-up, speechless men [which] is principally characteristic of Germans." He favorably compared Hippel's "depth and wealth of spirit" with that of the English novelist Laurence Sterne: high praise indeed for a writer often dismissed as a producer of sentimental potboilers. Hegel knew well that Hippel was also the posthumously disgraced author of a revolutionary 1792 tract on the liberation of women.

A successful bureaucrat and life-long friend of Immanuel Kant, Hippel was at the leading edge of the generation of German romantics who profoundly questioned accepted notions about the relationship between women and men (Vogel 1987). This movement reflected similar ferment in England, where Wollstonecraft's *A Vindication of the Rights of Woman*—published in the same year as Hippel's book—created an "immediate sensation," and in France, which witnessed among others, Condorcet's 1789 essay *Sur l'admission des femmes aux droits de cité* and Olympe de Gouges's pamphlet, *La déclaration des droits de la femme et de la citoyenne*, circulated in 1791 (Sellner 1979: 21). None of these early feminists survived the last turbulent years of the eighteenth century, but they strongly affected many key thinkers,[2] including Hegel.

Timothy Sellner declares that Wollstonecraft's and Hippel's "works, which complement each other in a remarkable way, ought perhaps to be considered *together* as comprising the first truly complete manifesto of feminism." Hippel's book, says Ruth Dawson (1980: 15), "began with the radical assumption that men and women are equal, a thought more drastic than even his English contemporary Mary Wollstonecraft was willing to assert clearly." In an argument that rejected the sexual division of labor, Hippel (1979: 80) claimed that patriarchal relations distorted the physical and mental differences between the sexes. Bourgeois society and the state provided men with outlets for their capacities that were forbidden women, who were treated "as mere parasitic plants."

Hippel averred that "pregnancy and childbirth," not physical and mental inferiority, were the "reason for the subordinate status of the female." The fact that women, and not men, gave birth to, and raised, children was itself evidence of women's superiority. He "found it inconceivable that an inferior being could be assigned this task" (Dawson 1980: 16). Hippel constructed a sophisticated anthropology to explain the origins of women's oppression. (Significantly, Hippel's version of the genesis of patriarchy was unknown to, or ignored, by Marx and Engels, who based their own theory on Lewis Henry Morgan's *Ancient Society*, a "rather unscholarly, and speculative book" [Barrett 1985: 13]). In early society, according to Hippel, both women and men hunted game. But by leaving hunting in order to invent agriculture, women offered men an historic opportunity. Males used their monopoly on weapons and warfare to turn women themselves into property, along with children and domestic animals. Wrote Hippel (1979: 89),

> Thus the woman gradually became mistress of the domestics, and before she realized it, the chief domestic animal herself. The poor woman—what could be more astonishing? By virtue of the very same revolution in which she brought freedom into the light of day, she herself became a slave!

Men, Hippel (1979: 110-11, 167, 147) opined, fear women; they realize that women have the capacity to achieve much more than their male coevals. As a result, men prevent women from speaking in public or from obtaining professional or state positions. "We do not wish to exert ourselves trying to keep step with the opposite sex," Hippel wrote. As if anticipating a theme in Virginia Woolf's (1986: 22-5) classic, *Three Guineas*, Hippel made fun of the pomp and ceremony indulged in by male elites, and claimed that elaborate masculine rituals were designed primarily to overawe women. By excluding the female sex from wider society, men had actually made it an enemy of the state. Familiar only with the private realm, and treated as "ciphers in political society," women could hardly be expected to become good citizens. Females in the families of powerful men, Hippel suggested, were tempted to use their "clandestine ... power of persuasion" to influence these men in favor of private, family interests rather than those of the state.

Hippel's argument pointed to the same contradiction Jane Roland Martin (1985: 62) outlines, when examining Rousseau's differential education for the boy, Emile, and the girl, Sophie.

> Sophie's domain is the home. By nature and education she is prevented from caring about any larger realm. Thus the only needs she will feel, the only desires she will have, the only aims she will pursue, will be personal and familial. When these are consonant with the public good the fact that she is accustomed to manipulating Emile to her own ends will be of no consequence. But when private and public purposes clash, as they inevitably must, Sophie's considerable manipulative skills will be directed to causing Emile to favor familial interests over his public obligations.

The answer to this domestic conflict, Hippel (1979: 167) felt, was to extend equal rights to women. "If you cease to withdraw from women those portions to which they have an undeniable right, you will automatically put an end to the insidious intrigues which women presently conduct to the disadvantage of their husbands and the state as well."

According to Hippel—in an argument that anticipated J. S. Mill's *The Subjection of Women*—bourgeois marriage was a masculine ruse for enslaving the opposite sex; and chivalrous notions of modesty and virtue were ploys designed to preserve female servitude. "The idea of chastity served a double purpose, first, to keep women out of competition with men and, second, to insure that paternity could be correctly identified" (Dawson 1980: 25). As a result of being treated "as [a] mere object[], without name and rights," said Hippel (1979: 132, 92), "the soul of the woman shrank ... into the limits of her household." Hippel condemned the view that the restriction of women was necessary to ensure the proper raising of children. Both parents, he thought, had an equal duty as caregivers. Hippel, an expert in German and Roman family law, wrote several editions of an anonymously published marriage manual, which reached a huge audience. The first two editions took a conventional view of marriage and the family, but in the third edition, printed in 1792—just after his feminist manifesto—Hippel called for absolute equality between women and men. Sellner (1979: 39) proposes that Hippel eventually came to realize that marriage "could not be perfected until equality between the sexes had been achieved."

Ute Frevert's (1989: 11, 57, 63-4) path breaking history of women in Germany applauds the contribution of Hippel's thought to feminism. German romantic thinkers like Hippel, Goethe, and Friedrich Schlegel, she writes, presented a vision of love and marriage as "a union of independent, individual people responsible for themselves. This daring blueprint envisaged free people who distanced themselves from preconceived ideas and shunned regulation by others." But Frevert sees Hegel as part of the backlash against Hippel and other progressive thinkers on women and the family. Indeed, portrayals of Hegel as an anti-feminist are now commonplace.

The strange connection between Hegel and Theodor Gottlieb von Hippel has never been explored. There are good reasons for this. Except for de Beauvoir's (1953) *The Second Sex*, important modern commentaries on Hegel's theory of the family date back only to the 1970s (e.g., Mills 1979, 1986; Moller Okin 1980; Elshtain 1981; O'Brien 1981, 1989; Landes 1981; Lloyd 1981; Easton 1987; Ravven 1988; Pateman 1988). Hippel's *On Improving the Status of Women* was out of print for about 140 years before it was rediscovered in the late 1970s (Sellner 1979: 17-18; Vogel 1987: 126; Frevert 1989: 11).

If timing is a factor, so is the tenor of Hegel's intervention and that of Hippel's. *On Improving the Status of Women* was a fiery attack on male privilege, in the style of the late Enlightenment, penned by an anonymous author. Hegel's discussion in the *Philosophy of Right* was an outwardly positive assessment of the bourgeois family, written in the stiff manner of a university course text, under the hypercritical eye of the Prussian censor. When read carefully, however, Hegel's account of domestic relations carries the same explosive charge as Hippel's.

3. *"Eve* and *Reason* Ought to Be Regarded as Synonymous"

An intimation of the parallels between Hegel and T. G. von Hippel appeared in their discussions about the psychological makeup of women and men, and their interpretation of the Biblical story of Adam and Eve. We have already seen that Hegel enjoyed Hippel's characterization of "buttoned-up, speechless men" in the comic novel, *Careers in an Ascending Line.* Hegel also learned from Hippel's discussion of the same topic in *On Improving the Status of Women.* One important difference between women and men, Hippel (1979: 117, 191) asserted, is that women seldom stay angry long; men are more often sulky, and tend to hold grudges. Generally, women have a sunnier disposition than their male partners, who are prey to "vanity, pride, avarice, and adulation." Hippel's characterization sounds remarkably like that of Virginia Woolf's in *Three Guineas* (1986: 86, 83-4), where she describes the transformation that takes place when men cross over into the public world, "with its possessiveness, its jealousy, its pugnacity, its greed." "What then remains," she asks, "of a human being who has lost sight, and sound, and sense of proportion? Only a cripple in a cave."[3]

In the *Philosophy of Right*, Hegel (1976: 114-15, 263-4) justified the sexual division of labor through an assessment of the emotional and intellectual capabilities of women and men that obviously parroted Rousseau's (1979) misogynist commentary (Pateman 1988: 176; Martin 1985: 38-69) on the traits of Sophie and Emile. Hegel's discussion of woman's nature in these paragraphs is rather odd, given that the model he explicitly offered for the feminine character was the heroic Antigone, who hardly resembles Rousseau's obedient but manipulative Sophie. Another discordant feature of the text is its overly positive portrait of man. After all, Rousseau's Emile differs radically from the brutal and insensate Kreon of Sophocles's drama. But by posing these two conflicting models of woman and man, Hegel demonstrated the underlying instability of traditional conceptions of gender.[4] As Howard Williams (1989: 118) suggests, "in Hegel's view . . . it is precisely the two contradictory meanings which are of genuine advantage to philosophy. . . . He positively favours the word [or concept—D. M.] with two contradictory meanings."

Significantly, in his lectures on state and politics Hegel—like Hippel—referred to unflattering characteristics of men, qualities reminiscent of the obstinate king of Thebes. In the 1818 Berlin lectures, for example, Hegel (1983b: 139; 1974: 523-9) described men as childishly morose and sulky, compared to women; there are analogous comments in the Berlin cycle of 1822/23. Hegel may have dropped disapproving remarks about men in the *Philosophy of Right* in order to elude censorship. In any case, his judgements about women's and men's capacities, including a notorious comparison of women with plants, and men with animals (1976: 263), recall passages in Hippel's (1979: 80, 168) revolutionary book. (The state, said Hippel, treated women as "plants"; "Without Eve, Adam is but an animal.") Hegel's (1976: 265, 263-4) contention that females are the best educators of young children, and his claim that "when women hold the helm of government, the state is at once in jeopardy" are features of Hippel's text as well. Pointing out that Socrates learned dialectic from his mother, a midwife, Hippel (1979: 126-7) wrote that women had more direct access to reason and morality than men, and were more successful in communicating these to children. As we have already seen, Hippel thought that by confining women to the family, men succeeded only in making them dangerous to the state.

Patricia Mills (1986: 152; also, Barber 1988: 7; Hodge 1987: 128) asserts that restricting women to the family undermines the supposedly universal basis of Hegel's theory. *But Hegel explicitly acknowledged woman's presence in civil society and the state.* After reaching maturity, he (1976: 118) declared, children of both sexes "become recognized as persons in the eyes of the law and as capable of holding free property of their own and founding families of their own, the sons as heads of new families, the daughters as wives." Benjamin Barber (1988: 13) ingeniously contends that the "tacked on" phrase about husbands and wives in this passage was somehow meant to exclude women from the public sphere. However, if this is what Hegel intended, he would have had to exclude females from the category of legal person, as was done in contemporary justice systems in England and elsewhere (Sachs and Hoff-Wilson, 1978). After all, more women remained single in Hegel's time than our own (9-12 percent of women in England, for example, and 20 percent of those in Scotland never married); and marriages did not last long, due to high death rates (about one quarter of marriages were broken up by death within ten years; "while around 56 per cent would not have lasted twenty-five years" [Anderson 1990: 28-9]).

The notion that Hegel excluded women from civil society is founded, I think, on a misplaced extrapolation of recent changes in the female labor force back to the early nineteenth century. Interpreters assume that Hegel's period was marked by exclusion of women from the workforce when, in fact, the level of married women's participation in paid employment was very close to late twentieth century levels; single women were a major component of the workforce throughout the last century. Married women's labor force participation rates," notes Joyce (1990: 139), "did not decline until the second half of the nineteenth century."

In any event, person is the founding category of the *Philosophy of Right*, everything in the text follows from it, and applies to it, regardless of gender or marital status. As I argue in this chapter,

Hegel's theory treats women and men as equal property holders in the family; thus, whether or not they marry, women never lose the status of person, property holder, and citizen.

Hegel was radically anti-essentialist; for him, both sexes are determined not by biological makeup, but by mind or reason. First and foremost, the family is a *structure of consciousness*, a structure that yields and changes with the course of history (Easton 1987: 34). Thus, "woman like man is a socially constructed personality" (Ravven 1988: 155). The mental structure belonging to family life, through which women are socialized, does indeed confine the female sex; but this consciousness is dissolved and transformed by the impact of civil society.[5] Hence, like Plato (1989), Hegel saw the breakup of traditional family relations as an inevitable result of the development of the ideal or social state. In the Platonic Republic, Hegel (1955: 112) observed, "women are no longer private persons, and adopt the manners of the man as the universal individual in the state. And Plato accordingly allows the women to take their part like the men in all manly labours, and even to share in the toils of war." In many respects, this is also the destiny of woman in Hegel's state.

What critics overlook is that Hippel and other contemporary supporters of women's rights would have concurred with the *Philosophy of Right*'s characterization of women's and men's capacities and social location. Wollstonecraft's theory stresses the power of socialization; her main argument for female emancipation was precisely the oppressive limitations of the patriarchal family, and its debilitating effect on women, who were "educated for dependence" (1967: 87). Similarly, in their 1825 *Appeal* for women's rights, the Owenite socialists William Thompson (1970: 191) and Anna Wheeler described women as passive, oriented toward the family, and starved of knowledge.[6] "An education of baby-clothes, and sounds, and postures, you are given," they wrote of woman, "instead of real knowledge." For Hegel (1976: 114), as for contemporary advocates of women's rights, the characteristics of both sexes are socially constructed. Within the patriarchal family, biological distinctions are magnified (and distorted) by social relations.

Other sources concerning Hegel's views on women tend to confirm Hippel's (and early feminism's) influence. In the *Lectures on the History of Philosophy*, for example, Hegel (1955, 3: 52) remarks that a few isolated women, along with "monks [and] other solitaries," were instrumental in keeping alive the spiritual and philosophical truth of Christianity during the Middle Ages (see also Easton 1987:

40-42). This matched Hippel's (1979: 134-5, 137) assertion that despite being shut out of centers of learning, women played "an important part . . . in the spread of Christianity." In Hippel's view, women "worship a religion of freedom, the will of God manifested in Spirit and in truth."

Leonore Davidoff and Catherine Hall (1987: 114) point out that in the nineteenth century, the Edenic myth was "the primary religious explanation for women's subordination to man." Mary Daly (1973: 45) asserts that "the malignant image of the male-female relation and the 'nature' of women" contained in Augustine's reading of the Fall "is still deeply imbedded in the modern psyche." But Hegel (1985: 107) scorned this misogynist rendering of the myth as "wholly prosaic and particular." Instead of signalling women's degradation, Hegel (1988: 217) saw Eve's acceptance of the apple as "the eternal story of human freedom." What the fable represents, said Hegel, is the emergence of reason, the escape from "the mere image of paradise . . . this stupefied innocence devoid of consciousness and will."

Hegel's account of the myth paralleled the one put forward thirty years earlier by Hippel. Hippel's version, in turn, resembles the radical interpretation of the story by early Christian Gnostics, (Pagels 1988: 66-7) and Daly's (1973: 67) feminist version of the myth, in which "women reach for knowledge and, finding it, share it with men, so that together we can leave the delusory paradise of false consciousness and alienation." For Hippel (1979: 66, 64), the Fall was

> a portrait of the emergence of man from the paradisal yoke of instinct, and the origin of the social condition for which the wise woman Eve was the intermediary and herald. . . . [I]t was she who shattered the bonds of instinct which had prevented human reason from rising up, and it was she who triumphed thereby. In memory of her the words *Eve* and *Reason* ought to be regarded as synonymous.

The symmetry between Hegel's thought and Hippel's *On Improving the Status of Women* goes much further than their harmonious accounts of the character of men and women, and the meaning of the Fall. Accordingly, in Hegel's *Phenomenology of Mind*, which provides the basis for many of his later writings, some complex and important passages on women and the family seem to refer directly to Hippel's feminist broadside.

4. Woman and the Family in the *Phenomenology of Mind*

The *Phenomenology's* sketch of Sophocles's *Antigone* provided the model for the sexes in the *Philosophy of Right.* According to Hegel, the Greek play captured the disjunction between the universality of the state and the ethical world of the family, as they are manifested in the conflicting "natures of man and woman." "This," Hegel (1976: 115) said, "is the supreme opposition in ethics and therefore in tragedy." As Hegel (1955, 2: 112) noted, Plato's philosophy abolished these contradictions by minimizing the differences between women and men, and shutting the family out of the Just State. In contrast, notes Jane Roland Martin (1985: 39), Rousseau admitted the family into his ideal community by confining the woman, Sophie, to the domestic realm, and leaving civil society entirely to Emile.

I maintain that Hegel's solution to the dilemma borrowed from both thinkers—although Hegel (1976: 261) ultimately favored Plato's approach over Rousseau's isolationist "educational experiments." Like Plato, Hegel separated the family from the state, and like Rousseau, he recognized the fundamental importance of the differences between the natures of women and men. Hegel accepted Wollstonecraft's and Hippel's (and Plato's) claim for political equality of the sexes. But while the two feminist thinkers hoped to empower women, and persuade men to give up their domination of the female sex, Hegel showed how the ethical disruption at the heart of the relationship between the private world of the family and the public realm of the state provided the conditions for the liberation of women.

Hegel deeply admired the "heavenly Antigone, the most magnificent figure ever to have appeared on earth," as he called her in the *Philosophy of History* (Quoted in Donougho 1989: 65). As Susan Easton (1987: 37) observes, Hegel's definition of tragedy relies on "tragic heroines with the capacity and desire for self-reflection." In Sophocles's drama, Antigone offended the gods by opposing the Theban king, Kreon, and burying her dead brother, Polyneices. For Hegel, Antigone and Kreon represented warring principles in Greek society. Antigone symbolized the private spirit of the family, Kreon the public spirit of the *polis*, or state. They were of equal power in the Greek context, though Antigone was for Hegel, far the nobler of the two. She not only preserved the memory of her dead brother, she uncovered, says Donougho (1989: 86), "the individualism at the heart of the *polis*, its male chauvinism, its overemphasis on the particular or male principle, its pretence that this is universal and natural." Hegel thought that the fate of Antigone presaged the destruction of Greece; the victorious male principle later fed the nascent civil society of Rome—which, incidentally, Hippel (1979: 99) called, "the very first of all great bourgeois societies."

Commentators rightly see *Antigone* as the guiding spirit in Hegel's outline of the ethics of the family and the nature of woman and man in the *Phenomenology*. Yet the Greek play was not the only source for these passages, which remain notoriously opaque even with *Antigone* as a guide (e.g. Solomon 1983: 538; Barber 1988: 16-17). The missing dimension is provided by Hippel's *On Improving the Status of Women*. Through his book, Hippel taught Hegel about the nuances of gender, and provided the anthropological theory that underlies Hegel's theory. For Hegel (1967: 477, 475-6, 497), Antigone's relationship with her brother, Polyneices, was the strongest possible for a woman within the "circumscribed life of the family." The relationships of daughter and father, or wife and husband, are clearly ones of (male) authority and (female) subordination. But the connection between sister and brother was potentially that of mutually self-affirming "free individualities"—a relation unaffected by what George Steiner (1984: 17) calls, "the paradox of estrangement inherent in all sexuality (a paradox which incest would only enforce.)" Hegel's claim is echoed by Alain Corbin (1990), who urges in *A History of Private Life*, that "brother and sister enjoyed a special relationship whose importance has too often been neglected." The connection between them constituted, says Corbin, the "one breech in the barrier between the sexes" so strictly enforced in the nineteenth, and early twentieth century.

Hegel (1967: 475-6, 497) felt that the relationship of mother and son would also be inadequate for expressing equal power relations. From a mother's point of view, the child is accidental—a contingent, and replaceable, result of her own circumstances and actions, which remain external to the child. The mother loves her child regardless of his concrete individuality, while the sister sees her brother as inevitable, no more of an accident than she is. Further, the relationship between mother and son, as in any parental relation, is based on separation. The child grows up to leave the mother, and for the mother, the independent existence of her child is "a foreign reality." Finally, the male supremacist character of Antigone's society meant, as Hegel noted, that the mother "extols a son as one who is the lord and master of the one who has borne him."

Antigone herself visits some of these themes, in explaining her duty to Polyneices:

> But I was right to honor you,
> and men who understand will agree.
> Suppose I had been a mother and widow.
> I would not have taken this burden on
> Or defied the nation in that case.
> The principle I followed is this:
> If my husband had died, there might be another,
> and a son by another man if I had lost my children.
> But my mother and father were gone.
> I could never have had a new brother
> (Sophocles 1973: 56).

The writer and composer Elizabeth Swados's (1991) attempt to rescue her brother—a schizophrenic street person lost to his parents and reviled by respectable society—and then her mission to disentomb and bury him, are a modern-day reminder of Antigone's struggle.

Goethe mocked Hegel's naivete about the supposed innocence of sister-brother relations (Donougho 1989: 71). However, what Hegel (1967: 477) argued was not that a brother was exempt from desire for his sister, but that Antigone's sisterly action did not stem from sexual attraction. Greek society was open to fathers, husbands, and brothers, but not to women. This gave men "the self-conscious power belonging to the universal life," and allowed them to acquire the "rights of desire," which they were liable to bring back with them when reentrying family life. Accordingly, incest is certainly not ruled out by Hegel's (1976: 115) theory.

In the quest to bury her brother, Antigone was expressing the essence of the family relation; her actions were not determined by selfish pursuit of power and wealth, or "blind obedience to authority" (Easton 1987: 40). In death, explained Hegel (1967: 469-72, 494-5), the individual fulfills the highest task set by nature, but even if the individual's demise were a direct result of work for the universal good, the political community itself is indifferent to the dead citizen, "who is merely unreal, insubstantial shadow." (Kreon could order the exposure to the elements of Polyneice's dead body without opposition from the people of Thebes, just as the New York neighbourhood, in which Lincoln Swados lived, was largely oblivious to his death.) It is the duty of the family to mediate the destructive processes of nature with consciousness, with ritual and ceremony. The individual is thus rescued from the decay and meaninglessness of death in nature. Nor is this service of love merely one owed to the individual family member. In a Durkheimian twist, Hegel contended that the family burial rite preserves the "mute, unconscious substance" of the community—or as Durkheim would say, provides the element of social solidarity, without which society would ultimately disintegrate.

While Antigone represents the ethics of the family, Kreon personifies "the self-conscious actuality" of the nation (Hegel 1967: 467, 473-4, 497-8), and (following Hippel's anthropology) the masculine principle of war. For Hegel, war is another means for developing social solidarity, for bringing the community together. Without the threat of death and destruction, the sphere of culture and wealth-creation that Hegel called civil society, would split into self-serving fragments. It is Polyneice's death in the civil war with his brother Eteokles (who was aided by Kreon) that leads Antigone to her tragic fate. Unlike Kreon, Antigone never achieves self-consciousness. She does the bidding of the family spirit without an awareness of herself as an independent personality.

According to Hegel (1967: 476), Antigone finds her substance and individuality within the family, but this relation is one of love and duty rather than "the natural one of pleasure." Yet, Antigone "premonizes and foreshadows most completely the nature of ethical life." In other words, she is the living embodiment of the ethical personality that will emerge (with Christianity) after the close of the family-centered Greek world. Like Hippel, Hegel sees the feminine character, and not the masculine one, as the most appropriate model for the fulfilled personality in an ideal community.

In Hegel's (1967: 481-2) feminist vision, the lesson of *Antigone* is clear. The fate of man is to spin downward into the "danger and trial of death," the fate of woman is to rise into the "daylight of conscious existence." He notes that there is an understandable tendency to see this double movement as two separate realities; but the female and male principles are actually interdependent, inseparable aspects of the whole. "Their opposition is rather the confirming and substantiation of one through the other; and where they directly come into contact with each other as actual factors, their mediating common element is the immediate permeation of the one with the other."

From the viewpoint of modern feminism (e.g., Chodorow 1978; Gilligan 1982), Hegel's insistence on mutual identity *and* difference in the natures of woman and man is just as acceptable as one that

contends against difference of any kind (Wood 1990: 245). Virginia
Woolf (1957: 101-2) writes that

> in each of us two powers preside, one male, one female; and in the
> man's brain, the man predominates over the woman, and in the
> woman's brain, the woman presides over the man. The normal and
> comfortable state of being is that when the two live in harmony
> together, spiritually cooperating. If one is a man, still the woman
> part of the brain must have effect; and a woman also must have
> intercourse with the man in her.

As we have seen, the female and male principles given agency in
the characters of Antigone and Kreon express the conflict between
ethical life in the family and the universality of the community. Yet
this contradiction is more complex than it at first appears. For Hegel
(1967: 496), the woman is manager of the household, while man
rules in the state. At the same time, however, *the principle of
individuality which infuses and enlivens the public realm is actually the
creation of woman.* The youthful male individual who advances from
the family into civil society is borne, socialized, and educated by
woman. For her brother, woman provides the closest approximation
to cross-sex equality that he will experience in the family, and for the
son marital partnership with a young woman provides a path of
escape from the confining parental home. Nevertheless, patriarchal
society's response to woman's vital contribution is to "suppress[]"
her (Hegel 1967: 496).

This "everlasting irony in the life of the community," as Hegel
(1967: 496) called the female sex, is what Rousseau forgot: if Sophie
has only private, family ends, and has the power to influence Emile
to follow these and not universal purposes, then she also has the
power to subvert the state.

It is useless, Hegel (1967: 496-7) observed, for patriarchal
sobersides to criticize woman for undermining the state, since
without her they and their precious community would not exist.
Woman, Hegel opined, makes the "grave wisdom of maturity . . .
the laughing-stock of wanton youth"; the brave young man "who
provides pleasure to woman" is also the instrument of war desperately required by the patriarchs to bind and protect their community.
This is part of Kreon's tragedy: he lost both of his sons, one in the
war to vanquish Polyneices, the other for love of a woman.

Hegel's lyrical argument about the nature of woman and man in
the *Phenomenology* is carried out within the context of ancient Greek

society. Yet he believed the lessons *Antigone* taught about family relationships are also largely applicable to the nature of the family in bourgeois society. Greek drama was a backdrop for the feminist theory he learned from T. G. von Hippel. Thus the trenchant passage from the *Phenomenology* describing how patriarchal society "creates its enemy for itself within its own gates, creates in it what it suppresses, and what is at the same time essential to it—womankind in general," while articulated nowhere in *Antigone*, reproduces a similar argument from Hippel (1979: 111):

> We do not take into account that the exclusion of the opposite sex from all serious public business must needs bring about in that sex the idea of dethroning all that is sacred, of degrading it, and of so spoiling the solemnity of life for the impertinent world of youth that when the young men finally begin to devote themselves to the affairs of the world, they will everywhere apply the maxim of absurdity that they learned at the feet of the fair sex. Few things will be able to withstand the blight of our pettiness and pedantry unless the women, the single possible preventive against the evil of our sex, are woven into the fabric of the state.

Unlike Hippel, Hegel did not expressly call for the liberation of women. What he did instead was to show how the clash of rival principles in the family and the public realm, as reflected in the sexual politics of *Antigone*, would eventually release women from domestic slavery. For Hegel (1967: 498-9), Greek reliance solely upon male strength and the hazards of battle to preserve the community meant "that its overthrow has come." But the family suffered from the same contradiction as ancient Greece; its dissolution "into a plurality of separate points" by civil society would yield the conditions for woman's freedom. To see how this result was achieved we now turn to Hegel's theory of the family in the *Philosophy of Right*.

5. "Ethico-Legal Love"

Social, or ethical, life for Hegel (1976: 110, 267, 155) consists of three separate spheres, each based on a distinct principle. The foundation of the modern family is love, which Hegel defines as, "mind's feeling of its own unity." The principle of civil society, the sphere of law, business, and trade, is the principle of self-interest. "In civil society each member is his own end, everything else is nothing to him." The final sphere, the state, transcends and unites these partial principles. The state achieves a concrete unity in which the individual "in virtue of its own sentiments towards the state finds in the state, as its essence and its end and product of its activity, its substantive freedom."

The Hegelian state is not reducible to government. Government is one part of the state, which also includes a national territory and a distinct culture. These in turn are broken up into regions, families, and individuals in civil society. For Hegel, the isolated individual of liberal theory is a myth. You are Canadian, Japanese, or Egyptian. Social identity marks you completely; it might as well be chiselled on your forehead. "Every aspect of people's mental and cultural possessions," notes Randall Collins (1985: 171), "becomes charged with significance as a marker of social membership." As a citizen of a country, you are also its "end." The state channels certain resources to your education, your health, and means of living. You are a product of the state, as the state itself results, in part, from your activity.

Compared to the state, both civil society and the family are limited, because their goals are private and self-regarding. Love in the family is restricted to its members and founded mostly on blood ties. Relative to other families, this unit may be as selfish as the possessive individual in civil society. Thus Weber observed that traditional kin groups in China, India and the ancient world saw outsiders as "objects of distrust and manipulation, to be ruthlessly cheated or oppressed when possible" (Collins 1986: 268).

For Hegel, the intense communalism of the family prevents emergence of individuality; and in civil society the competitive ethic stifles feelings of community. Further, family and civil society depend radically on the state. Domestic relationships are bounded by vicissitudes of law and culture, as are contracts in civil society. "Nothing," said Durkheim (1986: 196), "has fluctuated so much in the course of time as the idea of freedom of contract."

Yet there are similarities between the state and its subordinate levels. Like the state, civil society involves intense relationships, many on an equal footing, with all kinds of people, regardless of family background, religion, and race (Hegel 1976: 134). Accordingly, relationships in civil society are universalized. The family resembles the state because each person is a member, connected to the others by ties of love, responsibility and loyalty. Civil society is the sphere of contract; the family and the state go beyond this standpoint. A new-born baby makes no contract with her parents; the citizen is born or "naturalized" a citizen. The ties in each case are (or should be) absolute.

As we discussed in Chapter Four, property makes up one phase in the development of personality. But it is an abstract, restricted stage, and represents only an external relationship. Although an individual's property rights are confirmed by the community, they continue mostly to be a connection with external, dead things. Defined only in property terms, a person would be very poor indeed. Pierre Bourdieu (1984: 281) shows that the property relation extends to education, personal taste, and consumption of cultural products. "What is at stake," he writes, "is, indeed, 'personality', i.e. the quality of the person, which is affirmed in the capacity to appropriate an object of quality." Still, personality at this level remains an *acquisition*.

To become a completed personality, in Hegel's sense, an individual must form an image of herself. As we shall see more fully in the following section, this requires not only property, but an intimate relationship with another person. Relationships of marriage and family satisfy this need. The sociologist Nicholas Luhmann (1986) maintains that the need to develop an intense personal bond becomes irresistible in an acquisitive society which has obliterated the old ties of community, and which stresses the unique personal qualities which belong to the individual. "The code of love has evolved . . . as a mode of *interpersonal interpenetration*, which relies upon another person's view of the world" (Cheal 1991: 134).

The relationship between the sexes was the basis of tribes and early kin groups, as it is of the modern family. However, noted Hegel (1976: 131, 262), marriage is a social relation that first emerged, along with private property, in agricultural societies and rested on community approval. So, marriage is what Hegel called, "ethico-legal love." It is a legal relationship between two individuals, who freely choose one another through love.

Hegel (1976: 110-11) wrote that arranged marriages are "the more ethical way to matrimony" than marriages based on love between "two infinitely particularized individuals." Does this mean, as some commentators suggest (e.g., Steinberger 1986: 584), that Hegel preferred arranged unions? Arranged marriages, which were common practice in Hegel's Germany (Frevert 1989: 39), are more "ethical" because they bring the social moment, that is, the influence of parents and family, into marriage from the start. But these unions also violate the principle of individual freedom that is the basis of the modern world (Hegel 1976: 84, 262). Further, given male dominance in the family, arranged marriages are much more likely to harm the wife than the husband. As a result, noted Hegel (in a backhand critique of German mores), these relationships are common "amongst peoples who hold the female sex in scant respect."

Marriage—or some form of socially recognized, permanent bond based on sexual love—leads to growth of "substantive self-consciousness" (Hegel 1976: 176). Although Hegel applied his notion of marriage solely to individuals of the opposite sex, his model works as well for lesbian or homosexual unions. For example, "the socialist-feminist vision of an ideal society" put forward recently by Ann Ferguson (1990: 235-6) includes "the couple relationship that is sexual, committed to deep emotional intimacy, trust, and sharing." Ferguson advocates "ceremonies of commitment, which would be open to those of any sex;" these rituals "could supplant marriage ceremonies, and be based on a more limited time commitment (e.g., five years rather than life)."

While Hegel (1976: 118) saw marriage as important to the development of personality, remaining unmarried would not do an individual irreparable harm. "There can be no compulsion on people to marry." By contrast, social institutions forbidding marriage are corruptive of human relationships; Hegel regarded Luther's rejection of Roman Catholic celibacy rules for the priesthood as of world-historical significance.

What Hegel (1976: 112) said about marriage as liberation resembles Durkheim's discussion of the way social bonds protect individuals from depression and suicide. Yet Durkheim (1951: 188, 269) contended that marriage protected men from suicide, while predisposing women to take their own lives. Marriage gives men a place of spiritual repose and comfort unavailable to them in the work world. Women, however, never leave the protective bonds of family relationships, but simply proceed from their parental home to that of their husband, which is likely to be lonely and oppressive in comparison. Only the demands and joys of childbirth and childrearing can make up for the alienation of married women's lives. This was especially true if divorce was difficult to obtain, since the possibility of divorce militated against domestic satisfaction for men, and provided women with a chance to escape the confines of the nuclear family. Nevertheless, Durkheim felt that marriage was so important for society, that it was worth increasing the difficulty of divorce, even if that meant that more women might commit suicide (Sydie 1987: 32). The notion that bourgeois marriage favors men to the detriment of women is a critical part of Hegel's theory. Marriage can play the positive role Hegel claimed for it only if the marital partners are equal in other respects.

For Hegel, marriage is the first step or moment in the formation of a family. He was impatient with the belief that marriage is intended to satisfy sexual desire, or to procreate the species. Nor did he think that marriage simply means love between individuals, or—as Immanuel Kant supposed—a contract. Marriage concerns all these elements, but is wholly defined by none of them. The following sections discuss in detail Hegel's three elements of the family—love, marriage, property; the education of children; and the dissolution of the family.

6. "Love . . . the Most Tremendous Contradiction"

For Hegel (1971: 64; 1948: 307), love is the transcendence of property and pure personality, and therefore pivotal for an understanding of the family and the state. Sexual desire, he contended, is the root not only of the family, but also of "political, scientific, or artistic" pursuits in the universal community . No stranger to the popular culture of his period, the young Hegel based his notion of erotic love in part on Shakespeare's *Romeo and Juliet*. Hegel's opinions on love changed little as he grew older, and ideas in *The Early Theological Writings* reappeared in the *Philosophy of Right*. The account which follows draws on both texts.

Through love, wrote Hegel (1948: 305, 307; 1976: 261-2), the individual wins self-identity by yielding personal independence. When in love, you no longer see yourself as a single abstract being, but as a concrete unity with another person. You experience everything through the eyes of the beloved, and the world is transformed. Your definition of yourself becomes the definition your lover has of you. "In love, life is present as a duplicate of itself and as a single and unified self." In the initial moment of love, as Hegel characterized it, the individual is no longer happy alone, as he once was, but feels defective without the other. In the second moment, the individual realizes that her worth, her life, are now affirmed in the other, and the other has found the same affirmation in her. "The lover who takes is not thereby made richer than the other; he is enriched indeed, but only so much as the other is."

Losing one's personality turns out to be the moment of its creation; and marriage—the couple's decision to make themselves one person—is the validation of this new personhood. "Love therefore is the most tremendous contradiction. . . . As the resolving of it love is the unity of an ethical type" (Hegel 1976: 261). To say that two lovers are separate individuals, is only to acknowledge that they are mortal, that death may separate them. Thus, the question, "Who will die first?" tortured the post-modern married couple in Don Delillo's (1985: 100-1) apocalyptic novel about family life, *White Noise*. But Hegel (1948: 305-6) declared that love strives even to conquer mortality, "to annul this possibility [of separation] as a mere abstract possibility, to unite [with itself] even the mortal element [within the lover] and to make it immortal."

Later we shall see that the birth of children resolves the question of immortality. Moreover, we shall also discover a large worm in the Hegelian marital apple. The union of love should erase opposition between lovers (Hegel 1948: 308, 306). Unfortunately, this is not the case. Death enters the picture in the shape of property, objects that are dead, things without will or rights. "Since possession and property make up such an important part of men's life, cares, and thoughts, even lovers cannot refrain from refection on this aspect of their relations." Unequal property rights spell the death of love. "The one who sees the other in possession of a property must sense in the other the separate individuality which has willed this possession." The results can be frightful. "Love is indignant if part of the individual is severed and held back as a private property."

Love, Hegel (1948: 306, 304; 1976: 112) argued, can only exist between human beings who are "alike in power and thus in one another's eyes living beings from every point of view; in no respect is either dead for the other." There is no question that the married couple must be equals; love depends on symmetry between lovers. An unjust division of property and rights represents "a hostile power which hinders love's culmination."

In the *Phenomenology of Mind* Hegel (1967: 476-7) dissected the unequal power relationship inherent in traditional marriage—an analysis that may have influenced Engels's (1985: 110-13) critique of private property and bourgeois love. Hegel observed that the wife's love for her husband, as for her children, is founded on universal, ethical principles, as well as on physical pleasure and desire. But "in the husband, these two aspects get separated." The man finds sources of pleasure and desire outside the family, while the wife's own sexual longings call into question her ethical status in the family. Moreover, since the woman's erotic pleasures are supposed to be related solely to her universal duties, rather than to her own personal needs and satisfaction, "the wife is without the moment of knowing herself as *this* particular self in and through another." Hegel (1976: 115) referred to this line of reasoning again in the *Philosophy of Right*, where he observed that woman's life "has not yet attained its full actualization." *For Hegel, woman's predicament is the key dilemma of the family in bourgeois society.*

I will discuss Hegel's solution in later sections. For now, it is enough to see how women's subordination threatens the Hegelian ideal of erotic love and marriage. Uneven power diminishes lovers; the images they build and throw back to one another are distorted. One grows at the other's expense, and the result can only be an erosion of both. In marriage, stated the Owenites William Thompson (1970: 64) and Anna Wheeler, the woman loses her freedom. But man "loses the delights of the sweetest human intercourse, that of esteem and confidence between equals, heightened by the glow of sexual attachment." Instead of sharing love equally, said Virginia Woolf (1957: 35) woman's function in marriage is to reflect "the figure of man at twice its regular size." Along with these writers, Hegel saw that the system of inequality shrinks the husband's spirit so much that even a wife's life-long effort cannot restore the human dimension.

Hegel's ideal is reminiscent of "the feminist model of erotic love" recently put forward by the sociologist Roslyn Bologh (1990: 213). Bologh, like Hegel, suggests that if erotic love is contaminated by unequal relations of power it turns into its opposite. Instead of a mutually self-affirming connection, it becomes one in which the more powerful partner coerces the other. Moreover, this coercive connection applies, even if neither of the partners experiences it as such.

The brutality underlying a relationship based on coercive intimacy has led some contemporary feminist thinkers to reject heterosexual relations altogether. As Bologh (1990: 204) notes, this scholarship recalls in some respects the shunning of erotic love by religious thinkers, who equate sex with self-indulgence. Nevertheless, the radical feminist critique, though not its proposed solution of sexual separatism, actually follows from an analysis very similar to Hegel's.

For Hegel, a relationship based on unequal access to property is bound to be corrupt; the individual who benefits from inequality will always be tempted to see the other as property, as a dead object. For, as we have seen, property is inseparable from personality; and a personality without property is no personality at all. In modern patriarchal society, writes Bologh (1990: 203), "the man can objective-ly count on the submission and compliance of the woman (because of her objective dependence, her absence of objective rights) *more* than the woman can count on the submission and compliance of the man." Carole Pateman (1988: 15, 173) has shown how the concept of the state in western thought is intimately connected with modern marriage and heterosexual love. As the "greatest theoretical critic of contract," she opines, Hegel might have been expected to oppose the marital agreement. Instead, "Hegel's arguments are fatally compro-mised by his acceptance of the sexual contract." I argue the opposite. The *Philosophy of Right* is scathingly critical of women's oppression, their brutalization—and that of their children—by men, and their lack of property rights (Stillman 1989: 1045).

7. "A Contract to Transcend the Standpoint of Contract"

Marriage begins as a legal agreement between two people based on love for one another, but "it is precisely a contract to transcend the standpoint of contract" (Hegel 1976: 112). Every contract, Hegel affirmed, includes two people and an object. In the ideal marriage, though, the individuality of the contractors disappears and they become one. The lovers experience a unity of mind and feeling, and a closer understanding of one another than, as single persons, they once had of themselves. Hippel (1979: 167) presented a similar argument. "Man and woman together," Hippel noted, "constitute a complete human being."[7] Hegel insisted that in marriage no object is being exchanged, rather there is a change in consciousness. Where Kant (1974) believed marriage revolved around exchange of sexual organs (no wonder he never married!), Hegel (1976: 112, 163) contended that in an "actual" marriage union the "physical passion" of the partners "sinks to the level of a physical moment, destined to vanish in its very satisfaction." Even the quality of affection changes. Before marriage, lovers try to present perfect faces to one another; after marriage, intimacy includes actions and behavior that previously would have "produce[d] a sense of shame."

For Hegel (1976: 115), "The mutual, wholehearted, surrender of . . . personality" involved in marriage leaves no room for sex outside of it. Here Kant's idea of mutual exchange of sexual organs has some relevance, for with adultery there is a third set of organs making the rounds, which considerably confuses the exchange. Mutual surrender of personality would be impossible if one or both of the partners were having extramarital sex. Without monogamy, Hegel argued (a standpoint with which Engels [1985: 113] concurred) there can be no true freedom for the married couple, especially the woman.

Marriage is the first stage in the founding of a family; capital or a family's material holdings is the second. It is not enough, Hegel (1976: 116, 203) declared, for a couple to share a life together. They must also have "permanent and secure" material possessions. Shared possessions cancel the initial selfishness implicit in the concept of property. Therefore, every family must have adequate means of support. If many families lack property, then this reveals a profound social failure, not a failure of Hegel's theory.

> Security, consolidation, lasting satisfaction of needs, and so forth—things which are the most obvious recommendations of marriage . . . —are nothing but forms of universality, modes in which rationality, the final end and aim asserts itself in [this] sphere[].

Hegel was not denigrating families who lacked property. He was explaining the profound significance people place on their common holdings. This is why people dream of a home of their own, and harbor sentimental memories of a beloved household pet, or an old family car. The link between home and property is compellingly illustrated in Thomas Pynchon's (1966: 4) novel, *The Crying of Lot 49*, in which the used car salesperson Mucho Maas thought his customers trade-ins were "motorized extensions of themselves, their families, and what their lives must be like." Hegel's conception also captures the psychological devastation caused to family members by sudden loss of a home and personal possessions.

Shared conjugal property and personal relationships exemplify Marx's famous slogan about communism. Unfortunately, the patriarchal family perverted this principle. There it reads, as noted by the hero of Margaret Atwood's (1985: 127) *The Handmaid's Tale*, *"From each according to her ability; to each according to his needs."* The "collision" (*die Kollision*) as Hegel called it, between the rights of a husband and father in marriage, and those of a wife and children, is the subject of the next section.

8. A "Collision" of Rights

In his Heidelberg lectures, Hegel (1983a: 102-4) dealt with the ethical "collision" between the husband's rights and the rights of other members of the family, especially the wife. This conflict jeopardized conjugal equality, the essence of marriage. A solution lay in two related directions. First, civil society offers each member of the family an opportunity to earn a living, and elude domestic tyranny. Second, the state cancels the despotic rights of the male head, and guarantees security and property for each family member. Since Hegel discussed property ownership in the family before mentioning the birth of children, the rights of married women were the main focus of his remarks. He repeated the Heidelberg comments in the *Philosophy of Right*. However, the dialectical structure used in the later work separated parts of the discussion kept together in Heidelberg. But the main thrust stayed the same. Hegel's vigorous attack on patriarchal property relations emphasized issues that have informed a century and a half of struggle for women's and children's rights (e.g. Frevert 1989; Stetson 1982; Holcombe 1983).

As we saw earlier, private property undermines the equal relationship between lovers; a free union dictates equal sharing of property. For Hegel (1948: 308), however, this solution is unsatisfactory: law recognizes only individual property rights, not collective ones: "Community of goods is still only the right of one or other of the two to the thing." In the film version of Iris Murdoch's *A Severed Head* (1961), for instance, the estranged married couple quibble over each item in their luxurious household, as images of heirlooms, and other personal treasures are projected onto a movie screen.

In Hegel's theory, the family is legally one person, the male head. This was historically accurate—men were heads of family, and they did control property—and it also pinpointed the central conflict that would destroy the traditional family. The worm in the apple of conjugal love provided the motive for women to escape domesticity, and also gave them the means to do so.

The family is an immediate social institution, in Hegel's (1976: 117) terminology. Feeling and intuition are its basis, rather than reflective calculation (the structure of mind belonging to civil society) or reason (the consciousness of the state). It is a deeply flawed, rational organization, "exposed to partition and contingency." The family was initially formed within the agricultural mode of production, and founded on patriarchy, the rule of the father (e.g. Lerner

1986: 49-50). This is why Hegel (1976: 131) confined the principle of the patriarchal family to the agricultural class in civil society. The family is rational, but immediate; universal, but grounded on the arbitrary will of the male head; it is a general form that finds its archetypal expression in one social class.

Hegel observed (1976: 116-17) that it is the prerogative of the male head "to go out and work for [the family], to attend to its needs, and to control and administer its capital." Significantly, this idea is still a staple of "masculinist" sociology, which measures "the social class of households by the occupation of the male 'head'" (Hart 1989: 20). In Hegel's (1976: 116-17) theory, however, the father has no exclusive command over family property; each member of the family has a "right in the common stock." By restricting property to the male head, and permitting husbands and fathers to dispose of family capital without consulting spouse and children, the patriarchal principle provides "an occasion for breach of obligations and for mean exertions and equally mean subservience."

The law of property, Hegel (1976: 120) said, was grounded "on the father's arbitrary will within the family;" this was a wholesale violation of love and rationality. He condemned the law that "neither wife nor mother" could inherit the property of the family "she had helped to found, and which was properly her own." He also denounced similar prohibitions applying to daughters. Significantly, Hegel used the same terminology as the English feminists, William Thompson (1970: 77) and Anna Wheeler, to describe patriarchal power, i.e., "the arbitrary will" of the father or husband.

Few passages in the *Philosophy of Right* can match in vitriol Hegel's (1976: 119-20) caustic assessment of the "accident, arbitrariness, and shrewd self-seeking" that follow from giving husbands sole access to family property and its disposal. Legal subordination of women and children meant their helpless exposure to men's violence and cruelty, to "arbitrariness . . . mean exertions . . . folly . . . and malice." Lifting a page from *Antigone*, Hegel suggested that the ability of patriarchs to bequeath family property to whomever they pleased was especially ironic since "no respect would be forthcoming for his wishes after his death, if not from the family's love and veneration for its deceased fellow member."

If Hegel's condemnation of patriarchal rule was as strong as I have argued, why has it gone unnoticed by commentators, many of whom see him as "an unrepentant and often bitter misogynist"

(O'Brien 1981: 24)? One reason, I think, is that few interpreters have considered his theory within the context of nineteenth century family relations. Therefore, they fail to see that the relationships Hegel criticized are precisely ones which prevailed in his period. In addition, Hegel disguised much of his discussion as a historical critique of the Roman family, and a philosophical disagreement with Immanuel Kant.

When Hegel censured the "arbitrary will" of husbands and fathers, he was condemning the dominant family relations of his period. In both Prussia and England, for example, women had no right to property or inheritance, or to custody of their children (Stetson 1982: 5-6; Frevert 1989: 43-4). Wives in both countries required their husband's permission before they could earn money inside or outside the home. In England, writes Lee Holcombe (1983: 35, 26-7), money earned by women in the workforce "belonged legally not to her but to her husband who as the absolute owner could use and dispose of it however he pleased, both during his lifetime and by will after his death." Similarly, a woman's sexuality and companionability were considered to belong to her husband: a man could sue his wife's lover for damages involving loss of exclusive sexual access, or deprivation of a "wife's 'comfort and society.'" There was no equivalent right for the wife "for, having no legal identity apart from her husband, she could not sue at all."

Writing in the Owenite newspaper *New Moral World* in 1839, Catherine Barmby (1989: 99) outlined the family conflicts specified earlier by Hegel.

> There is much talk about family interests and family affection; but how are these dealt with in our code of laws? The law of inherit-ance, of marital settlements, and of dower; the law of divorce, and that which relates to the custody of infants, etc. etc., do they evidence a regard towards the promotion of family affection? Does it not frequently oppose the son to the mother, the brother to the sister, the husband to the wife, and the father against the mother of their children!

Modern sociological research suggests that wife abuse, marital rape, and incest, which occur in about one fifth of all North American families, are mostly committed by men who see wives and children as their own private property (e.g. Russell 1982: 2-3). In societies founded on absolute legal domination by husbands and fathers—as were nineteenth century Germany and England—a significant proportion of families must have contained violent,

sexually abusive husbands and fathers. Nevertheless, as Julie
Blackman (1989: 7) has shown, wife abuse and most other forms of
"intimate violence" did not emerge as a political issue until the
1970's.

By partially concealing his assault on the patriarchal family as a
critique of the Roman era, Hegel saved himself from the censors.
But this manoeuvre also underscored his belief, mentioned in
Chapter Two, that the system of industrial capitalism had created
social conditions reminiscent of Roman times. Hegel (1983a: 107;
1976: 266) knew that his account of Roman child slavery and
brutalization of women in the *Philosophy of Right* recorded not just a
terrible past, but also an ugly capitalist present. His 1817/18
Heidelberg lectures, for instance, made this connection directly,
comparing the system of child labor in England with the Roman
father's despotic authority over his children. Similarly, in the
Philosophy of Right he mentioned that the German law of inheritance
copied the "unethical legal system of Rome."

Here again Hegel appears to have been influenced by Hippel,
who believed that the inferior status of the female sex resulted
largely from importation of Roman statutes into the Germanic code.
The relative freedom women enjoyed in the early middle ages was
reversed, Hippel (1979: 108) claimed, and the woman placed under
"the legal dominion of her husband." Modern historians agree that
the revival of Roman law in the thirteenth century was "a significant
feature of the history of the West . . . [that] led to a loss of the old
financial and juridical autonomy of women" (Casey 1989: 78).

Although legislation on women changed several times in the long
history of the Roman Empire, it was constant on one point. Roman
law "gave severe control over family members, and especially
women, to the *pater*, the male head of the family, or to some other
male guardian" (Collins 1986: 317) The Roman legal code did not
have the same impact in England as in Germany; nevertheless, the
English male head of family traditionally enjoyed "absolute rights of
property" (Casey 1989: 78).

According to Hegel (1956: 286-7)—in an analysis that corresponded closely to Hippel's—the Romans transformed the family
from "a beautiful, free relation of love and feeling," into a sombre
unit guided by "the principle of severity, dependence, and subordination." Marriage was perverted into "a mere contract," where the
object exchanged was the wife herself. "The husband acquired a
power over his wife, such as he had over his daughter; nor less over

her property; so that everything which she gained, she gained for her husband." Men's cruel dominion over wives and children was a sop to make them forget their own subjugation by the state. "For the severity which the Roman experienced from the State he was compensated by a severity, identical in nature, which he was allowed to indulge toward his family—a servant on one side, a despot on the other."

These remarks from the *Philosophy of History* are more or less repeated in the *Philosophy of Right*, where Hegel (1976: 110) also told the story of "Cicero [who] divorced his wife as a business speculation in order to pay his debts with his new wife's dowry." Hegel doubtless was referring not only to Cicero, but to a great international scandal that was raging at the time. While Prince Regent, George IV married the German princess, Caroline of Brunswick. He did it mainly for her money. Once his prodigious debts were paid, he promptly left his wife and child. A notorious womanizer, the king tried to divorce Queen Caroline in 1820 on the grounds that she had committed adultery during the 25 years they were estranged. He failed, but Caroline died shortly after the infamous trial. For radicals of the period, writes Lee Holcombe (1983: 35-6), the case "became a symbol of all that was rotten in the state of England."

9. "Personal Right of a Real Kind"

The feminist current in Hegel's thought underpinned his disagreement with Kant's (1974: 108; Shell 1980: 151-2; Williams 1983: 85) idea that women and children are a form of property, which Kant called "Personal Right of a real kind." This *"most strictly personal of all rights,"* Kant opined, justified men's domination over wives and children: "The Man acquires a Wife; the Husband and Wife acquire Children, constituting a Family; and the Family acquire Domestics." Kant's theory expressed the strains inherent in the contemporary family which, suggests Alan MacFarlane (1986: 290), "maintained a precarious tension between separateness of property and legal person on one hand, and a very close emotional, psychological and spiritual identification." For Hegel (1976: 39-40), however, Kant's doctrine was the most barbarous aspect of his philosophy. He noted that Kant's "perverse" definition of personal property rights was drawn from Roman family law, which gave precedence to a person's particular capacity in the family "over the universal right of personality as such." "Objectively considered," declared Hegel, "a right arising from a contract is never a right over a person, but only a right over something external to a person or something which he can alienate, always a right over a thing."

As we have seen, Hegel was not merely finding fault with some queer notion of Kant's.[8] Hegel was challenging the basic property relationships of nineteenth century capitalism (many of which survive in our own period). The legal position of women and children reflected the madness Hegel (1976: 118, 39) saw running through the whole concept of private property. Capitalist society cannot decide what is a thing, and what is not. Thus, as in Rome, personality is confused with family status; a woman's rights as an individual are subordinated to her place in the family.

In Chapter Nine, I argue that Marx saw the struggle for workplace regulation in British industry as a fight for individual personality in Hegel's sense, especially the personality of women and children. The modern battle for women's right to their own bodies is another dimension of this conflict. Murder, incest, rape, sexual and physical assault, pornography, and other crimes committed by men against women and children are a measure of the latters' relative inability to exclude others from their own bodies. The same is true of prostitution. "Only through the prostitution contract," writes Carole Pateman (1988: 204), "does the buyer obtain unilateral right of direct sexual use of a woman's body."

The contest for control over reproduction may be the most glaring indicator of women's lack of property rights in Hegel's sense.[9] Even a being with the barest potential to have a potential for rights may be granted a higher priority than the woman to which this organism is attached. Pro-life ideologues use value-laden, but ultimately superficial terms, like "preborn child" and "unborn child," to describe indiscriminately the human fertilized ovum, blastocyst, embryo and fetus, and to privilege the "rights" of such entities against those of an adult woman, or female child (Morgentaler 1982). "We seem to be willing," writes Katha Pollitt (1990: 414; also Tribe 1990: 237) "to deny the basic right of bodily integrity to pregnant women and to give the fetus rights we deny children." So-called surrogate mother contracts, which are widespread in the United States, confuse a woman's ability to give birth with a thing. A pregnant woman is said to provide "services" to prospective "parents," the donors of sperm or fertilized ova (Pateman 1988: 213).

Hegel would have rejected the modern formulation of a woman's rights as somehow in opposition to those of her fetus. As Catharine

MacKinnon (1987: 93) argues, this is primarily a masculine standpoint, the perspective of a third party.

> On one level, men respond to women's rights to abort as if confronting the possibility of their own potential nonexistence—at *women's* hands no less. On another level, men's issues of potency, of continuity as a compensation for mortality, of the thrust to embody themselves or their own image in the world, underlie their relation to babies (as well as to most else).

Hegel (1971: 95-6, 99) saw that a mother and the child in the womb form a "an undivided psychic unity . . . a correlation of soul to soul." The notion that they are separate entities, he wrote, belongs to "the abstractive intellect which is unable to grasp the unity of distinct terms." There can be no justification for treating the embryo or fetus as a being with rights separable from those of the woman who bears it. The woman is the "self" of the fetus, which is as "yet no *self*, as yet nothing impenetrable, incapable of resistance." In contrast to the fetus, which "is only externally treated as an individual and has only a nominal independence," the pregnant woman "is the sum total of existence, of life, and of character, not as a mere possibility, or capacity, or virtuality, but as efficiency and realized activity, as concrete subjectivity;" she—not the "child in the womb"—is the "total mental self-hood" "whose decision is ultimate."

Given Hegel's concept of unity between expectant mother and fetus, it is unlikely that a woman would desire to terminate this relationship, except for good reason. In a recent ruling, Canadian Supreme Court Justice Bertha Wilson suggests the parameters for such a decision; these would conform to Hegel's (1976: 37-8) outline of the rights of personality:

> The right to liberty . . . guarantees to every individual a degree of personal autonomy over important decisions intimately affecting his or her private life. Liberty in a free and democratic society does not require the state to approve such decisions, but it does require the state to respect them.
>
> A woman's decision to terminate her pregnancy falls within this class of protected decisions. It is one that will have profound psychological, economic and social consequences for her . . . It is not just a medical decision; it is a profound social and ethical one as well (quoted in Conway 1990: 214-15).

If a woman did decide to abort—and assuming unimpeded access to the procedure—she would probably do so at an early stage, in order to avoid the terrible physical pain and risk of injury or death involved in a late term abortion, and the emotional cost of breaking a steadily maturing link with another being (Morgentaler 1982: 149).[10]

Hegel's critique of Kant's notion of family hierarchy affords a strong basis for understanding current patriarchal abuse, *even in areas (like abortion) upon which Hegel did not specifically comment*. From the standpoint of marital equality, for example, individuals joined by marriage ought to keep their separate identity; and children's names should reflect the psychic unity formed before birth between mother and child.[11] But in modern marriage, observes Lenore Weitzman (1981: 9, 13), "the . . . woman's loss of an independent identity is most clearly symbolized by the loss of her name." Children are commonly given their father's surname; and in the exceptional cases where a woman's surname is used, it usually occupies secondary status to the father's. In divorce cases, U. S. courts recognize a father's "protected 'property right' to have his progeny bear his name," even when the mother reverts to her own surname, and has custody of her offspring. "Naming customs and rituals like big weddings," Gillis (1985: 313) concludes, "reproduce basic inequalities in the marriage relationship that remain unresolved."

"Some decisive reforms in the legal standing of wives," attests Carole Pateman (1988: 120), "are so recent that most of us still bear marks of subjection, notably that we are known by our husband's names." As Stone (1986: 83) points out, the "peculiar English habit of wholly obliterating the woman's name at marriage" was unknown elsewhere in Western Europe in the seventeenth century. It is, he says, "remarkable evidence of English stress on patrilineal descent." With the spread of industrial capitalism, the English pattern was adopted in Germany and many other countries. Accordingly, in the 1817-18 Heidelberg lectures, Hegel (1983a: 98; also Frevert 1989: 43) wrote that a consequence of marriage is that "the wife loses her name."

A common justification for erasing a woman's surname at marriage—and naming her children after the husband—is that it assures continuity of the family name, although only the husband's is thought worthy of continuity.[12] For Hegel (1976: 116, 264), however, any family other than the immediate one has no claim at all on a new union. He observes that the tradition of patriarchal naming flows from feudal conceptions which favored the male line over matrimonial ties between woman and man. But modern marriage "brings into being a new family which is self-subsistent and independent of the clans or 'houses' from which its members have been drawn." The absence in many Western countries of legislation forcing a woman to take her husband's name is testimony to the continuing strength of male supremacist institutions. As Hippel (1979: 134) suggested, maintaining discriminatory practices against women by "tacit agreement [is] often even more inhuman and oppressive" than doing so by "formal legal means."

The family hierarchy supported by Kant has ominous implications for the development of personality, in Hegel's sense. A woman's name in itself is the supreme mark of her personality. "There is a great deal in a name," affirmed Elizabeth Cady Stanton in 1847. "It often signifies much and involves a great principle" (quoted in Stannard 1977: 4). The loss of a woman's name symbolizes the sacrifice of her personality in the family. Little girls grow up expecting to forfeit their identity, an expectation not shared by little boys. For a daughter or mother in the "gender differentiated nuclear family," writes Ann Oakley (1984: 201),

> an autonomous sense of self, a self which exists outside and independently of relationships with others, does not need to develop; there are no factors that encourage it and many that militate against it. Women's sense of identity is thus dangerously bound up from early childhood with the identities of others.

The subordination of women was only one aspect of Kant's philosophy; another motif in his theory was the father's absolute authority over his children. Hegel's critique of this position is considered in the next section.

10. "That System Even Gave a Father Power to Sell His Son"

Kant (1974) did not see children as a necessary part of the family. In his eyes, childless (or childfree) married partners made up a family just as much as fecund couples did. Hegel agreed (1976: 113, 131), and pointed out that children were hardly the main reason for marriage, since people had produced offspring long before the first appearance of the marital relationship. What, then, is the connection between marriage and children?

A married couple's love for one another, said Hegel (1971: 255; 1976: 264-5), lacks externalization. The lovers have each other, and the two are "in substance" one, but this is a fiction. Their "union of hearts" is "only a unity of inwardness or disposition; in outward existence, however, the unity is sundered into two parties." The married pair's love lacks external embodiment; and they come to experience this as a defect. Fear of losing the beloved grows because it means an eternal absence. True, the couple already have their love embodied in worldly possessions; but these are external, not spiritual. Lovers eventually desire to have their love objectified as a person, their child. "In the child, a mother loves its father, and he its mother. Both have their love objectified for them in the child." By having a child, Hegel contended, the married pair create a relationship "in which parents are loved and which they love."

The relationship Hegel sketched between children and parents is ideal. It expresses what is rational in the family connection.[13] This was hardly the situation for all families in Hegel's period, perhaps even most of them. Hegel (1976: 120-21, 41, 114) noted that in Rome, a father had legal control over his children's lives. "That system even gave a father power to sell his son." This had a corrosive effect on "the ethical relation of love." As we know, Hegel was not only describing Roman conditions. In France, for example, "a father could request that his child be arrested and held in state prisons. . . . Formalities were minimal, as were the guarantees against abuse" (Perrot 1990: 169-70). Similarly, the contemporary English legal system mostly saw children as their father's possession. Even today, many men perceive their offspring in this way; children provide men with social recognition, but few fathers give much personal time to child care (Gillis 1985: 316).

Hegel (1976: 114) described men's "tranquil" place in the family as "a subjective ethical life on the plane of feeling." He meant they don't do much at home. "Does not the portion of work allotted to women invariably entail a greater expenditure of energy?" asked Hippel (1979: 70-71). "With happy heart the harvester returns home to his hut to rest after his exhausting labor, while even in the simplest country household there still remain manifold tasks for the women to perform." The most onerous of these duties, of course, was childrearing. In some primitive tribes, observed Hippel, a man, not the woman,

> holds the celebration at the time of parturition. Hardly is the woman delivered of her burden, when she bathes it in the nearest river, offers the new arrival her breast—thereby saving herself from lacteal fever and the vexation of enlisting a wet-nurse—and performs

her household duties just as before; while the man, stretched out on his bed, lets himself be ministered to and receives visits as well as congratulations from his neighbors because he—just think of the effort—has borne a child by his wife.

The temptation to see the *couvade* merely as a primitive ritual may be dispelled by glancing through the birth notices in any city newspaper: as Una Stannard's (1977) *Mrs. Man* relates, these usually credit the father more than the mother for the happy event. Again, the woman's identity is often well camouflaged, e.g., "Mr. and Mrs. Peter Smith announce the birth . . ."

Men's lack of responsibility in child rearing was the least of the problems created by the nineteenth century outlook on family life. William Thompson (1970: 14, 18) and Anna Wheeler, admitted that some men might neglect the "almost despotic power" the law granted them over their wives. Most, however, "will . . . use power for their own exclusive, obvious and immediate benefit." The same argument applied to children. This was the reason, they said, for "regulations, as society advances in improvement, to protect children from the abuse of power on the part of their parents." Like these writers, Hegel realized that many English fathers sold or rented their children to employers (an issue explored in detail in Chapter Nine). Nor did this represent isolated acts of desperately poor people. Ivanka Kovacevic's (1975: 102) survey of the literature of the period, for example, indicates that it was traditional practice, even among relatively well-off families. F. M. L. Thompson (1988: 136) confirms that English parents were reluctant to send their offspring to school when there were "openings for young children to pick up a penny or two." Sale of children to capitalists belonged to the historic European trend of parent-child relationships which in earlier periods manifested itself in slavery, and mass child abandonment. Rousseau, for example, notes John Boswell (1988: 20, 424), casually abandoned all five of his children to probable death in foundling homes.

As shown in Chapter Four, Hegel knew about the masses of children flooding into English mills. He followed the long parliamentary debates that resulted in the Factory Act of 1819, which tried to regulate children's labor. "Here, then," Hegel (1976: 41, 118) wrote in the *Philosophy of Right*, ostensibly of Roman child slavery, "the two qualities 'being a thing' and 'not being a thing' were united, though quite wrongly." Hegel aimed his fury not just at Rome, but at English capitalism.

One of the blackest marks against Roman legislation is the law whereby children were treated by their fathers as slaves. This gangrene of the ethical order at the tenderest point of its innermost life is one of the most important clues for understanding the place of the Romans in the history of the world and their tendency towards legal formalism.

In Hegel's (1976: 117) view, children are entitled to their parent's love, trust and support, but parent's have no property claims on their offspring. "Children are potentially free and their life embodies nothing save potential freedom. Consequently they are not things and cannot be the property of their parents or others." A key purpose of the Hegelian family is to provide for children's education, for their "second, or spiritual birth." Hegel made no provision for separate education based on gender. Individuals of both sexes have an equal right to an education.

Today's large-scale use of teenage labor in the fast-food industry violates the fundamental right of a child to a proper education. According to Hegel, the duty of parents is to advance children's education and moral development, even though children may resist this effort. Parents have no right to money or services from children. Ironically, ideas that once supported sending poor children into factories now justify permitting middle and upper class children to work at "bad jobs" that "make them psychologically poor." "The belief that work—under virtually all circumstances—is 'good' for young people, and a good deal of work even better, is deeply entrenched" (Greenberger and Steinberg 1986: 235-8; also Zelizer 1985: 220-21)

Children must develop their potential in the family and then wrest themselves free of it. The parents' task is to make this process productive and enjoyable. They must not stand in the way once children are capable of leaving. Parents have "the negative aim of raising children out of the instinctive, physical, level on which they are originally, to self-subsistence and freedom of personality and so the level on which they have the power to leave the natural unity of the family" (Hegel 1976: 117, 265). This demanding process means that parents "on the whole" love their children more than their children love them. In the child parents see the culmination of their love; in her parents the child sees two people she must leave behind.

The decline of the family, which will be surveyed in the next section, means that education of children can no longer be solely a domestic responsibility. Education becomes a function of the state, which must provide schooling on a universal basis, in spite of the resistance of parents, "who talk and make an outcry about teachers and schools. . . . [S]ociety has a right to act on principles tested by its experience and to compel parents to send their children to school, to have them vaccinated, and so forth (Hegel 1976: 148, 277).

11. "The Dissolution of the Family"

For Hegel, the family is a natural form of reason whose destiny is to self-destruct. Provided parents do not abuse them, children find in its cosy haven means to develop their personality, and so escape parental influence. Growth of adult personality, however, is impossible within it. This is why women do not attain full self-consciousness as long as they are restricted to the family circle. Love is the basis of the family, and its members treat each other accordingly. Recognition and encouragement of independent ability by outsiders has no place in the family. This feature of civil society is vital for individual freedom. Your parents, or your spouse, may forgive you for behavior that others would not tolerate, and censor you for actions others are indifferent about. Young people particularly are likely to regard praise or blame from outsiders as more important than similar treatment from family members. These and other factors make it necessary for an individual to leave home, if she is to achieve self-actualization.

As I suggested earlier in this chapter, Hegel did not confine women to the family sphere. In fact, to read Hegel as restricting women from civil society and the state is to ignore the dialectic of his text. For women, the barriers to civil society dissolve. Some are cleared by education, death or divorce; the rest are blasted away by the destructive force of capital.

Absent in the family, universality is an axiom of civil society. Just as Plato did not bar women from the ideal Greek state, Hegel did not exclude them from modern civil society. "The concrete person" is the chief actor in civil society, and a "person" may be female or male. Moreover, in Hegel's theory every member of civil society is also a citizen of the state. Accordingly, his (e.g., 1983a: 113-14; 1983b: 152-3, 168-9) lectures featured gender neutral terms for the individual in civil society and the state—e.g., *das Individuen* (the individual), *die Person* (person), and so forth.

Women (with the exception of slaves) were kept within the walls of the home, and thus excluded from the public world of Plato's

Greece; they were not, however, barred from "the system of needs" in Hegel's Europe. There was no possible motive, in other words, for Hegel to exclude the female sex from this sphere, and scarcely any likelihood that this could be achieved. "As was the case in farming society, [German] women in the traditional artisan classes were fully integrated into the production process" (Frevert 1989: 31). Females were a substantial proportion of workers in England, and until 1832, some could vote in national elections. Jane Rendall (1990: 4) advises that manufacturing work done at home or in small workshops continued to be a important feature of women's work in the nineteenth century. "Of course working-class women had always worked in early modern England, though they normally received significantly lower wages than men. . . . The overlap between home and work" was a continuing "theme of women's work." Even if Hegel could have closed his eyes to an obvious reality, this would have been a very strange exclusion. His friends included some of the most talented and independent women of the age, and his own sister remained unmarried, working for a living as tutor and governess.

The family ideal of the bourgeoisie, for which Kant provided a partial blueprint, did indeed demand confinement of women to the home, and this pattern would spread with partial success from the bourgeoisie outwards throughout the nineteenth century (Hunt 1990: 45).[14] But at no point were women closed out of the workforce, although they certainly were excluded from the most desirable jobs. Even Kant did not seek to eliminate women from the world of work; his theory aimed only to ban them from citizenship—a big difference. Influenced by the first major wave of feminist thought, Hegel was concerned to show precisely that the patriarchal family was inherently unstable and impermanent; and that women were destined to become equal members of the state.

Education of male and female children "to freedom of personality" within the family prepares them for leaving it. They earn their own income, and begin new families. Similarly, the death of parents is a gateway to civil society for women. In Hegel's (1976: 111, 121) theory, daughters as well as sons may inherit a share of the family capital and become "self-subsistent persons." "Excluding daughters from inheriting," said Hegel, "is an infringement on the principle of the freedom of property." For Hegel, in contrast to the sexist attitudes of the day, "both the ethical disposition and family trees are much more likely to be preserved by freedom of property and equality of inheritance than the reverse of these." Hegel did not extend the privilege of inheritance to children in the landed aristocracy, other than first-born sons. He connected the institution of primogeniture, which discriminates against females and most males, to the realm of the state. I will look at this development in Chapter Ten. Meanwhile, it is worth pointing out that primogeniture was not a German tradition. Many German states of Hegel's day outlawed the practice. The foremost example of primogeniture was the English political system.

The route to civil society opened by education and parental death may be closed again for many females. Their property may be absorbed by husbands, and their personality swamped by enforced domesticity. This possibility is cancelled by divorce. Marriage is founded on love, but love is only a feeling. Marriage is a fragile institution because its only rational foundation is the couple's love for one another. Love can disappear as quickly and mysteriously as it began. Sexual love is capricious and accidental, no matter what its immediate origin. Hegel (1976: 118) insisted that divorce may be necessary to avoid enslavement of a couple by a union in which their love has vanished. "There is no merely legal or positive bond which can hold the parties together once their dispositions and actions have become hostile and contrary."

Hegel (1971: 256) urged that both partners should have an equal right to divorce; and that dissolution should be an option for any marriage in which love has disappeared. His stand on divorce resembled the "remarkably liberal" provisions of the French divorce law of 1792 (Hunt 1990: 33, 45), but it was at odds with contemporary legislation in many Western nations, and with the conservative trend that was building throughout Europe. The Napoleonic Code had already reversed the advances of the Revolution in France; only in the 1970s, writes Lynda Hunt, did "French law concerning family life return to the principles of 1792." The complex English law made divorce prohibitively expensive, "beyond the reach of all but the wealthiest classes," and overwhelmingly favored the interests of husbands over wives (Holcombe 1983: 94). The relatively lenient Prussian code was also biased towards men, and mostly allowed divorce only in the case of childless marriages (Frevert 1989: 54-5).

Because marriage is a social institution, Hegel felt that divorce must be granted only by the state. Obtaining a divorce should be made as difficult as possible, without infringing on individual rights. He was thinking of the rights of children and women, especially their right to property. As in Hegel's example of Cicero, (and the Prince Regent of England) Roman law (and that of contemporary bourgeois society) permitted men arbitrarily to leave their wives and steal family property. Women and dependent children had little defence against this practice. When the "father's arbitrary will" is given precedence in divorce, as in inheritance, "then a legal road is paved to the corruption of manners, or rather the laws themselves necessitate such corruption" (Hegel 1976: 121).

Love may not die; many couples enjoy a life of wedded happiness. The possibility of divorce, however, introduces a different mode of consciousness. No woman or man can depend on marriage lasting forever, and this brings a shift in marital relations. From now on, the partners must see themselves as one, but also as separate entities. The state has decisively entered the tranquil domain of the family. "In virtue of such fortuitousness," that is, the possible death of married love, wrote Hegel (1971: 256), "the members of the family take up to each other the status of persons; and it is thus that the family finds introduced into it for the first time the element, originally foreign to it, of *legal* regulation." As a free personality, a woman like a man encounters no bar to entering civil society. The change in women's position due to her recognition as a property holder, and to the chance she might lose her family ties, opens civil society to her. The nuclear family disperses into self-dependent units.

Final dissolution of the family results from the explosive intervention of bourgeois society into patriarchal relations. Hegel (1976: 148) is unequivocal about the effect of this on women's place. "Civil society tears the individual from his family ties, estranges the members of the family from one another, and recognizes them as self-subsistent persons." There is no reference here to a separate fate for wives than for other family members. The bourgeois social revolution "subjects the permanent existence of even the entire family to dependence on itself and contingency."

In Hegel's Europe, dissolution of traditional family relations created a system of independent persons bound together in civil society by their mutual needs. Hegel foresaw that people's alienated existence as autonomous individuals would continually renew desire for family life (Easton 1987: 36). The contending forces within the nuclear family, and outside of it, would eventually create a life of formal equals, regulated by law. Yet Hegel realized that abstract equality is insufficient for real freedom. Women might attain equality before the law, but as long as males are dominant in the family, men will also monopolize power in civil society and the state. Moreover, civil society itself sponsors inequality on a large scale, reinforcing gender hierarchy within the family, and throwing up a whole system of social classes. This system, as comprehended by Hegel and Marx, is the subject of the next two chapters.

Notes

1. Before moving to Hegel's theory of the family it may be useful to discuss briefly some details of his personal life. Hegel's (1984: 234) *Letters* suggest he formed valued relationships with women, including his friend and frequent correspondent, the novelist Caroline Paulus. Throughout his life, Hegel was close to his sister, Christiane Hegel, who worked as a governess and tutor, and never married. Christiane Hegel committed suicide shortly after her brother's death. Their bond may illuminate Hegel's theory of the sister-brother connection in the *Phenomenology of Mind*. Still a bachelor at the age of thirty-six, Hegel fathered a child by Christiana Burckhardt (nee Fischer). He refused to honor a promise to marry Burckhardt after the death of her husband. She gave their child her maiden name, and Hegel's brother's Christian name. Married friends of Hegel cared for his son, Ludwig Fischer. When the boy was eight, Hegel received permission from his bride, Marie von Tucher, to have him join the family. Aside from the young Fischer, whose presence must have scandalized respectable opinion, Hegel's family life was typical of the German burgher. He was twenty year older than his spouse, as was common among middle class couples in the early nineteenth century. Tucher took Hegel's name, and stayed at home, raising two boys. Their first child, a daughter, died at the age of three months. Apparently, Hegel enjoyed a loving relationship with his sons by Marie Hegel, one of whom, Karl Hegel, helped edit his father's collected works. In contrast with the record of male philosophers from Plato to Kant to Sartre, what stands out is the ordinary quality of Hegel's private life. His contented domestic affairs likely influenced the portrait of loving family relations in the *Philosophy of Right*.

2. Since the eighteenth century male philosophers have been aware of the movement for women's rights (Midgley and Hughes 1983: 45-6). Thus feminism influenced their work, though usually in an anti-feminist direction.

3. The similarity on this between Hippel and Woolf was pointed out to me by Jane Roland Martin.

4. Here is a partial list of contradictory characteristics of the two sexes drawn from Rousseau's *Emile* (1979) and Sophocles's *Antigone* (1973): Woman is passive (Sophie), woman is active (Antigone); woman lacks the ideal (Sophie), woman embodies and fights for it (Antigone). Man is active

(Emile); man is locked up in himself (Kreon); man is capable of the ideal (Emile); man falls far short of it (Kreon). A much longer list could be constructed, but the characters of Emile, Sophie, Antigone and Kreon are much too subtle and varied to be summarized in this way, however long the inventory of traits.

5.   Hegel (1976: 114, 118-19) remarked in the *Philosophy of Right* that women have their "substantive destiny" in the family and men have their "substantive life in the state." Later, however, he referred to both sexes as having their "substantive destiny in the new family." "Substantive" refers to the concept of "substance" which in Hegelian (1975: 213-14) logic concerns change and form-activity. Substance is "all content" but "this content . . . is nothing but that very revelation, since the character (being reflected in itself to make content) is only a passing stage of the form which passes away in the power of substance." Thus, substance, as an important but low stage of the Notion (or human individual), concerns inherently unstable, changing forms.

6.   The Irish aristocrat, vegetarian, and socialist, William Thompson was an associate of Thomas Hodgskin, and a prominent disciple of Robert Owen. "He was one of the earliest economists to argue for the right of the worker to the whole produce of his labour and work out the beginnings of a theory of exploitation" (Rowbotham 1974: 48). Together with Anna Wheeler, Thompson wrote probably the most important feminist book of the early nineteenth century: *Appeal of One Half the Human Race, Women, Against the Pretensions of the Other Half, Men, to Retain Them in Political, and thence in Domestic, Slavery.* It appeared in 1825, the same year as Thomas Hodgkin's *Labour Defended Against the Claims of Capital,* and four years after the *Philosophy of Right.* Both Taylor (1983: 22-3) and Pateman (1988: 160-61) provide interesting accounts of the *Appeal,* and the vexed questions surrounding its authorship.

7.   Rousseau suggested that marriage created a "harmonious whole" by bonding the "complementary traits" of man and woman. Unlike those of Hegel and Hippel, however, Rousseau's marital union was based on inequality. "Wholeness is achieved," writes Jane Roland Martin (1985: 53-4), "not because each finds fulfillment in the other's love, but because the two sets of traits when joined together form a perfect whole."

8.   A weakness of modern scholarship on Kant's theory (e.g. Mendus 1987) is precisely its tendency to see Kant's views as idiosyncratic "bourgeois narrow-mindedness" rather than the template for modern patriarchal conceptualizations of the relationship between women and men.

9.   The nineteenth century was marked by increased judicial interest in abortion (Brodie, Gavigan, Jenson 1992; Gavigan 1984). In England, Lord Ellenborough's Act of 1805 criminalized abortion before quickening for the first time, and made abortions performed after quickening punishable by death. (Quickening was defined as the first movement made by the fetus in the womb.) The Act of 1837 dropped both the death penalty and the use

of quickening as a juristic category. The *Offences Against the Persons Act* of 1867, which remained on the statute books for a century, made abortion a felony punishable by three years in prison. (Hegel fathered a child outside of wedlock in 1807.)

10. "Third trimester abortions remain highly unusual, representing just a 10th of a percent of all the abortions in the United States" (Kolata 1992: 12). Women usually choose to have late abortions only when their physical or mental health is endangered, or when the fetus is severely deformed.

11. Some argue that women who keep their surname upon marriage are merely upholding patriarchy at a different level, since they retain their father's surname. True, a child's name is mediated, in Hegelian terms, by her parents, and, therefore, includes its patriarchal origins. But once she is given a surname, that name *for her* is *immediate*, it becomes part of *her* personality. This is proven by the fact that she can now give her name to her children, who will then, indeed, bear their mother's name, and not their father's.

12. Another excuse is that a woman's refusal to take her husband's name might hurt his political chances with "family value voters" (Pollitt 1992: 221). Accordingly, Hillary Rodham Clinton gave up her name so that her husband Bill Clinton could have a better shot at the U. S. presidency. Her decision was celebrated as a brave "new womanism" by columnist William Saffire.

13. Nor is the family ideal merely "bourgeois." Joan Scott (1988: 111), for example, notes that the family ideal of the French utopian socialists, which was based on the writings of Saint-Simon, "was not an organizational structure but a fulfilling human experience, the collective happiness of utopian socialism that reconciled differences and harmonized opposites as exemplified by marriage." Utopian socialism shied away from detailing the actual structure of the family in order to avoid "the bourgeois view that the ideal family could somehow exist apart from and indeed resolve capitalism's alienating effect."

14. Harrison (1989: 145) argues that the domestic ideal "may have been encouraged among working people from outside, but it originated from within. The so-called 'embourgeoisement' of working people occurs less through their conversion to alien values than through the gradual encroachment of one long-standing working-class tradition on another."

6

Hegel's Theory of Property, Part I: Possession and Use

If it is true that there is a necessary correlation between persecution and writing between the lines, then there is a necessary negative criterion: that the book in question must have been composed in an era of persecution, that is, at a time when some political or other orthodoxy was enforced by law or custom.
—Leo Strauss, *Persecution and the Art of Writing* (1973: 32)

Hegel is still in hiding.
—Jacques D'Hondt, *Hegel in His Time* (1988: 1)

1. Introduction

Hegel's concept of the family, as we saw in the last chapter, uncovered profound domestic conflicts within the family's key tenets, including equality in love and marriage, common property holdings, and the education of children. By accepting the family ideal, Hegel's theory produced a more powerful critique of traditional domestic arrangements than that put forward later by Marx and Engels. In his 1884 classic, *The Origin of the Family, Private Property and the State,* for instance, Engels (1985) overlooked the role of state legislation in family matters, even though the English courts had by that time made some clear advances in favor of women's and children's rights (Barrett 1985: 23). Similarly, Engels idealized the proletarian family, and failed to see that gender conflict was inherent in the traditional model, regardless of social class (Coward 1983: 160; Pateman 1988: 134). Finally, he underestimated the specific character and influence of the family. As an autonomous social and economic unit, the family is a source not only of women's oppression, but also of meaning and personal identity lacking elsewhere.

Hegel followed the same strategy for understanding property relationships, as for comprehending the family. He admitted the validity of the concept, and then showed how the bourgeois notion of property came into conflict with the principles underlying it. We saw in Chapter Four that, for Hegel, property is intimately connected to the notion of personality, and work is the chief means for exercising and developing personality. However, the contemporary labor contract violated the rights of personality in two ways. The first of these external violations of contract was the employment of children, who lack a completed personality in Hegel's sense of the term. The second was the worker's inability to control the length of time she worked for the capitalist. The English Factory Acts were an initial attempt by the state to cancel these infringements on contract and personality. Yet even in the absence of child labor, and with strict regulation of the working day, the capitalist labor contract violates the intrinsic rights of personality. In this chapter, and in Chapter Seven, I will show that Hegel's theory of property is actually an argument for the right of the worker to the whole product of her labor.[1]

Section two compares Thomas Hodgskin's property theory with the general outlook of Marx and Hegel; subsequent sections provide a full treatment of the Hegelian concepts of possession and use. These property concepts are illustrated in section five by the work of two nineteenth century writers on English factory life, Harriet Martineau and Frances Trollope. The chapter concludes with a discussion of the process of recognition in Hegel.

2. Thomas Hodgskin

It is at least arguable that a direct line between Hegel's discussion of the wage contract and that of Marx may be drawn through the writings of Thomas Hodgskin. Hodgskin was a radical democrat and author of *Labour Defended Against the Claims of Capital* (1964), published in 1825, and two other volumes devoted to working class political economy. Along with Robert Owen, John Gray and William Thompson, Hodgskin "provided the theoretical substance of a distinctive, working-class political economy which was popularly accepted and popularly purveyed" (Thompson 1984: 222) Marx referred often to *Labour Defended* in his discussion of the labor theory of value, and—as Hodgskin's biographer, Élie Halévy (1956: 169-70) points out—the two may even have met in London, since Hodgskin had ties to the German expatriate community through his Hanoverian wife. Marx (1976: 1000) called Hodgskin, "one of the most important modern English economists."

Hegel and Hodgskin also probably knew of one another, although Hodgskin's writings contain no references to Hegel or the German idealist tradition (King 1983: 355). The English socialist travelled widely in north Germany, and in 1820 published a book about his experiences. His monograph presented the English with their first view of the Continent after two decades of war, and was widely read. A voracious consumer of the English press, Hegel would have heard of this working class ideologist in any event. For Hodgskin was sub-editor and contributor to Hegel's favorite English newspaper, the *Morning Chronicle*. Nor would it be surprising if Hegel was familiar with Hodgkin's *Labour Defended*.

> There was something in Hodgskin's writings well calculated to attract the attention of those who had any real insight into the signs of the times. No member of the English socialist group seems to have been more widely read on both sides of the Atlantic, and the significance of his position was instantly recognized (Foxwell 1962: lvi).

In any case, evidence exists that *Labour Defended Against the Claims of Capital* "seems to have attracted Hegel's attention" (Petry 1984: 298). Hegel's surviving papers contain a fragmentary record of his readings from the *Morning Chronicle*, including notices of newly published books. Hegel inscribed the publication date of Hodgskin's book (July 30th, 1825). Instead of copying out this notice, he filled in the details of a book published eleven days before (Petry 1976: 31). A curious coincidence involving this excerpt from the *Morning Chronicle* occurred five years later.

In the 1830 edition of the *Encyclopaedia Logic* Hegel (1975: 11) spoke warmly about the identity still drawn by the English between science and philosophy. The English accordingly preserved the original historical meaning of the term, philosophy. "Newton continues to be celebrated as the greatest of philosophers: and the name goes down as far as the price-lists of instrument-makers." Hegel goes on, "the recent science of Political Economy in particular, which in Germany is known as the Rational Economy of the State, or intelligent national economy, has in England especially appropriated the name of philosophy." What has this to do with Hodgskin? In a footnote to this passage, Hegel wrote, among the advertisements of books just published, I lately found the following notice in an English newspaper: "The Art of Preserving the Hair, on Philosophical Principles, neatly printed in post 8vo, price seven shillings." By philosophical principles for the preservation of the hair are probably meant chemical or physiological principles.

The publisher's notice for a hair restorer is the one transcribed by Hegel under the publication date of Hodgskin's book. Was the balding Hegel leaving a clue for future investigators? Perhaps not, but the conjunction of a reference to political economy and Hodgskin is intriguing. We shall see later that Hodgskin's formulations appear to have found their way into Hegel's *Philosophy of Mind*.

Hodgskin based his ideas on an understanding of Locke's philosophy of law (Neale 1981: 170, 189). R. S. Neale claims that the theories of Hodgskin and other English socialists were "primitive" compared to Marx's, and "tinged" to some degree "with ideas of bourgeois right."[2]   Gareth Stedman Jones (1983: 137) provides a more nuanced account, but ends up reducing Hodgskin's argument to a backward critique of capitalist usury which he unfavorably contrasts to "later social democratic analysis." I argue, on the contrary, that Hodgskin's system was, in a way, significantly less primitive and more radical than Marx's. It led Hodgskin beyond value and profit, and encouraged him to consider the juristic and philosophical foundations of the theory of property.[3]

Hodgskin (1964: 25) contrasted "natural" with "artificial" property rights. Artificial rights are those created by governments to justify and protect the power and privileges of the ruling classes; natural rights are common to all societies and are based on human nature. Hodgskin cited the English Combination Acts, which threatened severe punishment for workers who dared to form trade unions, as an example of a law to protect artificial property rights. "No other combination seems unjust or mischievous, in the view of the Government," he wrote,

> but our combinations to obtain a proper reward for our labour. It is a heinous crime in the eyes of a legislature, composed exclusively of capitalists and landlords, and representing no other interests than their own, for us to try, by any means, to obtain for ourselves and for the comfortable subsistence of our families, a larger share of our own produce than these our masters choose to allow us.

According to Hodgskin's (quoted in Halévy 1956: 115) anarchist view, there was no need for government to legislate natural property rights, since these are part of the makeup of every individual.

[Otherwise] parents had no right to the love and respect of their
offspring, and infants no right to draw nourishment from the breasts of
their mothers, until the legislator—foreseeing, forecalculating the
immense advantages to the human race of establishing the long list of
rights and duties . . . had established them by his decrees.

Hodgskin believed that Smith and Ricardo based their labor
theory of value on John Locke's conception of natural property
rights. In *Labour Defended* Hodgskin interpreted such rights as the
principle "that nature gives to each individual his body and his
labour; and what he can make or obtain by his labour naturally
belongs to him" (quoted in Ellerman 1985: 293, 295).

Hodgskin could not have accepted Marx's ideal of communism;
he regarded "fiscal and interventionist socialism" (Halévy 1956: 17,
177) with as much disgust as he felt for capitalist property relations.
He believed that this form of society might threaten individual
freedom to an even greater extent than capitalism did. If he was
sharply aware of the worker's rights, however, Hodgskin seemed
oblivious to the significance of "natural" relations of power and
property in the family.

There is no outcry in Hodgskin's work against the exploitation by
men of their children and wives. When Robert Owen and others
were already fighting for effective legislation against long hours for
factory children, and Anna Wheeler and William Thompson were
denouncing male domination, Hodgskin took for granted the sexual
division of labor. He (1966: 256-7) warned against intrusion by the
state into the affairs of the family, where "filial affection" conquers
all. "Those who would substitute parliamentary decrees and social
regulations, enforced by punishment, for this mutual affection . . ."
demurred Hodgskin, "must have more confidence in legislative skill
than in the wisdom of nature."

Despite its shortcomings, Hodgskin's theory offers a unique
perspective on the concealed Hegelian elements in Marx. His
property theory resembles that worked out earlier by Hegel but
largely absent in Marx. His rejection of state interference, which
accurately represented the feelings of a wide section of the working
class movement, contrasts not only with Hegel's position but also
with that articulated in *Capital*. For Hegel, the wage contract must
be understood within a socio-legal and philosophical framework; it
cannot be comprehended either as a natural relationship, as
Hodgskin thought, or as a reflection of material production relations,
as Marx appeared at times to believe.

In *Capital*, the contract of employment turns out to be the creation not simply of material factors, but of government legislation. This result is never theorized by Marx, but its Hegelian origin is apparent. No one else but Marx was paying systematic attention to the extraordinary development of government intervention in British industry; and no one knew Hegel better than the expatriate revolutionary.

The phases of the wage contract in Marx, and the rise of state intervention will be discussed further in Chapter Eight. The remainder of this chapter will look more deeply into Hegel's legal theory, *a theory that turns out to be much more radical than that of Marx*. Marx (1976: 341), as we have seen, displayed the contract of employment as a simple exchange of commodities, albeit one complicated by capital's propensity to stretch the working day, and the worker's desire to limit it. "The worker needs time in which to satisfy his intellectual and social requirements, and the extent and number of these requirements is conditioned by the general level of civilization." Hegel's position is similar, but he goes a step further, a step that brings him closer to Hodgskin than to Marx.

3. Three Moments of Property

If a pen were held in front of you, you would see a solid object, structured in space and set in time. The pen, however, is not only a tightly delineated material thing; it is also a mass of moving matter connected to its environment by a million invisible collisions and joinings. Social relationships, while solid enough, are even more an illustration and result of motion and transformation. Hegel sought to develop a language that would capture the movement as well as the stasis of reality.[4] His usage of the term "moment" is a good example. In its ordinary meaning moment has the connotation of time, but time connected to a flow of events moving backward and forward. A moment also describes a significant event in history or in a person's life, and a consequence of action. Finally, it refers to a stage in historical or logical development.

The Hegelian moment embraces most of these meanings. A moment is a phase or stage of development in a particular concept. In dialectical logic, a moment represents the point of sublation (or *aufheben*), when opposite meanings join to create a new one. Hegel (1989: 107) gave a prosaic example of a moment in the *Science of Logic*. "In the case of a lever," he wrote, weight and distance from a point are called mechanical moments on account of the sameness of their effect, in spite of the contrast otherwise between something real, such as a weight, and something ideal, such as a mere spatial determination, a line.

In Hegelian terminology, Hodgskin's system, as I have presented it, could be seen as a moment, a point of transition between the value theory of Marx and the property theory of Hegel, though the sequence here is the opposite of that in historical time. Interestingly, Hegel (1976: 35) observed that the moments of a concept are often ordered opposite to their appearance in history.

Typically there are three moments in any Hegelian concept, though not always. Each moment includes the others, like a circle that encompasses other circles.[5] Hegel employed terms with much the same meaning for him of "moment," such as "modification," "determination," "mode." All are aimed at conveying the idea of change and development in a concept.

Hegel's notion of property has three moments, taking possession, use, and alienation. These refer to an order in history, to a specific series of actions and events, and to logical development. Each determination of property is connected to the others, but in real life there is no rigid sequence; one may appear without another, and so forth. For the concept to be logically complete, however, each of the moments must make an appearance. Vital to them all is the notion of will, of intentional action. You possess something because you *will* to do so (Knowles 1982: 49). Even your body is something you possess; and your occupation of it is the more complete the more you develop and strengthen its capabilities. An animal does not occupy its body in the same manner as a human being. We live because we choose to live; we can withdraw our will to live in the act of suicide. Animals do not have this choice.

4. "Taking Possession"

The first moment of property, taking possession, includes three modes of its own. You can possess an object by physically grasping it, or by having access to it in some indirect manner, e.g. through the medium of tools and machinery. You can even possess something accidentally. Your house may turn out to be sitting on an oil deposit; in the theatre you may find yourself occupying a seat beside a famous movie star. Possession may also be obtained by imposing a form on a thing, by working on it and changing its character.

Finally, you possess something if you mark it as yours—put your signature on a book, for instance, or the family monogram on a jacket.[6]

The second form of taking possession already implies that the labor process is fundamental to the concept of private property. To work on something effects a unity between worker and thing such that the externality of the object is abolished: the thing becomes in concrete fashion a product of mind.[7] An artist, for example, takes up sketch board and pencil and creates a drawing that captures an idea formerly existing only in her imagination. "To impose a form on a thing," wrote Hegel (1976: 47), "is a mode of taking possession most in conformity with the idea to this extent, that it implies a union of subject and object, although it varies with the qualitative character of the objects and the variety of subjective aims." Hegel left no doubt he was referring to the labor process. Forming a thing, he wrote, includes contrivances for utilizing raw materials or the forces of nature and processes for making one material produce effects on another, and so forth." Hegel's concept is very close to Hodgskin's (1966: 237) definition of property as "man's right to the free use of his mind and limbs, and to appropriate whatever he creates by his own labour."

Since Locke (1980: 19), labor has been a primary element in the liberal canon; to have "mixed" our labour with something, "and joined to it something that is [our] own", he declared, is to make that thing our property. But Locke's justification of property became an excuse for its denial to most individuals and its accumulation by a narrow class of capitalists (Macpherson 1962, 1983). "*Ideologically* and *juridically*," wrote Marx (1976: 1084; also 272-3), "the ideology of private property is transferred without more ado to property founded on the *expropriation of the immediate producers.*"

Hegel, like Hodgskin, argued that the property rights of the individual are ultimately rights in herself, a claim to her own body and mind. Marx agreed with this position. Accordingly, he (1976: 271) called the worker's labor-power "his own property," something over which the worker has "rights of ownership." However, for Marx, the liberal concept of property refers to the relationship between an autonomous producer and her conditions of production. No sooner is this relationship established than it is transformed by ideologists of capital into something else. It becomes a justification of capitalist property rights, the exact system that destroys the livelihood of the independent worker (Booth 1989: 21). Marx forgot that the concept of property as developed by Locke had a goal other than justifying bourgeois property rights. As Alan Ryan (1987: 16) observes, it was also aimed at establishing legitimate claims of individuals against the absolutist state. This side of the notion of private property was always foremost in the mind of Hodgskin as it was in Hegel's.

Hegel, however, was no happier than Marx with the liberal concept. He too noted the difficulty bourgeois thinkers had in sorting out individual property rights from those of large capital. This complication has not disappeared. One modern solution hit upon by bourgeois ideologists, as Drucilla Cornell (1989: 1619) points out, is to suggest that there is simply no such thing as corporate power vis à vis the worker. The corporation is only a "nexus of discrete contracts between economic agents." Thus "the employment contract is just another transactional exchange that takes place in the 'nexus of contracts' that we call the corporation" (Cornell 1989: 1619). In this age of the omnipresent corporation the ingenuity of the bourgeois mind is much to be admired.

For Hegel, when the worker engages in the labor process she directly establishes a claim to the means of production. Liberal theory avoids this possibility. The worker simply joins her labor with the capital of the entrepreneur and is amply rewarded for her trouble. A fair day's pay for a fair day's work is the happy outcome of this bargain of equals. "The employer and employee meet as free individuals and can strike any deal they want," observes a modern representative of the liberal position, "presumably it will be mutually advantageous" (Posner 1989: 1630).

For most interpreters—including Marx (e.g. 1981: 753-3)—Hegel's theory is actually a justification of capitalist property rights. Alan Ryan (1987: 123) is one of the most recent and influential holders of this view. He admits that there are radical undercurrents in Hegelian property theory, but claims that Hegel failed to follow them up. Like many writers, Ryan (1984b: 196) complains that Hegel's theory lacks "internal coherence," but I would argue that the fault lies with the commentators and not with Hegel. Hegelian property theory is perfectly coherent, provided its radical implications are accepted rather than dismissed as untenable. Critics often assume Hegel was a conservative, and protect this view even if it appears to go against the evidence they are examining. In the following I will demonstrate the critical thrust of Hegel's theory of property, while keeping in mind scholarship that takes an opposing standpoint.

5. Harriet Martineau and Frances Trollope

The Hegelian moment of taking possession will be compared in this section with similar discussions in Hodgskin and Marx, and illustrated with the work of two Victorian literary women, Harriet Martineau and Frances Trollope. Both women were forced to earn their own living in the 1830s; both chose writing as a way to make an income; and both concentrated on the conditions of the industrial working class, though from opposite viewpoints.

Confusion in the bourgeois mind about the concept of property is inadvertently demonstrated by the writings of Harriet Martineau (Yates 1985: 3; Davidoff and Hall 1987: 186-7). Novelist, political economist, historian and fighter for women's rights, Martineau published *Illustrations of Political Economy*, nine volumes of stories demonstrating for working class and middle class readers the grand truths of economic science. Martineau's work, which appeared in the early 1830s, reflected the recognition then given by political economy to labor as a source of value, and also its stern insistence that the worker was fully compensated for her contribution.[8] *Illustrations of Political Economy* was inspired by a book that attacked the theories of Thomas Hodgskin; in later life Martineau was a tireless critic of Factory Inspector Leonard Horner.

> Such was her commitment to the sacred name of liberty, that she opposed all efforts to secure some degree of legal protection for women and children employed in factories and mines. Since she held that the freedom of the individual to enter into any agreement about labour should be absolute, it was possible for her to write about the Factory Acts that those who deprived workers "of the free disposal of their own labour would steal from them their only possession" (Kovacevic 1975: 218-19).

Today, few would agree with Martineau's position on child labor, but many feminists would accept her argument that state regulation of the workday interfered with women's ability to develop their human potential. I will return to this controversy in Chapter Nine.

One of Martineau's most famous stories is *A Manchester Strike*. According to David Skilton (1977: 125), it "gives the best description of a strike and of union organization in Victorian literature." This dark chronicle of a misguided labor action concludes with an explanation of Ricardo's wage-fund theory, which held that wages are a function of the relation between the size of the working population and the amount of capital. Wrote Martineau (1834: 13),

COMMODITIES, being jointly produced by capital and labour, are the joint property of the capitalist and the labourer.
The capitalist pays in advance to the labourers their share of the commodity, and becomes its sole owner.
. . . The portion thus paid is WAGES.

For Hegel, Martineau's claim would have seemed nonsensical. Capital, in his vision "produces" nothing; only the worker has a capacity to create things. The labor process itself abolishes the distinction between the means and object of labor. The commodities produced, therefore, belong to the worker, who should be Martineau's "sole owner," not the capitalist. "In laying hold of the means," Hegel (1975: 273) remarked in the *Encyclopaedia Logic*, "the notion [i.e. the worker—D.M] constitutes itself the very implicit essence of the object."[9]

Hodgskin (1964: 3-5) also rejected the idea that capital "works," observing that this was a widespread conceit among political economists. James Mill, for example, (a prominent source for Martineau's *Illustrations*)

speaks of capital as an instrument of production cooperating with labour, as an active agent combining with labour to produce commodities, and thus satisfies himself, and endeavours to prove to readers that capital is entitled to all that large share of the produce it actually receives.

Commenting on a set of propositions similar to those displayed by Harriet Martineau, Marx (1976: 734) wrote that with the development of capitalism, "the property laws of commodity production must undergo a dialectical inversion so that they become laws of capitalist accumulation."[10]

If Hegel rejected the doctrine that capital is an equal contributor in the labor process, as did Hodgskin and Marx, there is also a sense in which Hegel himself would have seen it as correct. Possession—the stage we have reached so far in his concept of property—is a relatively amorphous moment in the development of property rights. Possession can initially take place under any number of social conditions. It can be a simple relation between an individual and an external object, or a highly complex technological endeavor with great demands upon mind and skill. This important distinction for Hegel is rarely mentioned by interpreters, although it did have an impact on Marx (1976: 290-91), who remarked on a similar stage in his own concept of the labor processs.

> The process we have presented here does not reveal the conditions
> under which it takes place, whether it is happening under the slave-
> owners brutal lash or the anxious eye of the capitalist, whether
> Cincinnatus undertakes it in tilling his couple of acres, or a savage,
> when he lays low a wild beast with a stone.

In taking possession, the relationship of the laborer to the means
and object of work is wholly abstract. Whether she is physically
grasping something, working on it, or simply marking it, *the actual
presence of the worker's will and purpose may be very slight.* In fact,
possession is so abstract that it can take place under control of a
power apart from the worker. Accordingly, this relationship is
consonant not only with advanced capitalism, but also with slavery.
That is why Hegel discusses the institution of slavery at the end of
his commentary on the moment of possession. Slavery was
historically justified because it belonged to a period when individual
personality was undeveloped. The slave was a *conscious* being, but
not a *self-conscious personality*, with property rights.

The slave's self-consciousness had not developed to the point at
which she could perceive herself as a *thing*, her own possession and
no one else's. Self-consciousness requires the struggle between
master and slave, or—if we think of Hegel's Berlin lectures discussed
in Chapter Three—between capitalist and worker.

> This false, comparatively primitive, phenomenon of slavery is one
> which befalls mind when mind is only at the level of consciousness.
> The dialectic of the concept and of the purely immediate conscious-
> ness of freedom brings about at that point the fight for recognition
> and the relationship of master and slave (Hegel 1976: 48).

This brings us to Frances Trollope. Mother of the famous
novelist, and along with Martineau, one of the earliest contributors
to the genre now called English industrial fiction, Trollope was a firm
supporter of government intervention to protect factory children. It
is seldom recalled that when Hegel[11] and Marx were writing about
the labor process, many industrial workers were either children or
women; men were late entrants to industrialization (Engels 1969:
170).

Frances Trollope had this fact firmly in mind when in the late
1830s, outfitted with British government reports and statistics on
child factory operatives, she travelled from London to Manchester to
investigate conditions in the mills. In doing so, notes Skilton (1977:
123), she was "performing functions nowadays associated with

higher journalism and the social sciences . . . In the 1830s the novel
had a greater confidence in its own social and political role than ever
before or since."

Trollope's 1839 novel *The Life and Adventures of Michael Armstrong,
the Factory Boy* received bad reviews from the establishment press,
but sold well and was influential in the struggle for factory reform.[12]
Critics have argued that Trollope's story of Deep Valley Mill, "which
"gives the impression that almost all factory hands were children,"
(Gallagher 1985: 127-8), actually depicts "an earlier period when
factories were located in isolated valleys where rivers provided the
source of power" (Kovacevic 1975: 101).[13]   Still, the Hegelian
moment of taking possession refers, among other things, to the early
stages of industrialization, when the situation described by Frances
Trollope was dominant.

Imagine you are entering with Trollope (1840: 80-82) a "monster"
English cotton-spinning mill. "The ceaseless whining of a million
hissing wheels seizes the tortured ear." In this "horrid earthly hell"
there are "hundreds of helpless children divested of every trace of
health, of joyousness, and even of youth." Supervised by adult male
overlookers, "strap in hand," the exhausted little laborers stand mute
amidst the "thunder" of the machines. You observe "lean and
distorted limbs—sallow and sunken cheeks—dim hollow eyes, that
speak unrest and most unnatural carefulness, [and] give to each tiny,
trembling unelastic form, a look of hideous premature age."

You are captivated by the sight of "the whirling spindles urging
the little slaves who wait[] on them to movement unceasing as their
own." The novelist points out that "the whole monstrous chamber
[is] redolent of all the various impurities that 'by the perfection of
our manufacturing system,' are converted into 'gales of Araby' for
the rich, after passing in the shape of certain poison through the
lungs of the poor." Who could help but marvel at this "transmutation of life into gold"?   The visit has exposed for you "the secret
arcana of that hideous mystery by which the delicate forms of young
children are made to mix and mingle with the machinery, from
whence flows the manufacturer's wealth."

Your tour of the factory confirms the liberal doctrine on property.
In the moment of possession, the worker is merely—in Hegel's (1989:
715) words (which appear to deliberately echo those of
Locke)—"*mixing* and *aggregating*" her labour with the object[14], in the
same manner that a machine (or an animal) can be directed to carry
out numerous, complex functions on a pre-existing material. As

Trollope said, "the delicate forms of children are made to mix and mingle with the machinery."

The scene in Deep Valley Mill illustrates a relationship Hegel (1989: 715) called, "outward necessity." As in any mechanical process, "the active object has this its determination only by means of another object." The children's actions are determined by moving machinery and the equally mechanical control of adult overseers. A similar relationship is surveyed by Marx (1976: 449). Under the factory system, he observed, raw material and machinery "confront the wage-labourer as the property of another." The cooperation of the workers "is entirely brought about by the capital that employs them."

The terse but forceful language of the *Encyclopaedia Logic* advises that in the process of outward necessity "this whole is external to itself, it is self-externalized even in its own self and in its content, and this externality, attaching to the fact, is a limit of its content" (Hegel 1975: 212). Marx (1976: 450) put it more concretely:

> [the workers'] unification into one single productive body, and the establishment of a connection between their individual functions, lies outside their competence. These things are not their own act, but the act of capital that brings them together and maintains their situation. Hence the interconnection between their labour confronts them, in the realm of ideas, as a plan drawn up by the capitalist, and, in practice, as his authority, as the powerful will of a being outside them, who subjects their activity to his purpose.

"The necessary," as Hegel (1975: 212) said, "being through another, is not in and for itself: hypothetical, it is a mere result of assumption." This was the condition of a large part of the English working class in the first half of the nineteenth century: "it [was] not in and for itself."

Possession is a rudimentary mode of property; it is simple and arbitrary and can occur with only a modest expenditure of will, or even with a will that is coerced into being no will at all. Possession coincides with the slave system, not just the slavery of the ancients, but the slave system that was in full swing throughout the colonies of Hegel's time. For Hegel—as we have seen—the factory setup in Britain, where the employer "sought to leave workers only the choice between long hours of work or no work at all," (Rueschemeyer 1986: 8, 87) was also a form of slavery. The next determination of the concept of property—use—is vastly different from possession.

6. "The Process of *Recognition*"

Purpose is what distinguishes the second moment of property—use—from taking possession. To do something with a purpose is to work toward some self-determined goal. Property in a thing is achieved, according to Hegel (1976: 49), when we use the thing to satisfy some need or purpose of our own. "The use of the thing is my need externally realized through the change, destruction, and consumption of the thing." The Hegelian notion of will and purpose reappeared in Marx. He (1976: 284) compared the product of the actions of a spider with the work of a weaver, and a bee to an architect. The big difference between the automatic operations of an insect and the labour of a human being is the presence in the latter of will and purpose.

> What distinguishes the worst architect from the best of bees is that the architect builds the cell in his mind before he constructs it in wax. At the end of every labour process, a result emerges which had already been conceived by the worker at the beginning, hence already existed ideally. Man not only effects a change of form in the materials of nature; he also realizes . . . his own purpose in those materials.

Purpose is altogether lacking in the moment of possession; or at least the purpose may be that of someone other than the one doing the possessing. Children in the cotton mill were not creatures of purpose; they were acting in mechanical fashion at the command of someone else. This relationship, Marx (1976: 425) pointed out, is an "inversion," a "distortion" of what is supposed to take place in the process of production. "From the point of view of the simple labour-process the worker is related to the means of production, not in their quality as capital, but as being the mere means and material of his own purposive activity." Capitalism reverses this coin, so that the worker is the "mere means and material" of machinery. It then becomes sinful even to consider letting a large capital stock sit idle for lack of workers. "Hence furnaces and workshops constitute 'lawful claims upon the night-labour' of the labour-powers."

The moment of taking possession marks the beginning of self-consciousness in the worker. She starts to see herself as a person relative to the factory master, a person with rights. In other words, she implicitly becomes a being with will and purpose, capable of advancing to the second moment of property, use. Hegel (1971: 170, 165) called this the "process of *recognition*." "I am aware of the object as mine; and thus in it I am aware of me," wrote Hegel (1971: 165). "The formula of self-consciousness is I = I: —abstract freedom, pure 'Ideality.'" But the capitalist refuses the worker her self-identity; for him, she is only a *thing*. "When an individual feels herself excluded by another who takes no notice of her, as he takes possession of her things as if she were a thing herself," writes Cornell (1989: 1558), "she experiences a gap between her knowledge of herself and the lack of knowledge the other has of her." The struggle for recognition is not a battle merely for property; it is a battle for reciprocity, for mutual recognition: "the impulse to *show* itself as a free self, and to exist as such for the other" (Hegel 1971: 170; Cornell 1989: 1585).

In the first stage of this "life and death struggle" wrote Hegel (1971: 172-3), the worker "surrenders his claim for recognition," and the other becomes his master. This initial defeat prepares the basis for the social and economic life of both master and slave. "In the battle for recognition and the subjugation under a master, we see, on their phenomenal side, the emergence of man's social life and the commencement of political union."

Recalling Hegel's discussion of England before the Reform Bill in Chapter Two, we saw that the country lacked a political life; what it had was a life of wealth and poverty, of masters and slaves, a political existence based on force. Yet this essentially perverted political order was also a necessary stage in the development of freedom. "*Force* [is] . . . the necessary and legitimate factor in the passage from the state of self-consciousness sunk in appetite and selfish isolation into the state of universal self-consciousness" (Hegel 1971: 173). The dynamic of this Hegelian transition may be traced in the movement from possession to use.

The poor in civil society are without purpose; they lack freedom to develop their own capacities, to exercise their free will. Many commentators claim that Hegel threw up his hands over the condition of the poor. Hegel, they propose, did not know what to do about this huge mass of individuals without rights and property.[15] *I argue, on the contrary, that his answer to the problem is contained in the analysis of the concept of property.* The moment of use, in particular, points to the solution of poverty in civil society.

If the moment of use involves will, it also includes the *means* by which the individual's purpose is achieved. For Hegel (1976: 49), the highest form of mediation between purpose and its fulfilment is represented by the means of production, "a product which continually renews itself."

If my use of [a thing] is grounded on a persistent need, and if I make repeated use of a product which continually renews itself, restricting my use if necessary to safeguard that renewal, then these and other circumstances transform the single grasp of the thing into a mark, intended to signify that I am taking it into my possession in a universal way, and thereby taking possession of the elemental or organic basis of such products, or of anything else that conditions them.

The poor are barred access to the supreme achievement of civil society: the intermediating complex of mechanical and chemical processes called means of production, machinery, capital, and so forth. The propertyless worker is "mere immediacy" as opposed to the capitalist who possesses the means of production. "But this immediacy is at the same time the corporeity of self-consciousness [i.e. the master, D.M] in which as in its sign and tool the [master] has its own *sense of self*, and its being *for others*, and the means for entering into relation with them" (Hegel 1971: 171).

Hegel's concept of taking possession involves a relationship between persons and things, and debouches into a condemnation of slavery; the moment of use refers specifically to direct status or class relationships. The following chapter, which focuses on Hegel's "business class," will examine these relationships, and their connection with the third mode of property, alienation. In Hegel's view, alienation passes over into a more advanced stage called "contract." The Hegelian moments of property and contract provide an account of class consciousness, and a coruscating critique of bourgeois property relationships that surpass those of Marx.

Notes

1.   For Marxist critics newly won over to some significant Hegelian formulations—such as the importance of a justice system to protect human rights—the labor contract exposes Hegel's deepest flaw. "Wage labour is as such the surrender of an integral aspect of the self . . . to external control, and so it must contravene the basic meaning of freedom as self-determination" (McCarney 1991: 34; also Arthur 1986). These writers overlook the central place of the labor contract in Hegel's theory, which provides the entry point for the individual into the governing bodies of civil society and the state.

2.   At least since Perry Anderson's (1965: 17) germinal "Origins of the Present Crisis," which lamented the inadequacies of early proletarian ideology, Marxists have been skeptical about the contribution of the mid-

nineteenth century English socialists. R. N. Berki (1988: 114), for example, claims that "it is clear that Marx did not learn anything very important from [Hodgskin and the other] Ricardian socialists, as he undoubtedly did learn a great deal from Smith (mainly) and Ricardo."

3. Noel Thompson (1984: 87) ignores the juristic basis of Hodgskin's theory, and attributes Hodgskin's "essentially reformist policy prescriptions" to a misplaced faith in (bourgeois) private property.

4. I owe the discussion of Hegelian language to a conversation in 1976 with Professor Donald MacRae.

5. The importance of the circle for Hegel is emphasized in one of the best and most accessible discussions of Hegelian terminology, Walter Kaufmann's (1978: 237) *Hegel: A Reinterpretation.*

6. In Hegelian theory, possession of human beings is illegitimate. It is nevertheless noteworthy that traditional marriage and the patrilineal naming system are forms of "marking." Thus the patriarchal male impresses his surname on wife and child alike.

7. "How is something most completely taken into ownership? . . . One answer [for Hegel] is that things most fully become ours when our work transforms them. We endow a thing with a new essence by working on it, and this new nature supersedes the original nature; naturally, therefore, labour gives one solid title" (Ryan 1987: 125). Ryan's loose exegesis of Hegel will be discussed further below.

8. "The theories of political economy," writes Catherine Gallagher (1985: 56) in *The Industrial Reformation of English Fiction*, "made it possible to conceive of workers in tragic heroic terms, not just because it made them seem destined to suffer, but also because it made them seem important."

9. In *The Communist Ideal in Hegel and Marx* (1984) I suggested that the concept of "end" in *Logic* has the skilled worker as a primary meaning. Recently, David Lamb (1987: 177) has made a similar argument. "Hegel," he suggests, "is the philosopher of the Industrial Revolution."

10. Referring directly to *A Manchester Strike*, Marx (1976: 787-8) called Martineau an "old maid" who, on behalf political economy, "puts . . . words . . . into the mouth of her ideal capitalist."

11. "Reliance on women's labor and, more significantly, children's labor is now little remarked upon in reference to handicraft and even early factory industry." "The early factory cotton industry was . . . dominated by women's and children's labor. Most of the mills surveyed in 1816 were small scale and employed significantly more women than men, and roughly equal numbers of adults and children. The few large-scale mills at the time employed roughly equal proportions of men and women; adults and children" (Berg 1987: 68, 71).

12. "With its emphasis on documentation, its new role for women, and the new authority it gave to the female social novelist," writes Joseph Kestner (1985: 58) in his *Protest and Reform: The British Social Narrative by Women*, "Trollope's campaign for government intervention (contrary to the

beliefs of Harriet Martineau) advances the female social novel to a different plane by its care for sources and its involvement of a middle class woman in working class affairs"

13. For a counter-argument, see Kestner (1985: 51).

14. This passage is from a section in the *Science of Logic* called "mechanism," which provides the logical substructure of the concept of possession.

15. Observing that Hegel actually offers a number of administrative solutions to the problems of poverty, Norbert Waszek (1988: 22) allows that this criticism of Hegel "does not seem to be quite fair." In Chapter Seven, I claim that Hegel has an additional, structural solution to poverty: worker ownership of the means of production.

7

Hegel's Theory of Property, Part II: Class Consciousness

It is in the highest degree uncharacteristic that [Hegel] . . . should leave so important an issue [as poverty] hanging in the air, beyond the normally voracious grasp of the system. The explanation, as Marxists have repeatedly pointed out . . . is that we here come up against the bourgeois horizons of his thought.
—Joseph McCarney, *"The True Realm of Freedom"* (1991: 19)

Persecution, then, gives rise to a peculiar technique of writing, and therewith to a peculiar type of literature, in which the truth about all crucial things is presented exclusively between the lines. . . . The works of great writers of the past are very beautiful even from without. And yet their visible beauty is sheer ugliness, compared with the beauty of those hidden treasures which disclose themselves only after very long, never easy, but always pleasant work.
—Leo Strauss, *Persecution and the Art of Writing* (1973: 25, 37)

1. Introduction

The treatment of poverty in Hegel's Berlin lectures, and a similar approach in the *Philosophy of Right*, appear to be grounded in a radical critique of civil society. Yet commentators have discovered in Hegel only a conservative understanding of the basis of civil society—private property. This chapter presents a different account of Hegelian property theory. I shall argue that Hegel's concept includes a profound critique of bourgeois private property, a critique that underpins his position on poverty. My argument hinges on a neglected contrast Hegel made between the moments of property called respectively, taking possession and use. Possession was examined in Chapter Six; here we will look more closely at the moment of use, and the further determinations, alienation and contract.

The moment of use assumes power or status relationships between property owners. Accordingly section two examines Hegel's theory of social class. Following sections will show how the moment of use transforms the nature of property relationships within the business class. This Hegelian transformation—which resembles the property theory of Thomas Hodgskin, and echoes a pivotal idea in Rousseau—involves the rise of class consciousness in the worker, and a fundamental challenge to the supremacy of capital. At the same time, Hegelian theory provides the basis for a conception of the state that serves as a counterpoint to freedom of contract. The concluding section suggests that for Hegel the liberal doctrine on property leads to its own sublation (*aufheben*) by cooperative ownership of the means of production.

2. "The Business Class"

A major divergence between Marx and Hegel is thought to be the place of the working class in their respective social theories. While the proletariat is central in Marx, Hegel's theory was once held to be notable for the absence of workers. Recently, the tide has shifted. The working class is now admitted by some interpreters into Hegel's social theory, but only as a subordinate strata, excluded from the governing corporations and the state (Cullen 1988; Plant 1987). Others have gone further, and suggest that the proletariat has a political role in Hegel equal to that of other groups in civil society (Heiman 1971: 123; Ryan 1984a: 138; Winfield 1987; Bellamy 1987). The recently published Heidelberg lectures on politics, in which Hegel (1983a: 131-4) explicitly included workers in the business class, provides strong support for the latter position.   The political dimensions of Hegel's class theory will be discussed fully in the concluding chapter of this book. This section will elucidate Hegel's concept of the "business class," one of the three main classes or estates in the *Philosophy of Right*.

In contrast with Marx, Hegel (1976: 131) viewed ownership or non-ownership of the means of production as only one dimension of class. The other dimensions are functional and social psychological. Conceptually, the agricultural class of peasants and landlords has no real property dimension at all, since full-fledged property rights emerged only with the bourgeoisie. Nobles and serfs are tied to each other by lines of deference and necessity; they earn their living off the land, rather than on the market. This provides them not only with an agenda of labor and supervision, but also with a mode of life "which owes comparatively little to reflection and independence of will."

The family-centred agricultural way of life was mortally threatened by expansion of the market; its demise was inevitable. Dissolution of the agricultural class hinged on a contradiction: the relationships between its members were not property relations per se, yet "the soil . . . is capable of exclusively private ownership and . . . demands formation in an objective way and not mere haphazard exploitation" (Hegel 1976: 131). In England, as shown in Chapter Two, the landed interest survived and prospered as a governing class by adopting bourgeois property relations and production methods.

We have already encountered Hegel's universal class, identified by its relation to the state, and possessed of a form of consciousness suited to its role as guardian of universal interests. Here again there is no question of property ownership. "What anchors the civil servant in his world is not the ownership of the office, but tenure subject to good behaviour and the public's recognition of his official status" (Ryan 1984a: 132).

The business class is defined primarily in terms of property relationships; these in turn are intimately connected with its structure of consciousness and social function. "Whereas the ethical life of the family," writes Anthony Black (1984: 204), "is especially developed in the agricultural class, and that of the state by the class of civil servants, the ethics of civil society are especially developed in the business class."

This class earns its living through manufacture and trade; it is made up of individuals who possess varying amounts of capital or skill; and it is sub-divided among those who work as artisans, in mass production, or in banking and exchange.[1] Business life produces a particular mental structure, which Hegel calls "reflection," or "the understanding." The chief characteristics of the reflective consciousness are self-reliance, and a powerful desire for individual freedom.

As mentioned above, some commentators claim that Hegel's business class includes only wealthy capitalists. However, it would have been completely inconsistent to exclude workers from this stratum. The agricultural class retains the distinction between lord and serf; the universal class is divided between the bureaucracy and the commanding levels of the state executive. Similarly, the business class is split between those who have property, and those who have little or none; it embodies what Hegel (1976: 130) called, "the vast disparities of resources and ability" characteristic of civil society.

> Men are made unequal by nature, where inequality is in its element, and in civil society the right of particularity is so far from annulling this natural inequality that it produces it out of mind and raises it to an inequality of skill and resources, and even to one of moral and intellectual attainment.

Deep significance is attached to Hegel's use of a single term to include both workers and capitalists. The business class started out as a stratum of apprentices and masters united in guilds, and retained something of this characteristic when Hegel was writing (Black: 168-170). Moreover, in Hegelian political theory the tremendous divisions that emerged in this class during the industrial revolution are eventually healed by the coming of the modern corporation.[2]

In the early decades of the nineteenth century it was common practice to lump workers and capitalists together. They were allies against aristocracy, and the social origins of employers and workers were often very similar. It was not unheard of for a worker to become a capitalist, and there were plenty of unsuccessful entrepreneurs who lost their shirts and fell back into the working class. Owners often took a direct hand in the operation of their firms. Thus even the socialist Thomas Hodgskin declared that "masters are *labourers* as well as their journeymen. In this character their interest is precisely the same as that of their men." Hodgskin went on, "CAPITAL, or the POWER TO EMPLOY LABOUR, AND CO-EXISTING LABOUR ARE ONE; and . . . PRODUCTIVE CAPITAL AND SKILLED LABOUR are also ONE; consequently capital and a labouring population are precisely synonymous" (1964: 91).

Admittedly, Hodgskin (1964: 108) was making a point in this last sentence about ownership of property, and he specifically excluded the idle "capitalist, the oppressive middleman who eats up the produce of labour" from his definition of capital. Nevertheless, by linking workers and owners, both Hodgskin and Hegel were following a long tradition in economics. In 1766, for instance, the French economist Turgot placed "capitalist entrepreneurs and ordinary workmen" within his "industrial stipendiary class" (Quoted in Cullen 1988: 40).

Identifying labor with capital was common in the first third of the nineteenth century, although everyone knew, or sensed, that they represented opposed interests. Thus the *Westminster Review*, a journal read regularly by Hegel, referred in 1831 to "the two great divisions of the labouring order," which the *Review* distinguished from the governing aristocracy. This single "labouring order" was divided between "the manufacturers, at present in comparative comfort,"—i.e. capitalists and industrial workers—and "the agricultural labourers sunk to the last depth of misery" (quoted in Halévy 1961a: 17).

The business class is the centrepiece in Hegel's (1976: 271) analysis of the moment of use. Neither the agricultural class or civil servants are important at this stage. On one hand, property relationships are foreign to the universal class, "which must . . . be relieved of direct labour to supply its needs." On the other hand, the agricultural class is more or less stalled at the stage of possession, where dependence and submission have a place.

Hegel's business class must be one of the most intriguing concepts in the history of thought. A unity of capitalist and worker, whose members have an identical structure of consciousness, it is also an inwardly split social class, which—as we shall see in the following sections—contains opposing views on the nature of private property. Like Marx's proletariat, Hegel's (1976: 271) business class is the key actor in the historical drama unfolding in civil society. "The agricultural class is . . . more inclined to subservience, the business class to freedom." Yet its rapid, conflict-ridden progress is dogged by the growing presence of the universal class, the dour and dutiful servants of community interests who make such a spectacular entrance in *Capital*.

3. "The Use of the Thing"

The relationship of the worker to the means of production represents an advanced mode in the concept of property. Possession can be accidental, and can even occur without an actual will. Use of a single thing, like a child eating some candy, is also a limited relation. As the child says after the candy disappears, "all gone." It is different with a productive tool or machine. In the moment of use the worker not only takes possession of the means of production, she also steers them toward satisfaction of future needs and insures their renewal, for without her they would rot and decay. According to Hegel (1976: 49), in the simultaneously destructive and conserving action of labor, the worker goes beyond mere possession and asserts "universal" possession of the means of production, "and of anything else that conditions them."

A fatally twisted version of the Hegelian concepts of possession and use is now recognized as the dominant legal relation defining capitalist production (Woodiwiss 1987: 455-6). The capitalist enjoys unimpeded access to, and control over, the means of production and the finished product, and has the right to hire and fire, with little fear of intervention from employees or the state (Woodiwiss 1987: 456; Marx 1976: 996) This ability is hinged not on the fact that the capitalist "owns" the firm, but rather stems ultimately from the capitalist's position as an employer (or user) of factor inputs, especially labor. The capitalist need not even "own" the means of production. These can be rented, along with the services of workers, and used to produce a commodity that belongs solely to the capitalist (Ellerman 1991: Chapter Eight, pp. 2-3). The worker herself is considered by the bourgeois legal system as a *thing* like other factor inputs, a thing *used* by the capitalist to produce a certain commodity (Ellerman 1985: 313). The capitalist's *use* of the worker and other inputs in the production process gives him the right of ownership over the products of labor. Wrote Marx (1976: 996), "the owner of the capacity for labour owns that labour just as effectively as he owns the other material conditions of production that he has bought. And he does not just own the particular elements of the labour process; the entire process belongs to him."

4. "An Overlord to Nothing"

Much of Hodgskin's (1964: 71-2) *Labour Defended Against the Claims of Capital* is a demonstration that capital results from the worker's effort. The capitalist exercises property rights over raw materials, machines, and labor power, but all these are really claims on the labor of the worker. The worker's wages are expended on commodities produced by another worker; the raw materials and machines employed in the labor process result from the exertions of still others. The employer stands between the worker and her counterpart "separating them so widely from each other that neither can see whence that supply is drawn which each receives through the capitalist." The master "is the *middle-man* of all the labourers" and grows fat on their productive activity.

Hegel (1971: 257, 244; 1989: 749-50) made the same point. Capitalism is a system in which economic production "is conditioned by the ever-continued production of fresh means of exchange by the exchangers' *own labour.*" Compared to the "infinite self-determination of the Notion" (i. e. the worker), he suggested, the material and product of labor are only accidental, forms translated into other forms, none of which are (like the worker) ends in themselves. The individual realizes her personality in work, but the means of production are incorporated into the endless flow of commodities to the marketplace. "The conclusion or *product* of the purposive act is nothing but an object determined by an end external to it; *consequently it is the same thing as the means.*" In the *Philosophy of Mind* Hegel (1971: 244) expressed this in a slightly different, even more cryptic manner. "Possession is *property*, which as possession is a *means*, but as existence of the personality is an *end.*"

The revolutionary implications of Hegel's (1976: 49-50) analysis are brought home in the *Philosophy of Right,* where he insisted that by using or working with the means of production the worker is establishing a property right in them.[3]

> Since the substance of the thing which is my property is, if we take the thing by itself, its externality, i. e. its non-substantiality—in contrast with me it is not an end in itself . . . —and since in my use or employment of it this externality is realized, it follows that my full use or employment of the thing is the thing in its entirety, so that if I have full use of the thing I am its owner. Over and above the entirety of its use, there is nothing left which could be the property of another.

For Hegel, property defines the beginning and end of the bourgeois mind, the point at which the "understanding consciousness" splits wide open. In the capitalist conception, a person can "own" the means of production without ever having laid eyes on them, much less used them. Alan Ryan (1984a: 126-7) argues that Hegel would view this "control at extreme arm's length [as] a triumph of mind over matter." Insofar as workers are excluded from property rights, it might be seen as a triumph by Hegel—a triumph of greed and abstraction over rationality. A formal, abstract title extends to the master full rights of ownership while the worker has no claim at all. For Hegel (1976: 50), this is a total violation of the idea of property.

> If the whole and entire use of a thing were mine, while the abstract ownership was supposed to be someone else's, then the thing as mine would be penetrated through and through by my will . . . and at the same time there would remain in the thing something impenetrable by me, namely the will, the empty will, of another. As a positive will, I would be at one and the same time objective and not objective to myself in the thing—an absolute contradiction. Ownership is in essence free and complete.

The worker confronts an irreducible blockage in the movement from possession to use: the personality of the capitalist, the owner of property. In civil society, Hegel (1971: 257) wrote, "immediate seizure of external objects as means . . . exists barely or not at all: the objects are already property." The worker has no chance to gain property because everything is already monopolized by the owning class. It must be admitted, allowed Hodgskin (1964: 73), that "all savings in society are usually made by capitalists. The labourer cannot save; the landlord is not disposed to save; whatever is saved is saved from profits and becomes the property of the capitalist."

The entrepreneur has already "marked" the instruments of labor, asserted possession of them with title deeds, a company name, and so forth, that are supposed to be *"representative"* of his will. "In its objective scope and meaning," stated Hegel (1976: 49, 50), "this mode of taking possession is very indeterminate." The distinction between concrete, active possession and use of the means of production by the worker and their illusory use by what Hegel calls, an "overlord to nothing" is symptomatic of bourgeois "insanity of personality." Madness, Hegel explained, need not refer only to "the presence of a direct contradiction between a man's purely subjective ideas and the actual facts of his life." Insanity permeates the entire bourgeois system ("the world of fact") and emerges from a condition of *objective madness* in which "'mine' as applied to a single object would have to mean the direct presence in it of both my single exclusive will and also the single exclusive will of someone else."

In a later section we shall see that Hegel's concept of bourgeois insanity of personality is given definitive form in the third moment of property, alienation. I will also show that the connection Hegel made between insanity and the wage contract was drawn before him by Rousseau. Interestingly, one of the meanings of alienation for Hegel (1971: 115) is mental illness. Disease of any kind erupts from alienation of part of an organism from the whole. In congestive heart disease, for example, the choked valves of the heart threaten fatally to separate the organ from the rest of the body. Alienation of any sort ends in "impotence and dependence on an alien power."

The understanding consciousness is diseased in exactly this sense. Like a distorted mirror, it constantly reflects back contradiction and division in the objects of consciousness. "What disorganizes the unity of logical reason, equally disorganizes actuality," said Hegel (1971: 270, 128). With its attitude to property, the bourgeois mind, like that of an insane person, "is shifted out from the centre of its actual world and, since it also still contains a consciousness of this world, has two centres, one in the remainder of its *rational* consciousness and the other in its *deranged* idea."

Political economy—"one of the sciences which have arisen out of the conditions of the modern world"— represents both the rational and irrational aspects of bourgeois consciousness. On one side, economists like Say, Smith and Ricardo have discovered

> in the sphere of needs this show of rationality lying in the thing and effective there; but if we look at it from the opposite point of view, this is the field in which the Understanding with its subjective aims and moral fancies vents its discontent and moral frustration (Hegel 1976: 127).

5. "Two Owners Standing in Relation to Each Other"

The moment of use reveals the split in bourgeois consciousness brought about by the concept of private property. It also throws light on the structure of the business class. This class, insisted Hegel (1976: 51), is made up of "an owner on one hand" (the worker), "and an overlord who [is] the overlord to nothing on the other" (the capitalist).

Hodgskin (1964: 33) called the capitalist, "the oppressive middle-man, who eats up the produce of labour." Hegel did not use the term "middleman" in the *Philosophy of Right,* which was published before Hodgskin's book. However, the *Philosophy of Mind* was substantially revised in 1830, five years after publication of Hodgskin's classic. There Hegel (1971: 258) defined "the reflected estate" as consisting of, on one hand, "middle men .. mere agents" and, on the other, "the individual [who] has to depend on his subjective skill, talent, intelligence, and industry."

Hodgskin granted that many capitalists took a managerial role in production; for him, this is what brings together the interests of worker and capitalist. Both are interested in ensuring the most efficient possible organization of the workplace. The problem is that the capitalist rarely takes the worker into account, treating her not as an equal, but as a disposable commodity. Hegel (1976: 51) made the same concession to the capitalist. The entrepreneur's managerial role rescues the bourgeois system from absolute madness.

> Were there nothing in these two relationships except that distinction [between formal ownership and ownership through use] in its rigid abstraction, then in them we would not have two overlords . . . in the strict sense, but an owner on the one hand and an overlord who was the overlord of nothing on the other. But on the score of the burdens imposed there are two owners standing in relation to each other.

Marx (1976: 1022, 1019) also allowed for the managerial role of capital, calling it *"the formal subsumption of labour under capital"*: "the labour process is subsumed under capital . . . and the capitalist intervenes as its manager, director." However, he was not concerned, as were Hegel and Hodgskin, with the implications of this role for the concept of property since for Marx everything boils down to the extraction of surplus value.

In Hegel's conception of the business class, the two sides develop a similar consciousness. They share a world of production and exchange that builds a particular structure of thought. They are, of course, bitterly opposed to each other on issues relating to the employment contract and property rights, a conflict that spills over into ways of thinking. *Yet there are many areas of agreement between them, especially their suspicious attitude toward the state and the universal class.* In the final chapter, we will look at Hegel's recommendations on politics that take into account resemblances between the conflicting sides of the business class mind.

We have already discussed Hodgskin's hostility to government, a trait he shared with capitalist political economy. In the history of factory legislation we shall find the male workers' movement at some points almost as opposed to government intervention as the capitalists, often for the same reasons. In his account of factory law, Marx deliberately underplayed conflict between workers and factory inspectors, probably to avoid giving comfort to enemies of state intervention.

At this stage in the relation of use, capitalist and worker are nowhere equal in consciousness or power. Workers have not gained recognition in the eyes of the master. This phase of Hegel's property theory is similar to Marx's conception of the second stage of the employment contract, which is fully discussed in the next chapter. Both involve intensive division of labor and introduction of machinery; and both are concerned with the rise of class consciousness in the worker, what Hegel (1971: 174-5) called "the passage to universal self-consciousness."

6. "Universal Self-Consciousness"

The development of self-consciousness is a central theme in the section on civil society in the *Philosophy of Right*; but self-consciousness is essentially created within the framework of social class. "A man with no class is a mere private person and his universality is not actualized" (Hegel 1976: 271, 133). Thus when Hegel wrote about forms of consciousness, he did so in the context of the three classes of civil society. As the chief protagonist in civil society's system of needs, the business class is also the one in which the development of class consciousness—the dialectic of *recognition* between master and slave—is most salient. Accordingly, Hegel (1976: 126) referred often to the "Understanding," i. e. the mode of consciousness peculiar to the business class. The process of recognition—the development of self-consciousness—occurs primarily in the mode of property called use. In "the moment of liberation intrinsic to work" the laborer advances to the position of equal in consciousness and (ultimately) in power to the capitalist. At this point she is capable of asserting her rightful claim to the product of her labor, a claim that involves (as we shall see in the conclusion of this study) a struggle for power in the corporation and the state. Thus in Hegel's (1983b: 196; Avineri 1985: 207) Berlin lectures, the growth of class consciousness is two-sided; it isn't simply that the working class achieves a consciousness of itself, but also that the "ruffian-like behaviour" of the rich is tamed and controlled.

The worker could not assert herself at the level of possession, since this stage of property involves domination and control by an external power. For example, the factory children of Hegel's day could not have successfully claimed ownership of the means and products of their labor. As incomplete personalities, they were hardly able to assert control of themselves, let alone the production process. Similarly, owners could not advance in consciousness very far when their wealth depended on exploiting little children and powerless adults. Nevertheless, domination prepares the basis for a higher form of consciousness, "since it is by compulsion that the particular rises to the form of universality and seeks and gains its stability in that form" (Hegel 1976: 124).

The battle for property rights is primarily an "educational struggle"—*Bildung*, the self-development of consciousness. "The final purpose of education," writes Hegel (1976: 125) in a remarkable passage in the *Philosophy of Right*,

> is liberation, and the struggle for a higher liberation still; education is the absolute transition from an ethical substantiality which is immediate and natural to one which is intellectual and so both infinitely subjective and lofty enough to have attained a universality of form.

The "theoretical education" of the "understanding" concerns "not merely a multiplicity of ideas and facts," but a practice which encourages "flexibility and rapidity of mind, ability to pass from one idea to another, to grasp complex and general relations, and so on."

> Practical education, acquired through working, consists first in the automatically recurrent need for something to do and the habit of simply being busy; next, in the strict adaptation of one's activity according not only to the nature of the material worked on, but also, and especially to the pleasure of other workers; and finally, in a habit produced by this discipline, of objective activity and universally recognized aptitudes (Hegel 1976: 129).

Consciousness is hierarchically organized. The mind of the agricultural class falls well short of the mentality of the business class. The latter, in turn, is a mind concerned with the *particular*, rather than with the general interests that occupy the mental world of the universal class, the "thinking" estate, as Hegel (1971: 258) called it. Business class mentality is a product of civil society; so is that of the universal class. But the thinking estate possesses a greater capacity for comprehending the universal because its life and concerns are precisely those of the state. Nevertheless, the universal class has its own shortcomings. It is ultimately *dependent* on the state for an income; and government relies on revenues drawn from civil society. The growth and influence of the universal class, in other words, depends heavily on the fortunes of the business class. Moreover, its education may distance the universal class from the lives of ordinary people. Although the church is excluded from power in Hegel's (1983b: 194; Avineri 1985: 206) state, the education received by pastors—which makes them "more learned than able to speak to the heart and reveal the inner life"—probably bears resemblance to that received by the universal class.

On one hand, the routine, habit and comradeship of work contribute to the development of the understanding consciousness. On the other hand, the abstraction involved in producing standard goods for sale in an impersonal market allows work to be divided and sub-divided, infinitely simplified into a complex division of labor. Tasks become less intricate and output increases as the worker's abilities are simultaneously honed and narrowed. Localized skills and production disappear as the mass market makes each dependent on the work of everyone else. This has a positive side: work becomes "more and more mechanical, until finally man is able to step aside and install machines in his place." The negative dimension, however, is equally important. Brutalization of skill and separation of the means of production from the worker "results in the dependence and distress of the class tied to work of this sort, and these again entail the inability to feel and enjoy the broader freedoms and especially the intellectual benefits of civil society" (Hegel 1976: 129, 149-50).

Hegel's comments are echoed by Marx (1976: 375). Capital has no reason to care for the cultural, intellectual, and social life of the worker; all that matters is profit, the maximum possible in the shortest time. That means a minimal life and maximum working day for the proletariat. "Time for education, for intellectual development, for the fulfilment of social functions, for social intercourse, for the free play of the vital forces of his body and his mind, even the rest time of a Sunday (and that in a country of Sabbitarians!) what foolishness!"

Accumulation of wealth in civil society, Hegel (1983b: 195; Avineri 1985: 206-7) observed in his Berlin lectures, creates a huge mass of dispossessed individuals who feel "excluded and despised," and are filled with "an inner revulsion and revolt." We are now in a position to see that his analysis rested on a crucial distinction later borrowed by Marx: the difference between use value and exchange value. The uses to which a thing may be put are a function of its specific character or quality, Hegel (1976: 129, 51) noted, but its utility (given to it alone by human labor) is also a universal characteristic (its value) that allows the thing to be exchanged for other things. Thus it becomes "an abstract, universal thing or commodity." "As full owner of the thing," stated Hegel, "I am *eo ipso* owner of its value as well as its use."

To own something is in essence the ability to sell it. If you cannot sell something, then you do not really own it. Accordingly, the concept of property dialectically passes over from use into alienation and contract. For Hegel, the most important form of contract is the purchase and sale of labor power—i.e. the employment contract. In the *Philosophy of Mind*, for example, he (1971: 245) observed that contract concerns "thing, labour, and time."

Hegel (1976: 63) pointed out that a thing's *use* may also have exchange-value, apart from the value of the thing itself. Any form of rental makes this basic distinction. "In the contracts whereby I part with the *use* of a thing, I am no longer in possession of the thing though I am still its owner, as for example when I let a house." Accordingly, Marx's celebrated contrast between labor power and labor itself, can be applied to more than just the capacity to work.[4]

While the ability to work may be handed over to a buyer for a limited time, the value of human personality remains with the worker. Marx, as we saw in Chapter Three, cited Hegel's distinction in the *Philosophy of Right* between a person's labor and her labor power, since the capitalist merely purchases the ability to work for a specific period; a slave owner purchases labor, i.e. the entire substance of a slave.

Nevertheless, Marx's labor theory of value presented things upside down. For him, the worker's alienation proceeded from objective economic relations which systematically undercut the price of labor power. The root of alienation, however, is socio-legal, not economic. The worker's exclusion from property is not caused by her inability to obtain full value for her work, as Marx argued. In the contract of employment, the worker is excluded absolutely from property, and consequently also from the value represented by property ownership. "In property, the quantitative character which emerges from the qualitative is value" (Hegel 1976: 240). The next section will examine Hegel's argument more closely.

7. "Alienation" and "Contract"

My claim in this chapter has been that Hegel's theory of property, far from being a justification of the bourgeois order, actually entails the worker's right to the fruits of her labor. *This is the internal contradiction in the contract of employment: it is a contract to disbar the worker from the ownership of property.* I have also contended (in Chapter Four) that the wage contract may be violated *externally*, in two ways. First, to engage in contract, the worker must have a personality. Children lack a fully developed personality, and therefore must be excluded from the wage bargain. Second, as one of the contractors in the wage agreement, the worker should have control over its terms, especially regarding the length of the working day.

In Hegel's period the wage bargain exhibited all three contradictions: children were routinely exploited in factories; workers had no control over the conditions of their employment (including even the ability to find employment); and labor was separated from the ownership of property. These, according to Hegel, are the ultimate causes of alienation and poverty in civil society.

Hegel's solution to the dilemma of civil society, which involves development of democratic corporations and the social state, will be presented in the final chapter. Here, and in Section eight, I will complete the examination of Hegel's concept of property, and deal with some objections to my account of his theory.

For Hegel, the function of property is to assure freedom of the individual; personal freedom is property's foundation and goal. The right to property is based on individual personality, and just for that reason, a person's property in herself is inalienable. A singer may sell her ability to sing a song or two, but she cannot turn over her larynx; you may volunteer, or sell, a pint of your blood, but you cannot jeopardize your health by trading blood for lucre. Thus freedom is this contradiction: "I have property in myself; I do not have property in myself."

> Those goods, or rather substantive characteristics, which constitute my own private personality and the universal essence of my self-consciousness are inalienable and my right to them is imprescriptible. Such characteristics are my personality as such, my universal freedom of will, my ethical life, my religion (Hegel 1976: 52-3).

Hegel (1976: 11) did not draw up a complete list of things that are inalienable, (although he did mention in this context the whole of a worker's time and product of labor; sale—or rental—of children and sexual organs; taking one's own life; disqualification from holding property; alienation of political beliefs and civil liberties; leasing out one's religious feelings to a priest, and so on). Philosophy could never anticipate every possibility, and besides the business of theory is to lay out general principles, and thereby "save itself the trouble of giving good advice."

Despite the doubts of some commentators,[5] Hegelian theory provides a more thorough conception of inalienable rights than exists in any other philosophy of law. Contracts are a legal form ultimately enforced by the state; and government has an obligation to ensure that contracts do not infringe on individual personality (Cornell 1989: 1594). This is not a trivial matter. An important movement in jurisprudence is turning to Hegel for guidance on issues dealing with contract, such as marriage, abortion, prostitution, the futures market in new-born babies (so-called "surrogate motherhood"), the employer's right to hire and fire ("employment at will"), and so forth.[6]

A key argument of this book is that Hegelian theory demolishes the liberal belief in unlimited freedom of contract, including the ability to sell one's labor without time restrictions, and capital's right to appropriate the whole product of an employee's labor. Moreover, Hegel (1976: 130, 146) assailed even the *absence* of contract, when this means unemployment for workers. People must be guaranteed the right to work, otherwise they would lack the means to develop their personality, the absolute foundation of the right to property. As we saw in Chapter Four, other "social rights," such as access to good health care, and protection from pollution, follow from the broad Hegelian conception of individual property rights.

Two objections may be raised to my account of Hegel's property theory. One is that Hegel left open exactly what restrictions should be placed on the workday. This objection is intimately connected with another. While Hegel's theory appears to be a justification of the worker's right to the product of her labor, he blocked this possibility by stating that the worker may legitimately alienate her services for a wage.

Restrictions on time are a thorny affair. As we saw in Chapter Four, Marx (1976: 343) accepted Hegel's theory as an argument against the 14-hour day, six or seven day week common in the mid-nineteenth century English textile industry. These conditions indisputably violated the free development of human personality. Good Hegelian arguments (especially in view of the responsibility of working parents to care for their children, and parents' need to have some time of their own) could also be made for a five or six hour day, and a four day week, with two months holiday in the bargain. These arguments will no doubt be made in the future; indeed, some workers are already making them.[7]

We are on firmer ground with regard to the second problem.

Unquestionably Hegel saw the employment contract as a violation of freedom of personality. Nevertheless, wage labor was (or could be) a huge advance over slavery. Thus Hegel treated the labor contract as a means toward expression of individual personality, compared to slavery or serfdom. This judgement turned out to be accurate. A contract of employment gave workers the potential to improve its conditions (Woodiwiss 1987: 483); slaves lacked this capability. We shall consider the footing in the corporation provided to the worker by the employment contract in the concluding chapter.

If the employment contract is an advance over slavery, it is certainly not the ultimate expression of individual freedom. Offering workers a wage—even a good one—is no substitute for property, for a universal and permanent means of support for the individual and her family. In an important passage already cited in Chapter Four, Hegel (1976: 54) agreed that restricted alienation of an individual's services (within certain limits of morality and propriety) is an appropriate form of exchange, "because on the strength of this restriction my abilities acquire an external relation to the totality and universality of my being." This would justify, for example, the form of exchange exemplified by an independent contractor offering a finished product or services to a customer; but, as Hegel made clear, it does not support the capitalist employment contract. "By alienating the whole of my time, as crystallized in my work, and everything I produced, I would be making into another's property the substance of my being, my universal activity and actuality, my personality."

The contract of employment did just this. Workers alienated everything they produced, with no counterbalancing share in the means of production. Most were left with nothing once their term of employment was over; few gained property. As we have already seen, the ultimate expression of property is the means of production: something that renews itself, and is permanent and secure. Well-off workers in the nineteenth century may have owned consumer goods, and even family homes, but these do not count as property in Hegel's (1989: 750) terms. Consumption goods "fulfil their destiny only by being used and worn away and they correspond to what they are supposed to be only through their negation."

Yet the inference of Hegel's (1976: 237, 230) property theory is that "everyone must have property." Everyone, said Hegel, must have access to "the universal and permanent capital . . . which gives each the opportunity, by the exercise of his education and skill, to draw a share from it and so be assured of his livelihood, while what he thus earns by means of his work maintains and increases the general capital."

8. "Persons and Property Owners"

Hegel's analysis of the wage contract as "insanity of personality" was derived from Rousseau.[8] In *The Social Contract* Rousseau (1968: 54) rejected any contract in which a person "alienate[s]" or sells himself to another "in return for at least a subsistence." If a person was to be worth anything to the buyer, she or he would have to be fed and clothed anyway, so subsistence amounted to a sale of oneself for nothing.

> To speak of a man giving himself in return for nothing is to speak of what is absurd, unthinkable; such an action would be illegitimate, void, if only because no one who did it could be in their right mind. To say the same of a whole people is to conjure up a nation of lunatics; and right cannot rest on madness.

Unlike Hegel, Rousseau did not mention time restrictions on labor, so the French philosopher did not see the contract for wages as an advance over slavery. In other respects, however, their positions are very similar. Contract is based, noted Hegel (1976: 57), on "the moment of recognition," i.e. on the affirmation of the worker's personality versus that of the master. But the labor contract is grossly flawed. Rather than receiving recognition as a property holder, the worker is entirely severed from property ownership. She may be capable of alienating her labor power, but that ability is limited, subject to caprice, and will ultimately pass with time. Morever, she is unable to restrict the period she must work for the factory master, who has laid claim to her entire life and personality. True, she may earn enough to maintain a decent lifestyle, but as Hegel noted (following Rousseau), "subsistence is not the same as possession" of property. Totally unrecognized as a property owner, the worker is coerced into a contract that is no contract at all.[9]

By failing to give recognition to the personality of the worker, the wage deal violates the terms of contract in two ways: first, it subjugates the will of the worker vis à vis the employer; and second, it constitutes an unequal exchange of value, a "gift" from worker to capitalist.

The capitalist employment contract entails domination of the worker, her obedience to the will of the owner. Her will is circumscribed, even abolished, in the labor process. According to Hegel (1976: 58, 51), however, the purpose of contract is to validate equally the will of the contracting parties.[10] "This identity of their wills implies also . . . that each will still is and remains *not* identical with the other but retains from its own point of view a special character of its own." The process of contract is a co-operative one, in which the identity of wills is reached democratically, without coercion; each party "comes to its decision only in the presence of the other."[11] This is the relationship we saw earlier in the moment of use, which I argued pertains to the business class *once the worker has won equality with the employer*, i. e. "two owners standing in relation to each other." "This contractual relationship implies that each, in accordance with the common will of both, ceases to be an owner and yet is and remains one."

The wage deal is a formal contract only, a gift. In the gift contract one of the contracting parties "has the negative moment—the alienation of the thing—and the other the positive moment—the appropriation of the thing. Such a contract is a *gift*." Wage labor actually counts as a sub-category of Hegel's gift contract, "loan of a thing": "i. e. the gift of a portion of it or restricted use and enjoyment of it; here the lender remains the owner of the thing . . . [which] may be a thing which counts (like money [or labor power—D.M.]) as a thing universal in itself." As Marx (1976: 451) put it, "the socially productive power of labour develops as a free gift to capital whenever the workers are placed under certain conditions, and it is capital which places them under these conditions."

A real contract, unlike a gift, requires that the parties remain at its completion with the same value in property with which they started. "What remains identical in the contract," wrote Hegel (1976: 63), "is the value in respect of which the subjects of the contract are equal to one another whatever the qualitative external differences of the things exchanged. Value is the universal in which the subjects of the contract participate."

We have now returned full circle to Marx's analysis of the wage contract in Chapter Four. Here is a contract in which the worker gives up more value ("surplus value") than she received from the capitalist. But there is a vital difference between Marx's presentation and that of Hegel. Unlike Marx, Hegel never abandoned the concept of private property. He demonstrated that exploitation originates from perversion of the concept of property. The worker never gains property in the means of production, because the route to ownership

is sealed by capitalist property law. The unequal exchange represented by the employment contract is a result of a basic distortion in
the property relationship itself. Moreover, the property claims of the
worker provide the basis for transformation of the capitalist firm into
the worker-owned, democratic corporation (Ellerman 1990).

These are essentially the conclusions reached by Hodgskin as
well. Yet Marx must have been repulsed by the "hard and sad"
philosophy underlying Hodgskin's system. "It is a philosophy,"
explains Halévy (1956: 176), "which demands acceptance of the fact
that justice condemns to death the sick, the infirm and the old when
their natural vitality fails them." For Hodgskin, property rested on
natural law, on survival of the fittest. In his conception workers
owned their firms, but what would happen in the event of business
failure or some other disaster? Who is to ensure that work and
production are safely regulated?

Hodgskin's extreme individualism rejected communism through
fear of the role it would give the state. Replacement of private
property by worker-owned corporations, warned Anton Menger
(1962: 125), would have its own dangers.

> Indeed without the Utopian supposition that the labour associations
> would be guided by brotherly love, it must, on the contrary, be
> assumed that the separately organised trade societies . . . would
> thanks to their position of ascendancy, wring more unearned income
> out of the community than private individuals are able to do to-day
> in open market.

Admittedly, Menger was writing in 1899, well before the appearance
of the transnational corporation. Still, would there be much
difference, from the point of view of the consumer (Winfield 1987),
between a worker-owned General Motors and the present one?

Here Marx rejoined Hegel. Civil society must be subordinated to
the state. Particular interests of individuals and corporations have
to play themselves out within a framework constructed by government. Hegel reached this position through a critique of the liberal
theory of property; Marx came to it through his study of the English
factory legislation. I will conclude this chapter with a glance at the
fate of the liberal theory of property.

9. A *"Necessary Standpoint"* but *"Not the Highest Standpoint"*

The liberal concept of property achieved what Hegel (1989: 580)
called in the *Science of Logic* a *"necessary standpoint"* in the history of

thought. "Such a standpoint is not to be regarded as an opinion, a subjective, arbitrary way of thinking of an individual, as an aberration of speculation." To think through the notion of property in an emerging bourgeois society is inevitably to arrive at the concept propounded by Locke and his followers. "Speculative thinking in the course of its progress finds itself necessarily occupying that standpoint and to that extent the system is perfectly true, but *it is not the highest standpoint.*" Locke emphasized the importance of possession and labor in the concept of property; perhaps this concept lingered in the minds of the nineteenth century industrial bourgeoisie when they called themselves "factory occupiers." They wanted to underline their possession of the means of production, and so justify their wealth.

Workers in Hegel's period were virtual slaves of the factory system; they had not advanced to the stage Hegel called "universal self-consciousness," and could not yet assert their own interests against the factory masters. (Marx later used a related Hegelian term to express the same idea, i.e. a class "in and for itself.") According to Hegel, the workers had to advance from mere consciousness, to self-consciousness, to a full sense of their own identity and interests. Only in this way could they escape industrial slavery.

Marx abandoned liberal doctrine in favor of a "scientific" demonstration that bourgeois property concealed exploitation and injustice that would ultimately cause its downfall. This demonstration, though faulty, contained a grain of truth; but it did not go far enough. The only thing false about liberal doctrine "is its claim to be the highest standpoint." Denying the liberal principle, Marx replaced private property with its opposite, public property. But public ownership of the means of production is as one-sided and as liable to injustice as its liberal antithesis. "Consequently, the *true* system cannot have the relation to it of being merely opposed to it; for if this were so, the system, as this opposite, would itself be one-sided. On the contrary, the true system as the higher, must contain the subordinate system within itself."

Hegel (1989: 581) attacked liberal theory from within. He took seriously its initial premises, as articulated by Locke and others, and followed them through to their logical conclusion. "The genuine refutation must penetrate the opponent's stronghold and meet him on his own ground; no advantage is gained by attacking him somewhere else and defeating him where he is not."

The result of Hegel's strategy is two-fold. First, he demonstrated that liberal doctrine is *false in itself*, and that it generates a refutation of itself more violent and total than could ever be achieved by squarely opposing it. Next, he showed that sublating or transcending (*aufheben*) liberal theory involves identifying social institutions, such as the democratic corporation and the social state, that will bring about its own self-succession.

"Individuals," wrote Marx (1976: 92) in *Capital*, "are dealt with here only in so far as they are the personifications of economic categories, the bearers . . . of particular relations and interests." In Hegel's socio-legal perspective, however, personal action, whatever its external motivations, remains morally accountable. The entrepreneur acts within an array of bourgeois production relations and his actions are intelligible only within it; but he is nevertheless a creature of will and conscience. The culpability of the capitalist, in other words, is central to Hegel's theory. Accordingly, the concept of property in Hegel is followed dialectically by wrong, i.e. violation of contract.

In the Hegelian (1976: 122-3; 1983a: 134) scheme, wrong does not apply only to the actions of single individuals, but also to the behavior of whole classes of people. Civil society—"this sphere of particularity"—is the arena which "portrays the disappearance of ethical life." Civil society privileges self-interest and self-will; and evil consists wholly in actions based on pure selfish will. Liberal doctrine, and the "external state"—the "state of nature"—that enforces it, together underwrite the mechanism of evil. *"Der Gewinn,"* said Hegel, *"ist die Hauptsache."* ("Profit is the main thing.")

We have encountered Hegel's external state in earlier chapters. This is not a network of well-meaning individuals led irrevocably to take decisions harmful to some but ultimately beneficial to the majority. On the contrary, civil society offers individuals a license to practice selfish pursuits at whatever cost to others (provided these pursuits are within the plastic limits of bourgeois property law), and to have these projects rewarded with all the official praise and deference formally reserved for those of noble birth (Hegel (1983b: 196; Avineri 1985: 207).

Measured by its own yardstick capitalism is founded on systematic fraud. The bargain between equals called the employment contract is really one in which the worker is swindled by the entrepreneur. The worker is allotted some dubious recognition in subsistence wages, but these are not equivalent to property. The following passage in Hegel's (1971: 246-7) *Philosophy of Mind* sums up the bourgeois wage deal.

> If the semblance of right as such is willed *against* the right intrinsically by the particular will, which thus becomes *wicked*, then the external *recognition* of right is separated from right's true value; and while the former only is respected, the latter is violated. This gives the wrong of *fraud* . . . where the nominal relation is retained, but the sterling value is let slip.

Given unrestricted free enterprise subsistence wages are the best possibility; much more likely is a slide into destitution prepared by wages that fall below the most minimal level required for self-support, or which disappear in closures and unemployment. Whatever level wages might attain, workers are forced to work long hours at demeaning jobs that deprive them of an opportunity to participate in the social and cultural spectacle of civil society. As Hegel said in his Berlin lectures, greed and self-interest spawn immense wealth at one pole and the most despicable conditions among the masses at the other. Hegel (1976: 247) described the crimes of the rich against the poor in the *Philosophy of Mind*.[12]

> Finally, the particular will sets itself in opposition to the intrinsic right by negating that right itself as well as its recognition or semblance. (Here there is a negatively infinite judgement . . . in which there is denied the class as a whole, and not merely the particular mode—in this case the apparent recognition.) Thus the will is violently wicked, and commits a *crime*.

For many interpreters, Hegel was incapable of resolving the dilemma of poverty, a failure linked by some to an incapacity of the Hegelian system. "It is undeniably instructive," gloats a recent Marxist commentator, "to see a great thinker reduced . . . to evasion, inconsequentiality and, ultimately, silence. No greater tribute to the power of capital in the intellectual sphere could be conceived" (McCarney 1991: 37).[13] But it isn't that Hegel (1976: 277-8) lacked a cure for poverty; civil society itself is unable to correct an evil it perpetually reproduces. Here "poverty immediately takes the form of a wrong done to one class by another." How could civil society cure a condition for which it alone is responsible?

Civil society, lectured Hegel (1983b: 197; Avineri 1985: 207) in Berlin—an analysis later reproduced by Marx—is too rich to prevent poverty. The basic source of human want is maldistribution of property; too much is created to be consumed by the producers among the poor. "For it is the case that the poverty of the workers (*Arbeitenden*) consists in the fact that what they produce does not find a buyer. There is too much capital (*Kapital*), and more is being produced than the nation can consume."

Charity and public assistance, such as provided by the English "poor tax", degrade the poor by taking from them their only possession: their personality, their ability to work. Selling goods more cheaply so that workers can buy them leads to economic depression and even more poverty.

> It is lack of employment which . . . is the main cause for poverty. There always appears, under prosperous conditions of culture, an overpopulation. When the poor are given opportunities to work, all that happens is that the amount of commodities is increased. But it is precisely the surplus of commodities which has caused unemployment (Hegel 1983b: 197; Avineri 1985: 207).

Like the early socialist economists Robert Owen, William Thompson and John Gray (Thompson 1984: 163), Hegel was formulating a theory of capitalist economic crisis. Marx (1978: 486-7) recognized Hegel's achievement and in Volume Two of *Capital*, he repeated Hegel's diagnosis in almost identical terms. "It thus appears that capitalist production involves certain conditions . . . which permit the relative prosperity of the working class only temporarily, and moreover always as a harbinger of crisis." Hegel may have been influenced by Owen, who in 1817 explicitly linked worker exploitation with overproduction and stagnation (King 1981: 241) Certainly, Hegel could not have differed more radically with classical political economy, whose adherents claimed that depressions caused by overproduction were impossible (Hirschman 1981: 169). These "upheavals" and the conditions which eventually ameliorate them, Hegel (1976: 147-8) declared, are due to "the working of a necessity of which . . . the clashing interests [of civil society] . . . themselves know nothing." However, Hegel went much further than Owen, Hodgskin, Thompson and the others. They could say why economic crises occurred, but they had no explanation for the cyclical character of economic downturns. If depressions were caused by disparity between the amount of goods workers produced and the wages they received, as the early socialist economists argued, then capitalism should be in a "permanent and deepening state of economic crisis" (Thompson 1984: 160).

Hegel ((1976: 149-50), of course, did not provide a complete theory of business cycles, but he offered the rudiments for one (Hirschman 1981; MacGregor 1984: 223-8). Economic growth is promoted by creation and expansion of internal markets for goods, and manufacture of capital equipment necessary to satisfy these markets. "It is from this double process of generalization that the largest profits are derived." But internal markets are never likely to solve the problem of crisis, since they only reproduce the original predicament. The best solution is to generate external, foreign markets for commodities.

> The inner dialectic of civil society thus drives it—or at any rate drives a specific civil society—to push beyond its own limits and seek markets, and so its necessary means of subsistence, in other lands which are either deficient in the goods it has overproduced, or else generally backward in industry, &c.

Thus England turned to imperialism, the creation of colonies. "Between 1780 and 1820 some 150 million men and women in India, Africa, the West Indies, Java, and the China coast succumbed to British naval power" (Colley 1986a: 359). The English, Hegel (1983a: 134; 1983b: 199; Avineri 1985: 208) noted, employed ingenious methods to increase demand for their excess goods. One ploy, he observed, was to give the stuff away to the Chinese, thus creating among this distant populace a taste and desire for English goods. "Through colonization a double aim is being reached: that the impoverished gain property, and that in such a way a new market is found at the same time for the metropolis."

As Albert O. Hirschman (1981: 169) affirms, Hegel's "is nearly perfect as a statement of the theory" of imperialism. Marx ignored this Hegelian legacy, and when Hobson and Luxemburg developed their own theories eighty years later, they did so unaware of Hegel's intervention.[14] Although imperialism was one of the solutions Hegel had seen for poverty, it was a dangerous and self-limiting one (Walton 1984: 254-5). "Hegel sees that the colonies have to become liberated and emancipated at one point and will share the destiny of civil society, namely to be rich but never rich enough" (Schlink 1989: 1432). A far better resolution was offered by democratic corporations and the social state.

Bourgeois fraud and crime—as suggested in Chapter Four—must be curbed by the state. If government fails to challenge the ravages of capital—the evil of the "natural will"—then "revolt become[s] necessary." In the *Philosophy of Right* Hegel (1976: 67; McCumber 1986) called the necessity of revolt "the right of Heroes."

> The merely natural will is implicitly a force against the implicit idea of freedom which must be protected against such an uncivilized will and be made to prevail in it. Either an ethical institution is already established in family or government, and the natural will is a mere display against it; or else there is only a state of nature, a state of affairs where mere force prevails and against which the Idea establishes a right of Heroes.

This brings us back to England in 1831 when Hegel surveyed the scene prior to the Great Reform Act. Revolution was possible, and the only alternative was a political administration strong enough to curb the abuses of capital. Such a government could not be imposed upon civil society; otherwise it would resemble a form of tyranny rather than liberation. The material for the social state would have to originate within civil society, and be interconnected with the industrial system. For Hegel this meant growth and consolidation on one side of social class and the corporation; and on the other, development of an appropriate public authority.

Hegel's solution to the dilemma of civil society, and its relationship with Marx's communism, is the subject of the final chapter. The next two chapters will trace Marx's chronicle of the growth of the interventionist state in Britain.

Notes

1. Writes Heiman (1971: 123), "the 'business' group (including workers as well as managers, tradesmen as well as traders, apprentices as well as professionals) is . . . very large, and represents a substantial segment of the population."

2. We can safely dismiss as an ideological dream Peter Drucker's (1989: 76) contention that big capitalists have "become economically almost irrelevant," and that workers "through their pension funds are now the capitalists." This is another instance of the bourgeois desire to obscure the role of capital as a powerful force vis à vis workers. It is especially pernicious in light of the capitalist assault on the right of workers to their own pension funds. Nevertheless, Drucker has a point. Workers' control of pension funds may provide the opening for equal access to power in the corporation predicted by Hegel's social theory. This aspect of his thought, which diverges dramatically from that of Marx, will be surveyed below, and in the final chapters of this book.

3. Alan Ryan's (1984b: 193) stimulating account of Hegel's property theory is one of the few that recognizes its radical implications, although Ryan sees these as a shortcoming. "The problem is whether the self-expressive aspects of work are really consistent with the division of labour . . . [D]oes it make sense to say that the man who performs some small task in an elaborate process really comes to *occupy* the thing which forms the end result of the process?" Interestingly, the "small task in an elaborate process" represented by the exchange of shares in a company does not cause Ryan (1984a: 126-7) any similar difficulties about ownership. "When you receive three hundred shares in Ferranti from me, they become yours by a process which does not in the least involve your having to go anywhere near Ferranti's factories, products, or personnel."

4. "Marx attached great importance to his 'discovery' of the distinction between labor power and labor time. Yet that distinction is not even unique to labor. When one rents a car for a day, one buys the right to use the car ('car power') within certain limits every day. The actual services extracted from the car are another matter. The car could be left in a parking lot, or driven continuously at high speeds. To prevent being 'exploited' by heavy users of 'car time,' car rental companies typically charge not just a flat rate but have also a 'piece rate' based on the intensity of use as measured by mileage" (Ellerman 1990: 20-21)

5. Alan Ryan (1984a: 125), for example, wonders whether Hegel's theory would cover sawing off one's left hand.

6. See, for example, the excellent collection of essays in the "Hegel and Legal Theory Symposium," *Cardozo Law Review*, 10: 5-6, 1989; and Carole Pateman's (1988: 173-81) *The Sexual Contract*.

7. Although, as Juliet Schor observes in *The Overworked American: The Unexpected Decline of Leisure* (1992), the trend has recently gone the other way in the United States. Issues of work time in advanced countries, and the problem of overwork and child labor in the Third World (Fyfe 1989), underscore the relevance of Hegel's and Marx's focus on the labor contract.

8. Carole Pateman's important study, *The Sexual Contract* (1988), caused me to notice this connection between Hegel and Rousseau, although Pateman herself does not allude to it.

9. Hegel (1976: 54; 1975: 192, 213) observed that wage labor is akin to the relation between force and its manifestations, substance and accident, universal and particular. In *Logic*, force is the relationship we have already met at the stage of possession, i.e. "knowledge of a third person, alien force and the like." Substance refers to the divided stage of use. "Substance is accordingly the totality of Accidents, revealing itself in them as their absolute negativity (that is to say, as absolute power) and at the same time as the wealth of all content." Universal and particular are relations on a higher grade and belong to the state.

10. In a recent article, Peter Benson (1989) provides a thoughtful discussion of Hegel's notion of contract, though he does not mention its applicability to wage labor.

11. Carole Pateman (1988: 148) observes that the arrangement between equals required by contract theory does not apply to the wage deal. "If worker and employer negotiated the terms, duration and conditions of the employment contract until a mutually beneficial result were reached, all aspects of employment would have to be open to negotiation. No employer could accept such an arrangement."

12. In a noteworthy and provocative study of *Hegel's Ethical Thought*, Allen W. Wood (1990: 250, 253, 255) misses Hegel's point about wealth and poverty—a point documented, for example, by John McCumber (1986: 382). In civil society neither can exist without the other, yet in Wood's account it is the poor and not the rich who are the focus of Hegel's analysis. For Wood, Hegel is a "hard-headed" realist who "wastes little pity on the sufferings of the poor, and does not place moral blame for their condition on them, or on anyone else." The poor become criminals for whom punishment is "a bad piece of luck, another contingency to which the life of poverty is exposed." Poverty, says Wood, is a problem Hegel's system described, but could not solve. According to Wood, the mentality Hegel imputed to the poor is "an alienated mentality of envy and hatred, a derisive rejection of all duties and ethical principles, a contemptuous refusal to recognize anyone's rights, a bitter denial of all human dignity and self-respect." But this is precisely the mentality of the rich, as Hegel saw it. After all, the poor cannot "reject" or "refuse" anything; they have no choice. It is the rich who make decisions and who have the power of rejection and refusal.

13. Actually "no greater tribute" to the intellectual sloth of contemporary Marxism "could be conceived" than its treatment of Hegel. McCarney's version, and that of the modern "Hegelian Marxist" school, conforms in most respects to that reached by Shlomo Avineri, Raymond Plant, and Charles Taylor almost 20 years ago. The "new orthodoxy," as Bellamy (1986: 100) calls the work of Taylor and the others, has been superseded by more recent Hegel scholarship (surveyed in MacGregor 1989) that presents a radically altered portrait.

14. The 1991 Gulf War—fought to protect U. S. military and economic interests (Sifry 1992) in the region that Hegel knew as the "axis of world history" (1956: 171; MacGregor 1991), and "to divert the attention of the American public from the social and economic crisis resulting from Reagan-Bush domestic programs" (Chomsky 1991b: 29)—is a textbook example of the Hegelian theory of imperialism. "As a result of war," Hegel (1976: 295) said, "nations are strengthened, but peoples involved in civil strife also acquire peace at home through making wars abroad."

8

Dialectical Inversion
of the "Free Contract"

To the extent that commodity production, in accordance with its own immanent law, undergoes a further development into capitalist production, the property laws of commodity production must undergo a dialectical inversion so that they become laws of capitalist appropriation.

—Karl Marx, *Capital* (1976: 733-4)

1. Transformation of the Wage Contract in *Capital*

Despite significant differences with Hegel, Marx (1976: 90) employed Hegelian theory in his analysis of England, the "*locus classicus*" of the capitalist mode of production. The most striking instance of this is the transformation of the employment contract. Hegel emphasized the central place of the wage bargain in the bourgeois economic system, and its intimate connection with the state. He saw democratic corporations and government intervention as the solution to the dilemmas of poverty and economic crisis caused by the contract for wages. An identical strain emerges in *Capital*. This chapter explores the transformation of the employment contract in *Capital*, and points to the Hegelian motifs Marx used to isolate and examine this change.

The present section offers a model of the sequential transformation of the contract of employment in *Capital*. Succeeding sections examine this three-step process in detail. We shall see that the underlying (and related) causes of the metamorphosis of contract are large-scale employment of women and children, and substitution of machinery for human labor. These elements are connected by Marx to the emergence, and extension, of factory legislation.

The stages of contract resemble the movement in the Hegelian concept of property from taking possession, to use, and alienation.[1]

In Hegel's (1976: 48, 46) stage of *"taking possession"*, human will is merely implicit in the thing possessed; yet possession brings "potentiality, capacity, potency." This is a "positive" moment, because the will finds itself in the thing—yet for that very reason possession is "subjective, temporary, and seriously limited in scope." As we saw in Chapter Six, Hegel connected this mode of property with diverse forms of production, including slavery.

Possession conforms with Marx's (1976: 730, 301, 344) first level of the wage contract, an ideal, conflict-free stage in which buyer and seller of labor power see themselves as equals.

> One party to the contract sells his labour-power, the other buys it. The former receives the value of his commodity, whose use-value—labour—is thereby alienated to the buyer. Means of production which already belong to the latter are then transformed by him, with the aid of labour equally belonging to him, into a new product which is likewise lawfully his.

The fact that the employer gains much more from this arrangement than the employee does not affect the legitimacy of contract. "This circumstance is a piece of good luck for the buyer but by no means an injustice towards the seller." Creation of surplus value demands only that the worker is kept at the job longer than is necessary to recover the capital advanced, and her wages. No compulsion is required, and no laws are broken. Nothing is said about the age or sex of the worker, who is presented as the owner of a capacity to exert abstract human labor each day for a limited, though unspecified, time period. "Leaving aside certain extremely elastic restrictions," wrote Marx, "the nature of commodity exchange itself imposes no limit to the working day, no limit to surplus labour."

As already noted in Chapters Six and Seven, there is no direct evidence in *Capital* of Hegel's idea that the work process itself changes the character of property relations. "As long as the laws of exchange are observed," wrote Marx (1976: 733, 680) ". . . the mode of appropriation can be completely revolutionized without . . . affecting the property rights which correspond to commodity production." Nevertheless, he did rehearse a crucial idea from Hegel: the opposed participants in the bourgeois wage bargain share an identical structure of consciousness. The employment contract is founded on a basic imbalance of power, but it is perceived by *both worker and capitalist* as a relation between equals.

All the notions of justice held by both the worker and the capitalist, all the mystifications of the capitalist mode of production, all capitalism's illusions about freedom, all the apologetic tricks of vulgar economics, have as their basis the form of appearance . . . which makes the actual relation invisible, and indeed presents to the eye the precise opposite of that relation.

Hegel's (1976: 46, 49, 48) second moment of property—"*use*"—is a negative and conflict-ridden stage, in which the thing appears as something opposed to the will, something which has to be "change[d], dest[royed], consume[d]." This moment involves "the fight for recognition and the relation between master and slave."

Use coincides with Marx's (1976: 734, 716) second stage of the wage bargain—"the dialectical inversion" of contract. Here the mythical free contract dissolves. The independent seller of labor power is transformed into a factory slave; the owner of property in labor power is revealed as "a personal source of wealth, but deprived of any means of making that wealth a reality for himself."

This moment of contract is marked by "an antinomy of right against right, both equally bearing the seal of exchange" (Marx 1976: 344, 590, 411, 520) The worker grows aware of the exploitative character of capitalism and revolts against extended working hours. "The worker maintains his right as a seller when he wishes to reduce the working day to a particular normal length." Contract relations can no longer depend on an identity of will. "Between equal rights, force decides." At the same time, however, introduction of machinery allows children, women and unskilled men—"in short, 'cheap labour', as the Englishman typically describes it" to replace "the independent worker, a man who is thus legally qualified to act for himself." The (adult male) worker becomes an appendage of the machine, or is displaced by women and children, who are sold into slavery by the worker himself. In this stage, capital overturns all legal and traditional barriers to the exploitation of labor, and the independent male worker, "become[s] a slave dealer."

"*Alienation*" is the final form of Hegel's (1976: 46, 48, 54) concept of property. In this stage the will is reflected back from the thing into itself, and becomes fully self-conscious. Once it reaches self-consciousness, the will becomes aware of the things that negate it. Violations of inalienable human rights, such as slavery, are finally understood for what they are, and abolished. "Man's absolute unfitness for slavery . . . is something which does not come home to our minds until we recognize that the Idea of freedom is genuinely actual only as the state." Hegel put forward the terms of the labor contract in this phase, but with a crucial addendum later cited by Marx (1976: 272): the daily length of the wage deal must be restricted, otherwise the worker alienates her entire personality.

Hegel's moment of alienation resembles the third stage of the employment contract in *Capital*. At this juncture, Marx (1976: 344) brought in not only class struggle, but also government, which alone decides the final shape of the agreement between worker and capitalist. "In the history of capitalist production," wrote Marx (1976: 344) "the establishment of a norm for the working day presents itself as a struggle over the limits of that day, a struggle between collective capital, i.e. the class of capitalists, and collective labour, i.e. the working class." In earlier stages, the state weighs in heavily on the side of capital, legislating a prolonged working day and enforcing the will of the capitalist. But for Marx (1976: 93-3, 412-13, 551) the English Factory Acts registered "an unmistakable advance . . . a radical change in the existing relations between capital and labour." Here Marx definitively forged the link between the wage deal and the state.

> The history of the regulation of the working day . . . prove[s] conclusively that the isolated worker, the worker as "free" seller of his labour-power succumbs without resistance once capitalist production has reached a certain stage of maturity. The establishment of a normal working day is therefore the product of a protracted and more or less concealed civil war between the capitalist class and the working class.

Through government intervention, the employment contract gains for the first time a resemblance, however feeble, to a real bargain between equals.[2] This allowed Engels, for example, to report in the fourth German edition of *Capital* that, thanks to labor legislation of the 1870s, English workers could no longer be sent to prison for quitting a job. "With a few exceptions . . . the worker in England is now on an equal footing with the employer in case of breach of contract and can only be sued under civil law."

The transformation of contract has historical and organizational dimensions, as well as the theoretical one. The first stage of contract coincides with the mode of production Marx (1976: 455) called, manufacture—"which extends, roughly speaking, from the middle of the sixteenth century to the last third of the eighteenth century"—and includes a system of workplace organization labelled, the formal subsumption of labor under capital. The second moment of contract corresponds to the factory system, and involves an organizational mode termed, the real subsumption of labor under capital. The third level of contract belongs to the era of factory regulation, in which government intervention plays a role in the organization of work. State interference does not merely affect the outer limits of the working day; it transforms the workplace, and the quality of working life.

Marx, notes Maxine Berg (1985: 75, 77) provided "historical signposts" to his model of economic transformation, but it is by no means a strictly accurate historical chronicle. Thus, machinery, productivity gains, employment of women and children, and other characteristics of the second phase of contract were actually part of the economic landscape well before the advent of the factory system. Moreover, Marx neglected "the features of the putting-out system and other related domestic forms of manufacture."

Critics also argue that Marx exaggerated both the speed of mechanization and the strength of capital in the second stage of contract. Modern research indicates, for example, that employers often declined to invest in new machinery, taking advantage of the generous supply of labor, and relying on "tried and true methods . . . [which rested] on the skill and authority of workers" (Joyce 1990: 150; also Lazonick 1979; Samuel 1977).[3] Instead of capitalists dictating the pace of technological change, labor and capital often cooperated in the introduction of machinery and other alterations to the work process.

Marx (1976: 492) himself acknowledged that he was "concerned . . . only with broad and general characteristics [of] epochs in the history of society." As we shall learn in the final section of this chapter, his model of industrial transformation gave considerable scope to development of workers' skills and the possibility of collaboration between labor and capital.

For Marx (1976: 411-12, 416), there are two major implications of the transformation of contract. First, introduction of machinery and gross exploitation of women and children ultimately precipitate state intervention. Second, the English factory legislation demonstrates to the international proletariat that the worker is no free agent—a lesson of world-historical significance. A regulated working day must form the basis of any deal between capitalist and worker; and this fulcrum of "free contract" is a product of government legislation.

In the place of the pompous catalogue of the "inalienable rights of man" there steps the modest Magna Carta of the legally limited working day, which at last makes clear "when the time which the worker sells is ended, and when his own begins". *Quantum matatus ab illo!* (What a great change from that time).

Factory legislation itself undergoes a triadic development. It reaches first into textile production, and then follows the spread of factory methods into other forms of manufacture, and finally it invades domestic enterprises. This growth is important, for, as Marx (1976: 412) affirmed, the march of factory law far outdistanced the initial working class movement for reform, which had died out by the early 1850s. State intervention became automatic, or self-sustaining, starting as "legislation for exemptions" in the first half of the nineteenth century, and becoming generalized thereafter.

As we have seen, the transformation of free contract is abstract and theoretical, rather than a strictly historical account. The ideal stage of contract exists mostly as a powerful myth in the minds of workers and capitalists, and has only a vague relation to historical reality. Domination of labor by capital, as postulated in the second stage of contract, was never entirely accomplished. Similarly, government regulation of the workplace was hardly complete in Marx's time, and remains problematic in our own. Although it cedes some power to labor (Woodiwiss 1987: 518), even a state-regulated wage contract operates as a vehicle for exploitation of the proletariat.

Nevertheless, Marx's model provided an opening for his discussion of the growth of working class consciousness and something like a theory of corporations and the welfare state. Once introduced in Parts Three and Four of *Capital*, however, class consciousness and the state are not discussed much further. Instead, the final sections of the first volume of *Capital* deal with accumulation of capital and general immiseration of the proletariat; Volumes Two and Three primarily pursue complex economic topics. In other words, Marx's emphasis lies on the antagonistic moment in the transformation of contract, rather than the resolution offered by corporations and the state.

2. Formal and Real Subsumption of Labor Under Capital

Metamorphosis of the wage contract is intimately connected with changes in workplace organization. The arrangement of capitalist production revolves around two poles, which Marx called formal, and real, subsumption of labor under capital (Burawoy 1985: 89). These, as we have seen, are roughly similar to the Hegelian moments of possession and use. In fact, it is hard to escape the impression that Marx's analysis of labor organization is drawn directly from the paragraphs on property in the *Philosophy of Right*. A principal difference is that Marx does not linger on the implications for the property rights of the worker, which are of paramount importance for Hegel.

Formal subsumption of labor under capital, which "is the general form of every capitalist process of production," concerns simple possession by the capitalist of the factors of production, including labor power. Marx (1976: 1019-20) called this mode, manufacture. "In spite of allusions to rural industry and centralized production . . . Marx's model . . . seems to have been a large workshop in the hands of capitalists and organized on the basis of wage labour" (Berg 1985: 75). Production that is only *formally* subordinated to the capitalist can go on as it had previously under earlier systems. "With the growth of capitalist production all *services* become transformed into *wage-labour*, and those who perform them into *wage-labourers*" (Marx 1976: 1042). The workers in a guild, for example, become employees of an entrepreneur without significantly altering their work routines; independent fur traders in North America join the Hudson Bay Company while maintaining a conception of themselves as autonomous agents (Newman 1991); sailors become wage-laborers "whose wage relation might be concealed under the cooperative form of a share in the profit" (Marx 1981: 1042). Social relations of earlier systems of production have merely been transformed into contractual ones.

This transformation itself depends, of course, on monopolization by capital of the means of production, and the existence of a large mass of individuals with only their labor to sell. (Marx documents and analyses this process in the famous Part Eight of *Capital*, "So-Called Primitive Accumulation.") The most significant changes in the workplace brought about by capital, often in alliance with the state, are a spectacular increase in the scale of enterprise; enhanced intensity and continuity of labor; and, in many cases, extension of the working day (Marx 1976: 1021).

The formal moment of workplace organization corresponds to the first or ideal stage of the employment contract, where the capitalist and worker are negotiators in a free wage deal.

A man who was formerly an independent peasant now finds himself a factor in a production process and dependent on the capitalist directing it, and his own livelihood depends on a contract which he as a commodity owner (viz. the owner of labour-power) had previously concluded with the capitalist as the owner of money (Marx 1976: 1020).

Real subsumption of the worker under capital entails revolutionizing the workplace, substituting machinery and practical science for traditional methods. The use of machinery at this level does not refer simply to mechanized production. Real subsumption of labor under capital emerges when a vast number of machines, composing complex organs of production, are operated simultaneously by a single motive power. The early textile mills, driven originally by water, and then by steam, provide the classic example. Instead of an "isolated machine," wrote Marx (1976: 503), "we have . . . a mechanical monster whose body fills whole factories, and whose demonic power, at first hidden by the slow and measured motion of its gigantic members, finally bursts forth in the fast and feverish whirl of countless working organs."

The huge investment required at this stage transforms the nature of capitalism: "it assumes social dimensions, and so sheds its *individual* character entirely." (Marx 1976: 1035, 983). This second form of workplace organization (the "specifically capitalist mode of production") resembles the Hegelian moment of property called use, including its double-sided analysis of ownership.

On one side, the worker "takes possession" of the physical, mechanical and chemical properties of the instruments of production, and uses them in a purposeful manner so that the means of labor become nothing more than aspects of his activity. "In tanning, for example, he deals with the skins as his own simple object of labour. It is not the capitalist whose skin he tans" (Marx 1976: 1007, 981). Marx called this the "*real labour process*." Although it corresponds to the Hegelian moment of ownership through use, he does not draw out the implications for a theory of property. In his analysis, the means of production remain "the property of the capitalist."

On the other side of the relation of use, the worker is incorporated into the productive process as though she herself were only a tool or machine. The capitalist *uses* the worker, who *transforms* the means of production to achieve a certain predetermined goal, i.e. profit for the employer. "The means of production thus become no more than leeches drawing off as large an amount of living labour as they can." For Marx (1976: 988), this is "the *valorization process*," and it closely resembles Hegel's (1976: 50) notion of abstract ownership, where the capitalist appears as "empty will . . . an overlord to nothing."

This inversion, in which the worker becomes just another aspect of the machine, leads, for Marx (1976: 990, 1003), to a form of insanity, the fetishism of commodities, "the rule of . . . dead labour over the living." "The objective conditions essential to the realization of labour are *alienated* from the worker and become manifest as *fetishes* endowed with a will and soul of their own. *Commodities*, in short, appear as the purchasers of *persons*." Marx's account closely resembles Hegel's discussion of the "insanity of personality" created by the reversal of property rights under capitalism. As with Hegel, this form of insanity applies to both worker and capitalist. The employer comes to see everything, even the bodies of young children, as a means of profit-making; similarly the worker is only too glad to throw his offspring and wife before the juggernaut of capital. "In private property of every type," wrote Marx (1976: 1083), in a passage reminiscent of Hegel's critique of the family, "the *slavery* of the members of the family at least is always implicit since they are made use of and exploited by the head of the family."

Marx's "fetishism of commodities" and Hegel's "insanity of personality" are concepts that underlie their joint critique (MacGregor 1984) of "bourgeois thought," (Marx) and "the understanding consciousness" (Hegel). Enlistment of science and technology in the production process "greatly intensifie[s]" the illusion shared by employers and workers that the power of capital, and not the collective power of the workers, lies behind the enormous material progress of bourgeois society (Marx 1976: 1024). Hegel felt that the capitalist's supervisory role in the production process saved the bourgeois system of property rights from absolute insanity. In an analogous fashion, Marx (1976: 986) argued that subsumption of labor under capital requires the organizing activity of the employer. Moreover, this relationship contributes to the intellectual development of the worker.

Marx's dual concept of capitalist work organization—like Hegel's theory of property—involves on one hand, magnificent riches alongside poverty and degradation, and on the other, the growth of class consciousness. While the subsumption of labor under capital encourages rapid development of class consciousness, this depends on massive intervention by government: first, to curtail exploitation of children and women by employers and adult male workers; and second, to provide workers with the leisure time necessary to develop community and class interests. The twofold character of Marx's concept has been missed by commentators, such as Burawoy (1985), who have concentrated on its repressive aspect, and have overlooked what is almost a commentary by Marx on Hegel's notion of the rise of *Bildung* in civil society.

3. Absolute and Relative Surplus Value

Surplus value is the value created by the worker beyond that required to reproduce his or her wages; the proportion between the labor necessary to satisfy "the narrow circle of [the worker's] own needs" and surplus labor is called the *rate* of surplus value (Marx 1976: 425). Lengthening the working day is one way of increasing the rate of surplus value. For example, if the worker spends five hours to produce the value of commodities needed for her subsistence, and five hours for the capitalist, the rate of surplus value is 50 per cent. If the entrepreneur requires her to spend an additional hour in the factory, the rate of surplus value jumps to 55 per cent. Marx named the additional product created in this manner, absolute surplus value.

The rate of surplus value may also be enlarged by shrinking the time necessary for the worker to replace her wages. Relative surplus value arises from introducing more efficient machinery and/or intensifying the pace and organization of work, with no change to the working day. In other words, productivity of labor is improved (Marx 1976: 431). Under competitive market conditions, every capitalist has a clear motive "to cheapen his commodities by increasing the productivity of labour."

> The objective of the development of the productivity of labour within the context of capitalist production is the shortening of that part of the working day in which the worker must work for himself, and the lengthening, thereby, of that part of the day, in which he is free to work for nothing for the capitalist.

Increased relative surplus value does not entail decreased absolute surplus value; rather, the opposite is true. According to Marx (1976: 666), productivity increased enormously in the late eighteenth and early nineteenth century, "the period in which the right to prolong the working day without any restriction at all became accepted as one of the basic rights of the citizen." Moreover, increased productivity leads to reduced prices and ultimately lowers the cost of the worker's means of subsistence; as a result, wages fall. If productivity gains occur in industries supplying goods to workers, lower wages may be the direct consequence of improved productivity.

Marx (1976: 646) allowed that the difference between absolute and relative surplus value "appears to be illusory." Absolute surplus value cannot be produced unless the worker can create more product than she consumes in wages; relative surplus value depends on the worker laboring longer than it takes to reproduce her means of subsistence. But the distinction is central to an understanding of various strategies in the hiring and use of labor power. Given a certain level of productivity, "surplus-value can be raised only by prolonging the working day in absolute terms;" and if the maximum working day is set, changes in the quantity of surplus value depend on "a change in either the productivity or the intensity of labour."

Formal subsumption of labor under capital primarily concerns production of absolute surplus value; real subsumption involves both absolute and relative surplus value. The first stage of the labor contract belongs to the period of manufacture, and initially involves production only of absolute surplus value, and the formal subsumption of labor under capital. "Given a pre-existing mode of labour . . . surplus-value can be created only by lengthening the working day, i.e. by increasing *absolute surplus-value*" (Marx 1976: 1021, 645). The second stage of the wage deal begins with factory production, and the real subsumption of labor under capital. This mode—which generates both absolute, and relative surplus value—"completely revolutionizes the technical processes of labour and the groupings into which society is divided"

The production of absolute surplus value is the subject of Part Three of *Capital*; relative surplus value belongs to Part Four. Both parts, which make up more than a third of the book, include lengthy observations on the history of factory law. What explains the dual appearance of parliamentary legislation in *Capital*? The drive to create absolute surplus value began with manufacture, but reached its apogee under the factory regime, which produces both absolute and relative surplus value. The Factory Acts regulated production of absolute surplus value, so they belong in Part Three; but the Acts also influenced the terms of the labor contract within the workplace, by stimulating machine production—and thus creating relative surplus value. Shorter hours increased labor costs, and capital adapted by increasing the intensity of work[4] and replacing skilled operatives with machinery and less skilled workers (Marx 1976: 533-43).   Industries based on earlier modes of production rapidly succumbed to the new methods, and were placed under factory law. Machine production degraded the work environment, and brought speed-ups and accidents.   Factory legislation adapted to these circumstances by further reductions to the working day, and by strengthening clauses on health and safety. Improvements brought by law were reinforced by technical changes designed to protect machinery from a harsh environment; these alterations often had the unintended consequence of greatly improving conditions for workers as well.[5]

Marx's use of Hegelian categories in the transmutation of contract clearly reveals the revolutionary implications of "piecemeal" government reform. The plodding advance of English factory law ultimately transformed the relationship between capitalist and worker. "The worker knows now," wrote factory inspector Baker in 1859, "when that which he sells is ended, and when his own begins; and by possessing a sure foreknowledge of this, is enabled to pre-arrange his own minutes for his own purposes" (quoted in Marx 1976: 415-16; 1974:87). This was of enormous portent, Marx thought, for the world proletariat. Thus in 1866 the International Working Men's Association passed a resolution proposed by the London General Council affirming that state action to reduce the working day to eight hours "is a preliminary condition without which all further attempts at improvement and emancipation must prove abortive."   Marx himself drafted this resolution,[6] basing it on a similar statement by "the English factory inspector, R. J. Saunders; 'Further steps towards a reformation of society can never be carried out with any hope of success, unless the hours of labour be limited, and the prescribed limit strictly enforced.'"

The role of the state, however, is only one aspect of the concluding moment of contract. There are other Hegelian developments. First, Marx emphasized the progressive influence on class consciousness of the regulated contractual relationship. This is very close to Hegel's concept of *Bildung*, the educational function of work and struggle in civil society. Marx also pointed to the growth of corporations, workers' cooperatives, and the development of a world market. We will examine these in the concluding section.

4. *Bildung*, Corporations, and the World Market

Roslyn Bologh (1990: 267) argues that patriarchal masculinist themes loom large in the tradition of social theory, especially the notion of a dramatic resolution to conflict, as in Marx's idea of communist revolution. Marx, writes Bologh, "stresses external heroic action that aims at ending once and for all . . . the domination of labor by capital." Certainly, the abrupt end epitomized by Marx's (1976: 929) famous phrase, "the knell of capitalist expropriation sounds, the expropriators are expropriated" has exercised immense intellectual and political appeal. Scholars have called attention to Marx's Hegelian language later in this passage, i.e., the "negation of the negation." The climax to the wage contract, warns Bologh, involves "communal control of the means of production. However, community, like family, may be a gloss for relations of repression in which weaker individuals are dominated and coerced by stronger ones."

The alternative Hegelian outcome provided by Marx's *Capital* is quite different from the finish promised by the negation of the negation. The better phrase to sum up the results of the transformation of the employment contract may be Marx's (1981: 567) observation that "the abolition of capital as private property [comes] within the confines of the capitalist mode of production itself."

Along with other patriarchal theorists, Weber links control by the institutions of democratic government with boredom and impotence (Bologh 1990: 292-3).[7] It may be another indication of the "feminine" themes Bologh canvasses in Marx—which "stress[] caring and support for each individual"—that *Capital* offers a powerful endorsement of the activist policies of the Victorian state. (Significantly, the interventionist English political administration has been labelled in the historical literature as the "Nanny State.") In addition to government, however, the denouement of the Marx's wage contract includes an optimistic evaluation of alienated labor, money, large corporations, and the growth of a world market.

Both Hegel and Marx stressed the problems of poverty, unemployment, and dehumanization that plague civil society. Like Hegel, however, Marx also indicated the progressive features of the bourgeois wage deal. In contrast, Marx (1981: 375, 1047) affirmed, with the isolation of rural communities and the particularism of feudal manners, capitalism sponsors the growth of a many-sided individuality and something like a universal life. One aspect of this is the extension of market relations across the globe. The terrible costs involved, for example, in making Asia and Africa "a pure appendage of the stock exchange" are accompanied by immense cultural transformation and the creation of an international proletarian perspective within a global community.

Other positive results of the wage bargain are enrichment of working life, and the unprecedented autonomy money gives to workers. Hegel and Marx underlined the remarkable increase in skill and sociability that come with the development of civil society (MacGregor 1984). On one side, traditional skills are erased and the abilities of the worker are narrowed. But on the other, modern industry encourages efficient work habits, cooperation with others, and the proliferation of new, and broader skills. This overall development and education of consciousness is what Hegel called, *Bildung*. In an extraordinary section of "Results of the Immediate Process of Production," the originally planned Part Seven of *Capital*, Marx (1976: 1026-35) argued that the labor contract itself produces the demand for equality, and extinguishes particularism and exclusion. Workers—especially those in the United States—come to demand equal treatment on the basis of a formal understanding of the law, regardless of ethnic origin, race, sex, religion, or other factors. Selfless loyalty to a paternalistic employer is no longer required of workers when there are other firms to bid for their services. These are factors that Paul Berman (1991: 79) notices in the modern wage contract as well.

> In a free-market economy . . . with democratic rights, workers and society as a whole can express their preferences in at least limited ways . . . It sounds paradoxical . . . but there is more socialism today in the United States than there ever was in the Soviet Union—that is, more opportunity for society as a whole to influence the economy and government.

Increased personal freedom for the modern worker rests on money, the universal equivalent. In Marx's view, money makes possible the exchange of commodities, but it also bequeaths to the worker a vital source of social power (Marx 1976: 1032-3, 1973: 409-10, 420-21; MacGregor 1984: 205-18). On a quantitative scale, of course, the capitalist's access to money dwarfs the worker's. Qualitatively, however, money gives to each individual a degree of social movement that escapes the influence of any single capitalist. This is a fact well known to kidnappers and assassins of the rich, but it is also a feature of the lifestyle of individual workers. "It is the worker himself who . . . buys commodities as he wishes and, as the *owner of money*, as the buyer of goods, he stands in precisely the same relationship to the sellers of goods as any other buyer." Similarly, the opportunity to earn more money acts as an incentive for the worker to improve her position relative to others, to enhance her level of skill and knowledge, and to invest in the welfare and education of her children. All these factors, in other words, build "the worker's *individuality* . . . his actual personal achievement."

Money's most important role is to free the worker from the administrative machinery of the state, and to equalize her contributions to government with those of others.[8] Before the advent of capitalism, the state typically relied on coerced services, or goods in kind; these burdens were notoriously difficult to spread fairly among citizens. Money in the hands of ordinary people, however, means that this "universal form of all types of wealth . . . can be taken as [a] 'thing[].' Only by being translated into terms of this extreme culmination of externality can services exacted by the state be fixed quantitatively and so justly and equitably (Hegel 1976: 195-5). Advocates of the California's famous anti-tax Proposition 13 might have reconsidered if the alternative was the one available to the pyramid builders of Egypt, or the vassals of feudal monarchy. As Hegel suggested, the existence of money allows the state to do without coerced services except in wartime, when these become vital. Marx (1973: 157-8) remained silent on this aspect of the employment contract in *Capital*, but in the *Grundrisse* he referred to it directly.

> The less social power the medium of exchange possesses . . . the greater must be the power of the community which binds the individuals together, the patriarchal relation, the community of antiquity, feudalism and the guild system . . . Each individual possesses social power in the form of a thing. Rob the thing of this social power and you give it to persons to exercise over persons.

Many feminist scholars have insisted that the wage contract is a key means whereby women can escape patriarchal control, an argument also made by Marx (1976: 620-21), who saw it as "a new economic foundation for a higher form of the family and of relations between the sexes." In their classic work on the factory acts,

Hutchins and Harrison (quoted in Mark-Lawson and Witz 1988: 172) outline the importance of women's working for a wage.

> The wage contract, though not, we hope, the final or ideal stage in the evolution of women's position, is an advance from her servile state in the medieval working class, or parasitic dependence on the family. . . . Grievously exploited as her employment has been and still is, the evolution of the woman wage earner, her gradual independence, in however limited a degree, is certainly one of the most interesting social facts of our time.

The employment contract has direct implications for capitalists as well as workers. The huge investments required for industrial production, combined with the uncertainties and devastation of the business cycle, force the growth of giant companies. Large capital outlays foster increased productivity, enlarged production, lower prices, an expanding market—and even bigger firms (Marx 1976: 967). Most of these are owned by private shareholders, but Marx (and Hegel) saw the development of workers' cooperatives as well.

Unlike Hegel, Marx did not directly connect the structure of corporations with the state, a linkage discussed in the final chapter of this book. Nevertheless, he (1981: 569) did mention that the monopolization of certain sectors of the economy by big capital "provokes state intervention." Marx also referred to phenomena reminiscent of Hegel's (1976: 153) description of the corporation as "a second family" for the worker. The trade union, for example, is a product of the employment contract, as is the corporation, and both grow in lockstep. "The workers *combine* in order to achieve *equality* of a sort with the capitalist in their *contract concerning the sale of their labour*. This is the rationale (the logical basis) of the trade unions" (Marx 1976: 1070; 1981: 375, 572). Clearly, this arrangement gives some leeway to cooperation between labor and capital in the production process. Similarly, Marx observed that the joint-stock company entails separation of ownership and control. The petty tyranny exercised by small capitalists and their families yields to the business bureaucracy, or what Marx called, "social powers of production." Hegel's declaration that within the corporation the individual's work is "elevated to conscious effort for a common end" is matched by Marx's glowing assertion that "capitalist joint-stock companies as much as cooperative factories should be viewed as transition forms from the capitalist mode of production to the associated one."

Marx's brief discussion of cooperative factories in Volume 3 of *Capital* may have been influenced by the moment of use in Hegel's concept of property. As we learned in Chapter Seven, Hegel (1976: 51) contended that the worker's possession and use of the instruments of production supplied by the capitalist ultimately establish the worker's claim to ownership, so that there are "two owners standing in relation to one another." Hegel added that "although their relation is not that of being common owners of a property, still the transition from it to common ownership is very easy." This approximates the dynamic Marx espied in the employment contract, except that Marx (1981: 568)—unlike Hegel—was not prepared to grant the individual worker an ownership claim in the means of production. Such a claim could only belong to the "associated producers."

At first, Marx (1981: 510-11) noted, the worker (like Frances Trollope's little factory slave in Deep Valley Mill) "must have a master, to make him work and govern him. And once this relationship of domination and servitude is assumed, it is quite in order for the wage-labourer to be compelled to produce, besides his own wages, also the wages of supervision." But with the transition to "social labour . . . the cooperation and combination of many to a common result," the labor of management devolves from the capitalist to the factory manager. Now not only capital, but also workers' cooperatives, can purchase the labor of supervision. The capitalist becomes "a functionary in production."

This development clearly overturns the bourgeois claim that profit is due to the entrepreneur's control and direction of the workplace—these are simply costs of production that are subtracted from profits. For Marx (1981: 568), the capitalist's ownership claim to the product of industry is bogus, while that of the worker is real.

> This result of the capitalist mode of production in its highest development is a necessary point of transition towards the transformation of capital back into the property of the producers, though no longer as the private property of individual producers, but rather as their property as associated producers, as directly social property.

Failure to see this result of the employment contract, claimed Marx (1981: 511; 1976: 382), "means nothing more than that the *vulgus* cannot conceive that forms developed in the womb of the capitalist mode of production may be separated and liberated from their antithetical capitalist character." The most striking instance of

Marx's "liberated . . . forms"[9] is "the shorter working day which, in the second half of the nineteenth century, the state . . . here and there interposed as a barrier to the transformation of children's blood into capital." Marx's account of the English factory legislation and its implications for social theory are the subject of the following chapter.

Notes

1. Tony Smith (1990: 124) rightly contends that "the logic underlying Marx's categorial progression must be uncovered if we are to reply to the . . . assertion that *Capital* is a confused jumble of pseudo-systematic dialectics and empirical history."

2. This may explain why, as Woodiwiss (1987: 458) puts it, "the law [on property and contract] that the state enunciated only became capitalist as the state became democratic."

3. Raphael Samuel (1977: 11) has brilliantly shown that most industries in England relied heavily on hand technology in the mid-nineteenth century, a reality acknowledged in *Capital*. "As Marx's lengthy chapter on 'modern industry' unfolds . . . it becomes clear that modern industry incorporates older systems of production rather than superseding them, and that it is in fact a mixed development, in which 'modern' domestic industry and 'modern' manufacture play no less distinctive a part than the machine-based industries."

4. "The Factory Act has strikingly shown that the mere shortening of the working day increases to a wonderful degree the regularity, uniformity, order, continuity and energy of labour" (Marx 1976: 535).

5. A modern example of this is the ban on smoking in workplaces where smoke endangers sensitive machinery, or presents a fire hazard. The rapid drop in smoking over the past decade in North America may be due in part to the unfavorable effect of tobacco smoke on the computer, which is now almost everyone's favorite machine.

6. Although Marx did not attend the September, 1866 meetings of the International Working Men's Association in Geneva his draft resolutions "permeate[d] most of the congress's work" (Draper 1986: 134).

7. Because he did not advocate heroic masculinist solutions to the problems of civil society, Hegel has been accused of "passivity" and "resignation" by commentators, including Avineri (1972), Plant (1984), and Cullen (1979).

8. Montesquieu, as Hirschman (1977: 78) shows, argued that money in the form of liquid capital assets can offer opposing power to that of the sovereign; this became an important theme in eighteenth century political thought.

9. William James Booth (1991: 27) offers an important redefinition of the idea of time in Marx, which exposes the "possibilities of development as human being or citizen" involved in the shorter working day. "Marx's political economy of time raises again the question of real wealth: whether it ought to be considered as hours embodied in things, governed by the laws of the market and, above all economic efficiency, or . . . as free time under human control and used for freely chosen purposes."

9

Marx and the Factory Acts

Unprincipled parents were induced . . . to sell their children into bondage . . . children of an age at which those of the middling and upper classes of society are not permitted even to cross a street.

—*Edinburgh Medical and Surgical Journal, XLI (1834)*
(quoted in Gray 1991: 42)

A man cannot become a child again, or he becomes childish. But does he not find joy in the child's naiveté, and must he himself not strive to reproduce its truth at a higher stage? Does not the true character of each epoch come alive in the nature of its children?

—Karl Marx, *Grundrisse* (1973: 246).

The factory inspector of today, like the militiaman, is the child of the struggle of labor against capital. The factory inspector enforces the law for the worker against the capitalist, the militiaman shoots down the worker by command of the capitalist.

—Florence Kelley, *c. 1892*
(quoted in Roediger and Foner 1989: 169)

The success of the Factory Act owed a great deal to Horner's intelligence, honesty and indeed to his ruthlessness.

—Bernice Martin, "Leonard Horner" (1969: 434)

1. The First Interventionist State

For Marx (1976: 520, 621, 635), ferocious exploitation of children and women by capital and large-scale introduction of machinery decisively transformed the labor contract in the first half of the nineteenth century. The cruel metamorphosis of contractual freedom in the sale of labor-power prompted "state intervention into factory affairs." We shall see that Marx's history of state action relied heavily on reports of the English Factory Inspectorate. Government inspectors, however, do not appear simply as fact-gatherers and statisticians. The bureaucrats who designed, implemented, and defended the statutes regulating the working day are key figures in Marx's Hegelian account of the Victorian state. Many of the laws of capitalist political economy formulated by Marx originally appeared in the *Reports of the Inspectors of Factories*. The "general extension of factory legislation to all trades for the purpose of protecting the working class in mind and body," as documented and explained in the reports of Leonard Horner and the others, became for Marx "the general law for all social production." Factory law, Marx claimed, is the central force underlying the movement of capitalist production toward communism.

> By maturing the material conditions and social combination of the process of production, it matures the contradictions and antagonisms of the capitalist form of that process, and thereby ripens both the elements for forming a new society and the forces tending toward the overthrow of the old one.

As I argued in Chapter Three, the account of factory legislation in *Capital* has implications for a number of significant issues in political and social theory. First of all, it establishes Marx's Hegelian credentials. Briefly, the Hegelian elements are the character of the state as a "counterpoise" (Marx 1976: 91), and successor, to unregulated capitalism; the role of factory inspectors as professional agents of a policy-making, administrative, central government apparatus; and the nature of class struggle, which involves not only workers and capitalists, but also government bureaucrats, middle class reformers, and aristocrats.[1]

Another set of Hegelian influences, as I have demonstrated in previous chapters, includes the role played by time in the labor contract, and the supreme importance of the development of individuality. Without these notions Marx's (1976: 416) belief that "the modest Magna Carta of the legally limited working day" represented a huge contribution to human progress would be inexplicable.

Finally, Hegel's conception of the family and of the nature of childhood and education discussed in Chapter Five is central to understanding Marx's discussion of factory legislation. The egalitarian family ideal that sprang from the German enlightenment, and which found expression in Hippel's work and in Hegel's, swayed Marx's interpretation of the struggles surrounding factory legislation. Marx had no sympathy for claims made by working class men on the labor of women and little children; he was disgusted by the idea that parents had a right to live off exploitation of their progeny. For Marx (1976: 614, 523), as for Hegel, everything is secondary to the grand effort of education; work for children and infants only makes sense if it contributes to their becoming "fully developed human beings." The barbaric English tradition of sending poor children and infants into factories struck both Hegel and Marx as one of the greatest crimes in human history. Clauses on hours of work and education in the Factory Acts represented the beginning of English society's efforts towards remedying this evil.

> The intellectual degradation artificially produced by transforming immature human beings into mere machines for the production of surplus-value (and there is a very clear distinction between this and the state of natural ignorance in which the mind lies fallow without losing its capacity for development, its natural fertility) finally compelled even the English Parliament to make elementary education a legal requirement before children under 14 years could be consumed "productively" by being employed in those industries which are subject to the Factory Acts.

Important aspects of Marx's narrative correspond fairly closely to those of the school David Cannadine (1987: 172, 175, 183, 190) has called, "the welfare-state Whigs." This scholarship, which dominated British history in the 1960s and 1970s, describes a "dramatic" "revolution in government carried out by zealous Benthamite bureaucrats," and views Britain's past as "simultaneously unique yet exemplary." Recently the Whig outlook has been challenged by historians who "are mainly concerned to show that less happened, less dramatically, than once was thought." But the transformation of the labor contract discussed by Marx fits with the revised version of the Whig thesis suggested by Pat Thane (1990) and Peter Mandler (1984).

Thane (1990: 19, 21; also MacDonagh 1977: 9) contends that a new generation of activist bureaucrats "had an historically unique opportunity due to the demands of the 1830s." As a result, they pushed radical central government reform well past the mid-century mark. However, the "self-sustaining growth" model of government proposed by the Welfare State Whigs cannot explain the reversals suffered by Chadwick and his peers, including Leonard Horner, which checked "the momentum of growth" in the 1840s and altered its direction "in important respects in the 1850s." Marx certainly noted this change, recording dismay (as we saw in Chapter Three) at Leonard Horner's abrupt resignation in his New Year's, 1860 letter to Engels. According to Thane (also Mueller 1984; Gowan 1987), the Northcote-Trevelyan civil service reforms of the 1850s were "partially designed precisely to restrain public and innovatory activities in the style of Chadwick and his peers on the part of bureaucrats."

Regardless of the question of historical interpretation, however, the pivotal position of factory legislation in *Capital* indicates that Marx's social theory was far more state-centered than is generally acknowledged. In a recent ground-breaking article, Campbell and Lindberg (1990: 634-6) discuss the ways government "shapes the economy's *organizational structure*—the different institutional arrangements that actors use to coordinate exchange and production, such as markets." A key means of shaping the economy, they urge, is the manipulation and enforcement of property rights, including those established by the labor contract. "The state's ability to define and enforce property rights determines social relations, and therefore, the balance of power among a wide variety of economic actors in civil society." Marx's account of factory legislation is concerned precisely with, "political struggles outside and within the state [that] influence the state's property rights actions."

In this respect, *Capital* harmonizes with Karl Polanyi's classic *The Great Transformation* (1957: 132, 165-6, 234; Block 1987: 175). Like Marx, Polanyi thought the Factory Acts "were required to protect industrial man from the implications of the commodity fiction in regard to labor power." They constituted the initial "step in the movement to protect society from the devastation caused by the self-regulating market," a tendency Polanyi associated with democratic socialism. *The Great Transformation* has influenced writers engaged in "bringing the state back in," (Evans, Reuschemeyer, and Skocpol 1985) but Marx's contribution has been strangely neglected. Block (1987: 175; MacGregor 1989: 159), for example, claims that while Marx hailed the Factory Acts, he "did not address this critical state intervention in theoretical terms." The thrust of my argument is precisely that Marx did place the Acts in a theoretical framework, that provided by Hegel in the *Philosophy of Right*.

Factory legislation is only one aspect of Marx's state-centered approach. Another is the place of the factory inspectors themselves. Alvin Gouldner (1979: 9) compares Marx to a television camera operator recording an industrial conflict. "One is not supposed to ask the television audience, 'where does the cameraman fit in?'"

Similarly, Leonard Horner and his colleagues presented themselves as objective mediators in the contest between factory masters and operatives. But in Marx's narrative of factory reform they were much more than that.

What the inspectors represent in *Capital* is an "embryonic new 'universal class,'" to borrow a term from Gouldner's (1979: 5, 7) "left-Hegelian sociology." For Gouldner, the power of the New Class (a class to which Marx himself belonged) is founded on its cultural capital, its monopoly of specialized knowledge; a key organizational base of the New Class is the welfare state. Harold Perkin (1989: 10) usefully modifies Gouldner's concept, arguing that "professional control of the market" is the real power source of the New Class.[2] The professional class is employed by both corporations and government, but sources of employment and income demarcate a fault line of conflict. The contest documented in *Capital* between factory inspectors on one side, and factory masters and their ideologues on the other, is an early example of this modern form of class conflict. Paradoxically, then, we find in Marx's key text a view usually linked by political sociologists such as Theda Skocpol (1986-87: 31-2) with Weber rather than Marx.

Marx's narrative contains little support for the neo-Marxist view that factory legislation was "the result of attempts to defuse class-based opposition to industrial capitalism" (Katznelson 1985: 274; Lehrer 1987: 15-16).[3] But it does accord with the revised Marxist perspective of Gareth Stedman Jones (1983: 72; also Price 1986: 60), who argues that the "the principal of the normal working day . . . was . . . the first major victory of the working class and pointed towards the new political relationship that would have to be fought out between worker and state in the conditions of modern industry."

Marx saw the major opponents of factory law as the capitalist class and its faithful scribes, the political economists. Although initially opposed to the Inspectorate, factory reformers and the working class movement were among the bureaucracy's allies against capital. Yet, as Marx recognized, there was always a fundamental ambiguity about parliamentary legislation within the short-time movement. On one hand, supporters of the factory cause appreciated the diminution in working hours made possible by the Acts. But reformers must have resented their own displacement by bureaucrats ("it seemed that the Oastlerites had been 'outbidden in humanity'" [Ward 1970: 68]), and workers were indignant when factory law jeopardized their own exploitation of wives and children.

"The distrust of state action," notes Polanyi (1957: 101; also Harris 1990: 116-7), "the insistence on respectability and self-reliance, remained for generations characteristic of the British worker."

Marx offered some indirect guidance on an issue that produced much heat in his time, and which has gained prominence in our own. Did the Factory Acts relieve women of the right to sell their labor power at the best price? Few today (in the advanced capitalist countries, at any rate) would contend that children's ability to sell their labor power should be unrestricted, as did nineteenth century opponents of factory legislation. But some scholars insist that the Factory Acts belong to a stream of patriarchal legislation that biased the labor market in favor of men and forced women back into the home. This question will be examined in detail below.

The first four sections of this chapter explore the development of factory legislation up to the 1833 Factory Act and the establishment of the Factory Inspectorate. Section five examines the contradictory relationship between the working class movement and factory inspectors during the early stages of factory reform. Section six looks at the Act of 1844, which included women as a restricted group; and section seven probes arguments about patriarchy and protective legislation. The important education provisions of the Factory Acts are surveyed in section eight. Section nine considers the revolutionary transformation that took place in the consciousness of factory inspectors as they worked to implement the Acts, especially the famous Ten Hours Act of 1847. Sections ten to fourteen study factory occupiers' vigorous resistance to workday reform; and section fifteen charts the vital contribution of political economy to capital's attack on state intervention. The final section investigates the biographical similarities that created the peculiar union between the communist Karl Marx and the factory bureaucrat Leonard Horner.

2. Early Factory Legislation

Marx (1976: 382-390) found "two opposite tendencies" in the history of state intervention. Both involved class struggle between capital and labor, but the role of the state in this conflict changed dramatically. "While the modern Factory Acts compulsorily shorten the working day, the earlier statutes tried forcibly to lengthen it." Labor statutes dating back to the fourteenth century were aimed at increasing the workday; by the middle of the eighteenth century, however, these fell into disuse. Capital, Marx advised, had fixed its grip on the English economy and could stretch the hours of work without assistance from government. "Every boundary set by morality and nature, age and sex, day and night, was broken down . . . capital was celebrating its orgies."

The tide changed early in the nineteenth century. T. K. Djang (1942: 23), a historian of factory inspection, argues that "the Health and Morals of Apprentices Act of 1802 was the first blow struck" by the state "to protect the weaker partner of industry."[4] For Marx (1976: 903; also Fox 1985: 87), however, the initial sign of the English government's change of heart was the 1825 repeal of the "barbarous" Combination Acts, which made trade union membership illegal. Parliament, declared Marx, reluctantly "gave up the laws against strikes and trade unions, after it had itself, with shameless egoism, held the position of a permanent trade union of the capitalists against the workers throughout five centuries."

Scholars are divided on Marx's view (which he shared with Robert Owen, Richard Oastler, and other reformers) that the worst excesses of child labor, unsafe working conditions, and intolerable hours were introduced by large-scale manufacturing, since these evils existed in earlier handicraft and cottage industry systems (Cunningham 1990). Unquestionably, however, England in the mid-nineteenth century abounded with children, and many were gainfully employed (Levine 1985: 175). Population growth was astounding, reaching 16.7 million in 1851 from 5.75 million a century earlier, with about forty percent of the population age 15 or below (Anderson 1990: 1, 47, 51). According to the 1851 census, almost 30 percent of children "aged between 10 and 15 years worked . . . [and this] is undoubtedly an underestimate" (Joyce 1990: 138). In 1836, "there were 30,000 children working in the Lancashire mills alone" (Walvin 1982: 62).

While child labor was a feature of earlier forms of production, the industrial revolution changed the character of work for infants and children (Gregg 1982: 124). Agricultural toil, for example, was never systematized and set to the clock, without regard to day, night or season, as occurred in the factory system. Nor is it likely that any earlier regime of work followed economies of time and discipline so strictly as did the textile industry with its "grinding and unremitting working routines and hostile environment" (Walvin 1982: 64; Wright 1988: 101).[5] The industrial economy of time meant that parents could benefit from infant's and children's labor, as they could not in earlier periods. Unlike work in factories, most farm toil demanded more strength than little children possessed. Moreover, "families engaged in industry were less likely than agriculturalists to see their teenage children leave home and embark on an extended sojourn in service. Having paid the cost of raising children, industrial families enjoyed the benefits of their labour" (Levine 1985: 176). The political economy of time is what most attracted Marx's attention. For as William James Booth (1991: 8) argues, "no modern philosopher has been as concerned with the question of time and freedom as was Marx."

Working conditions in textiles were dramatically worse than those in most other industries. Thus Eric Hopkins (1982: 53; also Cunningham 1990a: 280; Bienefeld 1972)[6] argues that the strict discipline and long working hours which prevailed in northern textile factories were unknown in "a wide range of domestic and small master industries as well as ironworks, glasshouses, tanneries, brickworks, and coal, iron-ore, and clay mines," which kept to traditional, relatively relaxed patterns of labor regulation into the late nineteenth century.

Marx (1976: 812) maintained that legislation "brought into existence from 1847 to 1864" on working class housing and sanitation arose not from indignation about the conditions of the proletariat but from fear that epidemics among the poor would spread to "the frightened middle classes in certain towns, such as Liverpool, Glasgow and so on." Similar anxieties initially motivated factory legislation.

Near the close of the eighteenth century epidemics broke out among apprentices in Lancashire factories; an outbreak near Manchester sparked an inquiry, and in 1802 "the Health and Morals of Apprentices Act became law" (Thomas 1948: 10; MacDonagh 1977: 22-3). The Act forbade employment of infants, limited the workday of pauper apprentices over age seven to twelve hours, and contained provisions for cleanliness, education and adequate sleeping quarters in the factories. In addition, "apprentices were to attend church at least once a month." The law was poorly framed and its enforcement was left to volunteers among justices and clergy.

The second act regulating children's working hours was modelled loosely on proposals by Robert Owen and (like the 1802 Act) supported by Peel, the father of the Tory prime minister. Introduced in 1815, and finally passed in 1819, it covered all factory laborers, not just apprentices. The 1802 Act was designed for a rural factory system based on water-power, and run by apprentice labor imported from orphanages in the south; the 1819 law was for an urban industry based on steam and staffed with workers from teeming working class neighborhoods. "When the steam-engine transplanted the factories from the waterfalls of the countryside into the centres of the towns," commented Marx (1976: 924), "the 'abstemious' profit-monger found his childish material ready to hand, without having to bring slaves forcibly from the workhouses."

The birth of large-scale industry, said Marx (1976: 922) "is celebrated by a vast Herod-like slaughter of the innocents." Machinery exiled the skilled male worker (though, as we shall see, this was only partially achieved), replacing him with women and little children, who worked at a fraction of his wage. Since any item of machinery was constantly threatened with obsolescence, it was imperative for factories to work day and night. Maximum return on investment dictated that children and women should be at their posts in 24-hour shifts. A child's terrified reaction to the factory system appears in a haunting passage from Charlotte Elizabeth Tonna's novel about immature factory labor, *Helen Fleetwood*, first published in 1839-40.

> Everything is done by machinery: you see, they are great things, ever so high and big, all going about and about, some on wheels running up and down the room, and some with great rollers turning about as fast as steam can drive them; so you must step back, and run forward, and duck, and turn, and move as they do, or off goes a finger or an arm, or else you get a knock on the head, to remember all your lives. As to sitting down there's no such thing.
> . . . Move, move, everything moves. The wheels and the frames always going, and the little reels twirl round as fast as ever they can; and the pulleys, and chains, and great iron works overhead, are all moving; and the cotton moves so fast that it is hard to piece it quick enough; and there is a great dust, and such a noise of whirr, whirr, whirr, that at first I did not know whether I was standing on my head (quoted in Kovacevic 1975: 307).

An early and influential proponent of the second factory act was Francis Horner, "luminary of the Bullion Committee and intimate friend of David Ricardo" (Marx 1976: 924, 390). This famous Whig political economist and parliamentarian, who died in 1817, was the elder brother of Leonard Horner. Despite efforts by Francis Horner and other reformers, the earliest factory legislation entirely failed. "Parliament passed five Labour Laws between 1802 and 1833, but was shrewd enough not to vote a penny for their compulsory implementation, for the necessary official personnel, etc. They remained a dead letter." Marx's judgment accords with that of the administrative historian Oliver MacDonagh (1977: 23). "The crucial defect in almost all social legislation before 1830, and the sharpest divide between the old regulative order and the new, was the absence of any direct state involvement in the drafting, management and execution of such matters."

3. The Factory Act of 1833

In 1833, writes David Roberts (1960: 20), "the central government did very little about the social problems that beset England." In less than twenty-five years, however, Parliament built an "expanding, bureaucratic, centralized, interventionalist State (Perkin 1969: 321). The 1833 Factory Act and the Inspectorate created to administer it figured strongly in the growth of regulatory government. The Factory Inspectorate was Parliament's second central agency (the first was the inspectorate created by the 1832 Anatomy Act [Richardson 1988: 108]).[7] The Factory Act represented the government's determination to regulate business in the interest of working class infants and children. Little wonder at Dicey's (1914: 237-8) anguished remark that this Act and those that followed have "tended toward socialism, and [contain] within [them] the germs of unlimited revolution, of which no man can as yet weigh with confidence the benefits against the evils." Ironically, the 1833 Factory Act was the consequence of a scheme by manufacturers to gut a ten-hours bill proposed in 1831 by Michael Thomas Sadler. Here, as elsewhere, Marx's (1976: 527) warning—derived from a similar one by Hegel (1976: 291)—is apposite: it is a mistake "to regard the first empirical form of appearance of a thing as its cause."

Inspired by the fierce propaganda of Richard Oastler—the "Factory King"—and the militant working class short-time committees formed in the north of England, Sadler argued that capital's disproportionate strength over the worker meant that the labor contract was flawed, and that factory operatives, especially infants and children, did not resemble the "free agents" described in books on laissez-faire economics (Hutchins and Harrison 1966: 33). Sadler (whose works on political economy are cited approvingly in *Capital*) was forced by the manufacturing interest to submit his bill to a Select Committee over which he presided. The Committee's 1832 Report became "one of the most significant social documents of the nineteenth century" (Fraser 1984: 20), but by the time it was tabled the unfortunate Sadler had lost his seat in the newly reformed House. His bill was re-introduced by Lord Ashley, "the protagonist of the aristocratic philanthropic campaign against the factories" (Marx 1976: 831), and handily defeated. Although leaders of the new Whig government like Grey, Melbourne and Althorpe "had no strong feelings either way," their colleagues "Graham, Russell, Brougham, and Durham were fanatical opponents of regulation of the hours of adult labour; and they were under severe pressure from the manufacturers" (Finer 1952: 51).

Still, Sadler's bill "indicated the bankruptcy of the ten-hours partisans, for it was in some respects a retrograde measure" (Thomas 1948: 10, 39). The character of male working class struggles for the ten hour day is a subject to which we shall return. For now it is useful to note that, unlike the legislation of 1819, the Ten Hours Bill offered no provisions for education or effective enforcement, "and children of nine were to be condemned to work for the same hours as those twice their age."

In contrast to his 1831 bill, Sadler's Report marked a crucial advance for opponents of the exploitation of children. It aroused public opinion and incensed mill-owners. The Report was biased and exaggerated, argued factory occupiers (a position with which Marx apparently concurred[8]), and they demanded another investigation, one more sensitive to their concerns. The new Whig government, with "its delicate consideration for the manufacturers" (Marx 1976: 392) promptly complied. Headed by Edwin Chadwick, barrister of the Inner Temple and former secretary of the recently deceased Jeremy Bentham, the Commission was packed with staunch Utilitarians, including Thomas Tooke, Southwood Smith, and Leonard Horner. Most of them fitted the description given by S. E. Finer (1952: 52) of Chadwick himself. "He tempered humanity with prudence and believed if an evil could not be excised without damage to the economic fabric, then it could not properly be called evil."

Yorkshire and Lancashire short-time committees "determined not to give any evidence to the Commission, but to demonstrate against the Commissioners wherever they went" (Kirby and Musson 1975: 380). The moral case for regulating children's labor had been clearly made by Sadler's Report in any case, but manufacturers presented the Commissioners with a strong dissenting brief, which included five main arguments. "Naturally the first was the stock denunciation of interference with freedom of contract and labour" (MacDonagh 1977: 29). The second argument was that legislation would interfere with parents' rights; to this was added the disruption of poor families' budgets. Global competitive forces were also brought up, especially the threat from American textiles. A fourth objection was "the notorious claim that profit rested upon the last hour of factory work, and infant labour." Finally, mill-owners insisted that conditions for child workers were a great deal worse in a wide array of industries that would not be covered by the law, including calico-printing, armaments, pottery, mines and building.

"Three evangelical reformers, Richard Oastler, Michael Sadler, and Lord Ashley . . . had imparted the impulse to factory reform, the Benthamites now defined its form" (Roberts 1960: 37). These followers of the man Marx (1976: 758, 280) described as "the arch-philistine . . . that soberly pedantic and heavy-footed oracle of the 'common sense' of the nineteenth century bourgeoisie" were in no mood to accept Sadler's critique of the labor contract. For them the buying and selling of labor power was indeed "a very Eden of the innate rights of man. It is the exclusive realm of Freedom, Equality, Property and Bentham." Nevertheless, this committee of "disinterested men, cool, analytical and unsentimental . . . model social scientists" (Ward 1962: 94) surprised everyone by demanding legislation to protect factory children.

They argued that infants forced into work by their parents and guardians were in no sense free agents (Fraser 1984: 21). "We are of the opinion," wrote the Commissioners, "that a case is made out for the interference of the Legislature in behalf of children employed in factories" (quoted in Thomas 1948: 51). Marx (1976: 520) underlined the epoch-making implications of this judgement.

> The revolution effected by machinery in the legal contract between buyer and seller of labour-power, causing the transaction as a whole to lose the appearance of a contract between free persons, later offered the English Parliament an excuse, founded on juristic principles, for state intervention into factory affairs.

The Commissioners' radical proposal for a factory inspectorate (which resembled Robert Owen's original plan for the 1819 Act) was suggested to it by large "manufacturers who desired to see the hours of labour in other factories restricted to the level of their own" (Hutchins and Harrison 1966: 39). Their recommendations were speedily accepted and passed into law, with additional clauses for persons aged thirteen to eighteen, prohibiting night work and restricting the workday to twelve hours. The flinty-hearted Commissioners had maintained that youngsters fourteen years of age and over should be considered adults. Significantly, the government defeated a proposed amendment put forward by ten hours reformers "that children under thirteen should work not for eight, but for ten hours a day, since this would be better for masters and operatives" (Thomas 1948: 63-4). Marx (1976: 390-1) spelled out the meagre provisions of the 1833 Act, which

> lays down that the ordinary factory working day should begin at 5.30 in the morning and end at 8.30 in the evening, and within these limits, a period of 15 hours, it is lawful to employ young persons (i.e. persons between 13 and 18 years of age) at any time of the day, provided that no individual young person works more than 12 hours in any one day, except in certain cases especially provided for.

Children and young persons were allowed a minimum of one and a half hours for meals. "The employment of children under 9, with [some] exceptions . . . was forbidden; the work of children between 9 and 13 was limited to 8 hours a day."

The Commissioners' sympathy for child operatives was tempered by their desire to minimize interference with capital's exploitation of adult labor power. Accordingly, "they created a special system in order to prevent the Factory Acts from having such a frightful consequence" (Marx 1976: 391). Anxious that restricting child labor would leave older employees idle, the Commissioners proposed a scheme of working children in relays. This ingenious strategy, wrote Marx, "was therefore carried out, so that, for example, one set of children between 9 and 13 years were put into harness from 5.30 a.m. until 1.30 p.m., another set from 1.30 p.m. until 8.30 p.m., and so on."

4. The Factory Inspectorate

"For 'protection' against the serpent of their agonies," advised Marx, (1976: 416, 353) "the workers have to put their heads together and, as a class, compel the passing of a law, an all-powerful social barrier by which they can be prevented from selling themselves and their families into slavery and death by voluntary contract with capital." As Marx recognized, in the fight to regulate capital's "werewolf-like hunger for surplus-labour" the workers could not and did not present a united front. Construction of the social barrier between labor and capital was therefore left to the state. The Factory inspectorate was vital to adminstration of the law and to public knowledge of the atrocities committed by the bourgeoisie in its quest for profit. It constituted a significant, undivided force against factory occupiers from about 1836 onwards; after 1853, when the reform movement had dissolved, the Inspectorate was the single, consistent lobby for extension of the Acts beyond the textile industry. Accordingly, Marx (1976: 390) criticized the 1841 Factory Act of France's Louis Philippe, precisely because it lacked provisions for factory inspectors. "The supervision and enforcement of this law, in a country where even the mice are administered by the police, is left to the goodwill of the 'friends of commerce.'"

Modern historians agree that the most far-reaching aspect of the 1833 legislation was the appointment of factory inspectors, "paid professionals employed by a central agency" (Roberts 1960: 103). These "guardians" of the law, Marx (1976: 349) observed, are placed "directly under the Home Secretary, and their reports are published every six months by order of Parliament. They therefore provide regular and official statistics of the voracious appetite of the capitalists for surplus labour." Assisted by superintendents (later called sub-inspectors) the factory inspectors were responsible for supervision not only of working hours of restricted persons and the health and safety provisions applying to them, but also for implementing the education sections of the Act. These sections, which provided for three hours of schooling a day for children, were of great significance, though the House of Lords managed to render them almost useless by rejecting Chadwick's proposals for establishing and financing factory schools.

The son of an Edinburgh linen manufacturer, Leonard Horner's bourgeois origins distinguished him from the small cadre of upper-middle class individuals drawn from professional families who staffed the central agencies of the Victorian state; but in other respects he was typical of this remarkable group. The vast majority of inspectors were children of lawyers, physicians, school teachers, engineers, clergy, and military officers. They belonged to the "forgotten middle class," as Harold Perkin (1969: 252) has called it, "the non-capitalist or professional middle class, a class curiously neglected in social histories of the age, but one which played a part out of all proportion to its numbers in both the theory and practice of class conflict." An educated, even scholarly band, they became dedicated public servants. David Roberts (1960: 352-3) counts 300 books produced by the 140 inspectors employed between 1833 and 1854; many of these record the inspectors' struggles in favor of urban planning, public health, industrial training, the treatment of insanity, and so forth.

Polanyi (1957: 101) suggests that the "brutal shock" administered to English workers by hasty implementation of the recommendations of the Poor Law Reform Commission of 1834 "makes nonsense of the myth of British gradualism." The same is true for the Factory Acts; only in this case the icy water of the state was thrown on the capitalist class (Brock 1973: 337).[9] Within a few months of the Commission's report, Parliament pushed open the doors of "the hidden abode of production, on whose threshold there hangs the notice 'No admittance except on business'" (Marx 1976: 28). Inspectors (and after 1844, sub-inspectors as well) could enter at will the premises of factories employing child labor—and the schools attached to them—in order to investigate conditions of employment and education. They formulated rules and orders required for the Act, ensured school attendance, and demanded a public record in each factory of employed children and their hours of work. Until 1844, when these prerogatives were withdrawn, inspectors possessed "the same powers, authority and jurisdiction over constables and police officers as those possessed by justices of the peace" (Lubenow 1971: 142). Like justices, inspectors could preside over court actions to enforce factory legislation. "What further power remains to be granted," moaned R. H. Greg, textile magnate and anti-Factory Act publicist, "unless it be that of hanging a mill-owner without trial, and leaving his body to the surgeons for dissection?" (Quoted in Thomas 1948: 95-6).

An incident in 1852, when two sub-inspectors, Mr. Jones and Mr. Patrick, were sent by Leonard Horner to investigate illegal employment of restricted factory operatives, provides a rare glimpse of capital's rage at incursions by the state. Attempting to interview women and young persons found at their posts after the legal quitting time, the sub-inspectors were rudely interrupted by the owner, Mr. Sumner.

> Mr. Sumner entered the shed under great excitement; asked Mr. Jones, whom he first encountered, "What business he (Mr. Jones) had in his mill?" Mr. Jones replied, that he was a Sub-Inspector of Factories, and produced Mr. Horner's letter of the 7th instant. Mr. Sumner was very violent, would not hear any explanation, nor even

look at Mr. Horner's letter; seized Mr. Jones by the shoulders and thrust him out of the shed . . . Mr. Patrick, seeing Mr. Jones so roughly handled by Mr. Sumner, immediately followed, and added his remonstrations to those of Mr. Jones. Mr. Sumner denied our authority. Mr. Patrick told him we had authority from Mr. Horner, whose name Mr. Sumner had mentioned. Mr. Sumner became more violent, and said he did not care for that. Upon which Mr. Patrick said that he had his appointment from the Secretary of State, which he produced and read a portion of, but Mr. Sumner would not listen; struck it from his hand; said we had no business at his mill at such hours; left us very abruptly and rushed into the shed. Mr. Patrick followed, still reading his appointment, wishing to go with him, and was partly through the doorway, when Mr. Sumner swore nobody should enter his mill, pushed him violently back, shut the door in his face, and placed one or more men on the inside with orders to let nobody enter (Horner 1852c: 9-10).

Armed with extraordinary authority, the Inspectorate was chronically understaffed and underpaid. The whole of Great Britain and Ireland was divided among four inspectors assisted by fourteen superintendents. In 1836, for example, Horner, along with five superintendents, was responsible for "2700 factories manned by more than a quarter of a million workers." A reorganization in 1837 substantially reduced Horner's workload, but the responsibilities of inspectors remained very heavy. After 1837, Horner's area contained 1,484 mills, located in the four northern counties of England (Cumberland, Westmorland, Durham and Northumberland) and parts of Yorkshire, Cheshire, Derbyshire and Staffordshire. James Stuart was assigned all of Ireland and Scotland, which had between them 600 mills; the rest of England and Wales was shared between R. J. Saunders and T. J. Howell, each with over 1,000 mills (Thomas 1948: 106, 98-100). No great improvement came in the years that followed, as the government chose not to replace Horner and Stuart's successor, Kincaid, once they retired. "Thus the curious paradox: while the work of the Factory Department grew apace, the number of inspection staff was allowed to dwindle" (Djang 1942: 40; also Bartrip 1982: 613).

In 1871, wrote Marx (1976: 625), the Factory Inspectorate consisted of two inspectors, two assistant inspectors and forty-nine sub-inspectors. "The total cost of administering the Acts in England, Scotland, and Ireland amounted . . . to no more than £25,347, including legal expenses incurred in prosecuting offenders." Clearly, if the Inspectorate had relied on its enforcement capabilities alone, factory legislation would have been a bad joke. Bartrip (1982, 1983) argues that the small size of the Inspectorate throws doubt on the inspectors' ability effectively to have enforced the law.[10] Yet the effectiveness of Horner and his colleagues derived from something in addition to their quasi-police powers, a point sometimes missed by modern critics and defenders of the Inspectorate.[11] The factory inspectors belonged to the generation of activist bureaucrats personified by Edwin Chadwick, "hero-villain of social reform in the first half of the 19th century." For Chadwick and his band of Benthamite reformers, notes Rudolf Klein (1984: 8-9), "there was nothing inconsistent in holding administrative offices and engaging in the mobilisation of public opinion in support of their views. No pressure group . . . has every been more assiduous in using the media and its network of contacts to promote its ideas."

Reports and statistics produced by Leonard Horner and other inspectors supplied advocates of factory reform within and outside Parliament with powerful ammunition against the bourgeoisie (Martin 1969: 430-31). *Capital* itself—in which, as Marx (1976: 349) attests, "England figures in the foreground" partly because it "is the only country to possess a continuous set of official statistics relating to the matters we are considering"—is a monument to the success of the Inspectorate's endeavors. In addition, inspectors advised political superiors on changes necessary for improved regulation of the factories, and pressured backward manufacturers to adapt safe practices developed by industry front runners.[12]

By 1836, inspectors had devised a system of factory Time Records, "the accuracy of which, attested by the owner, could be checked by cross-examination of the operatives, who were given full opportunity of acquainting themselves with the provisions of the Act" (Thomas 1948: 142-3). The experience of inspectors also proved critical for improving factory legislation. Thus, more detailed procedures, including the use of public clocks, were put in place by the Act of 1844. These measures were a boon to workers in their struggle against mill-owners who defied the law. Indeed, public clocks must have had a critical impact since most factory operatives had no timepiece of their own. "How could the worker know," asks David Landes (1983: 230), "that he was working only the hours he was paid for and that the employer was not in some way slowing or setting back the clock so as to steal additional labor?"

Hegel (1976: 15) observed that in ancient Rome there could be no definition of the human individual because slavery contradicts the true meaning of individuality. Similarly, in Victorian England—where thousands of children toiled in factories and workshops—there was no widely accepted definition of childhood (Roberts 1985: 1). Without a notion of childhood and in the absence of statutes defending their rights, children were fair game for powerful adults, whether these were workers or capitalists, fathers or mothers.[13] In the absence of birth records (certificates of birth were not mandatory until 1874 [Sutherland 1990: 144]) factory inspectors struggled to define childhood in terms of age and physical structure. Leonard Horner felt he had invented an infallible technique to tell children's ages by the development of their teeth (Wusteman 1983: 12). "Factory inspectors," observes Gillian Sutherland (1990: 144),

> queried the activities of obviously under-age children when they noticed them. But this was less easy than it sounds. A glance at any twentieth-century primary school class will show you considerable variety in any given age group; and poverty and chronic undernourishment meant that working-class children were in general smaller, uglier, dirtier and smellier than their middle-class counterparts, confusing the issue further.

As we shall see below, the inspectors also put in place the beginnings of a universal system of education for working class children; by 1862 over half a million child operatives were in school. Horner and the others were instrumental, therefore, in developing the childhood rites of passage that Victorian England lacked (Corrigan and Sayer 1985: 178). "The extreme situation of the factory children," affirms Vincent (1981: 99), "eventually led to the first formal identification of a period of a working class child's life as being the period in which he or she should receive at least some education."

Demonstrations and strikes were the ace played by the Inspectorate whenever lawmakers balked at extension and improvement of the Acts. After a wave of Chartist-inspired strikes and government-initiated violence swept the north of England and Scotland in July and August of 1842, Horner (1843: 3, 6) dryly observed in his December report of that year, "that throughout a large part of my district there was a suspension of all work for a long time, by the riotous proceedings into which so many of the workpeople were betrayed." He recommended provision of "adequate means of education" for factory children, since "as a question of public policy, it is obvious that something effective ought to be done without loss of time." State-supported education, he urged, "would be evidence to the humbler classes of friendly disposition and kind sympathy in those above them, feelings of alienation between employer and employed would be checked, and the just influence of property and education would be strengthened."

"Alarmed at the ever-widening range of State intervention," (Thomas 1948: 206), a succession of governments resisted officially appointing Horner as head of the Factory Inspectorate, but there was hardly any doubt that he was the leading bureaucrat. "As early as 1842 Sir James Graham, an experienced and cautious Home Secretary is known to have referred to Horner as 'the Inspector-General of Factories'" (Martin 1969: 428). The "Censor of Factories," as Marx (1976: 334) called him, rapidly became an early version of a media personality. "He was cited in Parliament and press," writes Roberts (1960: 247, 228-30), "as an oracle and was consulted by ministers." *The Times*, in particular, developed "a solemn respect" for his findings, and—along with other newspapers and journals—regularly published his reports. Thus *Capital*, with its hundreds of pages drawn from Horner's reports, and those of other bureaucrats, merely reflected the fascination of the age.

5. The Working Class and the Factory Acts

Efforts of factory inspectors to carry out the law were opposed as much by workers as by politicians, capitalists, and political economists (Thomas 1948: 73; Smelser 1959: 392; Bartrip and Fenn 1980: 183). Many factory operatives did not fully appreciate humanitarian anxiety about child labor; their main concern was to limit their own hours of work. "The operatives," writes Cecil Driver (1946: 83-4, 249), "wanted shorter hours and better conditions as much as anyone . . . apart from any philanthropic conditions, therefore, the men would naturally support a cause that promised to redound to their advantage also."

Factory operatives suspected the motives of the 1833 Commission and the Factory Inspectorate. Established at the behest of the mill-owners, the Commission made little pretence of neutrality (MacDonagh 1977: 42-3). Its officials "were guilty of some gross indiscretions in the conduct of their inquiry" (Driver 1946: 231, 230). Commissioners wined and dined with mill-owners and hobnobbed among powerful opponents of the ten hours cause. The Commission, Oastler "kept repeating, was simply a trick of the

Government's, 'playing into the hands of their dear friends the capitalists.'" The 1833 Report vindicating factory occupiers argued "that the worst abuses were confined to the small mills, [and] . . . made a point of noting the paternal, considerate, gentle and beneficent approach adopted by many large factories" (Carson 1974: 133).

The 1833 law—which banned children under nine and legislated a staged reduction of hours for those under age 13 to eight hours per day—threw the short-time committees into disarray (Gray 1987: 155). They had imagined no special provisions for youngsters under nine. Combined with vehement opposition from mill-owners, working-class resistance nearly overturned the Act (Thomas 1949: 73; Smelser 1959: 392). Nevertheless, when the government backtracked in 1836 and attempted to reduce the age limit for the eight hour day from 13 to 12, textile workers were enraged (Kirby and Musson 1975: 390). They had become accustomed to the Act, and would accept no changes unless the 10 hour day was legislated for all workers under twenty-one.

The factory movement's willingness to abandon the eight hour day for little children in exchange for a uniform ten hours embarrassed Ashley, who withdrew in 1837 a Ten Hours Bill based on resolutions from the operatives. "He was reluctant to do anything which would involve an increase of child labour from eight to ten hours a day" (Hutchins and Harrison 1966: 60).

The first choice of the ten hours movement was always for legislation limiting the motive power of the mills, rather than the labor of any particular group. Operatives shared with their leaders a "naive confidence in the efficacy of simple prohibitive legislation [which] made administrative intervention not only unnecessary but undesirable" (Lubenow 1971: 145). Bringing bureaucrats into the equation threatened the ideology of free contract to which workers in the early 1830s subscribed almost as fervently as capitalists (e.g. Kirby and Musson 1975: 367-8). If the mill-owners could be compelled by law to shut down their factories after ten hours of operation each day, then all operatives would benefit, and no special state agency would be required. Movement activists argued strongly that limiting child labor would not be possible unless adult labor was similarly restricted (Hutchins and Harrison 1966: 47).

Initially, inspectors shared the outlook of mill-owners. For the first three years they rarely challenged the textile interest, and there were few prosecutions (MacDonagh 1977: 57). Horner and the others were more concerned that adult operatives were supplied with enough child helpers to keep them working 14 or 15 hours a day (Thomas 1948: 299). To that end, inspectors even recommended that the age limit for young persons should be dropped from thirteen to twelve, or even eleven (MacDonagh 1977: 57). Horner's sympathy for the manufacturers involved him in several clashes with John Doherty, the main spokesperson of the Lancashire operatives, who accused the factory inspector of failing to apply the law (Kirby and Musson 1975: 391-2).

Horner already had considerable experience with workers, having founded in 1821 one of the first Mechanics Institutes, which provided low cost instruction in science and mathematics to skilled workers (Wusteman 1983: 10). Nevertheless, class barriers dividing the proletariat from inspectors were difficult to overcome. The effectiveness of factory legislation rested in large part on acceptance by mill-owners of the inspectors as equals (Health and Safety Executive 1980: 2); this in itself was a source of suspicion for factory operatives. In Horner's case, industrialists were likely to be his social inferiors, and this enhanced the chief inspector's ability to persuade textile magnates to obey the law. In education and culture the other factory inspectors similarly outdistanced masters.

Inspectors realized that cooperation with workers was essential for enforcement of the Act. In 1834 Horner published a pamphlet addressed to operatives, explaining the new statute and the duties of inspectors. Along with his colleagues, however, he was especially solicitous of the factory occupiers, and followed Home Office instructions to treat industrialists as friends rather than potential violators of the law. In contrast with favorable treatment for the mill-owners, Whitehall issued strict orders that inspectors were to avoid any contact with workers' organizations. Stuart, the inspector for Scotland, was reprimanded in 1844 for a casual liaison with the secretary of a short-time committee (Thomas 1948: 75, 255).

In the early years of the Inspectorate, several of the cruelly underpaid superintendents were dismissed on charges of bribery; these incidents fanned resentment among operatives and deepened their misgivings about the Inspectorate. Relations were damaged further by Home Office orders in 1839 for inspectors and superintendents to engage in political spying.

These internal communications resulted in perhaps one of the earliest instances of bureaucratic whistle-blowing. A message from Stuart ordering a superintendent to observe Chartist and short-time committee activities was leaked to John Fielden, whose revelations in the House upset the Home Office and astounded Parliament; the superintendent was fired, but later reinstated under Horner (Thomas 1948: 107-12).

Even in Thomas's (1948: 258) hagiographic account of the factory inspectors, James Stuart is described as "something of an enigma." In Henriques (1971: 18) authoritative sketch he is revealed as something worse—a killer, a habitual liar and a thief. Short-time committees and other adherents of the factory cause accused Stuart of neglecting important provisions of the Factory Acts. Despite Stuart's attempts to demonstrate that his administration of the law was as strict as any other inspector's, well founded rumors multiplied that he was an agent of the Scottish factory occupiers. "Unlike the English factory inspectors," wrote Marx (1976: 426), James Stuart was "a complete prisoner of the capitalist mode of thought."

During the controversy in the late 1840s over the "false relay system" (discussed below) Stuart embarrassed his colleagues by siding with the Home Secretary and refusing to prosecute employers. His death in 1849 removed one of the largest obstacles between operatives and inspectors. "With a few more men such as he in key places," Henriques (1971: 46) advises, "the nineteenth century might well have become an epoch of revolution instead of a period which saw peaceful development of constitutional bureaucracy."

Well before the Scottish official's demise, however, factory inspectors had accomplished "the fusion of interests" with workers and reformers required for "real progress" in factory legislation (Thomas 1948: 88). A few years after passage of the 1833 Act, friendly relations between mill-owners and public servants had cooled markedly. R. H. Greg, manufacturer and opponent of the Inspectorate, could write in 1837 that enforcement of factory law tends *"to destroy all good feeling, and to aggravate misunderstandings where they exist."* He complained that "the inspectors' regulations are founded upon the principle of the master being a *tyrant and a cheat,* and that the operatives must look to the *Inspector,* rather than to *him,* for justice and protection." Greg was mortified by Horner's warning to superintendents that operatives were frequently cheated of meals and misled into making up for lost time. These instructions, said Greg, "necessarily throw the master into a false position, from which he can with difficulty extricate himself, and throw power into the hands of work-people, of which, it is too much to suppose, they will not sometimes avail themselves" (quoted in Thomas 1948: 144). After 1840, notes MacDonagh (1977: 61), inspectors "behaved as a separate interest . . . the interior momentum of government was carrying them increasingly beyond the limits of 1833."

Apart from suspicion about the humanitarian motivation of the Factory Acts and the role of inspectors, there were good economic, cultural, and social reasons for working class defiance of the law. The industrial revolution represented for many destitute households an economic bonanza, as wages earned by children and women could double family income (Levine 1987: 114). Marx (e.g. 1976: 519-20 613, 620, 795) protested that working class parents benefited from their children's labor, and speculated that prospective income from children encouraged early marriage.[14] Most parents prompted their offspring to enter the factories, and they rankled at state interference with what they felt to be their absolute parental right.[15] "Horner complained that the parents and operative spinners who employed the children, were generally most active in trying to defeat the law" (Thomas 1948: 125). The education provisions of the Acts were a particular sore point, especially since schools were partly financed from child earnings. "The majority of working class parents (and consequently their children) did not have a deep attachment to education or any great confidence in its advantages" (Roberts 1985: 21).

Children in the mills "were not independent workers, but family wage earners whose parents had hired them out" (Tilly and Scott 1987: 113; Burawoy 1985; Mark-Lawson and Witz 1988: 158). According to Viviana Zelizer (1985: 25-7; also Levine 1987: 193), the child-oriented and affectionate model of family life that emerged as an ideal for the upper and middle classes in the early nineteenth century was mostly absent among workers and the poor until the turn of the twentieth century.[16] Among the poorest layers of English society, children—where they were tolerated at all—were often targets of sexual and physical abuse (Stone 1977: 470). "Child destitution," affirms Levine (1987: 188), "was urban, industrial England's crying shame."[17]

The 1862 Children's Employment Commission revealed, lamented Marx (1976: 519-20), "that, in relation to this traffic in children, working class parents have assumed characteristics that are truly revolting and thoroughly like slave-dealing." Fathers and mothers made their offspring freely available to factory occupiers, as in "the notorious London district of Bethnal Green [where] a public market is held every Monday and Tuesday morning, at which children of both sexes from 9 years of age and upwards, hire themselves out to the silk manufacturers." From this contract, which lasted one week, the children received two pence and tea, the parents one shilling, eight pence. Children confined to workhouses were taken out by local women and sold to employers for two shillings, six pence.

The view that children's wages were necessary to prop up working class family income throughout the nineteenth century (e.g. Foster 1974: 95-6; Anderson 1976: 328) ignores the culture of money and leisure in many households.[18] The wages of subordinate family members belonged to the male head of family; how he spent them was his business (Levine 1985: 176).

Writes Nicky Hart (1989: 30), "drinking was a popular and costly male recreation increasing proportionately with the size of the family." Estimates of the amount of family income spent by the average nineteenth century English workman on alcoholic beverages range from 25 to 35 percent; recreational drinking and tobacco together must have drained close to half of the family wage packet. At the turn of the twentieth century around 30 percent of working class families were in "secondary poverty" caused largely by the male breadwinner's expenditure on drink (Thompson 1988: 311-12). Factory reformers said that capitalists coined gold out of children's blood; they might have added that working class fathers turned it into beer.

Drink and its aftereffects swallowed time, as did the perennial male working class leisure pursuits of dog- and cock-fighting (Reid 1986). Many adult male workers, including the high status Lancashire mule spinners[19] (Cohen 1985: 117), celebrated "Saint Monday," and did not work during the early part of every week; it is not clear that working children and women were so favored.[20] Certainly, subordinate family members did not enjoy the same diet as the family head, who ate a disproportionate amount of the meat available in the house (Oddy 1990: 271-3; Harrison 1989: 125-6; Seccombe 1986: 58; Oren 1974: 228).

Given the manifest displacement of time and money represented by male-dominated working class culture, it is difficult to accept the argument that child labor was absolutely necessary for family budgets. The fight against child labor, insist Hutchins and Harrison (1966: 39), "was not so much a war between manufacturers and operatives . . . as a disease from which the industrial community was suffering."

Relations on the factory floor mimicked those in larger, male-dominated society. "Men in general were more productive [as supervisors] than women because they could command more 'respect' from their assistants, particularly the younger ones" (Lazonick 1979: 239, 244; 1981: 500). Male spinners usually paid children's wages directly to parents; and "when an assistant had to be coerced physically [by the spinner] to perform his or her work, this was a matter settled with the child's parent (that person, of course, often being the operative employer himself)."

Skilled and semi-skilled male operatives, rather than the manufacturer, directly employed infants and children. In seventy Lancashire mills surveyed in 1833 "about half the number of workers under the age of 18 were employed by operatives instead of directly by factory occupiers" (Hutchins and Harrison 1966: 37). When these men were unsuccessful in the political battle against government regulation, they shamelessly evaded the law. Smelser observes that "the most frequent evasion was to introduce children into the factory at too early an age, working them more than eight hours, and thus eliminating the necessity of hiring adolescents at a higher wage" (1959: 244).

Infants and children supplied operatives with raw material and assistance in tending mule spinning machines.[21] They were also used for less desirable and dangerous work, such as cleaning machinery.

> Each operative required three or four children. The youngest, often between 7 and 10 years old, served as a scavenger, retrieving ends from beneath the mule, where the threads were only 18 inches off the ground so that the operatives could reach the top of the machine. The others were "piecers," or "pieceners," who followed the mule carriage in and out, tying broken threads (Henriques 1979: 69-70).

Adult male "minders," or operators of spinning mules, were paid piece rates from which they deducted their assistant's fixed wage. Increases in production augmented the minder's weekly pay; but he was not required or expected to pay child helpers any additional wage.

> Therefore if the minder could produce more than the normal production, by, for example, getting broken ends pieced more quickly and doffing done faster, by cleaning and oiling the mules outside engine hours, or cooperating with overlookers in time-cribbing (starting and stopping the steam engines outside the limits of the work day set by

the Factory Acts), he reaped all the benefits, to the exclusion of the piecers, who nevertheless had to work longer and harder for the same pay (Lazonick 1979: 247).

Since cleaning was not paid for when machinery was stopped, adult "minders" had considerable incentive to compel youngsters to clean up while the machines were in motion. While minders could easily stop the self-acting mule to allow children safe passage, many did not. A factory inspector's report quoted by Marx (1976: 547) stated that

> of machines, perhaps self-acting mules are as dangerous as any other kind. Most of the accidents from them happen to little children, from their creeping under the mules to sweep the floor whilst the mules are in motion. Several "minders" have been fined for this offense, but without much benefit.

In 1843, a sub-inspector described a gruesome but typical accident arising from what Leonard Horner (1843a: 3-4) called, "the dangerous custom of allowing children to clean self-acting spinning-mules while they are in motion."

> George Greenbank, aged 12 years, was killed on the 4th of January last at the mill of Mr. John Cronkshaw, in Accrington. He was caught while "fluking" or cleaning the machinery between the self-acting mule and the back of the frame. The self-actor "puts up" with great force and rapidity, and there is no check to it, as in the case of the hand-mule; so that without the greatest activity and watchfulness of the children, they are every minute liable to be crushed. In the adjoining factory of Messrs. Hargreaves, Dugdale, and Co., a very excellent invention of a brush is being used behind the bobbin-frames, which renders it unnecessary for the children to go under the mule.

The Factory Act of 1844 prohibited mill-owners from allowing children to clean self-acting mules while in motion, but most employers merely hung a copy of the clause in every workroom. Minders often ignored the law, and accidents were frequent. Horner (1849b: 9) argued that responsibility for such tragedies ultimately rested with the owner rather than the adult male operative, particularly as safety devices were available that made cleaning by children unnecessary.

Still, the terrible record of child death and injury does not reflect well on the male mule spinners' concern for their little helpers. Rather, it represents the "harshness and cruelty" of adult males toward factory children (Pinchbeck 1981: 195). Child piecers were commonly subject to six or eight "lickings" a day by male spinners; female spinners used gentler methods. According to one child who worked for women,

> they used to coax the piecers up . . . They used to ask them if they's mind their work, and then give 'em a halfpenny or a penny; and then the piecers was pleased and worked; and if the piecers hadn't meat, they used to give 'em meat, and marbles, and tops; and at any pastime here gives 'em money; 6d. or 1s." (quoted in Pinchbeck 1981: 187).

Unfortunately women spinners were rare.

After the Act of 1844, cleaning of machinery by little children gradually disappeared in favor of using "males over 18 years of age [who] offered the significant advantage of being able legally to clean the mules after engine hours" (Lazonick 1979: 239, 252; 1981: 502). Minders generally coerced these young men "to contribute their unpaid labour-time."

The regular working day imposed by factory legislation was itself perceived by adult male operatives as a hindrance, since their preference was often to work late into the night to make up for loafing earlier in the week (Reid 1986). The main victims of this brutal process, reproved Marx (1976: 607), were children and wives. Even after the Factory Acts came into effect in northern mills, it is likely that many skilled men continued to be absent on Mondays and Tuesdays, and thus were tempted to violate the law during the days they worked.

6. The Act of 1844

The 1833 factory law, Horner later admitted, "was in some degree legislating in the dark . . . much of it was found to have been ill-contrived and some positively so bad that it obstructed, and to a great extent prevented, the attainment of the object" (quoted in Thomas 1948: 74). In 1837, inspectors began lobbying the Whig government to amend the 1833 legislation; two years later, the government finally succumbed to pressure, and proceeded to amend the law. At the last moment, however, Lord John Russell, then Home Secretary, withdrew the factory amendment "almost certainly . . . because of the strength of the textile interest, and, behind them, the pens of the economists" (MacDonagh 1977: 59-60).

As a parting gesture, the Whigs agreed with a proposal by Ashley to establish a Commission on Children's Employment. The Commission—which for the first time surveyed both textile and non-textile industries (Neff 1966: 88) concluded in February 1841 that "what was needed was not a new law, 'but the fulfilment of the intention of the existing law.'" The government once again went through the motions to amend the Act, but with no expectation of success. Peel's second Tory administration took over after the Whig's defeat in a parliamentary vote in June, 1841. "Thus the factory act of 1833 was followed by eight years of liberal paralysis" (MacDonagh 1977: 60).

The Conservative government's Act of 1844—like the ill-fated Whig amendment bills—was based on knowledge gained by inspectors while administering the original factory legislation. Marx (1976: 393) observed that the new Act, which reduced the working day of children under thirteen to six and one-half hours and included women as a protected category, was the result of intensive manoeuvring by the Inspectorate and close relations between inspectors, reformers, and factory workers, who "especially since 1838, had made the Ten Hours Bill their economic, as they had made the Charter their political, battle cry." The Act's passage was also assisted by law-abiding manufacturers "who . . . overwhelmed Parliament with representations on the immoral 'competition' of their 'false brethren,' who were able to break the law because of their greater impudence or their more fortunate local circumstances."

For Marx (1976: 626), however, along with other historians (Hutchins and Harrison 1966: 62, 85; Halévy 1961b: 172) a key element in the success of the 1844 Act was antipathy between landowners and capitalists. This antagonism appeared, roughly, as a struggle in Parliament between Tories, representing landowners, who opposed free trade and deplored factory conditions, and Whigs, standing for the manufacturing interest, who favored abolition of the Corn Laws, and opposed factory reform.[22]

The Corn Laws, which were promulgated in 1815 by Lord Liverpool's Tory government, placed high duties on imported grain. They were meant to revive an English agricultural sector devastated by falling prices in the aftermath of the Napoleonic Wars. The Anti-Corn Law League was established in 1838 by the manufacturing interest to fight the tariff.

The League argued that the tariff kept prices high, and discriminated unfairly against workers, who spent a disproportionate amount of income on food. Throughout its history, the movement to repeal the Corn Laws was deployed against aristocratic critics of factory conditions (McCord 1991: 152-3, 165-70). However, the party lineup on the Corn Laws—as on factory legislation (Hutchins and Harrison 1966: 87)—was not a simple matter of Whigs versus Tories. Aydelotte (1954: 114, 1966) has shown that party affiliations in the 1840s "revolved around some of the principal political and social tensions of the age." Generally, Tories were more likely than Whigs to support factory legislation, and Whigs leaned toward repeal of the Corn Laws. Nevertheless, successive Whig cabinets left the Corn Laws intact, and the legislation was repealed in 1846 by Sir Robert Peel's Conservatives, partly in reaction to the potato famine in Ireland. Similarly, while the Factory Act of 1833 was a Whig measure bitterly opposed by many Tories, the 1844 law was enacted by Peel's government, with support from the Whig side of the House.

Aristocrats dominated both parties; some landed families favored the manufacturing interest for political or economic reasons; others opposed it. As Peter Mandler (1984: 85, 102-3) illustrates, the divisions in the aristocracy cut across party lines.

> For the tories the factory question posed a clear choice between the revived paternalism of Young England and the laissez-faire-oriented conservatism of Peel. . . . For the whigs the question was to what extent their alliance with middle-class liberals on constitutional questions need be extended to social questions as well.

Thus the leading Tory supporter of factory reform, Lord Ashley (later Earl of Shaftesbury), discomfited many Peelite Conservatives; and Lord Morpeth, a Whig who believed in the regulated working day, toned down his commitment to the factory cause in order to placate the manufacturers' lobby in his Yorkshire constituency.

Horner marvelled that the 1844 Factory Bill easily passed Parliament with "the extraordinary and unexpected majority of 135. Nothing could exceed the universal astonishment" (quoted in Thomas 1948: 216). The industrialists, Marx (1976: 394-5) explained, "had started their campaign to repeal the Corn Laws, and they needed the workers to help them to victory." Anti-protectionist political leaders were even promising "that the Ten Hours Bill would be enacted in the free trade millennium." Under these circumstances mill-owners could hardly "oppose a measure intended only to make the law of 1833 a reality." Protectionist landowners, on the other hand, were out to punish the capitalists for threatening "their most sacred interest, the rent of land," and a tougher Factory Act seemed suitable for this purpose. Whatever the origins of its success in Parliament, the 1844 law is unreservedly praised by Marx.

> These highly detailed specifications, which regulate, with military uniformity, the times, the limits and pauses of work by the stroke of the clock, were by no means a product of the fantasy of Members of Parliament. They developed gradually out of circumstances as natural laws of the modern mode of production. Their formulation, official recognition and proclamation by the state were the result of a long class struggle.

As Marx recognized, major changes contained in the Act followed directly from recommendations by inspectors (Hutchins and Harrison 1966: 85), particularly Leonard Horner. The chief factory inspector's reports repeatedly complained that the eight hour day permitted for children under the 1833 legislation was difficult to enforce and made it impossible for child operatives to attend school. The six and one-half hours required by the new Act—which had to be performed each workday on a "half-time" basis, either before or after 1 p.m.—simplified record-keeping and left factory children free for morning or afternoon classes. Opposition to the change was headed off by reducing the legal age of employment from nine to eight. Clauses spelling out the beginning and end of the factory day, and requiring that protected workers start work at the same time, effectively ended the relay system, and ensured that men would have to follow the same pattern as restricted employees. The Inspectorate explained that without these clauses, inspectors' own working day could not be limited. In addition, the law established a chain of command within the Inspectorate, linking it to the Home Secretary and creating a central headquarters in Whitehall (MacDonagh 1977: 67-8).

Extension of the twelve hour day to women operatives also had been canvassed by the Inspectorate. In his report of December 1843, Horner (1844a: 3-4) complained that female factory workers barely over 18 "having to be out of bed at five in the morning, and not getting home till half past eight at night, may be fairly said to labour fifteen hours and a half out of twenty-four." He suggested that women were without the physical capacity "for a continuance of work for the same length of time as men;" and that their health and well being were more important for society than that of males. Replacement of adult males by less well-paid female operatives "is attended with the worst consequences to the social condition of the working classes, by the women being withdrawn from domestic duties; and diminished comforts at home have the most corrupting influence upon the men." Horner did not advocate removal of women from the workforce, or confining them to domesticity.[23] Nevertheless, he hoped that reducing women's hours of work would create additional employment for men, and do something to relieve "a very anomalous state of things" in Lancashire, where wages for adult females were well in excess of those earned by "hundreds of young men, between 20 and 30 years of age." Insisting that a regulated working day for all mill-hands, regardless of age or sex, was the best alternative, Factory Inspector Saunders (1843: 19-20, 37;1844: 25) recommended that women under twenty-one especially should be protected along with children and young people. He pointed to the onerous "physical" and "moral" consequences of night work for females, and called for legislation to force employers to substitute men for women working late hours.

Still, Horner (1844a: 4) did not believe that the argument for the freedom of labor applied to women. "A theorist may say that these people are old enough to take care of themselves; but practically there can be no such thing as freedom of labor, when, from the redundancy of the population, there is such a competition for employment." In any case, women are "much less free agents" than men. His argument was repeated by Sir James Graham, the Home Secretary, during the debates in Parliament on the 1844 legislation.

> Did [women] decide and judge for themselves? So far as married women were concerned, the Law held distinctly the reverse. The Law held that they were under such control that they could not decide and judge for themselves, and to the female sex generally many of the rights of freedom are denied . . . Married women might clearly be influenced by their husbands, for the sake of gaining higher wages, thus to overwork themselves, and generally as to females considering that they were the weaker portion of the community, having a claim by nature on our compassion and on our care, he [Mr. Horner] thought the House would feel that they were more peculiarly entitled to protection of the legislature (quoted in Evans 1978: 51-2).

7. Patriarchy[24] and the Factory Acts

The Fabian socialist historians Barbara Hutchins and Amy Harrison (1966) saw the 1844 Act as an unmixed blessing for women workers; and until the 1970s their view, along with the analogous position of liberal legal historians, held the field (Shanley 1986: 68).

Modern feminist scholars, however, disagree on the impact of the 1844 Factory Act. The fundamental issue is whether this statute, and others like it, contributed significantly to the exclusion of women from decent jobs, and thus forced them back into the home. Among those who believe protective legislation handicapped women, some argue that the law represented a victory for men over women and capital (Hartmann 1981; Barrett 1980; Ursel 1986; Walby 1986; Bradley 1989)[25]; others, including Jane Humphries (1977; 1981), contend that by enhancing the "family wage" earned by the male head, and enforcing the sexual division of labor, it improved conditions for all members of the working class family (Humphries 1977, 1981). Those who doubt that factory law was a major factor in women's exclusion from well-paid jobs, accept the Fabian view that the legislation was a genuine victory for working women (Brenner and Ramas 1984). The safety provisions of the Factory Acts, which applied to all workers, are usually ignored in this controversy. Similarly, many critics of the Acts forget that factory reform opened up jobs for adult women who "faced competition from child labor increasingly into the nineteenth century" (Calhoun 1982: 192).[26]

Disagreements within modern feminist scholarship reflect arguments made by supporters and opponents of the law in the second half of the nineteenth century (Hutchins and Harrison 1966: 183-99; Lewis 1985: 110). While welcoming restriction of children's hours, mid-nineteenth century English feminists rehearsed Harriet Martineau's claim that protective legislation for women interfered with free contract, the open market, and the principle of self-help. "Because the tenets of classical liberalism adequately encompassed their demands for equality of treatment, feminists rarely suggested application of the factory acts to men" (Feurer 1988: 249, 255; also Lewis 1991: 6). When middle class feminist leaders grew more aware of the conditions of working women around the turn of the twentieth century, most reversed their opposition to the law. By contrast, the controversy over protective legislation raged into the 1920s in the United States (Cott 1987: 120-29; 134-42; Kessler-Harris 1982: 180-216).

The notion that adult females, especially married women, were not meant for industrial work, and should not compete with men for jobs, was forcefully held by some within male trade unions and short-time committees (Hutchins and Harrison 1966: 65, 82-3; Walby 1986: 116-19; Smelser 1959: 394).[27] But it was also the position of crusading mid-Victorian novelists, Charlotte Elizabeth Tonna and

Elizabeth Gaskell (Neff 1966: 86). A variation of this argument was made by some feminist activists late in the nineteenth century, such as Helen Bosanquet (Lewis 1991: 172). Yet most reformers, including many working class men, saw protective legislation as a clear benefit for all mill-hands, and did not perceive the law as a means of barring females from industry. Leonard Horner and the other inspectors shared this position; so did Marx. The reason was simple. Everyone at the time knew that the 1844 law would cover men as well as women. "One of the [Act's] first consequences," affirmed Marx (1976: 395), "was that in practice the working day of adult males in factories became subject to the same limitations, since in most processes of production the co-operation of children, young persons and women is indispensable." Moreover, observes Gray (1991: 41), "there was no provision [in the 1844 Act] for systematic surveillance of the health and morals of women workers, despite periodic moments of intensified public concern."

As Marx emphasized, the main object of the Act of 1844 was to bypass the ideology of free contract. By the 1840s many middle class supporters of the regulated workday, including inspectors, no longer desired age- or sex-based legislation, except in the case of young children. Along with workers' short-time committees,[28] they wanted a law that would limit the hours of everyone in textiles (Hutchins and Harrison 1966: 65-7). The only way to achieve this was to extend the legislation to women, the largest group working in the factories, and one for which a plausible case could be made in Parliament that protection was required. Inevitably, this argument appealed to patriarchal beliefs about women's domestic and reproductive role, which in turn were probably reinforced by the existence of protective legislation (Lewis 1984: 188; Humphries 1977: 253).[29]

The regulated working day was not the only impediment to women being free disposers of their own labor power. Ellen Ross (1982: 580) has shown that working class marriage was an economic contract between grossly unequal negotiators, punctuated by husband's physical and sexual violence against wives. Women's responsibility for child care and housework was taken for granted. "The failure of wives to provide such services, even for very good reason—such as a husband's refusal or inability to provide money needed for meals—was looked on by men as a major breach of their marital claims." Patriarchal tyranny stepped over from the family onto the factory floor.[30] Often women were subcontracted by their husbands or fathers or some other dominant male, so they never entered an employment contract (Lazonick 1979; Humphries 1981). But even if directly employed by the factory master, women's wages were in law and reality the property of their husbands or fathers; they rarely had an income of their own (Osterud 1986: 46).[31] Women's oppression at home helped ensure their docility at work, a quality many employers counted on (Walkowitz 1980: 20). Women, writes Wanda Neff (1966: 30), "were not restricted by the regulations of a labour union, and could be used to break strikes. They did not dispute the orders of overlookers as did the men. They would work at night when men insisted on a decent season of rest." Lacking "means of improving their condition, as the men had by their unions," and facing "the antagonism of [male] workers and the greed of employers" women's only recourse was "protection by the Government."

There were other reasons to support protective legislation. Death rates in England for female children and young women far exceeded those for males. Mortality connected with childbirth accounted for only a fraction of the difference, since females under 15, also died at a higher rate than males. "Much of the excess . . . was due to high levels of respiratory tuberculosis . . . [especially in] poor agricultural areas, and districts with large unskilled working-class populations." Compared to women and female children, males enjoyed better nutrition, had "better access to washing facilities and changes of clothing," and were not as likely to be exposed to poorly ventilated and poisonous indoor working environments (Anderson 1990: 19; also Davidoff 1990: 96; Seccombe 1986: 58).[32]

Similarly, although they applied to all factory operatives, safety regulations in the 1844 Act (discussed further below) were particularly important for female workers. The inspectors' reports are filled with harrowing descriptions of terrible injuries inflicted on female operatives by open machinery. Victorian fashion standards rather than innate sexual difference was an important factor (John 1984: 173-4; Neff 1966: 38). Girls and women with long hair were scalped by whirling gears and shafts; dresses and petticoats caught in the machinery, and dragged the helpless operative to her death or mutilation; little girls and adult women were tripped by machinery while on open factory floors and stairwells, and sent flying into the gearing several stories below.

Nineteenth century accident reports did not include worker stress and fatigue, to which overworked women and child operatives under strict male supervision were particularly susceptible (Storey 1990: 25-6, 15).[33] Brenner and Ramas (1984: 52) observe that these conditions must have had an especially harmful effect on pregnant women, who were unable "to regulate their work so as to take account of their different physical needs in pregnancy—for example, by taking frequent rest periods." Similarly, while factory inspectors fought for better ventilation in the mills, they were unaware of brown lung (byssinosis)—the deadly, long-term disease of cotton textile workers, which results in lack of oxygen, and is characterized in victims by breathing impairment and rapid ageing—or of deafness caused by the incessant roar of machinery.[34] Ailments reported by women operatives, but not considered industrial accidents, included "fallen arches, pains in the feet . . . turned in ankles and knees, . . . swelled legs . . . enlarged veins . . . general weakness . . . bad eyesight . . . wounds and ulcers on the legs" (Neff 1966: 39).

Code words like "seduction" and "loose morals" used by Victorian reformers to describe relations between children, women and men in the mills, were dishonest and incoherent gestures toward the reality of male violence, rape, and sexual harassment in the workplace (Clark 1987: 92-103; Tucker 1990: 36; Backhouse and Cohen 1978: 68-70).[35] Women daring enough to leave the confines of home were seen as wantons and social rejects (Lewis 1984: 184-6; Walkowitz 1980: 33-4). While it is likely that male oppression was no worse in textiles than elsewhere (Hewitt 1958: 48-61), the atmosphere of sexual abuse and economic exploitation may explain why most females operatives favored the 1844 law restricting night work, and limiting the working day. Thus Marx (1976: 394) quoted Horner's report of 1844-45 which "states ironically: 'No instances have come to my knowledge of adult women having expressed any regret at *their* rights being interfered with.'"

In a study of the movement for shorter hours in the United States, Roediger and Foner (1989: 165) suggest that women, burdened by housework and a paid job—and yet accustomed to setting their own pace of work at home—may been especially sensitive to the value of time, and "to the deadening aspects of capitalist labor discipline."[36] The history of working women's attitude toward factory legislation lends support to this argument. In 1848, Chief Inspector Horner (1849a: 14-15; also Neff 1966: 76) made the revolutionary decision to consult women on the matter. However, his survey of 1153 operatives—which is erroneously reported in *Capital*[37]—concerned the newly implemented ten hour day, rather than protective legislation itself. Respondents were asked to choose between a ten, eleven, or twelve hour day. A bare majority of women agreed with the new regime; 10 percent opted for eleven hours; more than a quarter desired a return to the twelve hour standard. None objected to the regulated workday.[38] Far more men than women favored the new law. But, as we shall see, the Ten Hours Act created chaos in the factories and led to dramatically increased exploitation of women and children (MacDonagh 1977: 70). Female operatives' unenthusiastic support for the 1847 Ten Hours Act may reflect unsettled conditions then prevailing in the mills.

While the factory cause was dominated by men, working class women likely played an important part in the struggle for shorter hours, just as they did in the Owenite and Chartist movements (Taylor 1982; Thompson 1984: 121). Throughout the second half of the nineteenth century most female workers (with the significant exception of women in coal mines [John 1984: 148]) much preferred sex-based workday legislation to the alternative of no legislation at all (Feurer 1988: 251; Lewis 1984). In the United States, women workers were in the forefront of the earliest campaigns to limit hours, and they made a powerful feminist argument for protective legislation, which "centered not on woman's 'biological' disadvantages but on her double oppression as a wage-worker and a homemaker, and on her subjection to sexual harassment" (Roediger and Foner 1989: 276).[39] In 1925, a comprehensive survey of 500 unorganized New York state women workers gave an "overwhelmingly affirmative vote" for protective legislation; a "much less precise" national study conducted in the same year produced comparable results (Hunnicutt 1988: 68-9).

The 1844 Act did not prevent or discourage women from working in textiles; nor is it likely that it caused women's exclusion from well-paying or skilled jobs, such as cotton spinning (Brenner and Ramas 1984: 41). Women were already designated as a cheap labor force prior to industrialization (Berg 1985: 140; Rose 1988: 197-8; Pinchbeck 1981); they were excluded from some forms of cotton spinning by men's spinning unions (Berg 1985: 150, 160), and by changes in the labor process (Freifeld 1986: 335-7), well in advance of the 1844 Act. However, women dominated weaving before the Acts, and continued to do so at relatively high wages once factory legislation was in place (Walton 1990: 360-61). Although women's skills were not adequately reflected in the size of their wage packet, employers (including working class male contractors of female labor) were well aware that women's skills were vital for the industry (Berg 1985: 151-2). Female employment in textiles increased throughout the nineteenth century; this trend was pronounced in the case of married women, and those with young children (Walton 1990: 388).[40]

8. "A Delusive Law" on Education

The Factory Inspectorate advocated state-funded education for child operatives, but an early version of the 1844 Act, which contained provisions for adequate financing of factory schools, was "opposed by the Dissenters on the ground that too much control was given to the Church, and it was consequently thrown out" (Hutchins and Harrison 1966: 79). Although Horner warned against the failed bill's religious bias, his advice was disregarded (Roberts 1960: 246-7); Engels (1969: 202) recorded at the time that workers' short-time committees were "divided on the question and therefore inactive." Nevertheless, the Inspectorate "arranged that fines inflicted for breaches of the law should be paid into a banking account to be applied . . . for the establishment and support of day schools for factory children" (Thomas 1948: 214). Marx (1976: 523) quoted Horner's own judgment in his 1857 *Report* on the illusory nature of the education clauses.

> For this the legislature is alone to blame, by having passed a delusive law, which, while it . . . provide[s] that the children employed in factories shall be *educated*, contains no enactment by which that professed end can be secured. It provides nothing more than that the children shall on certain days of the week, and for a certain number of hours (three) in each day, be enclosed within the four walls of a place called a school, and that the employer of the child shall receive weekly a certificate to that effect signed by a person designated by the subscriber as a schoolmaster or schoolmistress.

The fate of the education clauses illustrates both the importance and limitations of the Factory Inspectorate. Inspectors could depend on the workers' movement for support in extending regulations on the working day, but not for an efficient system of education. Before 1840, short-time committees opposed education for factory children; working men feared state intrusion on parental rights, including that of prying an income from offspring. But in the 1840s many came to accept classroom training, and the factory cause reflected this change. Education, however, never became a focus of workers' agitation against manufacturers (Smelser 1959: 297). Partly as a result, schooling after 1844 remained in many cases very poor.

Relying on the inspectors' reports, Marx (1976: 523-5) criticized the "tricks and dodges" employed by factory occupiers to elude the education clauses, including exclusion "from employment [of] children who are obliged to attend school." Conditions in factory schools were impossible, as children of various ages crammed into dim, noisy and damp rooms lacking books and furniture. Many teachers signed the weekly certificate of schooling required for each child "with a cross, as they themselves were unable to write." The exertions of inspectors to improve education facilities, said Marx quoting from government sources, "were successful only in this, that since the passing of the Act of 1844, 'the figures in the school certificate must be filled up in the handwriting of the schoolmaster, who must also sign his Christian and surname in full.'"

Still, Marx (1976: 613-14) was impressed by the "education clauses of the Act," which "do proclaim that elementary education is a compulsory pre-condition for the employment of children." These clauses (resembling measures advocated by Robert Owen) show that

> the germ of the education of the future is present in the factory system; this education will, in the case of every child of a given age, combine productive labour with instruction and gymnastics, not only as one of the methods of adding to the efficiency of production, but as the only method of producing fully developed human beings.

Education of children in the factories as a prelude to communism! Clearly, Marx was far from modern notions of "social control," according to which humanitarian efforts at education by middle class reformers and others are only disguised means of affirming the existing order (Van Krieken 1986: 403). Gillian Sutherland (1990: 129) counsels that "all education is social control . . . The interesting question is not *whether* a given educational scheme is designed as social control but *what* sort of society is it intended to produce?" As Craig Calhoun (1981: 224) submits, Marx, like Hegel, "believed that progress of social life was directly matched in the progress of consciousness, that what truly mattered in human history appeared as rational in human consciousness." This is why Marx inclined to Hegel's view of the importance of state-sponsored education for children: like other aspects of factory law the clauses on education represented for Marx (1976: 619, 411-12) a revolutionary alteration in the conditions of the working class.

Though the Factory Act, that first and meagre concession wrung from capital, is limited to combining elementary education with work in the factory, there can be no doubt that, with the inevitable conquest of political power by the working class, technological education, both theoretical and practical, will take its proper place in the schools of the workers.

Accordingly, Marx used the phrase "social control" not to describe capital's domination over the working class, but to explain the state's role in taming the bourgeoisie. Capital's unrestrained extension of the working day, said Marx, "called forth, in opposition to this, social control, which legally limits, regulates and makes uniform the working day and its pauses."

Was Marx wrong about the benefits of government intervention? The Factory Act of 1833 was the first major breakthrough in the effort to bring education to the working classes; the Act of 1844 improved on this by actually giving factory children the time to go to school. Sutherland (1990: 130, 143) acknowledges that factory legislation may have had no real impact on school attendance. Yet, it differed from Sunday school (which merely gave working class children something to do on a day they did not have to work), by actually offering child operatives time off for education; and it disclosed "at least" that "middle class enthusiasts" thought that poor children "should be in school, not work." By signalling the intention of the state to provide schooling for poor children, factory law set the stage for the Education Act of 1870 which "at last created a mechanism to provide an elementary school wherever needed."

9. "Revolutionizing People's Minds"

As they appear in *Capital* Horner and most of the other inspectors are exemplars of Marx's (1976: 614) dictum that "large-scale industry . . . is capable of revolutionizing people's minds through the transformation it brings about in the material mode of production and the social relations of production." A member of the stony-hearted Chadwick Commission into Factory Labour, Horner was imbued with unquestioning faith in the principles of political economy and the good will of cotton masters (Roberts 1960: 169). He shared with his brother Francis (whose untimely death Leonard called, "the greatest calamity of my life" [quoted in Martin 1969: 414]) a repugnance for exploitation of child labor, and also an unreserved belief in the free contract between "master and man." In his early days as an inspector Horner's chief concern was that enough children were available in relays to assist adult workers throughout the fifteen hour day. He sympathized with factory occupiers about "legislative interference," and expected only a few months would be required before capitalists recognized the importance and necessity of the 1833 Act (Thomas 1948: 75-6, 116).

Horner's views shifted radically after his first few years as an inspector. His reports were soon filled with complaints about evasions of the law by factory masters, and the "overworking" of adult operatives of both sexes. Horner was constantly aware of the danger of coming down too hard on controversial issues, lest he embarrass his political superiors and lose his own credibility (Thomas 1948: 255-6). He rarely neglected to mention law-abiding manufacturers who supported the principles of the Factory Acts. He knew reference to such individuals would be enormously helpful for advocates of the factory cause. Nevertheless, his cautiously worded reports made it clear that Horner had soon decided that the legislated working day should apply to adult female and male operatives, as well as to children and young people. In 1843, for example, he (1844a: 4) wrote that mill-owners were taking advantage of distressed conditions in the industry to employ workers beyond 12 hours at wages lower than they had previously earned. "Some of their workpeople get no more than they do for 12 hours, but they dare not object. As to freedom of labour, no such thing exists at present: it is employment on almost any terms, or starvation."

The most dramatic shift in the consciousness of the Inspectorate related to the ten hour day. The shorter workday for all operatives was a fundamental element of working class political agitation, one the inspectors were reluctant to embrace. As Perkin (1969: 264) observes, "it required extraordinary independence of mind [for middle class professionals] to adopt the working class ideal." However, once factory inspectors accepted the workers' position they became its most energetic and influential advocates. A consistent opponent of the ten hours cause on grounds that it would have a disastrous impact on industrial output, workers' income, and employment, Horner changed his mind in 1848 after his survey of mill-hands' attitude toward the reduced workday. Marx (1976: 538; Horner 1850b: 5) mentioned Horner's about-face, which the latter first recorded in his report of 1850.

I continue to receive favourable accounts of the working of the Ten Hours Act. That great experiment, dangerous as it appeared to so

many, and to myself among others, because of so sudden a change
from twelve to ten hours, has succeeded, so far as it has been tried,
beyond what the most sanguine of those who were favourable to it
ventured to anticipate.

After 1848 inspectors publicly abandoned belief in the validity of
the free contract between labor and capital. The contract could only
be "free" if the state were there to legislate and enforce its terms.
The Inspectorate's reversal was so complete that Marx (1976: 415)
could borrow from Inspector Saunders's 1848 report to back up the
International Working Men's 1866 resolution for the eight hour day.
"Further steps toward the reformation of society," declared the
English bureaucrat, "can never be carried out with any hope of
success, unless the hours of labour be limited, and the prescribed
limit strictly enforced."

The primary cause of the Inspectorate's change of mind was
reaction by the capitalist class to the 1847 Ten Hours Bill. Paradoxically, the bill's passage ended up threatening the entire edifice of
factory legislation so painfully built by inspectors since 1833.
Capital's bloodthirsty assault fixed the allegiance of inspectors with
the workers' movement, and determined the course of factory
legislation for the next fifty years.[41]

10. Tiger at the Gates

The sudden intrusion on the shop-floor of determined government agents ended forever the palmy days of the "factory code" in
which "the capitalist formulates his autocratic power over his
workers like a private legislator . . . [and the] overseer's book of
penalties replaces the slave-driver's lash" (Marx 1976: 549-50).[42]
The bright state tiger at the gates panicked mill-owners into howling
resistance that continued unabated for over thirty years. "Nothing
characterizes the spirit of capital better," advised Marx, "than the
history of the English factory legislation from 1833 to 1864." The
height of fury was reached in the decade following 1847, but dress-
rehearsals for the employers' maximum offensive began long before.

The 1832 Factory Commission report praised "the enlightened
large employer" and associated "the worst practices with backward
and marginal producers;" this argument, Gray (1987: 162) notes, was
repeated in "the subsequent debate and much more recent commentary." Gray's research on factory occupiers, however, and that of
others (Yarmie 1984; Howe 1984) find little support for this view.

The firm opposition of capital to factory regulation was evident as early as 1818 when mill-owners combined to defeat the efforts of the pioneering Stockport short-time movement (Glen 1984: 72). "Whatever the congruence between particular measures and the interests of sections of employers, and whatever benefits they might *ex post facto*, have perceived, most extensions of the factory acts were vigorously resisted" (Gray 1987: 166). This is also the picture that emerges from *Capital*.

Marx (1976: 392) showed that capital's first attacks were aimed at provisions in the 1833 Act calling for gradual increase from eleven to thirteen of the upper age limit for children restricted to an eight hour day. "The nearer the deadline approached for the full implementation of the Factory Act, the fatal year 1836, the wilder became the rage of the mob of manufacturers." In 1836 cowed legislators passed an amendment lowering the age limit from thirteen to twelve, but it succeeded by only two: effectively a defeat for the government.

Defeated in Parliament, mill-owners resorted to deception to circumvent the Act. Forged certificates were produced for under-aged children; physicians bribed to give false certificates of birth; parents induced to illegally put their infants "through the mill"; most pernicious of all, manufacturers set up the "false relay system," where children worked in teams staggered at random. Observed Marx (1976: 393),

> the beauty of this system [was] that it annulled the whole Factory Act, not only in spirit, but in the letter. How could factory inspectors, with this complex book-keeping in respect of each individual child or young person, enforce the legally determined hours of work, and compel the employers to grant the legal meal-times?

The manufacturers' guerilla tactics shocked Horner, who by 1838 felt that few mill-owners had genuine sympathy or regard for their employees (Ward 1962: 213-14). From the late 1830s his reports criticized shortcomings in the 1833 Act and wilful evasion by employers. In 1842, Horner (1842b: 3) wrote of offending mill-owners' "ingenuity . . . stimulated by gain and uncontrolled by any sense of honesty."

11. "A Pro-Slavery Rebellion in Miniature"

In the "protracted and more or less concealed civil war between the capitalist class and the working class," (Marx 1976: 412) the proletariat won what seemed to be a decisive victory with the passage of the 1847 Ten Hours Bill. Abolition of the Corn Laws by their leader Peel—who argued that protectionism no longer served the interests of the country—had thrown the governing Tories into disarray. After the Conservative government's defeat, victorious Whigs found themselves divided on the law to limit working hours. Working class agitation worried opponents of protectionist law, and the Ten Hours Bill, which narrowly failed in 1846, easily passed the next year (Halévy 1961b: 138, 171-2). The workers, Marx (1976: 395) opined, "found allies in the Tories, who were panting for revenge. Despite the fanatical opposition of the Free Traders, headed by Bright and Cobden, the Ten Hours' Bill, so long struggled for, made its way through Parliament." The Bill stated that by May, 1848 the working day for young persons and women (and, by implication, for adult males as well) would be limited to ten hours. Parliamentary success ignited huge celebrations throughout the mill districts.

> Broadsheets elaborately and expensively printed in black and gold setting out the terms of the new Act and commemorating the leaders of the struggle, were widely distributed. Medals were struck in honour of the great occasion, and the Queen herself accepted a gold medal presented to her by Lord Ashley on behalf of her grateful subjects in the mills and factories (Thomas 1948: 297).

Working class joy was more than matched by gloom among capitalists, who instantly embarked on a vicious campaign to undermine the law. Amidst the economic crisis of 1846-47, wages were slashed ten percent; to compensate for the coming reduction of hours, pay packets were to be slashed a further twenty-five percent. Mill-owners propagandized among operatives for repeal of the Act. Said Marx (1976: 397), "no method of deceit, seduction or intimidation was left unused; but all in vain. [The workers] felt themselves to be oppressed, but by something different from the Factory Act."

The Ten Hours Act came into force on schedule, but within months the bourgeoisie was wallowing in a high tide of reaction (Yarmie 1984: 144). The Chartist movement had been destroyed, its leaders arrested and its organizations dismantled. Defeat of the June insurrection in France "united, in England as on the Continent, all fractions of the ruling classes . . . under the common slogan of the salvation of property, religion, the family and society" (Marx 1976: 396).

Encouraged by the political climate, manufacturers took advantage of weaknesses in the Factory Acts to overturn all their provisions.

"At no time since the Act of 1833," Horner (1849b: 7) despaired, "has the factory law been in so unsatisfactory a state to all parties as it has been during the last year."

The initial victories of this "pro-slavery rebellion in miniature," as Marx (1976: 398) called it, depended on the English state's failure to restrict adult male working hours. After 1844, when protected groups left the factory for the evening, adult males usually stopped as well. While the 1844 law was being drafted, Horner urged that the best way to restrict illegal employment of protected groups was to limit the workday for everyone to thirteen-and-a-half hours: twelve hours for work, and the balance for meals. But Parliament resisted his proposal. The factory day remained from 5.30 in the morning to 8.30 at night, or fifteen hours. Working protected groups in relays was curbed by a complicated set of provisions on hours of beginning and end of work, meal-times, and so forth (Thomas 1948: 301). The Ten Hours Act, which ran concurrently with the laws of 1833 and 1844, retained this system for young persons and women, with no special clauses for children (Lubenow 1971: 145).

In the first heady days, factory occupiers sacked protected workers and restored night-work for men. Then they distorted provisions for meal breaks and used the false relay system[43] to run the factories until late in the evening with protected workers assisting at the machines. Marx and Engels must have been especially familiar with this system, since Engels's family firm (Erman and Engels of Seedly) was used as an example by Horner [1850a: 7] and successfully prosecuted for employing relays. Under capital's direction, the Factory Acts became black comedy. Children and other protected categories were dragged in and out of work-shops at various intervals during the entire fifteen hour factory day.

> As on the stage, the same persons had to appear in turn in the different scenes of the different acts. And just as an actor is committed to the stage throughout the whole course of the play, so the workers were committed to the factories for the whole 15 hours, without reckoning the time taken in coming and going (Marx 1976: 403).

12. "A Species of Revolutionary Commissioner"

Mill-owners fought the Inspectorate in press and Parliament, using terms that resembled those of Senator McCarthy and his supporters in their assaults a century later on "card-carrying

Communists" in the U.S. government.[44] "They attacked the factory inspector as a species of revolutionary commissioner reminiscent of the Convention, who would ruthlessly sacrifice the unfortunate factory workers to his mania for improving the world" (Marx 1976: 396). Manufacturers worried about "the implication that factory legislation might hold for their relations with the working classes . . . A Stalybridge manufacturer greeted the Ten Hours Act as 'one of the dilutions of communism'" (Howe 1984: 184). Horner (1848b: 3) responded with notices in local newspapers warning against illegal working of children through the false relay system. He also organized the survey of workers' opinions examined earlier in the chapter—"one of the first such surveys . . . ever undertaken in England" (Driver 1946: 482).

Besieged by manufacturers, Home Secretary Sir George Grey instructed factory inspectors not to prosecute "mill owners for a breach of the letter of the Act or for employment of young persons in relays" (Hutchins and Harrison 1966: 103). Three of the four inspectors ignored Grey, declaring "that the Home Secretary had no dictatorial powers enabling him to suspend the laws" (Marx 1976: 401, 404). Responding to "this revolt of capital," as Marx described it, Horner prosecuted offending manufacturers and ensured that violations of the law received local and national publicity. Horner (e.g. 1849b: 4; 1851b: 5-6) also pointed out that magistrates friendly to factory occupiers, or who were mill-owners themselves, were refusing to convict employers brought to court by the Inspectorate.

In desperation Horner took a test case on the relay system to the Exchequer court in 1850. Noting that any law restraining the free exercise of capital "must be construed stringently" (quoted in Fraser 1984: 27), the court turned him down. "Great remedial measure nullified," wrote Lord Ashley, Horner's parliamentary ally. "The work to be done all over again; and I seventeen years older than when I began" (quoted in Finlayson 1981: 295). Writing at the same time, Engels agreed: "This verdict was tantamount to an abrogation of the Ten Hours Bill" (quoted in Marx 1976: 404).

Triumphant mill-owners renewed a compromise offer which would end the relay system for women and young persons in exchange for a ten and one-half hour day (Finlayson 1981: 295-6). In the meantime, Marx (1976:405) recounted, a "great number of manufacturers, who until then had been afraid to use the shift system for young persons and women, now seized upon it enthusiastically." The flood of violations was met by rebellion in the northern mill districts. Threatening meetings were called in Lancashire and Yorkshire at which the Ten Hours Act was denounced as "a Parliamentary fraud. . . . [T]he factory inspectors urgently warned the government that class antagonisms had reached an unheard-of degree of tension." Even some manufacturers grumbled about a system that made equitable application of the law impossible.

A compromise was reached in "the supplementary Factory Act of 1850." The new Act added one-half hour to each weekday, and reduced Saturday labor by one half-hour. In exchange for a weekly increase of two hours, the workers achieved a decisive breakthrough. Following Horner's proposal of almost a decade before, the normal working day was defined to coincide with the legal period of employment for protected factory operatives. "The work had to take place between 6 a.m. and 6 p.m., with pauses of not less than 1½ hours for meal times . . . By this the relay system was ended once and for all."

While it marked a watershed in the history of factory legislation (Hutchins and Harrison 1966: 107), the Act did not terminate capital's campaign of sabotage. The laws of 1847 and 1850 applied only to young persons and women; children were still covered by the unamended 1844 Act, and could be legally employed anytime between 5.30 in the morning and 8.30 at night. "This was sharp practice indeed, for those who supported the compromise had been led to expect that the measure would apply to children equally with young persons and women, and that the mills would, in fact, close at six o'clock at night" (Thomas 1948: 323). Ashley's attempts to have children brought under the 1850 legislation were quashed in Parliament by critics who claimed he was really trying to protect adult male operatives under the guise of helping little children (Finlayson 1981: 299-300). The Factory Inspectorate reported in July 1850 that almost 4,000 children in 257 factories were being used in double shifts to assist males over eighteen after young persons and women left work.

> Workers and factory inspectors protested on hygienic and moral grounds, but Capital answered:
> "My deeds upon my head! I crave the law,
> The penalty and forfeit of my bond" (Marx 1976: 399).

Renewed agitation and resistance from short-time committees allowed Horner to prepare a bill, introduced by Lord Palmerston in

1853, that restricted children's hours to those of other protected categories. There was no mention of adult male "free agents," but the new law applied to them as well. "Henceforth, with few exceptions, the Factory Act of 1850 regulated the working day of all workers in all the branches of industry subject to it. By then, half a century had elapsed since the first Factory Act" (Marx 1976: 408). The Ten Hours Act was limited to the textile industry, and failed explicitly to cover adult males. Because of capital's mad resistance it took more than five years for the 1847 legislation to have real effect. Nothing about the Act or its implementation indicates that capital or its representatives welcomed state intervention, as some Marxist and social control theorists have suggested. If it could have done, "capital in general" would have resisted regulation of the working day until doomsday. As Gray (1987: 173) remarks, "if . . . factory legislation is in some sense in the logic of capitalism, there is nothing in that logic to fix the standard working day at ten hours."[45]

13. "Association for the Mangling of Operatives"

Beaten in its efforts to subvert legislation on the working day in the textile industry, capital turned its guns on the health and safety provisions of the Acts, which had become "constantly more particular, more detailed, and more scientifically directed" (Hutchins and Harrison 1966: 201). The bourgeoisie's "suppression of all precautionary measures as to the safety, comfort and health of the workers," Marx suggested, accounts for "a great part of the casualty lists that tot up the injured and dead of the industrial army" (1981: 182). In the middle of the nineteenth century, therefore, we find the same outlook that has sanctioned—to take only one example—the auto industry's twenty-year resistance to airbags and other government safety measures (Claybrook 1984), and the consequent slaughter of hundreds of thousands on the roads of North America alone: "'killing no murder' if done for the sake of profit" (Marx 1981: 183).

Safety provisions, unlike other forms of factory regulation, applied directly to adult males as well as to protected categories. This gave the mill-owners' "free agent" argument exceptional force. Writes Howe (1984: 188),

> the classic issues were raised, namely unequal treatment of the manufacturers at the hands of an aristocratic state, and the key issue

of *laissez-faire* in political theory, namely how far the individual should be protected from the consequences of his own carelessness. It was argued that while a child should be protected from dangerous machinery, to protect an adult would be a serious limitation upon his right of self-direction.

Capital, exclaimed Marx (1976: 611), displayed

> fanatical opposition . . . to those clauses which imposed on them a slight expenditure on appliances for protecting the arms and hands of their 'hands.' Here is yet another dazzling vindication of the free-trade dogma that, in a society of mutually antagonistic interests, each individual furthers the common welfare by seeking his own personal advantage.

Horner was at the center of this conflict, as in 1853 he had per-suaded Palmerston "to issue a circular requiring all shafts, even those seven feet above the floor to be fenced" (Roberts 1960: 248; Bartrip 1979: 29). Scores of workers had been caught and mangled or killed by unprotected shafts, even mechanisms located close to the factory ceiling.

Embittered manufacturers, who "during the entire period from 1844 to 1854 . . . had not taken the least bit notice of" safety provisions (Marx 1981: 184), formed Associations for the Amendment of the Factory Laws to fight the legislation. These were the first organized expression of English employers' interests. The umbrella body formed in 1855—the National Association of Factory Occupiers (nicknamed by Charles Dickens, the "Association for the Mangling of Operatives" [Hutchins and Harrison 1966: 116])—employed methods similar to those used by modern pressure groups. "Members of Parliament were solicited, campaign funds established, advertisements placed in prominent papers, pamphlets published and deputations organized" (Yarmie 1984: 149). A factory inspector estimated that individual membership costs for this alliance exceeded the expenditure necessary for most manufacturers to install safety devices required by law (Marx 1981: 183).

Inspectors found themselves battling not only manufacturers but also their political commanders at Home Office, Palmerston and his successor Sir George Grey, who were inundated with petitions from mill-owners abusing the Chief Inspector and calling for his immedi-ate dismissal (Bartrip 1979: 29-32).

Grey, observed Marx (1981: 184), "proposed a compromise solution in April 1855, by which the government would be content with safe-guards that were scarcely more than nominal, [but] the Association rejected even this." In 1856, after a series of reversals in court, factory occupiers managed—with help, Marx submitted, from "one of those pious persons whose prominently displayed religion makes them always ready to do dirty work for the knights of the money bag"—to put through an Act of Parliament that nullified important safety clauses and referred complaints by injured workers to the courts and an arbitration panel of expert machine makers and engineers (Bartrip 1979: 47). The legislation was influenced by testimony from "the celebrated engineer William Fairburn [who] used his reputation as an expert in the defence of economy and the violated freedom of capital" (Marx 1981: 184).

Substitution of mill-owners' paid experts for testimony by "intelligent and observant men who are daily employed in the factory" appalled Horner (quoted in Hutchins and Harrison 1966: 118-19). Engineers and machine makers, he remarked, "look only to the construction and working of the machine, which is their business, and not to the prevention of accidents, which is not their business." He refused to prosecute cases under the Act since their outcome was a foregone conclusion. Thereafter the Inspectorate "made little use of arbitration; and the system was abolished in 1891" (Djang 1942: 153). Manufacturers had won a round, but their "trade union" (Marx 1981: 183) failed to achieve its larger goal of erasing the Factory Acts. "It was the last occasion for concerted opposition among cotton masters, and so facilitated overall acceptance of legislation" (Howe 1984: 188-9).

Two years after its victory in Parliament the National Association of Factory Occupiers disappeared (Bartrip 1979: 47). Marx claimed in 1865 that accidents had dropped substantially "principally due to the introduction of new machines which were already provided with safety-guards, which the factory-owners could leave in existence as they did not cost them any extra" (1981: 184). Manufacturers were also chastened by costly court settlements on behalf of injured workers.

Bartrip and Fenn (1980) contend that safety inspection had a limited impact on accident rates; nevertheless until machinery that incorporated certain safety devices became available most factory occupiers evinced slight interest in preventing accidents. "So much," reflected Marx (1981: 185), "for economy in the means of protecting the lives and limbs of workers—including many children—from dangers that directly arise from their use of machinery."

14. "The Children Were Quite Simply Slaughtered"

Historians (e.g., Joyce 1980; Howe 1984; Gray 1987) agree with Marx (1976: 408-9) that once the principle of a regulated workday triumphed, the British textile industry flourished "hand in hand with the physical and moral regeneration of the workers." Capitulation by factory occupiers to the rule of law meant that capital's overall resistance to the Acts "gradually weakened, while at the same time the working class's power of attack grew with the number of its allies in those social layers not directly interested in the question." From 1860 onwards tremendous gains were made in the application of the Factory Acts. Levine (1987: 188) and Seccombe (1990: 184-5) suggest that the success of factory law led to the decline of the birth rate in England (which began in the textile districts in the 1870s) because "the cost of children rose as a result of their falling industrial participation." Still, as Marx (1976: 610) emphasized, "capital never becomes reconciled to such changes."

A steady drumbeat for workday regulation in industries other than textiles was raised by the English public service at least since the 1842 Report of the Children's Employment Commission had revealed, in Nassau Senior's words, "the most frightful picture of avarice, selfishness and cruelty on the part of masters and parents, and of juvenile and infantile misery, degradation and destruction ever presented" (quoted in Marx 1976: 623-4). Vicious practices recorded by the Commission were exceeded only by "the coldness and apathy" with which its Report was received (Hutchins and Harrison 1966: 129).

If improvement was rapid in textiles, everywhere else the industrial nightmare continued. Children and women, Marx (1976: 592-9) noted, did the "night-work in salt mines, candle factories and chemical works;" they sorted filthy, disease-ridden rags imported from around the world to be "used for manure, for making bedflocks, for shoddy, and [to] serve as raw material for paper." Others found jobs in mining, tile and brick-making industries. Marx quoted from the *Public Health Reports* of the chief medical officer of the Privy Council, who declared that workers are unable alone to effect changes in their miserable conditions. "The life of myriads of workmen and workwomen is now uselessly tortured and shortened by the never-ending physical suffering that their mere occupation begets." The worst conditions of all occurred in domestic industries. "The average age at which the children start work is 6 years, but in many cases it is below 5." The working day varied from twelve to eighteen hours, depending on the state of trade. Little children huddled and strained at their work in overcrowded, cold, airless rooms, supervised by women armed with canes. "Thus do the children enjoy life until the age of twelve or fourteen. The wretched half-starved parents think of nothing but getting as much as possible out of their children."

Even within textiles large exemptions had been granted to silk manufacturers who pleaded that the fragile texture of the fabric demanded the lightness of touch possessed only by the very young.

> The children were quite simply slaughtered for the sake of their delicate fingers, just as horned cattle are slaughtered in southern Russia for their hides and fat . . . Despite the protests of the factory inspectors, repeated every six months, this evil has lasted to the present day (Marx 1976: 406-7).

The first sustained advance of factory reform outside of textiles came in allied industries like print works, bleach and dye works, and lace factories. Sharing locality and workforce with regulated industries, these enterprises created resentment among mill-owners, who protested that competitors who escaped the law were stealing their business. Insisting upon equivalent conditions of exploitation of labor in every sphere of production "as its own innate right," Marx (1976: 520) explained, "capital is by its nature a leveller . . . the limitation by law of children's labour in one branch of industry results in its limitation in others." However, the struggle for regulation was no less bitter for all the apparent rationality of reform, which anyhow was lost on "the particular group threatened. The Bleachworks and Dyeworks Act of 1860, often cited as evidence for progressive extension of factory legislation, had been successfully postponed by bleachers after it was first proposed in 1854" (Howe 1984: 190). Stormy debate in Parliament over the Bill, observed Hutchins and Harrison (1966: 137) "reminds us of the factory crusades of earlier times."

Savage work methods in industries allied to textiles were common knowledge, particularly those in lace making where much work was done in private dwellings. Children's Employment Commissioners in 1842 discovered infants of three and four hired for wages in lace making. "Among the little embroiderers some were so young when they began that they could not reach the regular frame on which the work was being stretched and were therefore obliged to stand"

(Pinchbeck 1981: 233). In 1862 it was not unusual for children aged five and six, often younger, to be employed in crowded, stench-ridden chambers from eight in the morning until eight at night; girls aged twelve and older often toiled much longer. Dyeworks and bleachworks notorious for an overwhelming incidence of respiratory and nervous diseases among employees, were the first to be regulated under the Acts; lace factories, though not lace makers in private homes (who employed the vast majority of women and children in this sector) were covered in 1861.

In 1862, Shaftesbury (formerly Lord Ashley) got through a motion in Parliament for a new investigation of the employment of children and young persons, and a Commission was formed a year later (Finlayson 1981: 407). Marx (1976: 609) was so impressed with the "thoroughly conscientious investigations of the Children's Employment Commission" that he compared their understanding of "the spirit of the capitalist mode of production" with Engels's *The Condition of the Working Class in England*. Six separate reports were issued between 1863 and 1867; the concluding volume recommended extension of the Acts to almost 1.5 million children, young persons and women working in large and small industries and in private dwellings. These proposals, Marx enthused, "threaten to deprive all the important branches of English industry of their 'freedom,' with the exception of agriculture, mining and transport."

Public opinion had shifted far enough in favor of reform that the Commission's earliest proposals for regulation of earthenware manufactures (including glass and pottery), matches, percussion caps, hosiery and lace and other enterprises were readily accepted; its final recommendations were put into bills in early 1867 by the Tory government. However, the huge expansion of protected workers was coupled with a feeble increase in Factory Act personnel (Bartrip 1982: 613). Further, the legislation regressed from earlier law "by a mass of vicious exemptions and cowardly compromises with the masters" (Marx 1976: 625-6). An addition to *Capital* by Engels contrasted Parliament's "extraordinary and extensive measures" with the "hesitation, the unwillingness and the bad faith with which it actually put these measures into practice."

The battle to extend the Acts beyond textiles demonstrated once again that working class parents were among the major obstacles to workday reform. Application of the Factory Acts to domestic industries threatened not only capital's free contract with labor, but also the right of parents to treat children as property.[46]

As long as factory legislation is confined to regulating labour done in factories, etc., it is regarded only as an interference with capital's right of exploitation. But when it comes to regulating so-called "domestic labour" this is . . . viewed as a direct attack on the *patria potestas*, or, in modern terms, parental authority (Marx 1976: 620).

Marx (1976: 620) quoted approvingly from the Children's Employment Commission's 1866 report that "it is, unhappily, to a painful degree apparent throughout the whole of the evidence, that against no persons do the children of both sexes so much require protection as against their parents." He disagreed with the Commissioners that parental abuse was chiefly responsible for child labor.

It is not however the misuse of parental power that created the direct or indirect exploitation of immature labour-powers by capital, but rather the opposite, i. e. the capitalist mode of exploitation, by sweeping away the economic foundation which corresponded to parental power, made the use of parental power into its misuse.

Whatever the circumstances that led to it, Marx agreed with the Commissioners that working class parents were responsible for enslavement of their children. "The rights of the children," averred Marx, "had to be proclaimed."

15. "The Mental Functions of the Capitalists and Their Retainers"

Marx's account makes clear that in the crucial years after 1853 the pivotal source of movement for factory regulation passed over almost entirely to inspectors.[47] His narrative offers little support for the argument that use of state power followed the expressed (or even unconscious) wish of the English bourgeoisie and its aristocratic allies. Nor could Marx have agreed with the influential idea that the state was only relatively autonomous of the ruling classes. Parliament doubtless was a tool of landlord and capitalist, but the bureaucracy it created had Faustian dimensions (Roberts 1960: 96).[48] For Marx, Horner and the other inspectors carried the day through their alliances with the proletariat, the middle classes, and elements among the aristocracy and (to a lesser extent) manufacturers. Marx's assessment is shared by historians of the Acts. The shift in favor of factory regulation, write Hutchins and Harrison (1966: 122), "is doubtless to be sought in the factory inspectors' reports."

The bureaucracy's most dangerous enemy was always the "class loyalty" of the masters, who felt "a strong class animus" for the

Factory Inspectorate (Howe 1984: 184). Another key adversary of the Inspectorate was the school of "classical economics [which] takes the historical function of the capitalist in grim earnest" (Marx 1976: 742). Viewing the worker solely "as a machine for the production of surplus value," political economy, and especially its vulgarizers, became a chief instrument in capital's war against factory law. Novelist, historian and women's rights activist Harriet Martineau was one of the most effective propagandists against the Acts, assisting the National Association of Factory Occupiers in its vendetta against safety legislation. Martineau was joined by Mrs. Marcet "who wrote little volumes of fables illustrating the principles of political economy and the folly for the working class of strikes and combinations" (Martin 1969: 437). Both writers exemplified "the way capitalist production acts on the mental functions of capitalists and their retainers" (Marx 1976: 368), but there were plenty of others.

Manchester cotton tycoons in 1836 chose Nassau W. Senior, an Oxford economist, "as their prize fighter, not only against the newly passed Factory Act but against the Ten Hours' Agitation which aimed to go beyond it" (Marx 1976: 333). In a learned disquisition Senior attempted to show that net profits are made in the "last hour" of the factory day. Any reduction from twelve hours, he warned, would strike at the earnings of capital; a reduction of an hour and a half would eliminate them. Horner was the first into the lists against Senior, writing an Open Letter in 1837 which defended factory legislation and hotly disputed the economist's data and reasoning (Marx 1976: 333-4, 614; Hutchins and Harrison 1966: 88-90; Martin 1969: 437-9). Senior's mind was soon "revolutionized," as Marx put it, and he became an enthusiastic supporter of factory regulation, doubtless partly because of Horner's intervention. Unfortunately, before his conversion, Senior had invented the theory of abstinence which explained interest and profit as capital's reward for "waiting" on a return from investment. "Strongly attacked by Marx, [the theory] became the key element in the neo-classical economics that has dominated [the twentieth] century" (Fine and Harris 1987: 392).

Abandoned by its creator, Senior's last hour remained a deadly weapon in the struggle against factory reform. His arguments were revived to defeat Ashley's Ten Hours Amendment in 1844, and in 1848 "the battle-cry of the 'last hour' was raised once again" in the organ of free trade, *The Economist,* "by James Wilson, an economic mandarin of high standing, in a polemic against the Ten Hours Bill"

(Marx 1976: 338, 337, 413). Factory inspectors were unimpressed, and after 1848 "never tired of teasing the factory-owners about this 'last,' this 'fatal hour.'" Another noted economist, Andrew Ure joined the offensive against the interventionist state. He warned of the moral dangers offered by the life of vice and ease that must attend any decrease in the twelve hour day for children and young persons. "The philosopher of the factory" was especially eager to protect the right of workers to sell themselves for as long as the employer desired. For Ure, it was "a mark of indistinguishable disgrace on the part of the English working class that they wrote 'the slavery of the Factory Acts' on their banners, as opposed to capital, which was striving manfully for the 'perfect freedom of labour.'"

Richard Oastler judged that political economy "had become the new state religion of Britain with the Houses of Parliament as its cathedral" (quoted in Driver 1946: 294). Major parliamentary arguments against factory legislation were usually framed in the profit-and-loss language of political economy, although "for the most part Classical economic thinking was expressed at Westminster in the speeches of many with little direct knowledge of the writings from which they drew their ideas" (Taylor 1972: 30; Lubenow 1971: 153-60).

As Marx (1976: 688, 703-4, 1076) pointed out, these positions were countered repeatedly in *The Reports of the Inspectors of Factories.* Horner and the others argued that legislating hours of work would not bankrupt the country; instead factory law would improve the condition of workers, reduce class hostility, and increase economic productivity. In 1840 Horner published *On the Employment of Children in Factories,* which contained a comparative review of factory legislation in Europe (Wusteman 1983: 13). About twenty years later Factory Inspector Redgrave carried out one of the first cross-national surveys of the differential impact of social legislation on economic productivity in order to disprove political economy's laissez faire argument. The Inspectorate's critique of political economy found its way into *Capital,* where Marx used inspectors' reports to combat mistaken notions about the nature of capital and wage labor.

The political economists' most spectacular accomplishment in their contest with factory bureaucrats was to firmly implant the doctrine of free contract in amongst the other "thoughtless contradictions of the capitalist brain" (Marx 1976: 564, 411; Taylor 1972: 43). The principle allowed Ure to write an entire book extolling a working day with no legal bounds. "That Parliament," noted Marx, "should forbid children of 13 years of age to be exhausted by working 12 hours a day reminds his liberal soul of the darkest days of the middle ages."

Marx (1976: 409) commented with disgust that vulgar political economy never admitted defeat on the factory issue. Instead, after decades of stubborn resistance, "the Pharisees of 'political economy' now proclaimed that their newly won insight into the necessity for a legally regulated working day was a characteristic achievement of their 'science.'" Ironically, capital's nineteenth century apologists would have agreed with standard Marxist explanations of the Factory Acts which see them as "rationalizing and stabilizing existing power relations in the society" (Lehrer 1987: 15; Dickenson and Russell 1986; Walby 1986: 103; Müller and Neusüss 1975: 67-9). Marx (1976: 380-81, 532-3) acknowledged that "the interests of capital itself points in the direction of the regulated working day," but nothing in the system guarantees this result.

> Capital, which has such "good reasons" for denying the suffering of the legions of workers surrounding it, allows its actual movement to be determined as much and as little by the sight of the coming degradation of the human race, as by the probable fall of the earth into the sun. . . . *Après moi le déluge* is the watchword of every capitalist and of every capitalist nation. Capital therefore takes no account of the health and life of the worker, unless society forces it to do so.

16. The Communist and the Factory Inspector

We have already seen that Marxist scholarship has mostly ignored Horner (and the other factory inspectors) despite Marx's (1976: 334) claim that "his service to the English working class will never be forgotten." Hal Draper (1986: 96), for example, complacently dismisses Horner's twenty-five years as a factory inspector. "Although M[arx]'s encomiums on H[orner]'s incorruptible work as a factory inspector has given him a niche in social history, he was primarily a geologist and educator." The Marxist elision has its counterpart in the annals of the English bourgeoisie.[49] Leonard Horner appears in the Dictionary of National Biography but "it is significant that" his work as an inspector "is passed over in a line" (Health and Safety Executive 1980: 2). Nevertheless, in future histories of bureaucratic organization there will have to be some mention of the strange fact that the leading theorist of communism was inspired by the reports of English state officials, primarily Leonard Horner. Whole sections of *Capital* are indebted to Factory Inspectorate publications, or those of other state agencies. Marx's data and analysis, his flow of argument, even his phraseology are taken at many points from the *Reports of the Inspectors of Factories*. Strikingly, the major figures criticized by factory inspectors are also chosen for obloquy by Marx (1976: 97): the "hired prize-fighters" of the bourgeoisie, the political economists.

Like that of Marx, Horner's was a world of mind as well as action. His famous brother Francis was an intimate of Ricardo, and Leonard was included in their circle. In the early nineteenth century when there were virtually no courses on political economy in England, Horner took advantage of the rich offerings at the University of Edinburgh. His biographer Bernice Martin (1969: 413) writes that, among other things, Horner "studied Moral Philosophy under Professor Dugald Stewart (whom he greatly admired and whose children became close friends of the Horners)." The top factory inspector was a life-long friend of James Mill and the economist McCullough; he knew and recognized the significance of the work of his close friend Charles Darwin from its earliest conception.

S. S. Prawer's *Karl Marx and World Literature* (1976) has displayed the remarkable range of Marx's intellectual universe; Horner's intellectual horizons were also very wide. While at school he learned the classical languages; later he familiarized himself with German, French and Italian "in order to read scientific, political and literary works and converse with scholars, politicians and businessmen on his travels in Europe. . . . His letters to his wife and daughters were full of appreciative accounts of Scott and Charlotte Brontë, Dante and Schiller" (Martin 1969: 422).

Before becoming a factory inspector, Horner had already achieved prominence in business and academia. He spent ten years with Lloyds Insurance Office before rejoining the family's manufacturing firm in Edinburgh. Later he became the first Warden of the University of London (1827-1831), and one of the initiators of the Geological Society of Great Britain (1835) (Martin 1969: 416). His many publications in geology were widely known; he was elected "as fellow of the Royal Society at the age of 28 in 1813," and was Secretary and twice President of the Geological Society in London.

Horner's "progressive views about women in science . . . led him" to admit women into the Geological Society, a controversial policy that was promptly reversed once his term as president expired

(Martin 1969: 417).[50] "In 1861 he attracted a great deal of comment by devoting his Presidential Address to the Geological Society to a review of the evidence for the antiquity of the world and the inadequacy of Archbishop Usher's Bible chronology of creation." During the address, Horner, then 76, presented his own original evidence for the dating of ancient buildings in the Nile Valley.

Marx and Horner each had female children,[51] and no sons. They shared close and affectionate relationships with their daughters, who in an age of tremendous restriction for the female sex (Vicinus 1985), became accomplished intellectuals, published authors, scientists (Kapp 1972, 1976; Martin 1969).[52] These biographical details point to the identities of culture, intellect and feeling that brought Horner and Marx together in their intense hostility toward exploitation of children and adult workers, and their contempt for the narrow souls that dominated political economy. The political theorist and the Whitehall bureaucrat were much harder on economists than they ever were on capitalists. The latter assuredly cared only for profit, but the former, after all, were reputed to have minds.

In numerous letters to his wife and daughters, Horner rarely referred to political economy, but in 1850, at the height of capital's rebellion against factory law, there was a significant break with tradition. "It quite disgusts me," he wrote to his daughter Frances,

> to hear the cold, calculating economists throwing aside all moral considerations, and with entire ignorance of the state of people who work in factories, talk of its being an infringement of the principle to interfere with labour. Why interfere with the use of capital in any way then? and do we not see laws passed every year to abate the abuse of the application of capital when it is productive of great moral and social evils? If I were free to write I could from my experience make such a statement as would show the fallacious reasons, and bad political economy, of those very economists, who, with their extravagant extensions of the doctrine of laissez faire, bring discredit on the science they cultivate (quoted in Martin 1969: 440).

Actually, Horner's reports and publications on the Factory Acts, quoted liberally in *Capital*, helped Marx make precisely the statement on political economy the inspector had envisioned.

What Horner and Marx shared most of all, however, was a deep belief in the efficacy of government action to relieve the sufferings of the oppressed at the hands of the powerful in the family and civil society. I have argued that for Marx this reflected the Hegelian legacy in his thought. MacDonagh (1977: 8) contends that in

Horner's case, as in Chadwick's, the guiding thinker was Bentham, who "was extraordinarily inventive in devising universal administrative schemes to replace the existing inefficiencies" revealed by the "devastating test of utility to every branch of government." In our own period the optimistic view of the state associated with Hegel and Bentham has fallen into disrepute. Theorists on all points of the political spectrum have grown suspicious of state action, reflecting a general trend in capitalist countries, and in the newly market-oriented societies in what was once called the communist bloc. In the conclusion of this study I will discuss the contribution Hegel and Marx could make to our understanding of the modern state and its current difficulties.

Notes

1. Burawoy (1985: 89) argues that Marx's model of capitalist production was based on the assumption of "market despotism": "Marx . . . took for granted . . . that the state would preserve only the *external* conditions of production (conditions for the autonomous working of market forces)." Perhaps it is not surprising, therefore, that Burawoy's own study ignores the role of state intervention in the English factory system.

2. Factory inspectors did not, of course, represent any coherent professional interest. But then hardly anyone did in the mid-nineteenth century, even medical doctors. Yet, as Robert Gray (1991: 20) argues for physicians, the inspectors as a group were attempting "to project a professional self-image . . . Professional men might thus present themselves as the bearers of superior knowledge and rationality, dedicated to the public good and the improvement of society."

3. As Bartrip and Fenn (1980; also Arthurs 1985: 173) have shown, the Marxist perspective resembles the social control view that once dominated accounts of the mid-Victorian era (Thompson 1981; Donajgrodzki 1979; Carson 1974, 1979, 1980). Carson (1980: 187), for example, contends that "the emerging industrial order of the nineteenth century contained within itself a logic that generated an impetus *towards* . . . effective regulation. Such regulation . . . was seen as having important and beneficial implications for the competitive structure of the textile industry, for the creation of a disciplined workforce and, no less important, for the ideological representation of the social relations of the workplace."

4. E. P. Thompson (1968: 376) disagrees with Djang, and suggests that the 1802 law "was less a precedent for new legislation than an attempt to extend customary apprenticeship safeguards in a new context." Richard Price (1986: 40) shows that the justice system in eighteenth century England played an important role in regulating industrial wages and working conditions, and this continued well into the nineteenth century. "The

continuities with eighteenth century law remained virtually intact until the more radical displacement by the statutes of the 1870s."

5. E. P. Thompson's (1967: 73-9) classic study, "Time, Work-Discipline and Industrial Capitalism" is marred by sexist assumptions about females and domestic labor and a sanguine attitude toward the relationship between skilled male workers and their child subordinates. Joan Wallach Scott (1988: 68-92) offers a feminist assessment of Thompson's work in *Gender and the Politics of History*.

6. "Many workers in organised trades had successfully clung to the norm established in the eighteenth century, and in 1850 worked a sixty-hour week. Equally, the various pressures brought upon government by the factory movement had resulted in a return to the norm for textile factory workers by mid-century. In mining, agriculture, domestic service, in the 'dishonourable' sections of the artisan trades, and in all domestic work, the eighteen-century norm had been breached, and hours were longer" (Cunningham 1990a: 281).

7. The Anatomy Act became law in August, 1832; the first reformed Parliament was elected in December, 1832. The Anatomy Act inspectorate was created to ensure a fresh supply of paupers's unclaimed dead bodies for the medical profession, and thus put an end to grave-robbery. Richardson's (1988: 51) powerful study shows how "entrepreneurial medicine eventually transformed [the corpse]" from a thing of awe and veneration "into an object of commercial exchange: a commodity."

8. Engels agreed with factory owners about exaggeration in Sadler's report (Thomas 1948: 41); apparently so did Marx. There is only one reference to the document in *Capital*.

9. "The notion of state officials entering private premises and regulating the relations of employers and employed was still a staggering novelty in 1833" (MacDonagh 1977: 44).

10. The argument that a tiny inspectorate can do little to enforce a law that covers a vast number of establishments is a compelling one. But critics of the Factory Inspectorate need to look at this ratio for other forms of inspection activity before reaching a conclusion. For example, today every city in the advanced capitalist world employs food inspectors to investigate conditions in restaurants and other eating places. Usually the inspectorate so employed is pitifully small and underfunded. Yet, while some food servers undoubtedly violate the law with impunity, this does not mean that laws governing the serving of food are totally ineffective. Since they usually apply to almost universal activities, laws requiring government inspection would demand breathtaking numbers of personnel and unlimited funding to achieve total enforcement. Bartrip offers no estimate of how big the Factory Inspectorate should have been; nor does he speculate on whether government would have been willing to fund such an undertaking.

11. Bartrip (1982: 605), for example, concludes that "the importance of inspection has been exaggerated." This issue is explored further below.

12. A modern spokesperson for the Inspectorate writes that "throughout its 150 years the Inspectorate has had these four overlapping roles, of law enforcement, of pressure group to improve the law, of pressure group to encourage the development of safer techniques, and of information centre" (Russell 1983: 6).

13. Chimney sweeps are a tragic instance. Children were apprenticed to this trade at the age of five or six; usually it took six months for them "to learn how to climb a chimney so as to serve as a kind of human brush." Reluctant climbers were compelled by a fire lit below them to squeeze through awkward angles and narrow passages; "death from suffocation was not uncommon" (Finlayson 1981: 408; Turner 1950: 33-58). Sweeps remained blackened throughout the week and were allowed to wash only on Sundays. "As they soiled whatever they touched, they could not be admitted into a home, and hence these little outcasts spent their nights in the cellar on beds of straw." A half-century after Hegel (1983a: 107) condemned the practice, Marx observed (1976: 358) that "in spite of legislation, the number of boys sold in Great Britain by their parents to act as live chimney-sweeping machines (although machines exist to replace them) is at least 2,000." In houses locked to avoid detection by municipal inspectors, "work was begun at 2, 3 and 4 a.m." (Finlayson 1981: 408). As soot was an excellent source of carbon, "capitalist chimney-sweeps" reaped large profits by selling it to farmers for manure (Marx 1976: 358).

14. Levine (1987) and Seccombe (1990) contend that the decline in the birth rate, which began in the last third of the nineteenth century, may have been due to the fall in child labor caused by factory regulation. I will return to this issue later in the chapter.

15. Robert Glen (1984: 72) observes that workers with good incomes were the first to oppose child labor. Thus in Stockport around 1818, "relatively high wages allowed for the possibility of many families to do without the income of children under the age of nine or ten." The strength of the Stockport short time movement "also highlights emerging popular views about childhood as separate, special stage in human life and widespread concern about the health and education of children."

16. F. M. L. Thompson (1988: 28) dissents from this. "It might equally well be argued that the closely knit unitary family, moderately affectionate and caring, existed first among the working classes, and spread slowly upwards." In her short story, "The Little Pin-Headers" Charlotte Elizabeth Tonna (1974: 329) describes the working class family relationships involved in child labor. Some "of those poor little slaves . . . have fathers or mothers who love them dearly, and bitterly grieve over the hard necessity that compels them, perhaps in sickness or other infirmity, or the total inability to find employment themselves, to send their children out to labour; others have selfish unfeeling parents, who gladly use them as machines to make money for their own indulgence; and others, again, are orphaned or deserted creatures, feeling themselves alone in the world, toiling for

strangers; or to earn the price of a scanty meal for themselves if they be above the earliest age."

17. Abuse of children is condemned in modern Western societies, but it is endemic in Third World countries, such as Brazil, where child malnutrition, abandonment and prostitution is common, and business-financed death squads execute thousands of little children every year (Schepper-Hughes 1991).

18. McKendrick (1974: 208) argues that "female and child incomes" created a "consumer revolution" that powered economic growth in the nineteenth century. "What ensured that the income would be spent on clothing the family and supplying the home was that, for the first time on any major scale, women had access to an independent income."

19. "Factory mule spinning—the major technique of cotton yarn production . . . required initially a great deal of mechanical skill and experienced handweavers who ordinarily built their own looms were attracted by the high wages paid for mule spinning" (Cohen 1985: 102).

20. Work traditions varied in different parts of England in the mid-nineteenth century, but most English workmen did not toil on Mondays. The regular workday dictated by steam power, which prevailed in textiles, forced many men to give up the tradition of "Saint Monday," but it survived in industries not dominated by steam. Even where steam power ruled, skilled male workers saw it as their privilege to be absent early in the week, while unskilled laborers were at their posts. E. P. Thompson (1967: 74) writes that in the pottery trade, "children and women came to work on Monday and Tuesday, but a 'holiday feeling' prevailed and the day's work was shorter than usual, since the potters were away a good part of the time, drinking their earnings of the previous week." Of course, when women did enjoy the privilege of "Saint Monday," they usually spent the day doing exhausting domestic labor (Reid 1986). In Leicester, for example, "they cared for infants, supervised the work of children, prepared meals, and did the weekly washing while their husbands observed St Monday by rambling in the fields or drinking in neighbourhood beer houses" (Osterud 1986: 51).

21. "Even when attached to power, the mule [spinning machine] required skilled labor rather than merely substituting mechanical power for labor. The mule spindles were mounted on a moving carriage. The movement of the carriage away from the rollers drew and twisted the yarn, while the next step, winding, was performed during the backward motion. Neither the backward motion of the carriage nor the winding process were mechanized. Rather, until about 1840, power was applied solely to the drawing and twisting motions, that is, the outward movement of the carriage. Pushing the carriage back in a constant speed proportional to that of the rotating spindles while at the same time carefully coiling the thread onto the spindle required a considerable skill . . . Moreover, it required a great deal of strength as well because the carriage of spindles soon became very heavy. By the 1830s, a 1400- or even 1800 pound carriage was not

uncommon in Lancashire" (Cohen 1985: 102).

22. Significantly, both the 1833 Factory Act and the legislation of 1844 coincided with periods of astonishing growth in the cotton industry. While this sector expanded rapidly throughout the first half of the nineteenth century, the strongest "bursts of investment which substantially increased productive capacity and rejuvenated equipment" occurred in 1823-5, 1833-6, and 1843-5 (Crouzet 1982: 197). The boom period of 1823-5 also coincided with passage of factory legislation, though Sir John Cam Hobhouse's measure of 1825, and the amended version passed in 1831, turned out to be ineffective, mainly because they lacked administrative machinery for enforcement.

23. Walby (1986: 124) and Valverde (1988: 627) claim that inspectors wanted women's exclusion from the textile labor force, but offer little evidence for this. It is true, however, that in the mid-1840s inspectors indicated that a lower ratio of female to male workers was desirable, but this was hardly a key issue for them. They also mentioned that factory work conflicted with women's domestic responsibilities, especially nurturing children, a position with which Marx (1976: 522) agreed. However, identical arguments were made in 1844 by Engels (1969: 172-5), who certainly did not favor excluding women from industry. By the late 1840s, as we shall see, inspectors accepted the workers' argument that protective legislation should be extended to all factory operatives, regardless of sex. Although inspectors certainly made an argument for women's special needs in order to gain parliamentary assent for improved legislation, adult females are rarely singled out as a special category in the *Reports of the Inspectors of Factories*.

24. The term "patriarchy" is a controversial among feminist scholars. Generally, Marxist feminists eschew the term as too wide and descriptive, rather than analytical (Mark-Lawson and Witz 1988: 153). By contrast, many feminist social historians and sociologists "have sought to salvage the term . . . from theoretical neglect and recast it in such a fashion as to further our understanding of the ubiquity of male dominance and the complexity of gender relations and inequality in the family, the labour market and the state." In my view, the Marxist feminist distrust of the term is unfounded.

25. This is a feminist version of the social control argument, usefully summarized by van Krieken (1986: 407) (I have altered the following quotation, which deals with child reformers, to make it fit the feminist case): "The *evidence* for this view is almost invariably the words of the reformers and [factory act] bureaucrats themselves. The usual procedure is to bundle together the most colorful and strident quotations one can find about the [moral] evils of [females in] the lower classes and how this or that institution [i.e., protective legislation] will civilize and regulate them, and this is presented as conclusive proof that [factory legislation] was clearly part of a process of [patriarchal] social control." Van Krieken sensibly notes that very often bureaucrats and reformers were left with little choice but to frame their arguments to accord with the perceived interests of dominant social

groups. Certainly, the Factory Inspectorate would have made little headway in parliament if it had advocated workday reform as a chief means of socially liberating women factory operatives. "The political context of attempting to loosen the state's purse strings, made it essential that arguments be made in terms of the overall political-economic benefits to the state, and it is thus difficult to ascertain what reformers 'really' believed."

26. Osterud (1986: 59) reports that in Leicester married women "remained in the labour force when their children were young and stopped working for pay when their children were old enough to replace them as contributors to family income. Thus in 1851, 30 per cent of wives with children under seven were employed, but only 20 per cent of those whose children were all over seven were."

27. Concerns about the moral propriety of employing adult females underground led to their exclusion from coal mines in 1842 (MacDonagh 1977; Humphries 1981); similar sexual worries about women in textile factories was a large theme in the male-dominated short-time movement (Alexander 1984; Valverde 1988), as well as in Engels's *The Condition of the Working Class in England* (1969: 176-7). However, these anxieties were not a feature of the *Reports of the Inspectors of Factories* (except concerning night work). Generally, inspectors were more troubled about the devastating physical effects of long working hours upon factory operatives, whatever their sex; industrial accidents were another prevailing motif.

28. Throughout the nineteenth century skilled male workers had a special interest in "short hour working," which had nothing to do with restricting women's labor: restricted hours "protected them against the consequences of overproduction." Writes Huberman (1987: 188-9), "a common strategy thus emerged to force short-hour working on all firms since it would reduce pressure in the industry to cut rates of pay. Along with bringing fluctuations of production under control there was also a general consensus among workers, whether in cotton spinning, construction or mining, that reductions in hours would spread evenly the available work and employment over the year."

29. Brenner and Ramas (1984: 40) are undoubtedly right, however, in suggesting that "it is very difficult to make a convincing case that so precarious a social-political edifice [as protective legislation] could have played a major role in conditioning the sexual division of labour or the family household system, either in England or the United States."

30. "Employers needed a labour stability that could be achieved by transferring the family division of labour into the factory and endowing the male minder with his natural responsibility for discipline, supervision and entry into the trade" (Price 1986: 79).

31. Mark-Lawson and Witz (1988: 162; also Humphries 1981) point out, for example, that male workers opposed exclusion of children and women from coal mining precisely because of its economic and social benefits for working men, including their control over the labor process.

32. A report from factory inspector Saunders (1840: 10-11) on the plight of 18 "sickly" and "diminutive" female pauper children employed in a mill in Derbyshire (three of whom had died) blames their condition not on work in the mill, but on "their condition at birth, or their treatment during the early period of infancy." Nevertheless, Saunders urgently requested removal of the fifteen surviving girls from the mill, since this would afford "the only probability of their becoming useful members of society."

33. "Accidents," say Bartrip and Fenn (1990: 70), "are a social construction. For official purposes an accident is only an accident if it fulfills certain definitional criteria, is reported and recorded."

34. "Medical evidence can take one closer to the realities of industrial life than the Factory Inspectors' reports, as in Dr. Greenhow's 1861 survey of industrial lung diseases, or Dr. Edward Smith's report on sanitary circumstances of tailors, printers and dressmakers" (Samuel 1977: 15).

35. Thus Engels (1969: 176) writes of, "the permanent, less conspicuous influence of persons of dissolute character, upon the more moral, and especially upon the younger ones." Unfortunately, there is little research on sexual harassment in mid-nineteenth century English factories. Nevertheless, there was much contemporary concern about male violence (Pleck 1987: 63-4; Behlmer 1982: 13-15; Tomes 1978). In 1853, Parliament passed the first law against assault on children and wife beating (a term devised in England in 1856). While Canada lagged behind "the mother country" in factory law, it was among the first to legislate on sexual harassment in the workplace. "In 1890 the law was amended to make it a criminal offence for employers and supervisors in factories, mills, and workshops to seduce women employees of previously chaste character under the age of 21" (Tucker 1990: 124; Backhouse and Cohen 1978: 68-70).)

36. Brenner and Ramas (1984: 51-2) argue convincingly that long hours for women in the factory were incompatible with their extremely arduous and time-consuming domestic chores, let alone the rigorous demands of child care.

37. Horner's pioneering opinion survey technique apparently confused Marx (1976: 397). He gave the breakdown of adult male opinions in the survey correctly; but confused the source, and failed to mention the result for women. Marx claimed that 10,270 adult male factory operatives in 181 mills were interviewed, but this referred to men in Horner's area who were forced by manufacturers to work more than 10 hours after the 1847 Act.

38. Horner and five sub-inspectors also interviewed hundreds of factory operatives in depth. Here are a few replies recorded by Horner (1849b: 27, 40) from women workers: "No. 15. Three young women, *weavers*, conversed with together.—All said that they would rather 'stick to the 10 hours' than go back to 12, even though they might get higher wages. . . . . No. 18. Married woman with a family, a *weaver*.—She makes less wages, but prefers working 10 hours; thinks it quite long enough to work, and believes that the others think as she does. . . . No. 19 A young woman of

16, *works at the roving frame.*—Does not like the reduction in her wages; would rather go back to 12 hours to get more. . . . No. 64. Female of 30, married, and has one child. *Winder.*—Earns at 10 hours 8s 6d; if she worked 12 hours would earn 10s 6d per week; cannot afford the loss, and would gladly return to 12 hours of work. . . . No. 65. Female of 40; married, and has no children. *Winder.*—Earns 2s. per week less than she would earn during 12 hours, but thinks the additional leisure compensates for pecuniary loss."

39.   In the 1980s, as Nancy Cott (1987: 329) notes, many feminist historians saw protective legislation as a regressive measure. Yet working women's widespread support for state intervention was not disputed by this scholarship. Kessler-Harris (1982: 213), for example, explains that women workers "perhaps bowed" to contemporary opinion and reluctantly accepted protective legislation that was clearly opposed to their interests. Similarly, for English female workers who supported the factory acts, Walby (1986: 122) contends that "patriarchal hegemony" caused them to misconceive their own gender interests. These interpretations are reminiscent of Lukács's concept of imputed class consciousness, which dictates what workers should think about something according to a higher understanding of their interests than they themselves can attain. In the case of women and protective legislation, however, the tribunal of the free market, rather than Lucács's Communist Party, is the ultimate legislator of true consciousness.

40.   Seccombe (1986) and Mark-Lawson and Witz (1988) have cogently argued that male attitudes to female labor changed over the nineteenth century. When the 1844 Act was put in place many women operatives were part of the patriarchal family labor system. Later, as the family system broke down, females appeared as competitors with men, who began to demand their removal from the labor market.

41.   The positive relationship cemented by the Factory Inspectorate with the working class meant that in the 1880s, when depression and high unemployment "contributed towards the growth of socialism and created increasing concerns about conditions of labour, . . . [w]orking men not only saw the factory inspectors as potential allies but also wanted their own representatives within the inspectorate" (Pellew 1982: 151).

42.   Writes Bartrip (1982: 618), "of course, it was explicit in the legislation that management's freedom of action was circumscribed by factory and mines acts, since these specified particular ways in which relevant businesses should be conducted."

43.   The "false relay system" was originally designed by Leonard Horner. In 1834 he circulated to mill-occupiers a detailed plan for working sets of children in relays running between 6 in the morning and 8 at night. Horner's system aimed at efficient employment of both children and adult workers; but he was also concerned that the timing of children's work would allow the local schoolmaster to be employed only from 8.30 a.m to 3.30 p.m. "with an hour's interval for dinner" (Thomas 1848: 403).

44. McCarthy first came to prominence by attacking bureaucrats at a Republican women's club in 1950. "I have here in my hand a list of 205 that were known to the secretary of state as being members of the Communist Party and are still making and shaping the policy of the State Department" (quoted in Navasky 1980: 23).

45. Gray (1987: 173) attributes the "logic of capitalism" argument to Marx, as do many other commentators (e.g. Bartrip 1980: 175; 1983: 68; Tucker 1990: 119). Carson (1979: 37; 1980) claims that his own "social control" interpretation of factory law is drawn from Foucault.

46. Similarly, the French revolutionary government's 1848 legislation on the working day "exempted family workshops . . . from the proposed law on women's and children's work because legislators objected to the inspection of private households. Not only might privacy be violated, it was argued, but the common interest of the work unit made it impossible to assign responsibility, even to the head of the household, for enforcing the law" (Scott 1988: 101).

47. In an excellent study of factory law in Canada, Tucker (1990) disagrees with the view, put forward by Arthurs (1985) that factory inspectors in the new country acted as an autonomous force. However, as Linda Colley (1986a) suggests, there is a need to treat offshoots from Britain, like Canada and the United States, within the context of contemporary imperial politics. In the Canadian case, for example, inspectors may have benefited from the advice and example of the English Inspectorate. Thus while Canada's factory legislation of the 1880s lagged behind England's, the law appears to have been far ahead of developments in the U.S., which had long since broken ties with Britain.

48. Writes David Levine (1987: 173), "the state was not simply a handmaiden of the industrial capitalists. It had a life of its own and an inner logic which often set it against the very class which 'controlled' it. . . Because the working day was shortened, because the labour of women and children was restricted, because workers' right to organize were recognized, and because employers were held to be liable for injuries sustained by their employees, the entrepreneurial choice of extensive exploitation was less accessible."

49. Shamefully, the work of Leonard Horner and the Factory Inspectorate is ignored even by today's reform movement to ban child labor in the Third World. Alec Fyfe (1989: 143-4), for example, suggests a strategy for eradicating exploitation of immature labor in less developed countries that is based on the "Victorian child labour campaign," but this model does not include an activist public service; nor does it mention the Factory Inspectorate.

50. Horner's attitude contrasted markedly with that of his successor, Redgrave, who resisted bringing women into the Factory Inspectorate in the late 1870s. "Redgrave was highly conservative about the social role of women and unable to conceive of a woman factory inspector 'conducting

her case and having to submit herself to the witness-box to the cross-examination of an astute attorney'" (Pellew 1982: 155).

51. Marx had three daughters; Horner had six.

52. Interestingly, Marx's favorite child, Eleanor, made life-long friends with Clara Collet, the daughter of Marx's frequent correspondent, the newspaper editor C. D. Collet. Before Eleanor Marx died in 1898, Clara Collet would become one of England's leading bureaucrats. "In 1891 Clara had been one of four women asked by the Royal Commission on Labour to report on women's 'sweating'" (Miller 1990: 75). Beatrice Webb, another friend of Clara Collet, feared after meeting Eleanor "that chances were against her remaining within the pale of respectable society" (quoted in Kapp 1972: 284). No doubt, Eleanor's fiery socialist politics (and her father's notoriety) would have prevented her from following Clara Collet and Beatrice Webb into the English bureaucracy. Yet in their commitment to improving the lives of working class people, Eleanor Marx and Clara Collet made choices about life and career that were entirely in accord with those made earlier by Marx and the factory inspector.

10

The Rational State

At the very least the belief that further advances in human history will lead to the amelioration of human suffering has been massively contradicted by the experiences of Auschwitz and the gulag.
—Steven B. Smith, *"Hegel and the French Revolution"* (1989a: 233)

Even regarding History as the slaughter-bench at which the happiness of the peoples, the wisdom of States, and the virtue of individuals have been victimized—the question inevitably arises—to what principle, to what final aim these enormous sacrifices have been offered. . . . Two elements, therefore, enter into the object of our investigation; the first, the Idea, the second the complex warp and woof of the vast arras-web of Universal History. The concrete mean and unity of the two is Liberty, under the conditions of morality in a State.
—G. W. F. Hegel, *The Philosophy of History* (1956: 21)

The state is undeniably a messy concept.
—Michael Mann *"The Autonomous Power of the State"* (1986: 112)

In relation to men (of the ruling class) women's consciousness did not, and most probably generally still does not, appear as an autonomous source of knowledge, experience, relevance, and imagination. Women's experience did not appear as the source of an authoritative general expression of the world.
—Dorothy E. Smith, *The Everyday World as Problematic* (1987: 51)

1. Hegel, Marx, and the Debate on the State

Hegel and Marx shared an ardent belief in the inherent rationality and liberating potential of government. Their view reflects a long tradition in German thought (Ritter 1986: 17), but it contrasts deeply with doubts about the state that characterize our own period. In this concluding chapter I will bring together the main arguments of this book and show that the standpoint of Hegel and Marx is even more compelling today, when the state is much larger and more powerful than in their time. The present section will assess the current status of the Hegelian vision of the state; subsequent sections will consider Hegel's central propositions about political power.

Despite the conventional wisdom that "the collapse of world communism [has ensured] . . . that Marxism and even socialism [are] unlikely to possess much appeal in the future anywhere in the world" (Wrong 1991: 567), Marx will continue to be important for debates about government and democracy. However, the Hegelian thrust of his theory of the state is not widely appreciated. Starting with Althusser—whose "main achievement was to break out of the Hegelian strait-jacket" (Callinicos 1989: 4, 3)—followers of Marx have increasingly distanced themselves from Hegel. Marxists stress the apocalyptic version of Marx's theory, in which the capitalist state disappears under communism, rather than the gradualist Hegelian perspective where bourgeois government is both transcended and preserved—the outlook which emerges most clearly from Marx's treatment of the Factory Acts.[1] The apocalyptic bias is almost universal, even though both versions of communism, as Berki (1983: 166-7) has shown, have at least equal textual validity in Marx.[2]

Paradoxically, amidst widespread denial of Hegel, the recent Marxist debate on the state[3] evinced a strong trend toward Hegelian positions (MacGregor 1989a). Orthodox Marxism's conception of government as an instrument of the bourgeoisie was supplanted by the relative autonomy thesis, which granted the state a limited role in managing capitalist society. Proponents of relative autonomy unconsciously embraced a pivotal idea in the *Philosophy of Right*, i. e., that state and civil society are "conceptually different, in practice even antagonistic, forms of social life which are nonetheless dialectically related" (Pelczynski 1984: 265). Block (1987: 81, 173) went "beyond relative autonomy," insisting that state managers are "historical subjects," with a set of interests and a mode of consciousness that differs from both workers and capitalists. Block attributed his views to Polanyi's *Great Transformation* (1957), but the state manager thesis contains more than a hint of Hegel's universal class.

By the beginning of the 1990s, the "the major Anglo-American [Marxist] contributors" to the debate had surrendered the field (Block 1991: 871) to the non-Marxist state autonomy school led by Theda Skocpol (Skocpol 1980; Evans, Rueschemeyer, Skocpol 1985). Skocpol and the others see the state as the principal actor in history, and relegate social class to a supporting role (Jenkins and Brents 1989: 894; MacGregor 1989: 169). Despite the influence on this school of Heclo, Hirschman, and Gouldner, all of whom—like Polanyi (1957: 111)—acknowledge a debt to Hegel, its members see themselves in the tradition not of Hegel, but of "such major German scholars as Max Weber and Otto Hintze" (Skocpol 1985: 7).

Lack of enthusiasm for Hegel's theory of the state is understandable, given the ambivalence even committed Hegelians feel about the politics of the *Philosophy of Right*.[4] If Karl Popper's influence has waned, the myth persists that Hegel did not confront political challenges brought by the modern era. A powerful current in Hegel scholarship still contends that his political theory excluded the working class from government, and adopted a paternalistic attitude toward the poor.[5] The feminist critique adds to these difficulties by maintaining that women are among the huge crowd barred from the Hegelian state.

This study attempts to dispel such myths, suggesting that an interpretation of the *Philosophy of Right* must take careful account of the conditions of censorship and oppression under which Hegel wrote (McCumber 1986: 386).[6] Nevertheless, these objections to Hegel's politics are overshadowed by widespread skepticism about his idealistic view of the state, and the notion of bureaucracy as a universal class. Thus Weber—who had a much darker perspective on government (and who relied on Hegel at least as much as Marx did)—is the authority favored by most political theorists. Intriguingly, the very points on which Hegelian theory is acknowledged to have been most successful—i. e. its insistence on the growing role of the state and increased salience of the public service—are used as evidence against it. Writes Dallmayr,

> Since [Hegel's] time, the flaws and "imperfections of the modern-state—the degeneracy (or putrefaction) of its flesh" (to use Marx's terms)—have become evident in manifold ways. Reduced to an instrument of bureaucratic controls or to a vehicle of chauvinist ambitions, the state has increasingly lost its Hegelian sense (1989: 1358-9; also Arato 1989: 1375).

Anti-statist arguments like this usually end by invoking the powers of civil society against the state. Theorists look to "new social movements" or some other nebulous assembly—e. g. Dallmayr's (1989: 1360, 1357) "plural and heterogenous groupings cross-cutting social divisions (or inhabiting the margins of such divisions)"—as a defense against "the all-pervasive tentacles of the bureaucratic state."

There are signs that popular animus against government has

peaked. The right-wing attack on the welfare state, combined with a massive shift of power and wealth to the rich (a conflation that would not have surprised Hegel), created a backlash that accelerated with the economic crisis of the early 1990s. In the United States, for example, extremes of wealth and poverty generated by the Reagan boom years reminded some observers of "economically divided mid-nineteenth century Britain" (Phillips 1991: 7, 55).[7] The gulf between rich and poor in Victorian England was narrowed by interventionist government; a parallel movement may be under way in the American heartland of the free market. A more favorable attitude toward state intervention would facilitate reception of Hegelian theory,[8] but the notion that government is antithetical to individual freedom and autonomy was always wrong. Hinchman (1984: 15; also Wolfe 1989: 109) makes exactly this point.

> In practice, if not yet explicitly in theory, the state has tended to become an *ally* of those who feel that their rights have been diminished or denied, not enhanced, by the free play of market forces. At the same time, the duties of the state to ensure human rights even against strong property rights have expanded greatly as the former notion has embraced such things as the right to a job, an education, a clean environment, participation in a common culture. Whether or not they really *are* rights, people believe that they are and look to the state for help in securing them.

2. Logic and the State

For Hegel, political categories are logically interrelated (through the form of the syllogism—individual, particular, universal) so that each leads of necessity to the next (and back again). There is no absolute order in the logical syllogism; that is, what is universal in one go-round of the dialectic can become the particular, or the individual, in another (Williams 1989: 95-109; Bellamy 1987: 697-8). In line with this conception, Hegel's state is more than a form of government. Rather, the state is an all-inclusive universal, a totality; it includes everything that belongs to a nation or society—territory, culture, language, economy, and so forth (Vincent 1987: 336; MacGregor 1989b: 55). In the shape of a representative political institution, government is linked through civil society (the sphere of the particular) with the individual. Similarly, the individual within the family—as the absolute basis of the state—is the universal, which is linked to the particularity of civil society through the mediation of the head of state, the monarch.

The state belongs to the highest of the three levels of dialectical logic which Hegel called, being, essence, and the notion. As the foremost expression of concrete freedom—the "union of freedom and necessity" (Hegel 1976: 163)—the unity of state and individual forms the absolute idea, the pinnacle of Hegelian logic: "the Idea which thinks itself" (Hegel 1975: 292). Hegel's universal secular state, unlike the ideal spheres of art and religion (but like philosophy), contains nothing but rational thought, as concretely expressed in the nation's constitution and code of law, and as existent in the mind of the individual citizen.

> The Absolute Idea is for itself the pure form of the notion, which contemplates its contents as its own self. It is its own content, in so far as it ideally distinguishes itself from itself, and the one of the two things distinguished is a self-identity in which however is contained the totality of the form as the system of terms describing its content.

This Hegelian unity is the basis of Marx's vision of communism, a vision probably best articulated in Hegel's *Aesthetics* (1975a, I: 48): "the final end and aim of the state is that *all* human capacities and *all* individual powers be developed and given expression in every way and in every direction."

Hegel's critics complain that the state in the *Philosophy of Right* is an *a priori* construction, rather than a real political entity. However, Hegel (1975: 143-4) insisted that the chief alternative to his political theory—liberalism, which views political authority as coextensive with civil society—is also a logical construction, but one at the lowest level of thought, being. According to Hegel, the liberal perspective shares its major concepts with the atomic theory of the physicists. Individuals are pictured as atoms who make up basic units of the social universe, and are both attracted and repelled by one another. "The will of these individuals as such is the creative principle of the State: the attracting force is the special wants and inclinations of individuals; and the Universal, or the State itself, is the external nexus of a Compact."

The revolution in ideas that propelled the development of the modern state, argues A. O. Hirschman (1977), ultimately joined all the human passions within the single one (urged especially by Adam Smith) of self-interest. In liberal theory, the possessive individual became the chief economic and political actor (Macpherson 1962). While Hegel learned much from Smith and other Scottish thinkers (Waszek 1988), he disagreed that self-interest is the primary motive of action. The principle of love, as developed by Greek philosophy and brought to reality by Christianity, is as important for human behavior as the notion of self-interest. Accordingly, for Hegel (1971: 264), the state represents a union of the principle of the family—love, and the principle of civil society—self-interest. By embracing these apparently contradictory springs of human endeavor, the state is assured of the loyalty of its citizens. "This universal principle, with all its evolution in detail, is the absolute aim and content of the knowing subject, which thus identifies itself in its volition with the system of reasonableness."

In Hegel's formulation, family and civil society are the root of community and basis of the individual's positive sentiment toward the state; as such, they are the universal which brings together the particular individual on one side, and the individuality of the state on the other. The nation itself—as a totality of family, civil society and the state—appears as an individual in relation to other states, which combined form the universe of states and the ultimate court of world history. The inner constitution of states also follows the dialectical form, and includes the individual as leader of the state; particular interests that make up civil society are reconstituted as the legislature (or parliament); the universal body of government is the executive, which includes the state's leader, parliamentary representatives in the cabinet, and the public service or bureaucracy. Also taking a tripartite form, the legislature includes an upper and lower house, with the monarch at the head.

Hegel's constitutional system reflects the class structure of civil society. Not only an element of the state, the bureaucracy is also a social class within civil society. Representatives from civil society occupy seats in the lower legislature of parliament; most of these are drawn from the corporations of the business class. Members of the agricultural class fill seats in the upper house. Apart from the part played by constitutional monarchy and the landed class—both of which were elements of most advanced governments of Hegel's time—his version of the state resembles the constitution of many modern western democracies. A key difference that will be explored further below is that members of parliament are not selected through universal suffrage on a territorial basis (Taylor 1975: 445); instead they represent the functional interests of corporations, and are elected by their corporate colleagues (Heiman 1971).

Hegel (1971: 270; 1956: 448) rejected the concept of parliamentary supremacy, which sees the bureaucracy and head of state as simple instruments of a majority party in the legislature.[9]   This tenet sacrifices the interests of the individual to those of the universal, and thus contradicts "the first and supreme principle" of individuality. "The Few assume to be the *deputies*, but they are often only the *despoilers* of the Many. Nor is the sway of the Majority over the Minority a less palpable inconsistency." It is precisely the alienation of the individual from society inherent within the liberal vision of the state—its elective despotism[10]—that caused Hegel (1976: 195) to reject the model of universal manhood suffrage—a model which he noted "prima facie excludes children, women, &c.," and therefore could hardly represent *their* interests.   "Here we have a critique," Charles Taylor (1975: 445) points out, "which will come back in transposed form in Marx, where the alienation of the citizen from bourgeois is one of the contradictions of capitalist society."

According to Hegel (1976: 263), representative democracy places power into the hands of dominant elites and their political representatives in parliament—"and so of the particular and contingent interest which is precisely what was to have been neutralized." This distances the individual from politics, and prevents the state from surfacing as an autonomous force relative to civil society (Drydyk 1986). The result is government by revolving door; elites replace one another in national leadership roles, exactly in the way theorized by the Italian theorists, Mosca and Pareto (Bellamy 1987a), at the turn of the twentieth century.

3. Hegel and the "Delicate Watch"

A frequently rehearsed theme in this book is the difference between what Hegel called the external state, and the rational state. An external state is a political administration relatively identical with civil society; it resembles Marx's notion of a capitalist-dominated government (Bobbio 1988: 81). The state is external because it lacks essential linkages between the individual and political authority. Instead, it is controlled by a social class or dominant elites, and performs only basic tasks of national security and protection of private property, both of which are narrowly defined by the ruling group.   England in 1831 was a classic instance.[11] The external state represents a pact between individuals in civil society, but a pact gone wrong, a pact in which control is inevitably ceded to powerful interests.   In Hegel's view, every modern state contains some combination of external and rational elements.[12]

In an argument based on Adam Ferguson's *Essay on the History of Civil Society* (Hirschman 1977: 121-2), Hegel (1976: 175) warned against a strong state, if by that is meant one that relies heavily on armed force, internal security operations, countervailing constitutional powers, etc., to safeguard so-called national interests. Repressive institutions such as these are usually recommended by the wealthy to protect their privileges from attacks by the poor, or incursions by democratic elements within the state.

> To take the merely negative as a starting-point and to exalt to the first place the volition of evil and the mistrust of this volition, and then on the basis of this presupposition slyly to construct dikes whose efficiency simply necessitates corresponding dikes over against them, is characteristic in thought of the negative Understanding and in sentiment of the outlook of the rabble.

For Hegel the consciousness of the rabble has an exact counterpart in the mind of the rich. Since the poor have little influence on the state, *their* recommendations would have no official audience (unless a revolution occurred, and in *that* case, Hegel's strictures would apply to the dispossessed who made the revolution).

The externality of the state is a function of unrepresentative control, but it is also a result of dominant views and theories of government (Hegel 1971: 270). The understanding consciousness characteristic of bourgeois society views government as identical with civil society; since this system is dominated by the law of the market, there is a strong sense among many of its citizens that the state should also be so governed (Riedel 1984: 148). Clearly, if dominant elites and their ideologists have a view of the state that stresses government's forced compliance to the interests of the privileged (interests secured by the free market)—and that view is not effectively challenged—then such ideas will have an important effect on the nature of government.

This is why for Hegel (1976: 157) the theories of political economy were so dangerous. Economists saw government as almost a frill, "something optional." Government action was to be measured only by the economic criteria of civil society; the state's costs and benefits for individual citizens considered in isolation from one another. In other words, the moral element of government—its devotion to the abilities and self-expression of every individual within it—was lost. Hirschman (1977: 124) spells out the implications of rule by an "economist king" who forbids tampering with the "delicate watch":

If it is true that the economy must be deferred to, then there is a case not only for constraining the imprudent actions of the prince but for repressing those of the people, for limiting participation, in short, for crushing anything that could be interpreted by some economist-king as a threat to the proper functioning of the "delicate watch."

We saw that in mid-nineteenth century England the national debt was of great importance for politics. Whigs and Tories each claimed to have measures that would reduce the debt; even radical politicians were seduced by the clamor around fiscal difficulties. Throughout the nineteenth century attempts to deal with the problems of industrial society were hampered by inadequate financing; the Factory Inspectorate was a foremost example. The justification for limits on funding of government programs was always the dire need to reduce the burden of the national debt, and to lift the onerous load of taxation off the backs of the people. The ability of capitalists to easily move liquid assets across national borders—and thus avoid taxes and inconvenient state policies—was also used as a reason to restrain government. As Hirschman (1977) shows, these themes—which contain interesting parallels to current debates about the transnational corporation and government deficits—go back to the seventeenth and eighteenth centuries.

Hegel saw great danger, as well as triviality, in the parliamentary power to determine the budget. Parliament, in his eyes, should deal only with legislation (including, of course, tax law); to include finance within its general duties, was to smuggle a "strict executive" power into its hands. It was up to the executive—the head of state, senior public servants, and ministers of the Crown—to estimate the costs of administration and provide ways and means of paying for them. Hegel (1971: 274) agreed that the so-called "*financial law*" was a law "in the general sense of embracing a wide, indeed the whole, range of the external means of government." However, an annual law was superfluous; most items in the budget are permanent expenditures, and only a small part varies from year to year. The danger, of course, was that representatives from civil society would use the budgetary power to strangle government. New projects could be choked, and existing programs weakened, slashed, or moth-balled by legislators under the pretext of financial exigency.[13]

The theory behind this parliamentary power was supposed to be that it provided a check to government. On one hand, this was an empty and absurd threat. "The financial measures necessary for the state's subsistence," Hegel (1971: 275) maintained, "cannot be made conditional on any other circumstances, nor can the state's subsistence be yearly put in doubt." Parliament could just as well set a time limit on some judicial institution "and thus, by the threat of suspending the activity of such an institution and the fear of a consequent state of brigandage, reserve for itself a means of coercing private individuals." On the other hand, the notion that parliament requires means of compulsion against government is "partly based on the false conception of a contract between rulers and ruled, and partly presuppose[s] the possibility of such divergence in spirit between these two parties as would make constitution and government quite out of the question."

Here Hegel put his finger on a key problem of modern liberal democracy. The financial power vested in parliament has allowed it to keep government under the control of dominant elites and their ideologists, the economists. At best, this power twists executive authority into a game of musical chairs between elite-dominated political parties. At worst, (and as occurred in many parliamentary democracies in the period preceding the Second World War) it can mean "the derangement and dissolution of the state, in which there no longer would be a government, but only parties, and the violence and oppression of one party would only be helped away by the other." Financial control, in other words, has been a way for the dictates of the market to impinge on those of the state. Instead of planning by the state being imposed on civil society, dominant interests in civil society have imposed their own plan upon government. In the 1990s, the peril sensed by Hegel in this situation has expanded. In many countries, political leaders have lost control of their own economies, and have relinquished economic direction to international financiers who have little interest in the welfare of their citizens. "International investors," writes Linda McQuaig (1991: 208),

> are looking for a set of government policies that include high interest rates, tight control of credit, cuts to government spending, removal of trade barriers, export promotion and deregulation and privatization. Indeed, this is the agenda countries must adopt in order to receive loans from the International Monetary Fund (IMF) and the World Bank, the powerful international credit agencies set up by the U. S. after World War II to rebuild the international economy along lines favoured by private western capital.

A chilling example of the priorities of international capital was revealed in 1991 by an internal memo from World Bank chief economist Lawrence Summers who proposed "encouraging *more* migration of the dirty industries to the L[ess] D[eveloped] C[ountries]." The chief economist suggested, among other reasons, that since labor is cheaper, and life expectancy shorter, in poor countries, "the economic logic behind dumping a load of toxic waste in the lowest-wage country is impeccable." Moreover, initial increases in pollution "probably have low cost. I've always thought that under-populated countries in Africa are vastly *under*-polluted; their air quality is probably vastly inefficiently low [sic] compared to Los Angeles or Mexico City." While suitably shocked by the World Bank official's candor, *The Economist* (1992b: 66) magazine, which scooped the memo, admitted that "on the economics, his points are hard to answer."

Much as Hegel anticipated, even political parties that escape control by wealthy elites in civil society have great difficulty avoiding the ruling political agenda. David Braybrooke (1985: 78) warns of "the trap that Revisionism—the social democratic parties of western Europe—fell into . . . of seeking a majority in parliament and then of carrying out responsible government on the basis of such a majority." Without fundamental changes in the relationship between civil society and the state, such efforts are nugatory. "Acting as a political party in a parliamentary system, the social democratic parties have had to commit themselves to compromise programs that placate widespread fears of radical change and accordingly offer to temporize indefinitely with the entrenched interests received from the past." The result, of course, is that social democratic governments disappoint the expectations of their supporters, a fate that afflicts mainline capitalist parties as well. Hegel (1956: 452) diagnosed this problem of liberal democracy with remarkable prescience.

> Asserting this formal side of freedom—this abstraction—the party in question allows no political organization to be firmly established. The particular arrangements of the government are forthwith opposed by the advocates of Liberty as the mandates of a particular will, and branded as displays of power. The will of the Many expels the Ministry from power, and those who had formed the Opposition fill the vacant places; but the latter having now become the Government, meet with hostility from the Many, and share the same fate. Thus agitation and unrest are perpetuated. This collision, this nodus, this problem is that with which history is now occupied, and whose solution it has to work out in the future.

4. Hegel's Solution

Hegel (1976: 193-4) offered a solution to the problem of modern liberal democracy in the final pages of the *Philosophy of Right*. Generally, his alternative relied on already existing constitutions, especially that of the English state, which, despite his strong reservations, still had much to recommend it. But he proposed small changes that have very large consequences. Constitutions, he averred, do not stand still, they become "progressively more mature in the course of the further elaboration of the laws and the advancing character of the universal business of government." Moreover, constitutions usually advance in a much different direction than the original framers had in mind. Hegel argued that in Germany, for example, the conversion of royal "private property" into "public property" occurred "without any struggle or opposition." Yet this change took place as a result of selfish efforts of German princes to protect their private domains by seeking guarantees from the state. Similarly, in the Holy Roman Empire an independent judiciary grew up simply because the Emperor, in his role as judge, found it inconvenient to "travel[] the Empire on circuit" and thus delegated "more and more of his judicial functions to others." The same is true of modern constitutions; initially devised to protect the wealth and power of privileged groups, they come to represent the interests of everyone in civil society.

For Hegel (1976: 280, 181), the concept of the sovereignty of the individual must be paramount "since the state is nothing but the articulation of concrete freedom." Individual sovereignty implies three things: symbolic representation of individual will in the figure of the monarch, the nation's leader; recognition of the absolute rights of property ownership; and functional representation of individual will in institutions of the state.

5. Leadership

Some critics suggest that Hegel meant to deify the Prussian king; others point to strict limits he placed on the power of the crown. I have shown elsewhere (MacGregor 1984) that Hegel's ironic account should be seen as a critique, rather than blind acceptance, of monarchy. Unquestionably, however, Hegel (1976: 183) saw individual leadership as absolutely necessary for a rational state. A nation cannot be led by an amorphous institution or group. Every citizen has to see political power as representative of her or his own will, and this can happen only if power is personified. "Everything done and everything actual is inaugurated and brought to completion by the single decisive act of a leader." U. S. President Harry S. Truman said it best: "the buck stops here" (Augarde 1991: 218).[14] Similarly, relations with other countries are maintained and personalized through the head of state and her or his representatives. "A state stands in relation not with one other state only, but with many. And the complexity of their relations become so delicate that they can be handled only by the head of state" (Hegel 1976: 296).

The crucial sociological principle involved in personal leadership was well understood by Weber (Mommsen 1984: 420), but it is also exemplified in every leading democratic nation, where authority vested in a single individual is the rule. It also accounts for the eclipse of constitutional monarchs in favor of prime ministers in many parliamentary systems, and the increased power and display of democratic leaders generally. Paradoxically, Hegel would regard modern representative systems, such as the American one, as giving too much power to the nation's leader (Kelly 1978: 221). For Hegel (1976: 288), the beauty of constitutional monarchy was precisely that the monarch's discretion was tightly circumscribed. "He is bound by the concrete decisions of his counsellors, and if the constitution is stable, he has often no more to do than sign his name."

6. Private Property and Corporations

Hegel's notion of private property as a defense against arbitrary authority has deep roots in political philosophy, though in its modern guise as an argument for the democratic character of private property in the means of production it is associated with such thinkers as F. A. Hayek and Milton Friedman (Hirschman 1977: 127). Hegel would likely have agreed with the neo-conservative defense of property. After all, as Henry Adams observed, "a Hegelian is one who agrees that everybody is right, but acts as if everybody but himself were wrong" (quoted in Kronick 1986: 391). Nevertheless, as we have seen, Hegel (1976: 175, 189) would also insist that the bourgeois version of private property is risibly narrow, a typical product of the "abstract Understanding." Private property and everything that goes with it—money, the market, capital, taxes, corporations, and so forth—are absolutely necessary moments of the state. However, property rights must be extended to include the worker's right to the product of her labor, and thus to democratic ownership, and control of corporations and businesses through "popular election." Today this is no longer a dream of far-fetched idealism. It is a principle represented, for example, in German industry, where joint management by capital and workers is common; in worker-owned firms in Europe and North America; and in the newly "privatized" communist countries where many firms are adopting a worker ownership model (Nove 1983; Whyte and Whyte 1988). "The East and West," declares David Ellerman (1990: 214), "are . . . converging towards the common ground of the democratic worker-owned firm."

As "pillars of public freedom," corporations, including businesses, professional organizations, municipalities, churches, voluntary organizations, educational institutions, and so forth, must be autonomous of state authority (Hegel 1976: 163, 133-4, 147, 278; Black 1984: 202-9). This is a lesson drawn by the English pluralist school early in the twentieth century, but it is also a chief feature of Hegel's theory of the state. The individual finds her immediate source of identity and expression in the family, and her personality is fully developed and given expression through work and effort in a corporation. In Hegel's terms, the corporation is the particular through which the individual reaches out to the universal. Nevertheless, the state must have overall authority; "otherwise [corporations] would ossify, build themselves in, and decline into a miserable system of castes." Corporations are licensed by government; their leadership must be ratified by higher officials, and the state should have the final say in their operations, "especially in the case of the larger branches of industry, because these are dependent on conditions abroad and on combinations of distant circumstances which cannot be grasped as a whole by the individuals tied to these industries for a living." Thus, Harold Perkin (1989: 518) observes that absence of national control over the modern corporation may lead to a new form of corporate feudalism, a system very like the one Hegel foresaw. In this "decentralized" authoritarian regime "the feudal lords of the giant corporations, manipulate their multinational estates with scant regard to national government or the interests of local inhabitants, whose prosperity and survival they decide without consultation or compunction."

Recent scholarly work on the left has recommended worker-controlled corporations as the key social planning unit (Albert and Hahnel 1991a, 1991b); on the right, the private business model has long been hailed as the template for societal governance. Hegel would have been unimpressed by these ideas. Corporations should have a critical role in government, but not because of their superior organization and leadership.

Hegel (1976: 190, 290-1) felt that corporations are prone to poor management, and shortsightedness about wider national issues. Especially at higher levels, corporate work relationships are likely to be unstructured, and prey to nepotism and favoritism. Corporate leadership tends to a parochial authoritarianism and exaggerated vanity.[15] Although these faults disqualified the corporate mind from national leadership, they did not really threaten the state.

> This sphere of private interests . . . affords a playground for personal knowledge, personal decisions and their execution, petty passions and conceits. This is all the more permissible, the more trivial, from the point of view of the universal affairs of the state, is the intrinsic worth of the business which in this way comes to ruin or is managed more or less laboriously, &c.

The central role of the corporation in Hegel's state has nothing to do with corporate political acumen: it is there to provide political representation for members of the various classes[16] in civil society, especially workers and the poor, who would otherwise have no voice whatever in the state.

> It is of the utmost importance that the masses should be organized, because only so do they become mighty and powerful. Otherwise they are nothing but a heap, an aggregate of atomic units. Only when the particular associations are organized members of the state are they possessed of legitimate power.

7. The Universal Class

Modern understanding of bureaucracy has been largely shaped by Weber for whom the civil service was a menace to parliamentary democracy (Bendix 1962: 453; Collins 1986b: 68; Boudon and Bouricoud 1989: 49-54). While much of Weber's ideal-typical discussion was indebted to Hegel, he unwisely extended the concept far beyond government, ascribing a rationality to business organizations that Hegel would have rejected. A Harvard Business School professor unwittingly expressed Hegelian doctrine when he said, "if you pay the chief executives of big American companies like bureaucrats, then they will behave like bureaucrats" (*The Economist* 1992a: 20). (The obverse of this, of course, is that if you pay C. E. O.'s like privateers they will behave like privateers.) Marx, as

I have argued, borrowed quite a different concept of bureaucracy from the *Philosophy of Right*. Leonard Horner and the others are hardly the cold, impassive types who stare out from Weber's work, and populate the many texts on bureaucracy influenced by Weber. If anything Marx's factory inspectors resemble far more closely the rules-crazed socialist zealots portrayed in right-wing literature; or the dedicated nurses and doctors, teachers, military officers, law officials, and humanely patriotic secret agents of popular fiction, film and television.

Nurses, soldiers, spies, and the police are members of the universal class, of course, but in the popular mind the bureaucrat is a Kafkaesque clerk with a green eyeshade. Hegel (1976: 190-2) admitted that government duties can be boring and that "genius" is not a qualification for public service. Tenure is necessary to protect civil servants from "the personal passions of the governed"—as when, for example, a teacher gives a student a bad report card; and salaries and benefits must be generous enough to remove "the external compulsion which may tempt a man to seek ways and means of satisfying them at the expense of his official duties."

Unlike workers and capitalists, Hegel (1976: 192) observed, the civil servant is not engaged in production of an external thing, like a kitchen knife or an automobile.[17] "Work in the public sector," affirms Desmond King (1987: 842) in an insightful article on the welfare state, "is differentiated from employment in the private economy by its removal from a generalized commodity production form: in the public sector, labor is no longer treated as a commodity produced for exchange." In fact, many duties assumed by civil servants are ones which have historically been assigned to women in the family: the "unwaged," decommodified "labour of social care" (Taylor-Gooby 1991: xii). According to Hegel, members of the business class should be penalized for non-fulfilment of contractual obligations, such as supplying defective cutlery, but civil servants are under no such contractual obligations. The Factory Inspectorate, for example, was not under contract to ensure that no underage children worked in a particular textile firm in Lancashire. The civil servant, added Hegel (1976: 191-2), devotes her "main interest, not only [her] particular interest, but [her] mental interest also" on "affairs of state." He was pointing to an important element in the consciousness of the universal class. Experience in advanced western countries indicates, for example, that civil servants and their unions—like the factory inspectors in *Capital*—form political pressure groups in favor of the programs they administer. Moreover, they are also principal allies of the beneficiaries of such programs, and assist state clients in mobilizing to expand or defend welfare programs. "The expansion of public employment over the last thirty years," notes King (1987: 843), "combined with the formation of bureaucratic interests, constitutes significant support for the welfare state and its services." Thus, *organized public servants constitute the kind of concrete barrier Hegel thought was necessary to protect the state from the caprice of elite parliamentary rule.* Government projects may fail, Hegel (1976: 192) admitted, but even the effort itself has "value in and for itself." The educational project of the Factory Inspectorate was in many respects a lost cause, as Marx showed, but it exemplified the desire of the state to provide universal education, and became a pioneering example for subsequent initiatives.

For Hegel (1976: 191-2), deliberate breach of duty or corrupt practices by civil servants are in general far more serious than violation of contract, and constitute "a trespass or even a crime." Violations by factory bureaucrats in the early days of the Factory Acts, for instance, had a large impact on workers' perception of the role of the state, and imperiled the entire government effort.

Duties of civil servants include provision of social goods such as welfare, education and health; the administration of justice; and also prevention of injury and promotion of public safety in the sale and production of commodities (Hegel 1976: 146-52, 193). Thus, far more than with any other class, the work of civil servants demands thought, education, sensitivity, and manners. Recruited mainly from the educated middle class, the civil servant must be broadly educated and well-read. While essential, technical education in the mechanics of administration is not enough; a deep introduction to philosophy, literature, history and so forth are necessary qualifications for civil servants. The larger the state, the more likely it is that bureaucrats can escape mundane personal and family intrigues, and the hatred and revenge of citizens who perceive themselves as wronged. "In those who are busy with the important questions arising in a great state, these subjective interests automatically disappear, and the habit is generated of adopting universal interests, points of view, and activities."

Hegel's concept of the universal class, and Marx's focus on the Factory Inspectorate in *Capital*, point to a peculiar absence in scholarship on government, an absence only recently addressed by Skocpol and other state theorists. As Davidson and Lowe (1981: 280)

observe in relation to twentieth century British experience, "bureaucracy played a constructive role in inter-war social policy which
historians to date have tended to ignore or underplay." Scholars
have accepted the convention of "the anonymity of the civil service,"
assuming that one government department is pretty much like any
other, and that opinion within departments and branches of
government is monolithic. Literature on government frequently
makes no distinction between the pronouncements of leading
politicians and ministers, or the opinions of civil servants, "the
choice depending it would seem, on whichever portrays the
government machine in the most unfavourable light."

Alvin Gouldner (1979: 7) modeled his own "New Class" after
Hegel's civil servants, seeing the union of knowledge and power
they represent "as the best card that history has presently given us
to play." Yet for Gouldner, the New Class is "flawed." "The New
Class is elitist and self-seeking and uses its special knowledge to
advance its own interests and power, and to control its own work
situation." Similarly, Harold Perkin (1989: 518) worries that "well-
paid" public sector professionals devoted to "the ideal of an
egalitarian, caring and compassionate state" might construct "an
authoritarian regime in which individual differences are discouraged
and individual enterprise frustrated."

These factors also troubled Hegel (1976: 193), who saw that the
universal class (as indeed happened in the defunct Soviet Union)
might acquire "the isolated position of an aristocracy and us[e] its
education and skill as a means to an arbitrary tyranny." He pointed,
for instance, to rogue elements of the universal class, such as
lawyers, who use their professional position and technical language
to turn the administration of justice "into an instrument of profit and
tyranny." (Physicians in contemporary North America who have
ransomed and subverted the health care system with astronomical
fees and unnecessary procedures are another example.)

The danger of bureaucratic dictatorship is handled in two ways.
First, strict hierarchy within the bureaucracy and answerability to
senior ministers means that individual civil servants can be called to
account for dereliction of duty or unpleasant manners when dealing
with the public. Moreover, the authority granted private societies
and corporations "is a barrier against the intrusion of subjective
caprice into the power entrusted to a civil servant, and it completes
from below the state control which does not reach down as far as the
conduct of individuals" (Hegel 1976: 192). Szelenyi and Martin

(1988: 663) suggest that these bureaucratic controls may account for hostility in academia toward Gouldner's New Class project.

> The bourgeois society at least offers the freedom of the "professions libres," of the Academia with economic security and privileges for the highly educated. Statist bureaucratization, on the other hand, would endanger such privileges. Would the intellectuals and the highly educated, knowingly and willingly, forego these privileges?

8. Parliament and Public Opinion

While Hegel (1976: 197, 195) saw parliamentary supremacy as a reckless doctrine, he nevertheless viewed parliament as the crowning moment of the state, "a determination of the Idea once the Idea has developed to a totality." It is the key means of bringing individual will to bear upon governance ("the moment of subjective formal freedom"), and offers a critical arena for popular education. Parliament provides a legitimate center for criticism, and prevents the growth of "a powerful *bloc* in opposition to the organized state." From a dialectical standpoint, the estates "are a middle term preventing both the extreme isolation of the crown, which otherwise might seem a mere arbitrary tyranny, and also the isolation of the particular interests of persons, societies, and Corporations."

The estates bring the concerns of ordinary people about bureaucratic policy and behavior directly into government; they also ensure that bureaucrats do their job properly for fear of criticism from legislators. "This same compulsion is also effective on the members of the Estates themselves" (Hegel 1976: 196). However, "the highest civil servants necessarily have a deeper and more comprehensive insight into the nature of the state's organization and requirements," so superior knowledge is not the chief characteristic of the estates. Further, subjective self-interest rules in civil society, and this—rather than the interests of the whole (again better represented by bureaucrats)—is what delegates to the estates are likely to carry with them.

As in most modern legislative systems, Hegel's estates are divided into an upper and lower house. The upper house provides a second look at legislation that might have been hastily passed by a majority party in the lower house, and performs a mediating role between the sovereign and the executive on one side, and the people's representatives on the other. Hegel (1976: 293) justified the presence of the landed class in the upper house, and recommended primogeniture as a means of ensuring orderly political representation from this stratum. Yet there can be hardly any doubt that he expected the sway of the nobility in government "in due course [to] disappear," as did the Scottish thinkers like Steuart who influenced him (Waszek 1988; Winfield 1988: 151).

Hegel (1956: 454-5) was highly critical of the English practice of primogeniture in his lectures on the *Philosophy of History*, denouncing it as an instance of "incredible deficiency"; but he also recognized that in England at the time "knowledge, experience, and facility acquired by practice" were an almost exclusive possession of the aristocracy. Still, the mediating role Hegel gave the upper house vis à vis the monarch on one side and the lower house on the other could as easily be achieved by a mixture of business class and universal class members, as by aristocrats, especially since the chief qualification for upper house members was education and security of income.

Hirst (1989: 20) observes that the "acid test of how democratic a country is, is no longer *who* can vote but *where* they can vote." Thus for political thinkers like Robert Dahl and Norberto Bobbio, real democracy depends on breaking the autonomous power of big business over the electoral system. This effort partly involves democratizing the workplace, as Hegel urged. But another Hegelian idea—which resembles that of the English pluralists, and also Emile Durkheim's (Black 1984: 220-36) notion of the democratic state—is just as important. *Hegel's key recommendation for change in the constitution of states was replacement of universal suffrage by corporate representation.* In Hegel's state, candidates for election are chosen and voted on within corporations, so that issues which concern people directly are brought to parliament through representatives from their own workplaces (Heiman 1971: 131).

This system struck Hegel (1976: 293-4) as far more rational than majority voting, which required from voters an unreasonable amount of "trust" and "confidence" in machine-selected party candidates. He feared that in party systems, voting would be based merely on the candidate's personality as an "abstract single person," rather than on the political aspirant's "principles, or his demeanour, or his conduct, or his concrete mentality generally." Hegel would not have been surprised, for example, by the current state of American politics, in which "political commentators ponder such questions as whether Reagan will remember his lines, or whether Mondale looks too gloomy, or whether Dukakis can duck the slime flung at him by George Bush's speech writers" (Chomsky 1991ba: 18).

Hegel (1976: 201, 294, 205) was not enamored of democratic nostrums such as severely limited terms for legislators or automatic recall mechanisms. Legislators should certainly represent the views of their electors, and this is safeguarded by making deputies representatives of corporations. "The point is . . . that the interest itself is actually present in its representative, while he himself is there to represent the objective element of his own being." Members of parliament should be selected because they have a better idea of corporate and national interests than their electors; moreover, democratic assemblies are "meant to be a living body in which all members deliberate in common and reciprocally instruct and convince each other." If Hegel saw work and corporate membership in civil society as essential for individual self-development, so too is publicity surrounding national political debate. The legislature is "a great spectacle and an education for the citizens, and it is from them that the people learns best how to recognize the true character of its interests." While Hegel knew only "two modes of [public] communication, the press and the spoken word," he would have recognized modern film, radio, and television as performing much the same educational function. Significantly, he did not make a distinction between expression of opinion in mass media and in the public at large. Unalloyed truth can be found in scientific works, but the press and other components of public opinion are "a hotch-potch of truth and endless error."

"At all times," advised Hegel (1976: 294, 205), "public opinion has been a great power and it is particularly so in our day when the principle of subjective freedom has such importance and significance." In the form of common sense, the mind of a people contains "all-pervasive fundamental ethical principles (disguised as prejudices) . . . eternal substantive principles of justice, the true content and result of legislation, the whole constitution, and the general position of the state." However, when these are exposed and aired in public (usually through the organs of the powerful) they "become infected by all the accidents of opinion, by its ignorance and perversity, by its mistakes and falsity of judgement." The basic problem with public opinion is that it lacks self-consciousness, it is non-reflective: "in itself it has no criterion of discrimination, nor has it the ability to extract the substantive element it contains and raise it to precise knowledge." Truth cannot be gleaned from opinion, since truth is discoverable only in itself. (To determine, for example, whether the bombing of Baghdad by the U. S. and its "coalition" allies in 1991 was a good thing, it would be useless to sample public opinion about it.)

Living in a society in which scholarly and scientific work, as well as popular media, were under intense censorship by reactionary authority, Hegel (1976: 205) was keenly aware of the value of free expression of opinion. Freedom of speech is essential, he believed, in a rational state, since this is the only means of satisfying "the goading desire to say one's say and to have said it." Moreover, it is "innocuous" in a society with a rational constitution, "stability of government" and "publicity of Estates Assemblies."

Hegel (1976: 205) pointed to a major contradiction in the notion that powerful elites control public opinion. He granted that the masses can be "*self*-deceived about the manner of its knowledge of . . . things and about its corresponding judgement of its actions, experiences, etc." Since the mass media are part of public opinion, they could clearly play a major role in such "*self*-deception." Thus, Hegel would likely have agreed with the analysis of Noam Chomsky (1991a: 16, 12; 1989), who argues that "the manufacture of consent" "is *more* important for governments that are free and popular than for despotic or military states." Despotic governments can rely on force, says Chomsky, following an argument from David Hume, "but as the state loses this weapon, other devices are required to prevent the ignorant masses from interfering with public affairs, which are none of their business." Yet Hegel (1976: 205) observed that a nation cannot be "deceived about its substantive basis, the essence and specific character of its mind." No amount of propaganda can subvert fundamental cultural beliefs and principles. Accordingly, Chomsky's powerful and compelling critique of indoctrination by the mass media assumes that his readers will recognize the wrongs he points to, and act to remove them, despite the best thought control efforts of the ruling elite.

9. The State as Love

Love is the most remarkable, and little noted, aspect of Hegel's (1971: 263-4) theory of government. "The State," he wrote,

> is the self-conscious ethical substance, the unification of the family principle with that of society. The same unity, which is in the family as a feeling of love, is its essence, receiving, however, at the same time through the second principle of conscious and spontaneously active volition the *form* of conscious universality.

For Hegel, rationality includes love; he would have rejected conceptions of rationality, like those of Weber and his followers, in which self-interest is the underlying principle. Accordingly, a rational state is necessarily one in which the principle of love, of human caring and unity, is dominant. Bologh (1990: 242) shows that Weberian rationality excludes community and family relationships, and "presupposes repression: a certain conception of and relationship to women, a relationship in which women are expected to fulfil men's personal and domestic needs, needs which are then not recognized as essential to being a man." Hegel (1976: 153), however, insisted that the family principle that is vaporized in civil society must be restored by the state. This process begins with corporations, where the ethic of love and friendship becomes dominant.

Given the market principle upon which they are based, however, corporations must limit their efforts, and exclude the welfare of individuals, such as the poor and dispossessed, who are not members. In our time, for instance, powerful unions in the United States have been able to coerce employers into providing health care benefits and other services. "This success reduced the pressure on the American federal state to provide these services, especially because those workers excluded from trade unions constituted a less effectively mobilized pressure" (King 1987: 848).

For Hegel, the chief role of the state and the civil service is to provide for the welfare and happiness of everyone in society. Hegel used the term state "police," which brings to the modern mind visions of red flashing lights on converging patrol cars, and the cold clatter of prison doors (Swaan 1988: 236). Police in its original meaning, however, meant community benevolence, community care. Nevertheless, in Hegel's usage it also underlined the role of the state in preventing powerful groups from victimizing the helpless. "Welfare states are not simply about doing good to individuals by meeting their needs, they are about sanctioning, controlling and directing people's behaviour as well" (Taylor-Gooby 1991: 208). This, of course, was exactly the role of *Capital's* factory inspectors, and it is increasingly the function of modern civil servants. Government must curb what Hegel (1976: 121) called, the "the father's arbitrary will within the family," i. e., men's violence against women and children; and it has to prevent exclusion of women and minorities from the ruling circles of civil society and the state.

The Hegelian vision conflicts radically with the understanding's view of the state, which, in its modern neo-conservative phase, would restrict government largely to national defense and supervision of contracts in civil society, and forbid the state entirely from the realm of the family (except, of course, to protect the "rights" of the fetus). This perspective, as Carole Pateman (1988), Dorothy Smith (1987) and other feminist scholars have shown, is profoundly male-centered, and has resulted in domination of civil society and government by masculine interests. Hegel's standpoint also explains the (patriarchal) Understanding's extreme hostility to the state: "feminization of government" (MacGregor 1989b) is a necessary outcome of the role he assigned to political power. Alan Wolfe (1989: 153), indicates, for instance, that mid-twentieth century notions of the welfare state "were premised on the idea that men would work and women would stay home, thereby making unnecessary (to be correct, unthinkable) the idea of government substituting for . . . the family." But as child care, education, and other tasks formerly carried out entirely within the family pass over to the state, women will increasingly assume a leading role in government. Thus Norwegian social planners expect that by the year 2000 "women will come to dominate the public sector as men flee to the private sector." This process of feminization is likely to be considerably slower in the United States, where state employment accounts for only 20 percent of wage earners, compared to almost 50 percent of workers in Sweden (Wright 1985: 203).

The central principle in Hegel is unity: unity of one personality with and through another in love, marriage, and the family; unity of the individual with her colleagues through work and effort in the corporation and government; and finally, unity of all citizens within the state. The principle of rational love, Hegel (1971: 64) maintained, belongs to the nature of human beings. Like Fourier, he saw sexual desire as the mainspring of all human effort, all the accomplishments of civilization. Desire is satisfied first of all in intimate relationships of love and family; but it also has "an extreme *universal* phase, in purposes political, scientific, or artistic." In this "active" side, "the individual is the vehicle of a struggle of universal and objective interests with the given conditions (both of his own existence and that of the external world), carrying out these universal principles into a unity with the world which is his own work."

Hegel's vision of love, I have argued, is what motivated Marx's idea of communism as well as his exploration of interventionist government in Victorian society. Marx believed that the state should prevent children and women from being sold by their fathers and husbands; that it should rescue workers from the juggernaut of capital, and provide an education for all. Moreover, he saw Leonard Horner and other members of the Factory Inspectorate not as servants of an oppressive regime, but as instruments of this Hegelian vision of the state.

Notes

1. Thus even an anti-Marxist writer like Axel van den Berg (1988:86) sees only the apocalyptic version, and denies that Marx harbored any belief in "incrementalism." "Marx and Engels never believed that any lasting concessions could be won short of the final victory, let alone that socialism could be achieved gradually by cumulative, partial reforms under steady working class pressure." In step with most other interpreters of Marx, van den Berg's clear-headed survey of the Marxist theory of the state contains no references to the Factory Acts.

2. In one of the contradictory types of Marx's communism, says Berki (1983:166-7), "there is no politics, no government, separated offices of state or contending political parties; instead of class and class consciousness there is substantive, familial unity." This is the version of communism I have called apocalyptic. In the other form, communism is not "the transcendence of politics, but the most thorough-going *politicization* of human society. . . . Communism is the destruction of bourgeois society and the ending of class exploitation, but it is also the continuation and further extension of the historical tasks that the bourgeois epoch and capitalism *began* performing but could not successfully bring to a conclusion." Held (1989:36-7) also points to the two versions of Marx's politics.

3. The debate is surveyed in Carnoy (1984), Skocpol (1979, 1985), Alford and Friedland (1985), van den Berg (1988), and Mahon (1991) among others. Wrong (1991:567) claims that van den Berg's "witty demolition of Marxist theories of the state leaves those theories without any credible intellectual foundations." Perhaps the Marxist withdrawal from state theory came none too soon.

4. Richard Bellamy (1987:693), who offers a thoughtful and enthusiastic analysis of the *Philosophy of Right*, observes that "Hegel's defenders would appear to concede the liberal's accusation that his philosophy is implicitly conservative; the endorsement of existing social relations as the product of a benign, if unknowable demiurge, the 'cunning of reason.'"

5. In the excellent collection of articles in the *Cardozo Law Review's* special edition on Hegel, this current is represented by Dallmayr (1989), Arato (1989), and Cohen (1989), with an important, though only partial, dissent by Schlink (1989). Plant (1977b:111-13), Avineri (1972:147-54) and Cullen (1979:85-116) initiated the idea that Hegel was *logically* unable to come to grips with poverty; Walton (1984:253-5) Bellamy (1987:700-701), and Forbes (1988:xii) reject this view.

6. Hegel himself (1974,II:22) emphasized that philosophical discus-sions have an esoteric and exoteric side. Esoteric philosophy is for the initiated; it conveys dangerous and subversive ideas that must be kept within a small circle. Exoteric philosophy deals with non-controversial and conventional issues for public consumption. In the *Philosophy of Mind* (1971:305-13), he relied on this distinction to defend himself against accusations of atheism and pantheism. "I have believed myself obliged to speak at more length and exoterically on the outward and inward untruth of this alleged fact: for exoteric discussion is the only method available in dealing with external apprehension of notions as mere facts . . . The esoteric study of God and identity, as of cognitions and notions, is philosophy itself." Perhaps in the future scholars should consult Leo Strauss's *Persecution and the Art of Writing* (1952) before venturing an interpretation of Hegel. Strauss's book focuses on medieval philosophy, but his "sociology of philosophy" (p. 7) is applicable also to modern writers.

7. Perhaps the capstone of the era came with the comment of Jude Rich, the aptly named head of a Princeton consulting firm. Responding to critics of stratospheric salaries and benefits of chief executive officers of U. S. corporations (which in one celebrated case reached almost $100 million in 1991), Mr. Rich said, "the average worker is being eliminated in many ways by improving efficiency and automation. They are a dime a dozen. What we really need is leadership, and the good leaders are really scarce" (quoted in Cowan 1992:6).

8. I agree with Jameson (1990:241) that "any number of straws in the wind point to an impending Hegel revival, of a new kind." But he cannot be right that "the Hegel who emerges from this rereading will be an unfamiliar materialist-mathematical Hegel, one who comes *after* the *Grundrisse*; quite unlike the idealist-conservative Hegel who *preceded* the writing of Marx's first great work, the unpublished commentary on the *Philosophy of Right*." Certainly, the new Hegel will come after the *Grundrisse*, but his idealism was never "conservative" and always "material-ist." For this argument, see my *Communist Ideal* (1984).

9. Drawing on David Marquand's *The Unprincipled Society* (1988), Hirst (1989:7) outlines the main elements of the "Westminster model": "the doctrine of unlimited parliamentary sovereignty; the appropriation by the executive of the prerogative powers of the monarch; and the fiction that civil servants are merely executors of their masters' will and therefore ministers alone are accountable to Parliament for their actions."

10. Hirst (1989:5-6) points out that in the last decade many advanced western countries have endured tyrannical rule by an elective majority, even though the party in power gained only a minor fraction of the vote. Margaret Thatcher's years at 10 Downing Street typified the experience of countries such as Canada, where Brian Mulroney's Tory party pursued unpopular and destructive policies on the basis of a 43 percent vote. Similarly, President Bush's neo-conservative administration won the 1988

U. S. election, but narrow changes in a few states would have sent Dukakis to the White House; in any case almost half the electorate failed to vote.

11. Daniel Bell (1989:49-50,) suggests that Hegel was wrong on this. The United States, not England (which retained too many elements of a feudal order), was the chief instance of an external state, in Hegel's sense. Bell offers an instructive definition of the external state. "There was no 'State' in the United States, no unified rational will expressed in a political order, but only individual self-interest and a passion for liberty. . . . If there was no State, what was there? To make a semantic yet substantive distinction, there was a *government*. This government was a political marketplace, an arena in which interests contended (not always equally) and in which deals could be made. Almost by chance, the Supreme Court became the final arbiter of disputes and interpreter of rules that allowed the political marketplace to function, subject only to the amendment of the Constitution—which then again was interpreted by the Court. The Constitution and the Court provided the bedrock of civil society." Bell submits that the U. S. now possesses "the lineaments of a State—institutions to shape and enforce a unitary will over and above particular interests [which] . . . emerged in the United States, beginning with the New Deal of Franklin D. Roosevelt."

12. Walter Korpi (1983:192-3) develops something like the Hegelian distinction, arguing that modern welfare states may be seen as either "marginal" (Hegel's external state) or "institutional" (Hegel's rational state). A minimal welfare state, such as that of the United States, devotes relatively little of its resources to the welfare of its citizens, and relies on individualistic criteria to distribute these. By contrast, the Scandinavian countries are institutional welfare states, spending a large proportion of national income on welfare programs, which are based on universal criteria.

13. This is what right-wing parties have succeeded in doing in many Western countries. Heilbroner and Bernstein (1989) propose that governments should distinguish between operating costs, and investment expenditures, like education, road building, and so forth. Investments could be financed by deficit spending without undue gnashing of teeth; operating costs would be covered by normal revenue. By taking the deficit out of the political arena, and treating it like an accounting problem, their proposal might help resolve the fiscal dilemma flagged by Hegel.

14. As Hegel (1976:288) put it, the signature of the monarch "is important. It is the last word beyond which it is impossible to go.

15. A discussion of modern corporate culture with many parallels to Hegel's appears in Alex de Jonge's brilliant *Stalin* (1986:14-15). "I have come to understand that in the world of the nontenured, administration by fear, with the firing squad replaced by instant dismissal, is closer to the rule [in business corporations] than the exception. Indeed, it appears to be the norm for any organization in which the administrators are not accountable to those under their authority and in which there is no job security."

16. Nothing in Hegel's scheme would prevent groups of civil servants from forming their own autonomous corporations, or unions, as indeed many have in the advanced capitalist countries. "State officials . . . are more highly unionized and organized than other sections of the workforce" (King 1987:855).

17. Richard Dien Winfield (1988:152, 227) sees Hegel's universal class as "extraneous" and "an anomaly" because it does not produce commodities! And certainly only in America could a "Hegelian" construct an ideal society that lacks a state and is governed by "interdependent decisions of autonomous market agents."

References

Albert, Michael and Hahnel, Robin. 1992a. *Looking Forward: Participatory Economics for the Twenty First Century*. Boston: South End Press.
_____. 1992b. *The Political Economy of Participatory Economics*. Princeton: Princeton University Press.
Alexander, Jeffrey C. 1987. "The Centrality of the Classics." Pp. 11-57 in *Social Theory Today*, ed. Anthony Giddens and Jonathan Turner. Stanford, California: Stanford University Press.
Alexander, Sally. 1984. "Women, Class and Sexual Differences in the 1840s: Some Reflections on the Writing of a Feminist History." *History Workshop Journal* 17 (Spring 1984): 123-49.
Alford, Robert, and Roger Friedland. 1985. *Powers of Theory: Capitalism, the State, and Democracy*. Cambridge: Cambridge University Press.
Anderson, M. 1971. *Family Structure in Nineteenth-century Lancashire*. Cambridge: Cambridge University Press.
_____. 1976. "Sociological History and the Working-class Family: Smelser Revisited." *Social History* 3 (Oct.): 317-34.
_____. 1990. "The Social Implications of Demographic Change." Pp. 1-70 in *The Cambridge Social History of Britain, 1750-1950*, ed. F. M. L. Thompson. Vol. 2, *People and Their Environment*. Cambridge: Cambridge University Press.
Anderson, Perry. 1965. "Origins of the Present Crisis." Pp. 11-52 in *Towards Socialism*, ed. Perry Anderson and Robin Blackburn. London: The Fontana Library.
_____. 1976. *Considerations on Western Marxism*. London: NLB.
_____. 1987. "The Figures of Descent." *New Left Review* 161 (Jan): 20-77.
Arato, Andrew. 1989. "The Reconstruction of Hegel's Theory of Civil Society." Hegel and legal theory, part 1. *Cardoza Law Review* 10(5-6)(Mar.).
Archibald, W. Peter. 1989. *Marx and the Missing Link*. Basingstoke: Macmillan.
Arthur, Chris. 1986. *Dialectics of Labour: Marx and His Relation to Hegel*. Oxford: Basil Blackwell.
Arthurs, H. W. 1985. *"Without the Law": Administrative Justice and Legal Pluralism in Nineteenth Century England* . Toronto: University of Toronto Press.

Ashton, Rosemary. 1989. *Little Germany: German Refugees in Victorian Britain.* Oxford: Oxford University Press.

Augarde, Tony, Ed. 1991. *The Oxford Dictionary of Modern Quotations.* Oxford: Oxford University Press.

Avineri, Shlomo. 1972. *Hegel's Theory of the Modern State.* Cambridge: Cambridge University Press.

_____. 1985. "Feature Book Review: The Discovery of Hegel's Early Lectures on the Philosophy of Right." *The Owl of Minerva* 16(2)(Spring): 199-208.

Aydelotte, William O. 1954. "The House of Commons in the 1840's." *History* 137 (Oct.): 249-62.

_____. 1966. "Parties and Issues in Early Victorian England." *The Journal of British Studies.* V: 95-114.

Backhouse, Constance, and Leah Cohen. 1978. *The Secret Oppression.* Toronto: Macmillan.

Barber, Benjamin. 1988. "Spirit's Phoenix and History's Owl or the Incoherence of Dialectics in Hegel's Account of Women." *Political Theory* 16(1)(Feb.): 5-28.

Barmby, Catherine Isabella, "Woman and the Laws." Pp. 96-101 in *Political Women 1800-1850*, eds. Ruth and Edmund Frow. London: Pluto Press.

Barrett, Michèle. 1980. *Women's Oppression Today.* London: Verso Editions.

_____. 1984. "Rethinking Women's Oppression: A Reply to Brenner and Ramas." *New Left Review* 146 (July - Aug.): 123-8.

_____. 1985. Introduction to *The Origin of the Family, Private Property and the State*, by Friedrich Engels. Harmondsworth, Middlesex: Penguin Books.

Bartrip, P. W. J. 1979. "Safety at Work: The Factory Inspectorate in the Fencing Controversy, 1833-1857." Centre for Socio-legal Studies Working Paper no. 4. Mar.

_____. 1982. "British Government Inspection, 1832-1875: Some Observations." *Th Historical Journal* 25(3): 605-26.

_____. 1983. "State Intervention in Mid-nineteenth Century Britain: Fact or Fiction?" *The Journal of British Studies* XXIII(1)(Fall): 63-83.

_____. 1985. "Success or Failure? The Prosecution of the Early Factory Acts." *Economic History Review* 38.

Bartrip, P. W. J., and P. T. Fenn. 1980. "The Administration of Safety: The Enforcement Policy of the Early Factory Inspectorate, 1844-1864." *Public Administration* LVIII: 87-102.

_____. 1980. "The Conventionalization of Factory Crime—a Re-assessment." *International journal of the sociology of law* 8: 175-86.

_____. 1983. "The Evolution of Regulatory Style in the Nineteenth-century British Factory Inspectorate." *International Journal of the Sociology of Law* 8.

_____. 1990. "The Measurement of Safety: Factory Accident Statistics in Victorian and Edwardian England." *Historical Research* 63(150)(Feb.):

58-72.

Baynes, Kenneth. 1989. "State and Civil Society in Hegel's *Philosophy of Right*: Comments on Dallmayr and Arato." Hegel and Legal Theory, Part I. *Cardozo Law Review* 10(5-6)(Mar.): 1415-26.

Beckett, J. V. 1986. *The Aristocracy in England 1660-1914*. Oxford: Basil Blackwell.

Behlmer, George K. 1982. *Child Abuse and Moral Reform in England, 1870-1908*. Stanford, Calif.: Stanford University Press.

Bell, Daniel. 1989. "'American Exceptionalism' Revisited: The Role of Civil Society." *The Public Interest* 95: 38-56.

Bellamy, R. 1986. "Hegel's Conception of the State and Political Philosophy in a Post-Hegelian World." *Political Science* 38(2): 99-112.

_____. 1987. "Hegel and Liberalism." *History of European Ideas* 8(6): 693-708.

_____. 1987a. *Modern Italian Social Theory*. Oxford: Basil Blackwell.

Bendix, Reinhard. 1962. *Max Weber: An Intellectual Portrait*. New York: Doubleday & Company Inc.

Benhabib, Seyla. 1984. "Obligation, Contract and Exchange: On the Significance of Hegel's Abstract Right." Pp. 159-77 in *State and Civil Society: Studies in Hegel's Political Philosophy*, ed. Z. A. Pelczynski. Cambridge: Cambridge University Press.

Benson, Peter. 1989. "Abstract Right and the Possibility of a Nondistributive Conception of Contract: Hegel and Contemporary Contract Theory." Hegel and legal theory, part 1. *Cordozo Law Review* 10(5-6)(Mar.): 1077-1198.

Bentley, Michael. 1984. *Politics Without Democracy 1815-1914: Perception and Preoccupation in British Government*. London: Fontana Paperbacks.

Berg, Maxine. 1985. *The Age of Manufactures: Industry, Innovation and Work in Britain, 1700-1820*. London: Fontana Press.

_____. 1987. "Women's Work, Mechanisation and the Early Phases of Industrialisation in England." Pp. 64-98 in *The Historical Meanings of Work*, ed. Patrick Joyce. Cambridge: Cambridge University Press.

Berki, R. N. 1983. *Insight and Vision: The Problem of Communism in Marx's Thought*. London: J. M. Dent & Sons Ltd.

_____. 1988. *The Genesis of Marxism: Four Lectures*. London: Dent.

Berman, Paul. 1991. "Still Sailing the Lemonade Sea." *New York Times Magazine*, Oct. 27.

Bienefeld, M. A. 1972. *Working Hours in British Industry*. London: London School of Economics and Political Science

Black, Anthony. 1984. *Guilds and Civil Society in European Political Thought from the Twelfth Century to the Present*. Ithaca, N.Y.: Cornell University Press.

Block, Fred. 1987. *Revising State Theory: Essays in Politics and Postindustrialism*. Philadelphia: Temple University Press.

_____. "Bringing the State Back to Its Proper Place," *Contemporary Sociology* 20(6)(Nov.): 871-3.

References 303

Block, Fred, and Somers, M. "Beyond the Economistic Fallacy: the Holistic Social Science of Karl Polanyi." Pp. 47-84 in *Vision and Method in Historical Sociology*, ed. Theda Skocpol. New York: Cambridge University Press.

Bobbio, Norberto. 1988. "Gramsci and the Concept of Civil Society." Pp. 73-100 in *Civil Society and the State: New European Perspectives*, ed. John Keane. London: Verso.

Bohme, H. 1978. *An Introduction to the Social and Economic History of Germany: Politics and Economic Change in the Nineteenth and Twentieth Centuries.* Oxford: Oxford University Press.

Bologh, Roslyn W. 1990. *Love or Greatness: Max Weber and Masculine Thinking—A Feminist Inquiry.* London: Unwin Hyman Limited.

Booth, William James. 1989. "Gone Fishing: Making Sense of Marx's Concept of Communism." *Political Theory* 17(2)(May): 205-22.

_____. 1991. "Economies of Time: On the Idea of Time in Marx's Political Economy." *Political Theory* 19(1)(Feb.): 7-27.

Boswell, John. 1988. *The Kindness of Strangers: The Abandonment of Children in Western Europe from Late Antiquity to the Renaissance.* New York: Pantheon Books.

Boudon, Raymond, and François Bourricaud. 1989. *A Critical Dictionary of Sociology.* Chicago: The University of Chicago Press.

Bourdieu, Pierre. 1984. *Distinction: A Social Critique of the Judgement of Taste.* Trans. Richard Nice. Harvard: Harvard University Press.

Braybrooke, David. 1985. "Contemporary Marxism on the Autonomy, Efficacy and Legitimacy of the Capitalist State." Pp. 59-86 in *The Democratic State*, ed. Roger W. Benjamin and Stephen L. Elkin. Lawrence, Kansas: University Press of Kansas.

Brenner, Johanna, and Maria Ramas. 1984. "Rethinking Women's Oppression." *New Left Review* 144 (Mar. - Apr.): 37-71.

Brock, Michael. 1973. *The Great Reform Act.* London: Hutchinson University Library.

Brodie, Janine,

Buchwalter, A. 1991. "Hegel, Marx and the Concept of Immanent Critique." *Journal of the History of Philosophy* xxix(2)(Apr.): 253-80.

Burawoy, Michael. 1982. "Introduction: The Resurgence of Marxism in American Sociology." *American Journal of Sociology* 88 Supplement:S1-30.

_____. 1985. *The Politics of Production: Factory Regimes Under Capitalism and Socialism.* London: Verso.

Bush, M. L. 1984. *The English Aristocracy: A Comparative Synthesis.* Manchester: Manchester University Press.

Butler, Clark. 1984. "Commentary." *Hegel: The Letters.* Trans. Clark Butler and Christiane Seiler. Ed. Clark Butler. Bloomington, Indiana: Indiana University Press.

Calhoun, Craig. 1982. *The Question of Class Struggle: Social Foundations of Popular Radicalism During the Industrial Revolution.* Chicago: University of

Chicago Press.

Callinicos, Alex. 1989. "Introduction: Analytical Marxism." Pp. 1-16 in *Marxist Theory*, ed. Alex Callinicos. Oxford: Oxford University Press.

Campbell, John L., and Leon N. Lindberg. 1990. "Property Rights and the Organization of Economic Activity by the State." *American Sociological Review* 55 (Oct.): 634-47.

Cannadine, David. 1984. "The Present and the Past in the English Industrial Revolution, 1880-1980." *Past and Present* 103: 131-72.

_____ . 1987. "British History: Past, Present - and Future?" *Past and Present* 116: 169-91.

_____ . 1989. *The Pleasures of the Past*. London: Fontana Press.

_____ . 1990. *The Decline and Fall of the British Aristocracy*. New Haven and London: Yale University Press.

Carnoy, M. 1984. *The State and Political Theory*. Princeton: Princeton University press.

Carson, W. G. 1974. "Symbolic and Instrumental Dimensions of Early Factory Legislation: A Case Study in the Social Origins of Criminal Law." *Crime, Criminology and Public Policy: Essays in Honour of Sir Leon Razinowicz*, ed. Roger Hood. London: Heinemann.

_____ . 1979. "The Conventionalization of Early Factory Crime." *International Journal for the Sociology of Law* 7 (37-60).

_____ . 1980. "Early Factory Inspectors and the Viable Class Society--a Rejoinder." *International Journal for the Sociology of Law* 8: 187-91.

Casey, James. 1989. *The History of the Family*. Oxford: Basil Blackwell.

Chester, Norman. 1981. *The English Administrative System 1780-1870*. Oxford: Oxford University Press.

Chodorow, Nancy. 1978. *The Reproduction of Mothering: Psychoanalysis and the Sociology of Gender*. Berkeley: University of California Press.

Chomsky, Noam. 1989. *Necessary Illusions: Thought Control in Democratic Societies*. Toronto: CBC Enterprises.

_____ . 1991a. "Force and Opinion." *Z Magazine*, July/August, 10-24.

_____ . 1991b. "Middle East Diplomacy." *Z Magazine*, Dec., 29-41.

Clark, Anna. 1987. *Women's Silence, Men's Violence*. London: Pandora Press.

Clark, Sam. 1991. "The Institutionalization of Aristocratic Status in Western Europe." Unpublished paper.

Claybrook, Joan. 1984. *Retreat from Safety: Reagan's Attack on American Health*. New York: Pantheon.

Cohen, Isaac. 1985. "Industrial Capitalism, Technology, and Labor Relations: The Early Cotton Industry in Lancashire (1770-1840) and New England (1790-1840)." Pp. 89-140 in *Political Power and Social Theory*, ed. Maurice Zeitlin. Greenwich, Connecticut: JAI Press.

Cohen, Jean. 1989. "Morality or *Sittlichkeit*: Toward a Post-Hegelian Solution." Hegel and legal theory, part 1. *Cardoza Law Review* 10(5-6)(Mar.).

Cohen, Leonard. 1988. "First We Take Manhattan." New York: Columbia

Records.

Colley, Linda. 1984. "The Apotheosis of George IIIrd: Loyalty, Royalty and the British Nation, 1760-1820." *Past and Present* 102 (Feb.).

_____. 1986. "Whose Nation? Class and National Consciousness in Britain 1750-1830." *Past and Present* 113 (Nov.).

_____. 1986a. "The Politics of Eighteenth-century British History." *Journal of British Studies* 25 (Oct.): 359-79.

Collins, Randall. 1985. *Three Sociological Traditions*. Oxford: Oxford University Press.

_____. 1986. *Weberian Sociological Theory*. Cambridge: Cambridge University Press.

_____. 1986a. *Max Weber: A Skeleton Key*. Newbury Park, California: Sage Publications.

_____. 1987. "A Micro-macro Theory of Intellectual Creativity: The Case of German Idealist Philosophy." *Sociological Theory* 5(1)(Spring): 47-69.

_____. 1988. *Theoretical Sociology*. San Diego: Harcourt Brace Jovanovich, Publishers.

Conway, John. 1990. *The Canadian Family in Crisis*. Toronto: James Lorimer & Company, Publishers.

Corbin, Alain. 1990. "Backstage." Pp. 451-668 in *A History of Private Life*, trans. Arthur Goldhammer, vol. 1. Ed. Paul Veyne. *From the Fires of Revolution to the Great War*. Ed. Michelle Perrot. Cambridge, Massachusetts: The Belknap Press of Harvard University Press.

Cornell, Drucilla. 1989. "Dialogic Reciprocity and the Critique of Employment at Will." Hegel and legal theory, part 2. *Cardoza Law Review* 10(5-6)(Mar. - Apr.): 1575-1623.

Corrigan, P., , and D. Sayer. 1985. *The Great Arch: English State Formation as Cultural Revolution*. Oxford: Blackwell.

Cott, Nancy F. 1987. *The Grounding of Modern Feminism*. New Haven: Yale University Press.

Cowan, Alison Leigh. 1992. "The Gadfly C. E. O.'s Want to Swat." *New York Times*, Feb. 2.

Coward, Rosalind. 1983. *Patriarchal Precedents: Sexuality and Social Problems*. London: Routledge & Kegan Paul.

Crouzet, François. 1982. *The Victorian Economy*. London: Methuen and Company Limited.

Cullen, Bernard. 1979. *Hegel's Social and Political Thought: An Introduction*. Dublin: Gill Macmillan.

_____. 1988. "The Mediating Role of Estates and Corporations in Hegel's Theory of Political Representation." Pp. 22-41 in *Hegel Today*, ed. Bernard Cullen. Aldershot, Hants.: Gower Publishing Company Limited.

Cunningham, H. 1990a. "Leisure and Culture." Pp. 279-339 in *The Cambridge Social History of Britain, 1750-1950*, ed. F. M. L. Thompson. Vol. 2, *People and Their Environment*. Cambridge: Cambridge University Press.

_____. 1990. "The Employment and Unemployment of Children in

England C. 1680-1851." *Past and Present* 126: 115-50.

D'Hondt, Jacques. 1988. *Hegel in His Time: Berlin, 1818-1831*. Trans. John Burbidge, Nelson Roland and Judith Levasseur. Peterborough, Ontario: Broadview Press.

Dallmayr, Fred. 1989. "Rethinking the Hegelian State." Hegel and legal theory, part 1. *Cardoza Law Review* 10(5-6)(Mar.).

Daly, Mary. 1973. *Beyond God the Father: Toward a Philosophy of Women's Liberation*. Boston: Beacon Press.

Davidoff, Leonore. 1990. "The Family in Britain." Pp. 71-130 in *The Cambridge Social History of Britain, 1750-1950*, ed. F. M. L. Thompson. Vol. 2, *People and Their Environment*. Cambridge: Cambridge University Press.

Davidoff, Leonore, and Catherine Hall. 1987. *Family Fortunes: Men and Women of the English Middle Class, 1780-1850*. London: Hutchinson.

Davidson, R. 1985. *Whitehall and the Labour Problem in Late-Victorian and Edwardian Britain: A Study in Official Statistics and Social Control*. London: Croom Helm.

Davidson, R., and R. Lowe. 1981. "Bureaucracy and Innovation in British Welfare Policy 1870-1945." Pp. 263-95 in *The Emergence of the Welfare in Britain and Germany*, ed. W. J. Mommsen. London: Croom Helm.

Davis, H. W. Carless. 1964. *The Age of Peel and Grey*. Oxford: Oxford University Press.

Dawson, Ruth P. 1980. "The Feminist Manifesto of Theodor Gottlieb von Hippel (1741-96)." Pp. 13-32 in *Gestaltet und Gestaltend: Frauen in der Deutschen Literatur*, ed. Marianne Burkhard. Amsterdam: Rodopi.

De Beauvoir, Simone. 1953. *The Second Sex*. Trans. H. M. Parshley. New York: Alfred A. Knopf.

De Jonge, Alex. 1986. *Stalin and the Shaping of the Soviet Union*. Glasgow: William Collins Sons & Co. Ltd.

Delillo, Don. 1985. *White Noise*. New York: Viking.

Dicey, A. V. 1914. *Lectures on the Relation between Law and Public Opinion in England in the Nineteenth Century*. Second edition. London: Macmillan.

Djang, T. K. 1942. *Factory Inspection in Great Britain*. London: Allen.

Doctorow, E. L. 1989. *Billy Bathgate*. New York: Random House.

Domhoff, G. William. 1967. *Who Rules America?* Englewood Cliffs, N.J.: Prentice Hall.

_____ . 1987. "The Wagner Act and Theories of the State: A New Analysis Based on Class-segment Theory." Pp. 159-85 in *Political Power and Social Theory*, ed. Maurice Zeitlin. Greenwich, Connecticut: JAI Press.

Donajgrodzki, A. P. 1977. "'Social Police' and the Bureaucratic Elite: A Vision of Order in the Age of Reform." *Social Control in Nineteenth Century Britain*, ed. A. P. Donajgrodzki. London: Croom Helm.

_____ . 1977. "'Social Police' and the Bureaucratic Elite: A Vision of Order in the Age of Reform." *Social Control in Nineteenth Century Britain*, ed. A. P. Donajgrodzki. London: Croom Helm.

Draper, Hal. 1977. *Karl Marx's Theory of Revolution.* Vol. 1, *State and Bureaucracy.* New York: Monthly Review Press.

_____. 1985a. *The Marx-Engels Cyclopedia.* Ed. Hal Draper. Vol. I, *The Marx-Engels Chronicle: A Day-by-day Chronology of Marx and Engels' Life and Activity.* New York: Schocken Books.

_____. 1985b. *The Marx-Engels Cyclopedia.* Ed. Hal Draper. Vol. II, *The Marx-Engels Register: A Complete Bibliography of Marx and Engels' Individual Writings.* New York: Schocken Books.

_____. 1986. *The Marx-Engels Cyclopedia.* Ed. Hal Draper. Vol. III, *The Marx-Engels Glossary: Glossary to the Chronicle and Register, and Index to the Glossary.* New York: Schocken Books.

Driver, Cecil. 1946. *Tory Radical, the Life of Richard Oastler.* Oxford: Oxford University Press.

Drucker, Peter. 1989. "The Next Workplace Revolution." *Report on Business Magazine* 6(3).

Drydyk, Jay. 1986. "Hegel's Politics: Liberal or Democratic." *Canadian Journal of Philosophy* 16(1): 99-122.

_____. 1991. "Review of Norbert Waszek's Hegel's Account of Civil Society." *The Owl of Minerva* 22(2)(Spring): 230-34.

_____. 1991 a. "Capitalism, Socialism, and Civil Society." *The Monist* 74(3)(July): 457-77.

Duquette, David. 1990.

Durkheim, Emile. 1986. *Durkheim on Politics and the State.* Ed. Anthony Giddens. Stanford: Stanford University Press.

Dyson, Kenneth H. F. 1980. *The State Tradition in Western Europe: A Study of an Idea and an Institution.* New York: Oxford University Press.

Easton, Susan. 1987. "Hegel and Feminism." Pp. 30-55 in *Hegel and Modern Philosophy,* ed. David Lamb. London: Croom Held.

The Economist. 1992a. "Bosses' Pay." Feb. 1st, 19-22.

_____. 1992b. "Let Them Eat Pollution." Feb. 8th-14th, 66.

Ellerman, David P. 1983. "Marxian Exploitation Theory: A Brief Exposition, Critique." *Philosophical Forum* XIV(4)(Summer): 293-326.

_____. 1985. "On the Labor Theory of Property." *The Philosophical Forum* 4(16)(Summer): 293-326.

_____. 1989. *Foundations of Economic Democracy.* Unpublished ms.

_____. 1990. *The Democratic Worker-owned Firm: A New Model for East and West.* Boston: Unwin Hyman.

_____. Forthcoming. *The Labor Theory of Property.* Unpublished ms.

Elshtain, Jean Bethke. 1981. *Public Man, Private Woman.* Oxford: Martin Robertson.

Elster, Jon. 1989. "Self-realisation in Work and Politics: The Marxist Conception of the Good Life." Pp. 127-58 in *Alternatives to Capitalism,* ed. Jon Elster and Karl Ove Moene. Cambridge: Cambridge University Press.

Engels, Frederick. 1969. *The Condition of the Working Class in England.*

London: Grafton Books.

_____ . 1985. *The Origin of the Family, Private Property and the State.* Introduction by Michèle Barrett. Harmondsworth, Middlesex: Penguin Books.

Esping-Andersen, G. 1985. *Politics Against Markets: The Social Democratic Road to Power.* Princeton: Princeton University Press.

Evans, Eric J., ed. 1978. *Social Policy 1830-1914, Individualism, Collectivism and the Origins of the Welfare State.* London: Routledge & Kegan Paul.

_____ . 1983. *The Forging of the Modern State.* London: Longman.

Evans, P. B., D. Reuschemeyer, and T. Skocpol. 1985. *Bringing the State Back In:.* Cambridge: Cambridge University Press.

Evans, Richard J. 1990. "Epidemics and Revolutions: Cholera in Nineteenth-century Europe." *Past and Present* 120: 123-46.

Ferguson, Ann. *Sexual Democracy: Women, Oppression, and Revolution.* Boulder, CO.: Westview Press.

Feurer, Rosemary. 1988. "The Meaning of 'Sisterhood': The British Women's Movement and Protective Labor Legislation, 1870-1900." *Victorian Studies* 31(2)(Winter): 233-60.

Fine, B. and L. Harris. 1987. "Ideology and Markets: Economic Theory and the 'New Right.'" Pp. 365-392 in *Socialist Register*, eds. Ralph Miliband, Leo Panitch and John Saville. London: Merlin Press Ltd.

Finer, Herman. 1961. *The Theory and Practice of Modern Government.* London: Methuen & Co. Ltd.

Finer, Sidney. 1952. *The Life and Times of Sir Edwin Chadwick.* New York: Barnes and Noble Inc.

Finlayson, Geoffrey B. A. M. 1981. *The Seventh Earl of Shaftesbury, 1801-1885.* London: Eyre Methuen.

Foner, Eric. 1992. "She Didn't Know Her Place." Review of *Ahead of Her Time*, by Dorothy Sterling. *New York Times Book Review* (Jan 26).

Forbes, Duncan. 1975. Introduction to *Lectures on the Philosophy of World History: Introduction*, by G. W. F. Hegel. Cambridge: Cambridge University Press.

_____ . 1988. Introduction to *The Scottish Enlightenment and Hegel's Account of "Civil Society"* By Norbert Waszek. Dordrecht: Kluwer Academic Publishers.

Foster, John. 1974. *Class Struggle and the Industrial Revolution.* London: St. Martin's Press.

Foster, R.F. 1988. *Modern Ireland 1600-1972.* London: Viking.

Fox, Alan. 1985. *History and Heritage: The Social Origins of the British Industrial Relations System.* London: Allen & Unwin.

Foxwell, H. S. 1962. Introduction to *The Right to the Whole Produce of Labour: The Origins and Development of the Theory of Labour's Claim to the Whole Product of Industry*, by Anton Menger. New York: Augustus M. Kelley.

Fraser, Derek. 1970. "The Agitation for Parliamentary Reform." Pp. 31-53 in *Popular Movements, c. 1830-1850*, ed. J. T. Ward. London: Macmillan and Co. Ltd.

_____. 1984. *The Evolution of the British Welfare State*. Second edition. London: Macmillan Press.

Freifeld, Mary. 1986. "Technological Change and the 'Self-Acting' Mule: A Study of Skill and the Division of Labour." *Social History*. 11(3)(October): 319-42.

Frevert, Ute. 1989. *Women in German History: From Bourgeois Emancipation To Sexual Liberation*. New York: Berg.

Fyfe, Alec. 1989. *Child Labour*. Cambridge: Polity Press.

Gallagher, Catherine. 1985. *The Industrial Transformation of English Fiction: Social Discourse and the Narrative Form 1832-1867*. Chicago: University of Chicago Press.

Gash, Norman. 1953. *Politics in the Age of Peel: A Study in the Technique of Parliamentary Representation 1830-1850*. London: Longmans, Green and Co. Ltd.

_____. 1979. *Aristocracy and People: Britain 1815-1865*. London: Edward Arnold.

_____. 1986. *Pillars of Government and Other Essays on State and Society, c. 1768-1880*. London: Edward Arnold.

Gilligan, Carol. 1982. *In a Different Voice: Psychological Theory and Women's Development*. Cambridge, M. A.: Harvard University Press.

Gillis, John R. 1985. *For Better, for Worse: British Marriages 1600 to the Present*. Oxford: Oxford University Press.

Glen, Robert. 1984. *Urban Workers in the Early Industrial Revolution*. London: Croom Helm.

Globe and Mail. 1989. Aug. 17.

Gouldner, Alvin. 1979. *The Future of Intellectuals and the Rise of the New Class: A Frame of Reference, Theses, Conjectures, Arguments, and an Historical Perspective on the Role of Intellectuals and Intelligentsia in the International Class Contest in the Modern Era*. New York: Continuum.

Gowan, Peter. 1987. "The Origins of the Administrative Elite." *New Left Review* 162 (Mar.).

Gray, Robert. 1987. "The Languages of Factory Reform in Britain, c. 1830-1860." Pp. 143-79 in *The Historical Meanings of Work*, ed. Patrick Joyce. Cambridge: Cambridge University Press.

_____. 1991. "Medical Men, Industrial Labour and the State in Britain, 1830-50." *Social History* 16(1)(Jan): 19-43.

Grebing, Hilda. 1985. *A History of the German Labour Movement*. Werwickshire: Berg.

Greenberger, Ellen , and Laurence Steinberg. 1986. *When Teenagers Work: The Psychological and Social Costs of Adolescent Employment*. New York: Basic Books, Inc.

Gregg, Pauline. 1982. *A Social and Economic History of Britain, 1760-1980*. Eighth edition revised. London: Harrap Limited.

Halévy Élie. 1956. *Thomas Hodgskin*. London: Ernest Benn Limited.

_____ . 1961a. *A History of the English People*. Vol. 3, *The Triumph of Reform (1830-1841)*. Trans. E. I. Watkin. New York: Barnes and Noble Inc.

_____ . 1961b. *A History of the English People*. Vol. 4, *Victorian Years (1841-1895)*. Trans. E. I. Watkin. New York: Barnes and Noble.

_____ . 1987a. *A History of the English People*. Vol. 1, *A History of the English People in 1815*. Trans. E.I. Watkin. New York: Ark Paperbacks.

_____ . 1987b. *A History of the English People*. Vol. 2, *The Liberal Awakening (1815-1830)*. Trans. E. I. Watkin.

Hamerow. T. S. 1958. *Restoration, Revolution, Reaction: Economics and Politics in Germany: 1815-1871*. Princeton: Princeton University Press.

Harris, H. S. 1983. "The Social Ideal of Hegel's Economic Theory." Pp. 49-74 in *Hegel's Philosophy of Action* edited by S. Stepelevich and D. Lamb. Atlantic Highlands, N. J.: Humanities Press.

_____ . 1988. "Preface." *Hegel in His Time*. By Jacques D'Hondt. Peterborough, Ont.: Broadview Press.

Harris, José. 1990. "Society and the State in Twentieth Century Britain." Pp. 63-118 in *The Cambridge Social History of Britain, 1750-1850*, ed. F. M. L. Thompson. Vol. 3, *Social Agencies and Institutions*. Cambridge: Cambridge University Press.

Harris, Laurence, V. G. Kiernan, and Ralph Miliband, eds. 1983. *A Dictionary of Marxist Thought*. Harvard: Harvard University Press.

Harrison, Brian. 1989. "Class and Gender in Modern British Labour History." *Past and Present* 124 (Aug.): 121-58.

Hart, Nicky. 1989. "Gender and the Rise and Fall of Class Politics." *New Left Review* 175 (May/June): 19-47.

Hartmann, Heidi. 1981. "The Unhappy Marriage of Marxism and Feminism: Towards a More Progressive Union." *Women and Revolution*, ed. Lydia Sargent. Montreal: Black Rose Books.

Hawkins, Angus. 1989. "'Parliamentary Government' and Victorian Political Parties, C. 1830-c. 1880." *English Historical Review* (July): 638-69.

Health and Safety Executive. 1980. *A Brief History of HM Factory Inspectorate*. London: Health and Safety Executive.

Hegel, G. W. F. 1948. *Early Theological Writings*. Trans. T. M. Knox. Philadelphia: University of Philadelphia Press.

_____ . 1955. *Lectures on the History of Philosophy*, volume 2. Trans. E. S. Haldane and Frances H. Simson. London: Routledge and Kegan Paul.

_____ . 1956. *The Philosophy of History*. Trans. J. Sibree. New York: Dover Publications, Inc.

_____ . 1964. *Hegel's Political Writings*. Trans. T.M. Knox. Oxford: Oxford University Press.

_____ . 1971. *Philosophy of Mind: Being Part Three of The Encyclopaedia of the Philosophical Sciences*. Trans. William Wallace and A. V. Miller. Oxford: Oxford University Press.

_____ . 1974. *Vorlesungen Uber Rechtphilosophie*. Ed. K. -H. Ilting. Stuttgart: Frommann Verlag.

_____ . 1974. *Lectures on the History of Philosophy*, volume 3. Trans. E. S. Haldane and Frances H. Simson. New York.

_____ . 1975. *Hegel's Logic: Being Part One of the Encyclopaedia of the Philosophical Sciences (1830)*. Trans. William Wallace. Oxford: Oxford University Press.

_____ . 1975a. *Aesthetics*, vol. 1. Trans. T. M. Knox. Oxford: Oxford University Press.

_____ . 1976. *Philosophy of Right*. Oxford: Oxford University Press.

_____ . 1977. *Phenomenology of Spirit*. Trans. A. V. Miller. Oxford: Oxford University Press.

_____ . 1980. *Lectures on the Philosophy of World History: Introduction*. Trans. H. B. Nisbet. Cambridge: Cambridge University Press.

_____ . 1983a. *Vorlesungen Ausgewahlte Nachschriften Und Manuskripte*. Vol. 1, *Vorlesungen Ber Naturrechtund Staatswissenschafts: Heidelburg 1817/18 mit Nachtragen Aus DerVorlesung 1818/19 Nachgeschrieben von Peter Wannenmann*. Ed. W Bonsiepen, Gethmann-Siefert A., F. Hogemann, W. Jaeschke, Ch. Jamme, H.-Ch. Lucas, K.R. Meist, and H. Schneider C Becker. Hamburg: Felix Meiner.

_____ . 1983b. *Philosophie Des Rechts, die Vorlesung von 1819/20 In einer Nachschrift*. Ed. D. Heinrich. Frankfurt am Main: Suhrkamp.

_____ . 1983c. *Philosophie Des Rechts: Die Mitschriften Wannenmann (Heidelberg 1817/18) und Homeyer (Berlin 1818/19)*. Ed. K. H. Ilting. Stuttgart: Klett Cotta.

_____ . 1988. Trans. R. F. Brown, P. C. Hodgson, J. M. Stewart and H. S. Harris. Ed. Peter C. Hodgson. Berkeley: University of California Press.

_____ . 1988. *Lectures on the Philosophy of Religion* . One Volume Edition: Lectures of 1827. Trans. R. F. Brown, P. C. Hodgson, J. M. Stewart and H. S. Harris. Ed. Peter C. Hodgson. Berkeley: University of California Press.

_____ . 1988. *Lectures on the Philosophy of Religion* . One Volume Edition: Lectures of 1827. Trans. R. F. Brown, P. C. Hodgson, J. M. Stewart and H. S. Harris. Ed. Peter C. Hodgson. Berkeley: University of California Press.

_____ . 1989. *Science of Logic*. Atlantic Highlands, N. J.: Humanities Press.

_____ . 1990. *Lectures on the History of Philosophy*. Vol. 3, *The Lectures of 1825-26: Medieval and Modern Philosophy*. Trans. R. F. Brown, J. M. Stewart and H. S. Harris. Berkeley: University of California Press.

Heilbroner, Robert, and Peter Bernstein. 1989. *The Debt and the Deficit: False Alarms/Real Possibilities*. New York: W. W. Norton & Company.

Heiman, G. 1971. "The Sources and Significance of Hegel's Corporate Doctrine." Pp. 111-35 in *Hegel's Political Philosophy: Problems and Prospects*, ed. Z. A. Pelczynski. Cambridge: Cambridge University Press.

Heiss, R. 1975. *Hegel, Kierkegaard, Marx: Three Great Philosophers Whose Ideas Changed the Course of Civilization*. Trans. E. B. Garside. New York: Dell Publishing Company.

Henriques, Ursula R. Q. 1971. "An Early Factory Inspector: James Stuart of Dunearn." *Scottish Historical Review* 50(18): 18-46.

——. 1979. *Before the Welfare State: Social Administration in Early Industrial Britain*. London: Longman Group Limited.

Hewitt, Margaret. 1958. *Wives and Mothers in Victorian Industry*. London: Rockliff.

Hinchman, Lewis P. 1984. "The Origin of Human Rights: A Hegelian Perspective." *Western Political Quarterly* 37(1)(Mar.): 17-31.

Hippel, Theodor Gottlieb von. 1979. *On Improving the Status of Women*. Trans. Timothy F. Sellner. Detroit: Wayne State University Press.

Hirschman, Albert O. 1973. "On Hegel, Imperialism, and Structural Stagnation." Discussion Paper 280 (March). Harvard Institute of Economic Research. Cambridge: Harvard University.

——. 1977. *The Passions and the Interests: Political Arguments for Capitalism Before Its Triumph*. Princeton: Princeton University Press.

——. 1981. *Essays in Trespassing: Economics to Politics and Beyond*. Cambridge: Cambridge University Press.

Hirst, Paul Q. 1989. "Introduction." Pp. 1-45 in *The Pluralist Theory of the State: Selected Writings of G. D. H. Cole, J. N Figgis, and H. J. Laski*, ed. Paul Q. Hirst. London: Routledge.

Hobbes, Thomas. 1966. *The English Works of Thomas Hobbes of Malmesbury*. Vol. 4, *De Corpore Politico, or the Elements of Law*. Germany: Scientia Verlag Aalen.

Hobsbawm, E. J. 1972. *Industry and Empire: From 1750 to the Present Day*. Harmondsworth, Middlesex: Penguin Books.

Hodge, Joanna. 1987. "Women and the Hegelian State." Pp. 127-58 in *Women in Western Political Philosophy: Kant to Nietzche*, ed. Ellen Kennedy and Susan Mendus. Brighton, Sussex: Wheatsheaf Books.

Hodgskin, Thomas. 1964. *Labour Defended Against the Claims of Capital, or the Unproductiveness of Capital Proved with Reference to the Present Combinations Among Journeymen*. Ed. G. D. H. Cole. London: Hammersmith Bookshop.

——. 1966. *Popular Political Economy*. New York: Augustus Kelley.

Holcombe, Lee. 1983. *Wives and Property: Reform of the Married Women's Property Law in Nineteenth-century England*. Toronto: University of Toronto Press.

Hopkins, Eric. 1982. "Working Hours and Conditions during the Industrial Revolution: A Re-Appraisal. *The Economic History Journal*. XXXV(1):52-66.

Horner, Leonard. 1841. *Reports of the Inspectors of Factories*. For the half-year ending 30th June 1841. Parliamentary Papers, vol. 342, no. xxiii. : 1-27.

——. 1842a. *Reports of the Inspectors of Factories*. For the half year ending June 30, 1842. Parliamentary Papers, vol. 31, no. xxii.

——. 1843a. *Reports of the Inspectors of Factories*. For the half-year ending December, 1842. Parliamentary Papers, vol. xxvii. 289-96.

——. 1843b. *Reports of the Inspectors of Factories*. For the half-year ending

30th June, 1843. Parliamentary Papers, vol. 424, no. xxvii.

_____. 1844. *Reports of the Inspectors of Factories.* For the half-year ending December, 1843. Parliamentary Papers, vol. 524, no. xxviii. : 533-8.

_____. 1846a. *Reports of the Inspectors of Factories.* For the half-year ending 31st October, 1845. Parliamentary Papers, vol. 681, no. xx. : 565-77.

_____. 1846b. *Reports of the Inspectors of Factories.* For the half-year ending 30th April 1846. Parliamentary Papers, vol. 721, no. xx.

_____. 1847a. *Reports of the Inspectors of Factories.* For the half-year ending 31st October 1846. Parliamentary Papers, vol. 779, no. xv. : 441-57.

_____. 1847b. *Reports of the Inspectors of Factories.* For the half-year ending 30th April 1847. Parliamentary Papers, vol. 828, no. xv. : 489-95.

_____. 1848a. *Reports of the Inspectors of Factories.* For the half-year ending 31st October 1847. Parliamentary Papers, vol. 900, no. xxvi. : 105-17.

_____. 1848b. *Reports of the Inspectors of Factories.* For the half-year ending 30th April 1848. Parliamentary Papers, vol. 957, no. xxvi. : 149-65.

_____. 1849b. *Reports of the Inspectors of Factories.* For the half-year ending 30th April 1849. Parliamentary Papers, vol. 1047, no. xxii. : 283-97.

_____. 1850a. *Reports of the Inspectors of Factories.* Half-year ending 31st October 1849. Parliamentary Papers, vol. 1141, no. xxiii. : 181-204.

_____. 1850b. *Reports of the Inspectors of Factories.* For the half-year ending 30th April, 1850. Parliamentary Papers, vol. 1239, no. xxiii. : 261-80.

_____. 1851a. *Reports of the Inspectors of Factories.* For the half-year ending 31st October, 1850. Parliamentary Papers, vol. 1304, no. xxiii. : 217-35.

_____. 1851b. *Reports of the Inspectors of Factories.* Half-year ending 30th April, 1851. Parliamentary Papers, vol. 1396, no. xxiii. : 293-313.

_____. 1852a. *Reports of the Inspectors of Factories.* For the half-year ending 31st October, 1851. Parliamentary Papers, vol. 1439, no. xxi. : 353-70.

_____. 1852b. *Reports of the Inspectors of Factories.* For the half year ending 30th April 1852. Parliamentary Papers, vol. 1500, no. xxi. : 377-89.

_____. 1852c. *Reports of the Inspectors of Factories.* For the half year ending 31st October 1852. Parliamentary Papers, no. xl. : 461-95.

_____. 1853. *Reports of the Inspectors of Factories.* For the half year ending 30th April 1853. Parliamentary Papers, no. xl. 533-55.

_____. 1860. *Reports of the Inspectors of Factories.* For the half year ending 31st October 1859. Parliamentary Papers, no. xxi.

Howe, Anthony. 1984. *The Cotton Masters, 1830-1860.* Oxford: Oxford University Press.

Huberman, Michael. 1987. "The Economic Origins of Paternalism: Lancashire Cotton Spinning in the First Half of the Nineteenth Century." *Social History* 12(2)(May): 177-92.

Humphries, Jane. 1977. "Class Struggle and Persistence of the Working Class Family." *Cambridge Journal of Economics* 1(1): 241-58.

_____. 1981. "Protective Legislation, the Capitalist State and Working Class Men: The Case of the 1842 Mines Regulation Act." *Feminist Review* 7 (Spring): 1-33.

Hunley, Dillard. 1991. *The Life and Thought of Friedrich Engels: A Reinterpretation*. New Haven: Yale University Press.

Hunnicutt, Benjamin Kline. 1988. *Work Without End: Abandoning Shorter Hours for the Right to Work*. Philadelphia: Temple University Press.

Hunt, Lynn. 1990. "The Unstable Boundaries of the French Revolution." Pp. 13-46 in *A History of Private Life*, vol. 4. Ed. Philippe Aries and Georges Duby. *From the Fires of Revolution to the Great War*. Trans. Arthur Goldhammer. Ed. Michelle Perrot. Cambridge, Massachusetts: The Belknap Press of Harvard University Press.

Hunt. R. N. *The Political Ideas of Marx and Engels*. Volume 2. *Classical Marxism: 1850-1895*. Pittsburgh: University of Pittsburgh Press.

Hutchins, B. L., and and A. Harrison. 1966. *A History of Factory Legislation*. Third edition. London: Frank Cass & Co. Ltd.

Hyman, Stanley. 1962. *The Tangled Bank: Darwin, Marx, Frazer and Freud as Imaginative Writers*. New York: Athaneum.

Ilting, K.-H. 1984a. "Hegel's Concept of the State and Marx's Early Critique." Pp. 93-113 in *The State and Civil Society: Essays on Hegel's Political Philosophy*, ed. Z. A. Pelczynski. Cambridge: Cambridge University Press.

_____. 1984b. "The Dialectic of Civil Society." *The State and Civil Society: Essays in Hegel's Political Philosophy*. Cambridge: Cambridge University Press.

Ingham, Geoffrey. 1984. *Capitalism Divided? The City and Industry in British Social Development*. London: Macmillan.

Jameson, Fredric. 1990. *Late Marxism: Adorno, Or, the Persistence of the Dialectic*. London: Verso.

Jenkins, J. Craig, and Barbara G. Brents. 1989. "Social Protest, Hegemonic Competition, and Social Reform: A Political Struggle Interpretation of the Origins of the American Welfare State." *American Sociological Review* 54 (Dec.): 891-909.

John, Angela V. 1984. *By the Sweat of Their Brow: Women Workers at Victorian Coal Mines*. London: Routledge & Kegan Paul.

Jones, Gareth Stedman. 1983. *Languages of Class: Studies in English Working Class History, 1832-1982*. Cambridge: Cambridge University Press.

Joyce, Patrick. 1980. *Work, Society and Politics: The Culture of the Factory in Later Victorian England*. Sussex: Harvester Press Ltd.

_____. 1990. "Work." Pp. 131-94 in *The Cambridge Social History of Britain, 1750-1950*. Vol. 2, *People and Their Environment*. Cambridge: Cambridge University Press.

Kant, Immanuel. 1974. *Philosophy of Law*. Clifton, N. J.: Augustus M. Kelley Publishers.

Kapp, Yvonne. 1972. *Eleanor Marx*. Vol. 1, *Family Life (1855-1883)*. London: Lawrence and Wishart.

Kaufmann, Walter. 1978. *Hegel: A Reinterpretation*. Notre Dame: University of Notre Dame Press.

Kelly, George Armstrong. 1978. *Hegel's Retreat from Eleusis: Studies in Political Thought*. Princeton: Princeton University Press.

Kessler-Harris, Alice. 1982. *Out to Work: A History of Wage-earning Women in the United States*. New York: Oxford University Press.

Kestner, Joseph. 1985. *Protest and Reform: The British Social Narrative by Women, 1827-1867*. Madison: University of Wisconsin Press.

King, Desmond S. 1987. "The State and the Social Structures of Welfare in Advanced Industrial Democracies." *Theory and Society* 16: 841-68.

King, J. E. 1981. "'Perish Commerce!' Free Trade and Underconsumption in Early English Economics." *Australian Economic Papers* 20 (Dec.): 235-57.

_____. 1983. "Utopian or Scientific? A Reconsideration of the Ricardian Socialists." *History of Political Economy* 15(3): 345-73.

Kirby, R. G., and A. E. Musson. 1975. *The Voice of the People: John Doherty, 1798-1854, Trade Unionist, Radical and Factory Reformer*. Manchester: Manchester University Press.

Klein, Rudolf. 1984. "Edwin Chadwick." Pp. 8-16 in *Founders of the Welfare State*. London: Heinemann Educational Books Ltd.

Knowles, Dudley. 1982. "Hegel on Property and Personality." *The Philosophical Quarterly* 33(130): 45-62.

Knox, T. M. 1975. "Translators Notes." *Hegel's Aesthetics*. By G. W. F. Hegel. Oxford: Oxford University Press.

Kocka, Jürgen. 1986. "Problems of Working-class Formation in Germany: The Early Years, 1800-1875." Pp. 279-351 in *Working-class Formation: Nineteenth Century Patterns in Western Europe and the United States*, ed. Ira Katznelson and Aristide R. Zolberg. Princeton: Princeton University Press.

Kolata, Gina. 1992. "In Late Abortions, Decisions Are Painful and Options Few." *New York Times*, Sunday, Jan 5.

Korpi, Walter. 1983. *The Democratic Class Struggle*. London: Routledge and Kegan Paul.

Kovacevic, Ivanka. 1975. *Fact Into Fiction: English Literature and the Industrial Scene 1750-1850*. Leicester: University of Leicester Press.

Kronick, Joseph G. 1986. "The Limits of Contradiction: Irony and History in Hegel and Henry Adams." *Clio* 14(4): 391-410.

Laclos, Choderlos de. 1903. *De L'éducation Des Femmes*. Ed. Edouard Champion. Paris: Librairie Léon Vanier.

Lamb, David. 1986. "Hegel on Civil Disobedience." *Hegel-studien* 21: 151-66.

_____. 1987. "Teleology: Kant and Hegel." Pp. 173-84 in *Hegel's Critique of Kant*, ed. Stephen Priest. Oxford: Oxford University Press.

_____. 1987a. "Teleology: Kant and Hegel." *Hegel's Critique of Kant*, ed. Stephen Priest. Oxford: Clarendon Press.

_____. 1987b. "Hegelian-Marxist Millenarianism." *History of European Ideas* 8(3).

Landes, David. 1983. *Revolution in Time: Clocks and the Making of the Modern World*. Cambridge, Mass.: Harvard University Press.

Landes, Joan B. 1982. "Hegel's Conception of the Family." *Polity* 14(1)(Fall): 5-28.

Lazonick, William. 1979. "Industrial Relations and Technical Change: The Case of the Self-acting Mule." *Cambridge Journal of Economics* 3: 231-62.

_____. 1981. "Production Relations, Labor Productivity, and Choice of Technique: British and U.S. Cotton Spinning . " *The journal of economic history* 41(3)(Sept.).

Lehrer, Susan. 1987. *Origins of Protective Labor Legislation for Women, 1905-1925.* Albany: State University of New York Press.

Lerner, Gerda. 1986. *The Creation of Patriarchy.* Oxford: Oxford University Press.

Levi-Strauss, Claude. 1987. *An Introduction to the Work of Marcel Mauss.* Trans. Felicity Baker. London: Routledge and Kegan Paul.

Levine, David. 1985. "Industrialization and the Proletarian Family in England." *Past and Present* 107 (May): 168-203.

_____. 1987. *Reproducing Families: The Political Economy of English Population History.* Cambridge: Cambridge University Press.

Lewis, Jane. 1985. "The Debate on Sex and Class." *New Left Review* 149 (Jan - Feb.): 108-20.

_____. 1991. *Women and Social Action in Victorian and Edwardian England.* London: Edward Elgar Publishing Company.

Lichtheim, George. 1971. *Marxism: An Historical and Critical Study.* London: Routledge and Kegan Paul.

Locke, John. 1980. *Second Treatise of Government.* Ed. C. B. Macpherson. Indianapolis: Hackett Publishing Company.

Lubenow, William C. 1971. *The Politics of Governmental Growth: Early Victorian Attitudes Toward State Intervention, 1833-1848.* Newton Abbot, Devon: David & Charles (Publishers) Limited.

Luhmann, Nicholas. 1986. *Love as Passion.* Cambridge: Polity Press.

Lukacs, Georg. 1975. *The Young Hegel: Studies in the Relations Between Dialectics and Economics.* Trans. Rodney Livingstone. London: Merlin Press.

MacDonagh, Oliver. 1958. "The Nineteenth-century Revolution in Govern-ment: A Reappraisal." *The Historical Journal* I(I): 52-67.

_____. 1977. *Early Victorian Government.* London: Weidenfeld and Nicolson.

MacGregor, David. 1984. *The Communist Ideal in Hegel and Marx.* Toronto: University of Toronto Press. 320.

_____. 1989a. "Marxism's Hegelian Blind Spot: The Theory of the State in Hegel and Marx." Vol. 9, *Current Perspectives in Social Theory: An Annual.* Ed. John Wilson. Greenwich, Conn.: JAI Press.

_____. 1989b. "The State at Dusk." *The Owl of Minerva* 21 (Fall): 51-64.

_____. 1991. "Hegel and Metatheory in Sociology: Reflections on the War in the Persian Gulf." Paper presented at the 26th Annual Meeting of the Canadian Sociology and Anthropology Association in Kingston, Ontario, Canada, 4 June.

MacKinnon, Catharine A. 1987. *Feminism Unmodified: Discourses on Life and Law*. Cambridge, Massachusetts: Harvard University Press.

Macpherson, C. B. 1962. *The Political Theory of Possessive Individualism: Hobbes to Locke*. Oxford: at the Clarendon Press.

_____, ed. 1983. *Property: Mainstream and Critical Positions*. Toronto: University of Toronto Press.

Macy, Michael. 1988. "Value Theory and the 'Golden Eggs': Appropriating the Magic of Accumulation." *Sociological Theory* 6(2): 131-53.

Mahon, Rianne. 1991. "From "Bringing" to "Putting": The State in Late Twentieth-century Social Theory." *The Canadian Journal of Sociology* 16(2)(Spring).

Maker, William. 1987. "Introduction." Pp. 1-28 in *Hegel on Economics and Freedom*, ed. William Maker. Macon, Georgia: Mercer University Press.

Mandler, Peter. 1984. "Cain and Abel: Two Aristocrats and the Early Victorian Factory Acts." *The Historical Journal*. 27(1):83-110.

Mann, Michael. 1986. "The Authonomous Power of the State: Its Origins, Mechanisms, and Results." Pp. 109-36 in *States in History*, ed. John A. Hall. Oxford: Basil Blackwell Ltd.

Marcuse, H. 1973. *Reason and Revolution: Hegel and the Rise of Social Theory*. Second Edition. London: Routledge and Kegan Paul Ltd.

Marcus, Stephen. 1985. *Engels, Manchester, and the Working Class*. New York: W.W. Norton.

Mark-Lawson, Jane, and Anne Witz. 1988. "From 'Family Labour' to 'Family Wage'? The Case of Women's Labour in Nineteenth-century Coalmining." *Social History* 13(2)(May): 151-74.

Marquand, David. 1988. *The Unprincipled Society*. London: Cape.

Martin, Bernice. 1969. "Leonard Horner: A Portrait of an Inspector of Factories." *International Review of Social History* 14(412-43).

Martin, Jane Roland. 1985. *Reclaiming a Conversation: The Ideal of the Educated Woman*. New Haven: Yale University Press.

Martineau, Harriet. 1834. *Illustrations of Political Economy*, vol. 3. *A Manchester Strike*. London: Charles Fox, Paternoster Row.

Marvel, Howard. 1977. "Factory Legislation: A Reinterpretation of Early English Experience." *Journal of law and economics* 20 (Oct.): 379-402.

Marx, Karl. 1970. *Critique of Hegel's "Philosophy of Right"*. Trans. Annette Jolin and Joseph O'Malley. Ed. J. O'Malley. Cambridge: Cambridge University Press.

_____. 1973. *Political Writings*. Vol. 2, *Surveys from Exile*. Ed. David Fernbach. Harmondsworth, Middlesex: Penguin Books.

_____. 1974. *Political Writings*. Vol. 3, *The First International and After*. Ed. David Fernbach. Harmondsworth, Middlesex: Penguin Books.

_____. 1976. *Capital: A Critique of Political Economy*. Vol. 1. Trans. Ben Fowkes. Harmondsworth, Middlesex: Penguin Books.

_____. 1978. *Capital: A Critique of Political Economy*. Volume 2. Trans. David

_____. 1981. *Capital: A Critique of Political Economy*. Vol. 3. Trans. David

Fernbach. Harmondsworth, Middlesex: Penguin Books.

Marx, Karl, and and Friedrich Engels. 1953. *On Britain*. Moscow: Progress Publishers.

———. 1978. *The Marx-Engels Reader*. New York: W. W. Norton.

———. 1985. *Collected Works*. New York: International Publishers.

Mathias, Peter. 1969. *The First Industrial Nation: An Economic History of Britain, 1700-1914*. New York: Charles Scribners' Sons.

Mayer, Arno. 1981. *The Persistence of the Old Regime: Europe to the Great War*. New York: Pantheon Books.

McCarney, Joseph. 1991. "The True Realm of Freedom: Marxist Philosophy After Communism." *New Left Review* 189 (Sept. - Oct.): 19-38.

McCord, Norman. 1991. *British History: 1815-1906*. Oxford: Oxford University Press.

McCumber, John. 1986. "Contradiction and Resolution in the State: Hegel's Covert View." *Clio* 15(4)(379-90.).

McKendrick, Neil. 1974. "Home Demand Economic Growth: A New View of the Role of Women and Children in the Industrial Revolution." Pp. 152-210 in *Historical Perspectives: Studies in English Thought and Society*, ed. Neil McKendrick. London: Europa Publications Limited.

McLellan, David. 1973. *Karl Marx: His Life and Thought*. London: Macmillan.

McNeill, William H. 1992. "History Over, World Goes on.". Review of *The End of History and the Last Man*, by Francis Fukuyama. *New York Times Book Review* (Jan 26): 14-5.

McQuaig, Linda. 1991. *The Quick and the Dead: Brian Mulroney, Big Business and the Seduction of Canada*. Toronto: Penguin Books Canada Ltd.

Mendus, Susan. 1987. "Kant: An Honest but Narrow-minded Bourgeois?" Pp. 21-43 in *Women in Western Political Philosophy: Kant to Nietzche*, ed. Ellen Kennedy and Susan Mendus. Brighton, Sussex: Wheatsheaf Books.

Menger, Anton. 1962. *The Right to the Whole Produce of Labour: The Origin and Development of the Theory of Labour's Claim to the Whole Product of Industry*. Trans. M. E. Tanner. New York: Augustus Kelley.

Midgley, Mary, and Judith Hughes. 1983. *Women's Choices*. London: Weidenfeld and Nicolson.

Miliband, Ralph. 1977. *Marxism and Politics*. Oxford: Oxford University Press.

Miller, Jane. 1990. *Seductions: Studies in Reading and Culture*. London: Virago.

Mills, Patricia Jagentowicz. 1979. "Hegel and "The Woman Question": Recognition and Intersubjectivity." Pp. 74-98 in *The Sexism of Social and Political Theory: Women and Reproduction from Plato to Nietzche*, eds. Lorenne M. G. Clark and Lynda Lange. Toronto: University of Toronto Press.

———. 1986. "Hegel's Antigone." *The Owl of Minerva* 17(2)(Spring): 131-52.

Mingay, G. E. 1986. *The Transformation of Britain*. London: Routledge & Kegan Paul.

Mishra, Ramish. 1990. *The Welfare State in Capitalist Society*. Toronto: University of Toronto Press.

Moller Okin, S. 1980. *Women in Western Political Thought*. London: Virago.

Mommsen, W. J. 1984. *Max Weber and German Politics 1890-1920*. Trans. M. Steinberg. Chicago: University of Chicago Press.

Moore, D. C. 1961. "The Other Face of Reform." *Victorian Studies* 4 (Sept.): 7-34.

_____. 1966. "Concession or Cure: The Sociological Premises of the First Reform Act." *Historical Journal* IX: 139-59.

_____. 1976. *The Politics of Deference: A Study of the Mid-nineteenth Century English Political System*.

Morgentaler, Henry. 1982. *Abortion and Contraception*. Toronto: General Publishing.

Mueller, Hans-Eberhard. 1984. *Bureaucracy, Education, and Monopoly: Civil Service Reforms in Prussia and England*. Berkeley: University of California Press.

Munzer, Stephen R. 1990. *A Theory of Property*. Cambridge: Cambridge University Press.

Murdoch, Iris. 1961. *A Severed Head*. London: Chatto and Windus.

Nairn, Tom. 1977. "The Twilight of the British State." *New Left Review* 101-102 (Feb. - Apr.): 3-61.

_____. 1988. *The Enchanted Glass: Britain and Its Monarchy*. London: Hutchinson Radius.

Nardinelli, C. 1985. "The Successful Prosecution of the Factory Acts: A Suggested Explanation." *Economic History Review* 38.

Navasky, Victor S. 1980. *Naming Names*. New York: Viking Press.

Neale, R. S. 1981. *Class in English History 1680-1850*. Totowa, New Jersey: Barnes and Noble Books.

Neff, Wanda F. 1966. *Victorian Working Women: An Historical and Literary Study of Women in British Industries and Professions, 1832-1850*. London: Frank Cass and Company Limited.

Newman, Peter C. 1991. *Merchant Princes*. Toronto: Penguin Books Canada Ltd.

Nove, Alec. 1983. *The Economics of Feasible Socialism*. London: George Allen and Unwin.

O'Brien, Mary. 1981. *The Politics of Reproduction*. London: Routledge and Kegan Paul.

_____. 1989. *Reproducing the World: Essays in Feminist Theory*. Boulder, CO: Westview Press.

O'Gorman, Frank. 1986. "The Unreformed Electorate of Hanoverian England: The Mid-eighteenth Century to the Reform Act of 1832." *Social History* 111: 513-33.

Oakley, Ann. 1984. *Taking It Like a Woman*. New York: Random House.

Oddy, D. J. 1990. "Food, Drink and Nutrition." Pp. 251-78 in *The Cambridge Social History of Britain, 1750-1950*. Ed. F. M. L. Thompson. Vol. 2, *People and Their Environment*. Cambridge: Cambridge University Press.

Oren, L. 1974. "The Welfare of Women in Labouring Families: England, 1860-1950." *Clio's Consciousness Raised: New Perspectives on the History of Women*, ed. M. Hartman and L. W. Banner. New York: Harper Colophon.

Osterud, Nancy Grey. 1986. "Gender Divisions and the Organization of Work in the Leicester Hosiery Industry." Pp. 45-70 in *Unequal Opp.ortunities: Women's Employment in England, 1800-1918*, ed. Angela V. John. Oxford: Basil Blackwell.

Pagels, Elaine. 1988. *Adam, Eve, and the Serpent*. New York: Random House.

Pateman, Carole. 1988. *The Sexual Contract*. Stanford: Stanford University Press.

Peacock, A. E. 1985. "Factory Act Prosections: A Hidden Consensus." *Economic History Review* 38.

Peacock, E. A. 1984. "The Successful Prosecution of the Factory Acts, 1835-55." *Economic History Review* 37.

Pelczynski, Z. A., ed. 1964. "An Introductory Essay." *Hegel's Political Writings*. By G. W. F. Hegel. Trans. T. M. Knox. Oxford: Oxford University Press.

_____ . 1984. "Political Community and Individual Freedom in Hegel's Philosophy of State." Pp. 55-76 in *The State and Civil Society: Studies in Hegel's Political Philosophy*, ed. Z. A. Pelczynski. Cambridge: Cambridge University Press.

Pellew, Jill. 1982. *The Home Office, 1848-1914: From Clerks to Bureaucrats*. London: Heinemann Educational Books Ltd.

Perkin, Harold. 1969. *Origins of Modern English Society*. London: Routledge and Kegan Paul.

_____ . 1981. *The Structured Crowd*. Sussex: The Harvester Press Limited.

_____ . 1989. *The Rise of Professional Society: England Since 1880*. London: Routledge.

Perrot, Michelle. 1984. "The First of May 1890 in France: The Birth of a Working Class Ritual." Pp. 143-72 in *The Power of the Past*, ed. Pat Thane, Geoffrey Crossick and Roderick Floud. Cambridge: Cambridge University Press.

Perrot, Michelle, and Anne Martin-Fugier. 1990. "Roles and Characters." Pp. 295-338 in *A History of Private Life*, vol. 4. Trans. Arthur Goldhammer. Ed. Philippe Aries and Georges Duby. *From the Fires of Revolution to the Great War*. Ed. Michelle Perrot. Cambridge, Massachusetts: The Belknap Press of Harvard University Press.

Petry, M. J. 1976. "Hegel and the *Morning Chronicle*." *Hegel-Studien* 11.

_____ . 1984. "Propaganda and Analysis: The Background to Hegel's Article on the English Reform Bill." *The State and Civil Society: Studies in Hegel's Political Philosophy*. Ed. Z. A. Pelcynski. Cambridge: Cambridge University Press.

Phelan, Sean. 1989. *Identity Politics: Lesbian Feminism and the Limits of*

Community. Philadelphia: Temple University Press.

Phillips, Kevin. 1990. *The Politics of Rich and Poor: Wealth and the American Electorate in the Reagan Aftermath*. New York: HarperPerennial.

Pinchbeck, Ivy. 1981. *Women Workers and the Industrial Revolution 1750-1850*. With new introduction by Kerry Hamilton. London: Virago.

Plamenatz, John. 1963. *Man and Society. A Critical Examination of Some Important Social and Political Theories from Machiavelli to Marx*. Volume 2. London: Longman Group Limited.

Plant, Raymond. 1977a. "Hegel and Political Economy, I." *New Left Review* 103 (May - June): 79-93.

_____. 1977b. "Hegel and Political Economy, II." *New Left Review* 104 (July - Aug.): 103-13.

_____. 1984. "Hegel on Identity and Legitimation." Pp. 55-76 in *The State and Civil Society: Studies in Hegel's Political Philosophy*, ed. Z. A. Pelzcynski. Cambridge: Cambridge University Press.

_____. 1984a. *Hegel: An Introduction*. Second edition. Oxford: Basil Blackwell.

_____. 1984b. "Hegel on Identity an Legitimation." Pp. 227-43 in *The State and Civil Society: Essays on Hegel's Political Philosophy*, ed. Z. A. Pelczynski. Cambridge: Cambridge University Press.

_____. 1987. "Hegel and the Political Economy." Pp. 95-126 in *Hegel on Economics and Freedom*, ed. William Maker.

Plato. 1989. Republic. *The Collected Dialogues of Plato, Including the Letters*, ed. Edith Hamilton and Huntington Cairns. Trans. Paul Shorey. Princeton University Press.

Pleck, Elizabeth. 1987. *Domestic Tyranny: The Making of Social Policy Against Family Violence from Colonial Times to the Present*. New York: Oxford University Press.

Polanyi, Karl. 1957. *The Great Transformation: The Political and Economic Origins of Our Time*. Boston: Beacon Press.

Pollitt, Katha. 1990. "'Fetal Rights': A New Assault on Feminism." *The Nation* 250(12)(Mar. 26): 409-18.

_____. 1992. "Clinton's Affair?" *The Nation*. 254(7)(Feb. 24): 220-1.

Posner, Richard A. 1989. "Hegel and Employment at Will: A Comment." Hegel and legal theory, part 2. *Cardoza Law Review* 10(5-6)(Mar. - Apr.): 1625-36.

Prawer, S. S. 1976. *Karl Marx and World Literature*. Oxford: Oxford University Press.

Price, Richard. 1986. *Labour in British Society*. London: Routledge.

Pynchon, Thomas. 1966. *The Crying of Lot 49*. New York: Bantham Books.

Raddatz, Fritz. 1978. *Karl Marx, a Political Biography*. Toronto: Little, Brown and Company.

Raff, Diether. 1988. *A History of Germany: From the Medieval Empire to the Present*. Trans. Bruce Little. Hamburg: Berg.

Ravven, Heidi. 1988. "Has Hegel Anything to Say to Feminists?" *The Owl of Minerva* 19(2)(Spring): 149-68.

Reid, D. A. 1986. "The Decline of Saint Monday, 1766-1876." Pp. 98-125 in *Essays in Social History*, ed. Pat Thane and Anthony Sutcliffe. Vol. 2. Oxford: Oxford University Press.   ◆

Reinarman, Craig. 1988. "The Social Construction of an Alcohol Problem: The Case of Mothers Against Drunk Drivers and Social Control in the 1980s." *Theory and Society* 17: 91-120.

Rendall, Jane. 1990. *Women in an Industrializing Society: England 1750-1880*. Oxford: Basil Blackwell.

Ricardo, David. 1966. *The Works and Correspondence of David Ricardo*. Volume 1. *Principles of Political Economy*. Ed. P. Sraffa. Cambridge: Cambridge University Press.

Richardson, Ruth. 1988. *Death, Dissection and the Destitute*. Harmondsworth, Middlesex: Penguin Books.

Riedel, Manfred. 1984. *Between Tradition and Revolution: The Hegelian Transformation of Political Philosophy*. Trans. Walter Wright. Cambridge: Cambridge University Press.

Ritter, Gerhard A. 1986. *Social Welfare in Germany and Britain: Origins and Development*. New York: Berg.

Ritter, Joachim. 1982. *Hegel and the French Revolution: Essays on the* Philosophy of Right. Trans. Richard Dien Winfield. Cambridge, Mass.: The M.I.T. Press.

Roberts, David. 1960. *Victorian Origins of the British Welfare State*. New Haven: Yale University Press.

———. 1979. *Paternalism in Early Victorian England*. New Brunswick, N. J.: Rutgers University Press.

Roberts, Elizabeth. 1985. "The Family." Pp. 1-35 in *The Working Class in England, 1875-1914*, ed. John Benson. London: Croom Helm.

Roediger, David, and Philip S. Foner. 1989. *Our Own Time: A History of American Labor and the Working Day*. London: Verso.

Rose, Sonya. 1988. "Gender Antagonism and Class Conflict: Exclusionary Strategies of Male Trade Unionists in Nineteenth Century Britain." *Social History* 13(2)(May): 191-208.

Ross, Ellen. 1982. "'Fierce Questions and Taunts': Married Life in Working Class London, 1870-1914." *Feminist studies* 8 (Spring 1983).

Rousseau, J.-J. 1968. *The Social Contract*. Trans. Maurice Cranston. Harmondsworth, Middlesex: Penguin Books.

———. 1979. *Emile*. Trans. Allan Bloom. New York: Basic Books.

Rowbotham, Sheila. 1974. *Women, Resistance and Revolution: A History of Women and Revolution in the Modern World*. New York: Vintage Books.

———. 1991. "The Greater London Council, Part One: Forming Democratic Policy." *Z Magazine* 4(12)(Dec.).

Rubinstein, W. D. 1981. *Men of Property*. London: Croom Helm.

Rueschemeyer, Dietrich. 1986. *Power and the Division of Labor*. Stanford: Stanford University Press.

Runciman, W. Garry. 1989. *A Treatise on Social Theory*, vol. 2. *Substantive Social Theory*. Cambridge: Cambridge University Press. 493.

Russell, Diana E. H. 1982. *Rape in Marriage*. New York: Collier Books.

Russell, J. R. 1983. "Introduction." Pp. 5-8 in *Her Majesty's Inspectors of Factories, 1833-1983: Essays to Commemorate 150 Years of Health and Safety Inspection*. London: Her Majesty's Stationery Office.

Ryan, Alan. 1984a. *Property and Political Theory*. Oxford: Basil Blackwell.

_____. 1984b. "Hegel on Work, Ownership and Citizenship." Pp. 178-96 in *The State and Civil Society: Studies in Hegel's Political Philosophy*, ed. Z. A. Pelczynski. Cambridge: Cambridge University Press.

_____. 1987. *Property*. Minneapolis: University of Minnesota Press.

Sachs, Albie, and Joan Hoff-Wilson. 1978. *Sexism and the Law: A Study of Male Beliefs and Legal Bias in Britain and the United States*. New York: Free Press.

Sagarra, Eda. 1977. *A Social History of Germany 1648-1914*. London: Methuen & Co Ltd.

Sakwa, Richard. 1991. "The Hegelian Triumph." *Times Higher Educational Supplement*, July 12.

Samuel, Raphael. 1977. "The Workshop of the World: Steam Power and Hand Technology in Mid-Victorian Britain." *History Workshop* 3 (Spring): 6-72.

Saunders, R. J. 1840. *Reports of the Inspectors of Factories*. For the quarter ending 30th September 1840. London: Her Majesty's Stationery Office.

_____. 1843. *Reports of the Inspectors of Factories*. For the half-year ending 30th June, 1843. London: Her Majesty's Stationery Office.

_____. 1844. *Reports of the Inspectors of Factories*. For the half-year ending 31st December 1843. London: Her Majesty's Stationery Office.

Schepper-Hughes, Nancy. 1991. "Social Indifference to Child Death." *The Lancet* 337 (May 11): 1144-7.

Schlink, Bernhard. 1989. "The Inherent Rationality of the State in Hegel's *Philosophy of Right*." Hegel and legal theory, part 1. *Cardoza Law Review* 10(5-6)(Mar.).

Scott, Joan Wallach. 1988. *Gender and the Politics of History*. New York: Columbia University Press.

Seccombe, Wally. 1986. "Patriarchy Stabilized: The Construction of the Male Breadwinner Wage Norm in Nineteenth-century Britain." *Social History* 11(1)(Jan): 53-75.

_____. 1990. "Starting to Stop: Working-class Fertility Decline in Britain." *Past and Present* 126: 151-88.

Seigel, Jerrold. 1978. *Marx's Fate: The Shape of a Life*. Princeton: Princeton University Press.

Sellner, Timothy F. 1979. "Introduction." *On Improving the Status of Women*. By Theodor Gottlieb von Hippel. Detroit: Wayne State University Press.

Seymour, Charles. 1915. *Electoral Reform in England Wales: The Development and Operation of the Parliamentary Franchise, 1832-1885*. New Haven: Yale

University Press.

Shanley, Mary Lyndon. 1986. "Suffrage, Protective Labor Legislation, and Married Women's Property Laws in England." *Signs: Journal of Women in Culture and Society* 12(1)(Autumn): 62-77.

Shell, Susan Meld. 1980. *The Rights of Reason: A Study of Kant's Philosophy and Politics.* Toronto: University of Toronto Press.

Schor, Juliet B. 1992. *The Overworked American: The Unexpected Decline of Leisure.* New York: Basic Books.

Sifry, Micah L. 1992. "Cloud Over Zion." *The Nation* 254(4)(Feb. 3).

Simmel, Georg. 1971. *On Individuality and Social Forms.* Ed. D. Levine. Chicago: University of Chicago Press.

Skilton, David. 1977. *Defoe to the Victorians: Two Centuries of the English Novel.* Harmondsworth, Middlesex: Penguin Books.

Skocpol, Theda. 1980. "Political Response to Capitalist Crises: Neo-Marxist Theories of the State and the Case of the New Deal." *Politics and Society* 10(2): 155-201.

_____. 1985. "Bringing the State Back In: Strategies of Analysis in Current Research." Pp. 3-43 in *Bringing the State Back In,* eds. P. B. Evans, D. Reuschemeyer, and T. Skocpol. Cambridge: Cambridge University Press.

Smelser, N. J. 1959. *Social Change in the Industrial Revolution.* London: Routledge and Kegan Paul.

Smith, Dorothy E. 1987. *The Everyday World as Problematic: A Feminist Sociology.* Toronto: University of Toronto Press.

Smith, Steven B. 1989. *Hegel's Critique of Liberalism.* Chicago: University of Chicago Press.

_____. 1989a. "Hegel and the French Revolution: An Epitaph for Republicanism." *Social Research* 56(1)(Spring): 233-61.

Smith, Tony. 1990. *The Logic of Marx's Capital: Replies to Hegelian Criticisms.* Albany: State University of New York Press.

Sophocles. 1973. *Antigone.* Trans. Richard Emil Braun. New York: Oxford University Press.

Stannard, Una. 1977. *Mrs. Man.* San Francisco: Germainbooks.

Steinberger, Peter J. 1986. "Hegel on Marriage and Politics." *Political Studies* 34 (Dec.): 575-91.

Steiner, George. 1984. *Antigones: How the Antigone Legend Has Endured in Western Literature, Art, and Thought.* New York: Oxford University Press.

Stetson, Dorothy M. 1982. *A Woman's Issue: The Politics of Family Law Reform in England.* Westport, Connecticut: Greenwood Press.

Stillman, Peter G. 1989. "Hegel's Analysis of Property in the *Philosophy of Right.*" Hegel and legal theory, part 2. *Cardoza Law Review* 10(5-6)(Mar.): 1031-72.

Stone, Lawrence. 1977. *The Family, Sex and Marriage in England, 1500-1800.* New York: Harper and Row.

_____. 1986. *An Open Elite? England 1540-1880.* Abridged edition. Oxford: Oxford University Press.

Storey, Robert. 1990. "'Injurious to Her Health': Protecting Women Factory Workers in Canada, 1880-1920." Meetings of the Canadian Sociology and Anthropology Assocation. University of Victoria, May.

Strauss, Leo. 1973. *Persecution and the Art of Writing*. Westport, Connecticut: Greenwood Press, Inc.

Sutherland, Gillian. 1990. "Education." Pp. 119-70 in *The Cambridge Social History of Britain, 1750-1950*, ed. F. M. L. Thompson. Vol. 3, *Social Agencies and Institutions*. Cambridge: Cambridge University Press.

Swaan, A. de. 1988. *In Care of the State: Health Care, Education and Welfare in Europe and the USA in the Modern Era*. New York: Oxford University Press.

Swados, Elizabeth. 1991. "The Story of a Street Person." *The New York Times Magazine*, Aug. 18.

Sydie, R. A. 1987. *Natural Women, Cultured Men*. New York: New York University Press.

Szelenyi, Ivan, and Bill Martin. 1988. "The Three Waves of New Class Theories." *Theory and Society* 17: 645-67.

Taylor, Arthur J. 1972. *Laissez-faire and State Intervention in Nineteenth Century Britain*. London: The Macmillan Press Ltd.

Taylor, Barbara. 1983. *Eve and the New Jerusalem*. London: Virago.

Taylor, Charles. 1975. *Hegel*. Cambridge: Cambridge University Press.

Taylor-Gooby, Peter. 1991. *Social Change, Social Welfare and Social Science*. Toronto: University of Toronto Press.

Thane, Pat. 1990. "Government and Society in England Wales, 1750-1914." Pp. 1-62 in *The Cambridge Social History of Britain 1750-1950*, vol. 3, ed. F. M. L. Thompson. *Social Agencies and Institutions*. Cambridge: Cambridge University Press.

Thomas, Maurice Walton. 1948. *The Early Factory Legislation: A Study in Legislative and Administrative Evolution*. Leigh-on-Sea, Essex: The Thames Bank Publishing Company Limited.

Thomis, Malcolm I., and Peter Holt. *Threats of Revolution in Britain 1789-1848*.

Thompson, Dorothy. 1984. *The Chartists*. Hounslow, Middlesex: Maurice Temple Smith Ltd.

Thompson, E. P. 1967. "Time, Work-discipline, and Industrial Capitalism." *Past and Present* 38 (Dec.): 56-97.

_____ . 1968. *The Making of the English Working Class*. Harmondsworth, Middlesex: Penguin Books.

Thompson, F. M. L. 1963. *English Landed Society in the Nineteenth Century*. London: Routledge and Kegan Paul Ltd.

Thompson, F. M. L. 1977. "Britain." Pp. 22-44 in *European Landed Elites in the Nineteenth Century*, ed. David Spring. Baltimore: Johns Hopkins University Press.

_____ . 1981. "Social Control in Victorian Britain." *The Economic History Review* 34(2)(May): 189-208.

_____ . 1984. "English Landed Society in the Nineteenth Century." Pp. 195-214 in *The Power of the Past*, eds. Pat Thane, Geoffrey Crossick and Roderick Floud. Cambridge: Cambridge University Press.

_____ . 1988. *The Rise of Respectable Society: A Social History of Victorian Britain 1830-1900*. London: Fontana Press.

Thompson, Noel W. 1984. *The People's Science: The Popular Political Economy of Exploitation and Crisis, 1816-34*. Cambridge: Cambridge University Press.

Thompson, William, and Anna Wheeler. 1970. *Appeal of One Half the Human Race, Women, Against the Pretensions of the Other Half, Men, to Retain Them in Political, and Thence in Civil and Domestic Slavery: In Reply to a Paragraph of Mr. Mill's Celebrated "Article on Government"* New York: Burt Franklin.

Tilly, Louise A., and Joan Scott. 1987. *Women, Work & Family*. New York: Methuen.

Toews, John Edward. 1985. *Hegelianism: The Path Toward Dialectical Humanism, 1805-1841*. Cambridge: Cambridge University Press.

Tomes, Nancy. 1978. "A Torrent of Abuse: Crimes of Violence Between Working-class Men and Women in London, 1840-1875." *Journal of social history* 11(3)(Spring): 328-45.

Tonna, Charlotte Elizabeth. 1975. The Wrongs of Woman. Pp. 303-58 in *Fact Into Fiction: English Literature and the Industrial Scene, 1750-1850*, ed. Ivanka Kovacevic. Leicester: Leicester University Press.

Tribe, Laurence H. 1990. *Abortion: The Clash of Absolutes*. New York: W. W. Norton & Company.

Trollope, Frances. 1840. *The Life and Adventures of Michael Armstrong, the Factory Boy*. London: Henry Coburn.

Tucker, Eric. 1990. *Administering Danger in the Workplace: The Law and Politics of Occupational Health and Safety Regulation in Ontario, 1850-1914*. Toronto: University of Toronto Press.

Turner, E. S. 1950. *Roads to Ruin: The Shocking History of Social Reform*. London: Michael Joseph.

Ursel, Jane. 1986. "The State and the Maintenance of Patriarchy: A Case Study of Family, Labour and Welfare Legislation in Canada.", Pp. 77-98 in *Family, Economy and State*, ed. James Dickinson and Bob Russell. London: Croom Helm.

Valverde, Marianna. 1988. "'Giving the Female a Domestic Turn': The Social, Legal and Moral Regulation of Women's Work in British Cotton Mills, 1820-1850." *Journal of Social History* 21(4): 619-34.

Van den Berg, Axel. 1988. *The Immanent Utopia: From Marxism on the State to The State of Marxism*. Princeton: Princeton University Press.

Van Krieken, Robert. 1986. "Social Theory and Child Welfare: Beyond Social Control." *Theory and Society* 15: 401-29.

Vincent, Andrew W. 1987. "The State and Social Purpose in Idealist Political Philosophy." *History of European Ideas*. 8(3): 333-47.

Vincent, David. 1981. *Bread, Knowledge and Freedom: A Study of Nineteenth*

Century Working Class Autobiography. London: Europa Publications Limited.

Vogel, Ursula. 1987. "Humboldt and the Romantics: Neither *Hausfrau* Nor *Citoyenne*." Pp. 106-26 in *Women in Western Political Philosophy: Kant to Nietzche*, ed. Ellen Kennedy and Susan Mendus. Brighton, Sussex: Wheatsheaf Books.

Walby, Sylvia. 1986. *Patriarchy at Work: Patriarchal and Capitalist Relations in Employment*. Minneapolis: University of Minnesota Press.

Walkowitz, Judith R. 1980. *Prostitution and Victorian Society: Women, Class, and the State*. Cambridge: Cambridge University Press.

Walton, A. S. 1984. "Economy, Utility and Community in Hegel's Theory of Civil Society." Pp. 244-61 in *The State and Civil Society: Essays in Hegel's Political Philosophy*, ed. Z. A. Pelczynski. Cambridge: Cambridge University Press.

Walton, John K. 1990. "The North." Pp. 350-90 in *The Cambridge Social History of Britain, 1750-1950*, ed. F. M. L. Thompson. Vol. 1. *Regions and Communities*. Cambridge: Cambridge University Press.

Walvin, James. 1982. *A Child's World: A Social History of English Childhood, 1800-1914*. Harmondsworth, Middlesex: Penguin Books.

Ward, J. T. 1962. *The Factory Movement, 1830-1855*. London: Macmillan & Co. Ltd.

_____. 1970. "The Factory Movement." Pp. 54-77 in *Popular Movements c. 1830-1850*, ed. J. T. Ward. London: Macmillan and Co. Ltd.

Waszek, Norbert. 1988. *The Scottish Enlightenment and Hegel's Account of Civil Society*. Boston: Kluwer Academic Publishers.

_____. 1988. *The Scottish Enlightenment and Hegel's Account of "Civil Society"* Dordrecht: Kluwer Academic Publishers.

Webb, Sidney. 1966. "Preface to the New Edition." *A History of Factory Legislation*. By B. L. Harrison and A. Hutchins. London: Frank Cass & Co. Ltd.

Weitzman, Lenore J. 1981. *The Marriage Contract: Spouses, Lovers, and the Law*. New York: The Free Press.

Whyte, William Foote, and Kathleen King Whyte. 1988. *Making Mondragon: The Growth and Dynamics of the Worker Cooperative Complex*. Ithaca, New York: ILR Press.

Williams, Howard. 1983. *Kant's Political Philosophy*. Oxford: Basil Blackwell.

_____. 1989. *Hegel, Heraclitus and Marx's Dialectic*. Hemel Hempstead, Hirtfordshire: Harvester Wheatsheaf.

Winfield, Richard Dien. 1987. "Hegel's Challenge to the Modern Economy." Pp. 29-64 in *Hegel on Economics and Freedom*, ed. William Maker. Macon, Georgia: Mercer University Press.

_____. 1988. *The Just Economy*. London: Routledge.

Wolfe, Alan. 1989. *Whose Keeper? Social Science and Moral Obligation*. Berkeley: University of California Press.

Wolff, Robert Paul. 1984. *Understanding Marx*. Princeton: Princeton

University Press.

Wollstonecraft, Mary. 1967. *A Vindication of the Rights of Woman, with Strictures on Political and Moral Subjects*. Ed. Charles W., Jr. Hagelman. New York: W. W. Norton & Company, Inc.

Woodiwiss, Anthony. 1987. "The Discourses of Production (Part II): The Contract of Employment and the Emergence of Democratic Capitalist Law in Britain and the United States." *Economy and Society* 16(4): 441-525.

Woolf, Virginia. 1957. *A Room of One's Own*. New York: Harcourt Brace & World, Inc.

———. 1986. *Three Guineas*. London: The Hogarth Press.

Wright, D. G. 1988. *Popular Radicalism: The Working Class Experience, 1780-1880*. London: Longman.

Wright, Erik Olin. 1985. *Classes*. London: Verso.

Wrigley, E. A. 1987. *People, Cities and Wealth*. Oxford: Basil Blackwell.

Wrong, Dennis. 1991. "Review of Axel Van Den Berg's *The Immanent Utopia: From Marxism on the State to the State of Marxism*." *Contemporary Sociology* 20(4)(July): 567-9.

Wusteman, P. 1983. "Leonard Horner: Inspector General of Factories." Pp. 9-13 in *Her Majesty's Inspectors of Factories, 1833-1983: Essays to Commemorate 150 Years of Health and Safety Inspection*. London: Her Majesty's Stationery Office.

Yarmie, Andrew H. 1984. "British Employers' Resistance to 'Grandmotherly' Government, 1850-80." *Social History* 9(2)(May): 141-69.

Yates, Gayle Graham. 1985. *Harriet Martineau on Women*. New Brunswick, N. J.: Rutgers University Press.

Zelizer, Viviana A. 1985. *Pricing the Priceless Child: The Changing Social Value of Children*. New York: Basic Books, Inc.

About the Book and Author

In this radically revised intellectual portrait of Hegel and Marx that challenges standard interpretations of their political theory, David MacGregor considers the nature of the state in capitalist society. This is the first book to place Marx's and Hegel's political thought directly into social and historical context. Revealing the revolutionary content of Hegel's social theory and the Hegelian themes that underlie Marx's analysis of the English state in *Capital*, the author shows how the transformation of the Victorian state in the nineteenth century influenced the mature Marx to reclaim Hegelian arguments he had earlier abandoned. These ideas included a theory of politics and social class that colored Marx's view of capitalist and working-class opposition to government reform initiatives.

MacGregor criticizes interpretations of state action that present government solely as a tool of capitalist and patriarchal interests. Noting the essential significance of child labor in the growing industrialization during Hegel's and Marx's time, the author contends that "alienation," as the two philosophers understood the term, assumes a labor force in which many workers are socially powerless children and women. Given these conditions, the centrality of the English Factory Acts to workers' lives becomes obvious, a centrality acknowledged by Marx but forgotten by his followers. The author concludes his discussion with an assessment of current arguments about the state and civil society, relating these debates to Hegel's conception of the rational state.

David MacGregor is professor of sociology at King's College, the University of Western Ontario. His previous book, *The Communist Ideal in Hegel and Marx*, received the John Porter Memorial Prize of the Canadian Sociology and Anthropology Association.

Index